WENDELL WILLKIE

WENDELL WILLKIE

1892-1944

MARY EARHART DILLON

J. B. LIPPINCOTT COMPANY

PHILADELPHIA AND NEW YORK

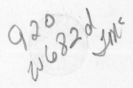

CONTENTS

PREFACE

IN THE year 1940 a new leader appeared upon the American political scene. Within an incredibly short time, he won the confidence of millions of American voters, only to disappear from the arena of politics as suddenly as he had come. Nevertheless, in a few years he had changed the course of American political thought and had developed a new relationship between the political parties which contend for the control of the United States Government.

Wendell Willkie was one of the most spectacular episodes in American history. He never held public office. He was almost totally inexperienced in the tactics of political parties, and yet he was nominated by one of the major parties as its candidate for the presidency. The defeat of Wendell Willkie as nominee of the Republican Party in 1940 was not accomplished by President Roosevelt and the Democratic Party. The presidential election was determined on the seashore of Dunkirk in France, when the fragments of the Allied armies, defeated by the Nazi war machine, made their tragic escape to England. It was the grim battle in Europe rather than the political contest in the United States which guided the American people to the decision that the Commander-in-Chief of the American Army and Navy, at this critical period, should not be changed.

Notwithstanding his defeat at the polls, Wendell Willkie clarified American thinking upon the New Deal. Without question, this economic and political revolution brought immense good to the American people, both in the way of promoting social security and in harmonizing the national and state governments. At the same time, the New Deal carried within itself elements of bureaucratic control contrary to the American way of life.

At the critical period, when the New Deal's impact had confused and almost annihilated its opponents, Wendell Willkie, by his courage and common sense, brought clearness of vision to the American people. By his intelligent leadership, he put timely limits to the aggressive inroads of the New Deal upon the liberties of the American people. At the same time, during a great international crisis, when democratic countries were threatened by the Axis Powers, he possessed the courage to oppose small-minded isolationists and to rally a large segment of the nation behind the foreign policy of his political opponent, the New Deal President, in an effort to make the United States an effective instrument of world peace.

After all these accomplishments, as suddenly as he had appeared in American politics, death removed Willkie from the political arena. Almost immediately his career began to take the form of a myth compounded of stories, rumors, propaganda, misconceptions and exaggeration, with the result that the picture of Wendell Willkie today is considerably confused and often far from the truth. With a desire to obtain, before it is too late, an account of Willkie as seen by his contemporaries, and particularly by the men and women who stood closest to him, the author has sought out and talked with a large number of persons who personally knew Willkie or participated in the great events among which he moved. Among his immediate family, the author has conferred several times with Edith Willkie, the wife of Wendell Willkie, and with other relatives.

Among Willkie's associates in the public utilities, the author has had numerous conversations with Justin Whiting, president of the Commonwealth and Southern Corporation; the late A. C. Watt, public relations expert and a director of C&S; John C. Weadock, general counsel for C&S; A. Chambers Oliphant, owner of Oliphant Washington Utility Service; Purcell L. Smith, president of the National Association of Electric Companies, in Washington, D.C.; Rowland George, Wall Street broker; and Oswald Ryan, general counsel for the Federal Power Commission, later vice-chairman of the Civil Aeronautics Board; and Bernard Capen Cobb, organizer of C&S.

Among members of the Republican Party, the author has talked with John D. M. Hamilton, National Chairman of the Republican Party in 1940; Frank Altschul, Wall Street banker and chairman of the Finance Committee of the Republican Party in 1936; Ernest T. Weir, chairman of the National Steel

Corporation and chairman of the Finance Committee of the Republican Party in 1940; Sinclair Weeks, former Republican Senator from Massachusetts and National Committeeman; Charles A. Halleck, Congressman from Indiana and Majority Floor Leader in 1946; Joseph W. Martin, Jr., Congressman from Massachusetts and Speaker of the House of Representatives, 1946-1948; Homer Capehart, Senator from Indiana; Samuel F. Pryor, vice-president of Pan American Airways, Connecticut political leader and chairman of Arrangements of the Republican National Convention of 1940; Harold E. Talbott, vice-president of Chrysler Corporation and chairman of the Finance Committee of the Republican Party in 1948; John B. Hollister, former Congressman from Ohio, assigned to the Willkie campaign train by the Republican Executive Committee; Styles Bridges, Senator from New Hampshire; and Ralph F. Gates, Governor of Indiana, 1944-1948, and an old family friend.

Other Republican leaders whom the author has consulted include: Joseph N. Pew, Jr., political leader of Pennsylvania; Raymond E. Baldwin, Governor of Connecticut, later a United States Senator and then a Federal Judge; Harold E. Stassen, Governor of Minnesota and later president of the University of Pennsylvania; Robert A. Taft, Senator from Ohio; John Foster Dulles, Wall Street lawyer, adviser to Governor Dewey on foreign affairs, member of the United States delegation to the United Nations and consultant to the Secretary of State; Oren Root, Jr., organizer of the Willkie Clubs; Mrs. Henry Breckinridge, philanthropist and organizer of the woman's division of the Willkie Clubs in 1940; Milton R. Polland, insurance broker at Milwaukee, Wisconsin, and influential in local politics; John E. Dickinson, vice-president of the Amity Leather Products Company in West Bend, Wisconsin, and chairman of all Republican County Committees in 1944; Ralph H. Cake, National Committeeman from Oregon and manager of the Willkie primary campaign in 1944; the late Ralph E. Church, Congressman from Illinois; Elliott V. Bell, former editorial writer of the *New York Times*, appointed Superintendent of Banks in 1943 by Governor Dewey; Charles A. Wolverton, Congressman from New Jersey and member of the Joint Committee on the Investigation of the Tennessee Valley Authority; Wat Arnold, Congressman from Missouri; and Robert Rolfs, of West Bend.

Among members of the Democratic Party, the author has consulted James A. Farley, National Chairman of the Democratic Party in 1932-1940 and Postmaster-General in 1933-1940, as well as Henry A. Wallace, Vice-President of the United States in 1940-1944; Raoul Desvernine, New York lawyer and active in the Jeffersonian Democrats; Elbert D. Thomas, Senator from Utah; Harold J. Gallagher, New York lawyer and active in the Jeffersonian Democrats; John W. Hanes, Under-Secretary of the Treasury, later organizer of the Democrats-for-Willkie; Alan Valentine, formerly president of the University of Rochester, and active in the Democrats-for-Willkie; Bainbridge Colby, Secretary of State under Woodrow Wilson; and Harold Young, political secretary to Henry A. Wallace.

Among journalists, the author has conferred with James Hagerty of the *New York Times;* Raymond Moley of *Newsweek;* Arthur Krock of the *New York Times;* Gardner Cowles, Jr., editor and owner of *Look;* Thomas Stokes, syndicate writer, and Roscoe Drummond of the *Christian Science Monitor.*

State Department and other officials the author consulted included Stanley K. Hornbeck, adviser on political relations in the Department of State in 1937-1944; Clarence E. Gauss, Ambassador to China in 1941-1944; General Patrick J. Hurley, personal representative of President Roosevelt in Soviet Russia in 1942, in the Near and Middle East, India and China in 1943, and Ambassador to China in 1944; General Claire Lee Chennault, commander of the Flying Tigers and in 1943 commander of the 14th U. S. Air Force in China; Loy Henderson, Foreign Service officer; and Llewellyn E. Thompson, Foreign Service officer.

Finally, a large number of persons who were friends or associates of Willkie have offered valuable information. These included Kenneth Colegrove, professor of political science at Northwestern University; Walter F. Dodd, author of *Cases and Materials on Constitutional Law;* and Walter Kahoe, former administrative assistant to the Chairman of the Board of TVA, Arthur E. Morgan; Gerald F. Winfield, member of the Associated Board of Christian Colleges in China; Irita Van Doren, literary editor of the *New York Herald Tribune Book Review;* Elisha M. Friedman, consulting economist of New York; Lepha McCurda, school friend of Wendell Willkie in Elwood, Indiana; O. D. Hinshaw, owner of the Hinshaw Drug Store at Elwood, Indiana; W. S. Woodfill, president of the Grand Hotel, Mackinac Island, Michigan; Harvey Firestone, Jr., president of the Firestone Tire and Rubber Company; Arthur E. Morgan, first Chairman of the Board of TVA; and Dr. Lillian Gay Berry.

None of the people listed above is responsible for any opinions or conclusions of the author.

The biography of Wendell Willkie is the old American story of a boy of average American parents and background, brought up on the Indiana prairie, rising to be one of the great men of his generation. Attaining a position of power and prestige in the metropolis of the nation, he made a contribution in three fields; business, politics, and foreign relations.

Despite his many blunders and great inexperience in public service, he did well for his country. His greatest talent was to dramatize a situation or a policy in such manner as to win public support. In business, although merely a private citizen, he defended Free Enterprise, and led the opposition to the New Deal program. Politically he revitalized the Republican Party and gave it a new type of leadership based on courage, imagination and the recognition of the need for new formulas. In so doing he stiffened the morale of the other liberal Republicans in the party. His vibrant leadership also took the Republican Party out of the bog of isolationism and committed it to international co-operation. With Willkie's patriotic efforts, President Roosevelt was able to win the unified support of the American people to the policy of making America the arsenal of democracy in the contest with Hitlerism. Willkie's invention of the Loyal Opposition led to the bipartisan foreign policy which helped win the Second World War and finally enlisted world-wide interest for the United Nations.

Willkie was a curious and contradictory personality. He broke many precedents. He made friends by the hundreds and almost as many enemies. Thus he became something of an enigma. How can one account for the Willkie episode in American politics? What was his secret of personal leadership? What was the origin of his defense of American Enterprise and Big Business? Did Willkie possess a consistent and logical philosophy of American life or was he a mere opportunist? Did he present the soundest opposition to the New Deal program? How shall the historian account for Willkie's indifference to the time-honored techniques of American politicians and political parties? Why was he unable to substitute personal leadership for party organization and tactics? And finally, what was the significance of Willkie as the founder of the bipartisan foreign policy which was developed in the last Administration of President Roosevelt and continued under his successor? These are the fundamental questions which have guided the investigation of this story. As a result, this biography is essentially a study in public opinion, party politics, and public relations.

WENDELL WILLKIE

CHAPTER I

A Young Man
From Indiana

IT WAS the first of March, 1919. Spring had not yet driven winter from the Indiana prairie. A sharp western wind was blowing. In the day coach of a Pennsylvania Railroad train hurrying through the midlands, sat a young man in the uniform of a first lieutenant of artillery. Two days earlier, at Camp Sherman, he had been honorably discharged from the United States Army. His name was Wendell Willkie.

The journey to his native town, Elwood, was rich in associations. He vividly recalled the day on which Congress had declared war on Germany, April 6, 1917. On that very day, he had enlisted as a private in the Army. About a month later he had reported to the first Reserve Officers' Training Camp at Fort Benjamin Harrison, and was there commissioned a first lieutenant. After a training period at Harvard University under French military instructors, he was assigned to the 325th Field Artillery.

There were other things to recall: his happy wedding to the charming blue-eyed girl from Rushville, which occurred during a brief leave from duty in January, 1918. He had been caught in a snowstorm and was late for the ceremony. But his bride, Edith, was understanding. He had taken her back to camp with him, and during the intervening months before his departure overseas, they had spent precious hours together. Then, on September 28, 1918, he had been shipped to France where his regiment was stationed at Camp de Souge, serving with the American Expeditionary Force under General Pershing.

Now the time had come to adjust himself to the future. His plan was to return to his father's law office in Elwood. After taking his law degree from the University of Indiana in 1916, he had practised with his father for a few months before the outbreak of war. He had admiration for his father's legal ability, and looked forward to being associated with him again in the little law office of Willkie & Willkie on the second floor of the old building on Anderson Street.

The train was nearing Elwood. The young soldier recognized the familiar farms with their red barns and meadow lands. Then came a cluster of ugly houses, and finally the well-remembered railway station, as small and drab as when he had left Elwood for the Army. The train jerked to a stop, and he alighted to be clutched in the embrace of his family. A soldier boy had come home. There was no brass band, no shouting, or waving of flags. The Army was now a thing of the past.

The absence of friends and neighbors at the station reminded him that he was almost a stranger in his home town. After he had graduated from high school, he had spent four years at the state university at Bloomington. Each summer he had embarked on some jaunt to a distant section of the country. Then, after receiving his bachelor's degree, he had taught history for one year at the high school of Coffeyville in Kansas before returning to the university for the law course. A few months after securing his law degree, he had left Elwood for military training camp. In the last ten years, therefore, he had lived in Elwood only for brief intervals. This was sufficient to account for the lack of a parade and cheers at his home-coming. There were, however, still other reasons.

The parents of Wendell Willkie were apart from the other folk of the community. They were different in the way they lived, the way they dressed, and what they thought and spoke.

His mother had been the first woman in Indiana admitted to the bar. Through many years she had continued to practise law with her husband. Hence, the second "Willkie" in the firm's name stood for Henrietta Trisch Willkie. She was a strange woman, and the sharpness of her views and her eccentricities had alienated the townspeople one by one. No one doubted her ability, but few claimed her as a friend. She was the first woman in Elwood to smoke cigarettes. Such conduct in a small community caused tongues to wag. Even at home she was an American matriarch. Adamant in any opposition to her plans, she exercised a dread power at the family hearth. She was goaded by one outstanding ambition: her children must succeed. This she continually dinned into their young minds.

As Mrs. Willkie was ever more deeply engrossed in her legal work, the household responsibilities were early imposed upon her eldest child, Julia. Indeed, it was she who gave the Willkie brood love and tenderness, preparing the meals, keeping the cookie jar filled, and getting the younger children merrily off to school. There were six children spaced only a year or so apart: Julia, Robert, Fred, Wendell, Edward, and Charlotte. Although Julia was only one year older than Robert, he and the others respected and looked up to her.

His father, Herman Willkie, was a man of fine ability with a lilt in his soul. He loved books and owned the largest library in the town. During the long winter evenings, he tried to awaken the imagination of his children by reading aloud to them from the classics. Fun-loving and gay, he awoke his family early in the mornings by singing lustily bits of verse and jingles. All of Willkie's neighbors agreed that he was a clever and shrewd lawyer. In fact his talents might have won for him a better practice in a larger community.

Young Willkie was deeply devoted to his father. The boy grew up with the firmly fixed idea that his father was the best lawyer in the state. Even many years later when Wendell had moved to New York City and had become an important figure on Wall Street, he frequently telephoned his father by long distance to ask his opinion on some legal problem. There was also a close spiritual bond between father and son. They engaged in long conversations on political and economic subjects. In these discourses, justice was a favorite theme. Through his father, the lad became keenly aware of the inequalities suffered by the underprivileged classes which were found even in a town like Elwood.

Both had a natural predilection towards politics. The elder man at one time even joined the Socialist Party, although he usually voted the Democratic ticket. Wendell early tied himself to the Democratic Party. Woodrow Wilson, who was elected the Governor of New Jersey the year that Wendell graduated from high school, was to become his political idol. The boy was attracted to civic affairs and greatly admired his father for the time and devotion he gave such matters. Herman Willkie led almost every civic movement in town. He had been instrumental in establishing the high school, the public library and the new building for the Methodist Church.

The community was proud of its public school system and churches, which the Willkies had helped develop. They had moved to Elwood in 1888, four years before Wendell was born. Herman Willkie had come to the town to serve as superintendent of schools while he read law. After establishing the high school he secured the money for the building which finally housed the entire school system. This was the school Wendell entered in 1899 as a first-grader, and from which he was graduated as a high school senior in 1910. The town also proudly possessed an "Opera House."

Elwood had its ups and downs. When the Willkies came to Elwood it still retained the characteristics of a frontier boom town. Natural gas had been discovered the year before. This turned the farming village into a thriving industrial center. In 1890 the Pittsburgh Plate Glass Company selected the town for the branch site of one of its factories. Two years later the American Sheet and Tin Plate Company was established which later became a subsidiary of the United States Steel Corporation. During the decade of the nineties the population grew from three thousand to fifteen thousand. Other industries were attracted to the town and the future of Elwood seemed well assured. Herman Willkie believed the boom would last indefinitely and bought real estate extensively, expecting to make large profits.

Before the boom collapsed he was able to secure a comfortable home for his large family. He chose a beautiful corner plot at 19th and North A streets which was a nice section with many trees and fine houses. Here he built a three-story frame structure with a stone foundation and a gabled roof, containing eight large rooms and an attic. The family moved into their new home about June, 1900. This was a rapturous experience for the children, since there was room both in the yard and the house for all their activities. The remainder of their childhood was spent in this happy spot.

In 1903 the gas wells suddenly petered out. At once the Pittsburgh Plate Glass Company closed its branch factory at Elwood and the tin-plate factory suspended operations. Thereafter it reopened from time to time as conditions fluctuated from good to bad. When the mills were opened, a fleeting prosperity returned to the community, and when they were closed times were bleak. With these reverses in the financial conditions of the town several thousand workers left Elwood to seek more stable employment elsewhere. Property values accordingly collapsed.

Herman Willkie suddenly found his law practice dwindling and his real estate holdings a liability. His one important client was the Amalgamated Association of Iron, Steel and Tin Workers. This was the only important labor union in the town. The fees from a labor union in these early days were not large. But they added very nicely to the family income, and the connection with the union, moreover, brought a discussion of labor problems into the family circle. Wendell, although still quite young, became much interested in the social ills of the workers. Several years later he came to know the men in the mill and learned of their conditions by working with them for one summer. When the big strike took place in 1909, his father showed him every step in the preparation of the legal case against the injunctions which the steel company was seeking. Through all these contacts with labor, he constantly heard his father say that some day "management would become enlightened."

The strike lasted intermittently for several years. In his effort to win for the union, Willkie thought it might be wise to enlist additional counsel, and he visited Clarence Darrow in Chicago, taking Wendell with him. But the great man wanted $20,000 as a retainer and $1,000 for each day in court. When the union officials learned of this price they thought Herman Willkie was doing all right for them. His fee was twenty-five dollars a day. Finally the case was ended and Willkie won. The injunction was denied. With this unique victory Wendell looked upon his father as without a superior in the field of law. But in reality the long court fight proved a hollow triumph as it weakened the union and reduced its membership.

By the summer of 1906 the family financial situation had become somewhat easier, so it was decided to send Wendell to the Culver Military Academy summer camp. He was not robust at the time and it was thought the experience would help to develop him physically. But Wendell did not enjoy the military discipline or the rugged life of a training camp, although he did learn to swim and he acquired some skill in handling a sailboat.

Wendell was fifteen when he found his first love. She was an attractive girl of Welsh extraction, Gwyneth Harry. Her beauty was unusual compared with the other girls in the town. She was gifted with a magnificent high soprano voice as vibrantly appealing as her rare loveliness. Wendell first saw her in the choir of the small Episcopal Church where he had been taken by a friend to meet her. After the service he was introduced to her and "walked" her home. It was the beginning of a long friendship. So devoted did he become to Gwyneth that he shortly deserted the large Methodist Church where his father was a leading member to join the simple little white church of the Episcopalians. To please her he even became a lay reader of the Church. For the rest of his life he accounted himself an Episcopalian.

During the remainder of his high school days, Wendell was accustomed to leave his house half an hour early so as to hurry across town to pick up Gwyneth and walk her to school, although he lived within two blocks of the schoolhouse. His love for her cost him much of his popularity, also. In his junior year he was made president of the local fraternity, the Beta Phi Sigma. But Gwyneth, new to the community and of immigrant parents, was not acceptable to the Delta sorority. "Wen" was so deeply hurt by the rebuff to the girl he loved that he decided

to resign from his fraternity in protest against the snobbishness
of fraternal organizations. It was a gallant gesture. He carried
this resentment against fraternities with him long after graduation from high school. In fact, he first attracted attention at
the university by his loud denunciation of fraternities as anti-
democratic.

When Wendell went to Bloomington, Indiana, to matriculate
in the state university he did not enter as a lonely freshman.
Already there were his sister Julia, and his brothers Robert and
Fred. Julia, the first to go to college, had established herself in
a small apartment on the ground floor of an old house. Here
she welcomed her brothers as one by one they came to Bloomington. Although she had finished her undergraduate work by
the time Wendell arrived, she had remained at the university
to take a master's degree. Always the home-maker of the family,
she continued this activity during the college days of her
brothers.

It was in January, 1910, that Wendell entered Indiana University. He had come to the university with an excellent high
school education showing four years of English composition and
literature, three and a half years of Latin, three years of history,
and two years of science, including short courses in botany,
zoology, and physics. Willkie entered college determined to
prepare for law school. Fortunately, he came under the benign
influence of Dr. Lillian Gay Berry, professor of classical lan-
guages and a kind friend of Julia's. She stressed the importance
of the classics as a broad cultural base for his law work. In after
years, he never forgot this training, which constantly enriched
his understanding of world events. In the early forties he wrote
her: "If Latin did nothing else for me, it helped me to learn
to read and no matter how much the battle rages, I can still
forget completely while re-reading the stories of ancient Rome,
and this is true even though these days I have to do it by the
'pony' route." Although his courses included mathematics,
chemistry and philosophy, it was history and economics which
most appealed to him. In these subjects he made a distinguished
record.

Wendell was the most constructive of the brothers in his
activities at the university. He hastened to participate in campus

affairs and soon became one of the leaders of the independent students. In his senior year, he was elected a director of the Union board. In 1912 he worked very hard to organize a mock political convention. This proved to be a failure because he had neglected to check the university calendar and his affair was scheduled for the same day as the Indiana-Purdue baseball game at Lafayette, Indiana. He won a place on the university debating team and had the experience of traveling through the state for intermural contests. He sometimes carried his love of argumentation into the classroom, however, and "debated" with his teachers.

Meanwhile, Gwyneth had entered Butler University at Indianapolis. As often as his bank account would permit, Wendell went to see her, taking a little bunch of flowers or a box of candy. But small differences kept popping up to cool their ardor for one another. "Wen" lacked a sense of rhythm and consequently was unable to dance, which was a great disappointment to her. Moreover, the fraternity situation bobbed up again, only this time it was the other way round. Gwyneth had done very well at Butler University and joined Kappa Alpha Theta sorority. Finding him outside her social orbit, she demanded that he join a fraternity or else lose her. It was said that he long debated between losing his "soul or his sweetheart." At last he compromised by joining Beta Theta Pi fraternity at the end of his last semester in college, and then sent his Beta pin to Gwyneth.

Early in life, Wendell had made contacts with all kinds of people. At the age of nine he sold newspapers in the streets of Elwood. During summer vacations, he variously labored for a junk dealer, drove a bakery wagon, worked as a fruit and vegetable man, and tended the blast furnaces of the tin-plate mill. College vacations were spent in the wheat fields of North Dakota, in the oil fields of Texas or some frontier place in the Dakotas. In fact it was the custom of Mr. Willkie to give each of his sons a one-way ticket to some distant point with the expectation that they would not only be self-sustaining during the summer months but would save enough for the return ticket home in time for the fall opening of college. One summer Wendell had bad luck as all his savings were stolen just as he was ready for the trip east to Indiana. His ingenuity saved him the embarrassment of wiring his father for money. He persuaded the local banker to give him a loan for his transportation which he later repaid from his own earnings. Certainly these summers gave him unusual experience and an acquaintance with provincial America.

Graduating from Indiana University in June, 1913, with an A.B. degree, Wendell had to earn the money before continuing with his law work. He had taken a number of law courses while completing his undergraduate requirements, so that one year in the law school was all he needed for his degree.

His history professor recommended him to the Board of Education of Coffeyville, Kansas, where he promptly received an appointment to teach history in the high school. Here Wendell spent a busy year which was a preview of his spectacular public career a decade later. He plunged into many activities and readily impressed his personality upon the school and the community. In a few short weeks he had organized a debating team called "The Senate," which followed the rules of procedure of the United States Senate. He delighted his team by taking them on frequent trips to neighboring towns for forenic contests. He coached the basketball team, which won the state championship, and he even found time to organize a high school branch of the YMCA which had occasional suppers. Only twenty-one years old, he was the youngest member of the teaching staff, and the idol of all his students.

By autumn, shortly after his return for the second year, he received a letter from his brother Fred who was doing very well in Puerto Rico and wanted Wendell to join him. Fred, who had become head chemist at the Fajardo Sugar Company, promised a good job with three times the salary Wendell was earning in Kansas. The prospect of adventure and financial increment were too tempting to refuse. He left at once. The students were so disappointed to lose such an exciting teacher that the entire school went to the station to see him off. When he reached Elwood there was another letter from Fred saying that he need not hurry as the sugar crop was a month late that year. Wendell decided to fill in the time by taking a short refresher course in chemistry. As his younger brother Edward was at Oberlin College, Wendell decided to go there. Accordingly he spent the fall weeks of 1914 at Oberlin in preparation for his new work. Wendell sailed for Puerto Rico in January.

Although Wendell only spent a few weeks there, Oberlin College proudly felt it had a kind of claim on him and in 1943 conferred upon him the honorary degree of LL.D.

His work in the sugar company at Puerto Rico was tedious. He made up for the dullness of his laboratory duties by exploring the island and was especially attracted to the old military roads, in the ancient Spanish sections. He was also interested in the modern life of the island and visited the sugar cane fields, where he talked with the workers.

By July, 1915, he had saved enough money to finish law school and accordingly returned to Elwood. He discovered that two years in Coffeyville and Puerto Rico had cooled the romance with Gwyneth. The break came rapidly. Gwyneth married another man and moved to California. Yet Wendell wasted no time in grieving. Life always moved rapidly for him.

In September, 1915, he entered the law school at Indiana University to complete his law work. Hardly had the semester begun when an old friend and fraternity brother from home, George DeHority, came to see him. George was going to be married to a girl in the neighboring town of Rushville, and he wanted "Wen" to be his best man. Understanding his social uneasiness, George hastened to assure Wendell that he would not be required to dance with anyone. So, several weeks later, the two journeyed to Rushville for the great occasion. At one of the bridal parties, Wendell found himself sitting next to his hostess, a most charming girl with chestnut curls and blue, laughing eyes. She was, he discovered, to be the maid of honor. He had met so many girls in rapid succession that he had to ask her for her name.

"I'm Edith Wilk, but people here call me Billie," she replied.

"Wilk and Willkie—it ought to be a good firm," he declared.

That was the beginning of a new romance that eventually led to marriage. He returned to law school and saw Edith only a couple of times during the year. Then, in June, 1916, came graduation.

Wendell was chosen orator for Class Day. A number of the

seniors had joined together to plan the kind of speech he should give, and its radicalism was in effect a dare to the speaker. The title was "The New Freedom," a slogan which so recently had been made famous by Woodrow Wilson. The speech was a diatribe against the conservatism of the law school, its faculty and the state supreme court. The effect was intended to be provocative and entertaining.

Just as Willkie began to speak, in walked the Chief Justice of the state supreme court with the President of the university and some members of the law school faculty. Now Willkie's fellow students became so frightened by the audacity of the speech they had helped prepare and egged him on to give, that no one applauded at the conclusion. Only a frigid silence prevailed as he took his seat. The boys had gone back on him. Immediately after the exercises he was summoned to the President's office and told never again to attempt to be "amusing." When the class on Commencement Day arose to receive their diplomas he was the only one to be passed over. His diploma was privately awarded to him several days later. Although he failed by a narrow margin to receive Phi Beta Kappa, his high scholarship was recognized by the gift of a twenty-volume set of *Encyclopedia of Law and Procedure,* sent to him by the faculty. In 1943, when he had become famous, the chapter elected him to membership. Several years earlier he had visited the university to be honored by an LL.D. degree. An afternoon reception was held for him. As he advanced into the crowded room with President-Emeritus William Bryan on one side of him and President Herman Wells on the other, all eyes fastened upon him. Suddenly he saw Professor Lillian Berry. He rushed forward, lifted her up high and kissed her on both cheeks. Professor Berry was amazed and delighted. The students, though a little stunned, were enraptured and applauded excitedly.

But as he left the campus in 1916, without applause or triumph, he was a little dejected. However, now that he had secured his law degree he was ready at last for admission to the bar and the beginning of practice. He returned to Elwood and his father's law office. Above all others he still admired his father for his legal wisdom and his grasp of judicial analysis. Moreover, Wendell loved the town, the streets and the trees and his old companions. It was the place he wanted to live always. It was home.

No sooner had he returned to Elwood than he became involved in politics and was promptly elected president of the Young Democratic Club of Elwood. The presidential campaign of 1916 was just getting under way. Oswald Ryan, of Madison County, was campaigning that summer for the office of state's attorney on the Republican ticket. He conducted his speechmaking tour in a dray and made his speeches from it in the streets. Thus he came to Elwood. When he finished speaking Willkie came up to him and reaching up his hand said: "I like your style. If you will get down from up there I will take you to the Democratic headquarters and introduce you to my friends." Ryan was elected prosecuting attorney, and his first case was against a man whom young Willkie was defending. Willkie lost the case to Ryan. Years later they met frequently in Washington. But Ryan never forgot that first meeting and how politically alive Willkie was, even in 1916.

During this exciting summer an old friend came to Wendell with another idea. How nice it would be to get Edith Wilk to move over to Elwood. Willkie promptly agreed that it was a wonderful idea, but how could it be achieved. The friend had it all figured out. A place in the Elwood Library would soon be vacant, and Edith was the assistant librarian at Rushville. All they had to do was to win over the library board, and didn't they have influence? Weren't their fathers on the board? So it was arranged that Edith Wilk should be offered the position, which she promptly accepted.

Once Edith was in Elwood, Wendell began to court her in earnest. Mrs. Willkie was rude to the young stranger. Edith stood it for three months and then she rushed home. Wendell rushed after her, but she could not be persuaded to return. So he continued his courting by trolley car. Then suddenly America entered the war, and they were all shaken out of their happy-go-lucky world.

These were the events that filled the mind of the young soldier as he sat in the train carrying him back to his home town. Now these things seemed far away as if they belonged to another world. The war had so completely raised a barrier to all things past.

The return of Wendell Willkie to his home town was not auspicious. There was something sweet and engaging about this young man who expected to bring his bride to the town of his birth to launch his career, but his mother promptly told him that there was not enough legal practice in Elwood for three Willkies and that he should look elsewhere. Perhaps this was her way to goad him into larger fields. Perhaps she feared that if he settled down in Elwood he would never achieve the success that she had envisaged for him. Whatever may have been her motive, it was a cruel realization for the young officer that there was no place for him in his own home town.

Herman Willkie was disappointed by the turn of events. He had long looked forward to the time when his son would join him in legal practice. Bowing to his wife's point of view, he now wrote his old friend, Frank C. Dailey, of the Indianapolis bar, to seek his help in finding a place for Wendell. Meanwhile Dale Crittenberger, Democratic boss of Anderson County, asked Willkie to come to see him. He told the young veteran that the Republican Congressman, Bert Vestal, could be defeated, and promised that he could make Willkie the Democratic candidate for the Eighth Congressional District of Indiana. To a young man always fascinated by politics, this was a dazzling proposal. He asked for time to think about it. With his head in the clouds, he returned home already decided in his own mind that he would soon be representing his district on Capitol Hill in Washington. But his father persuaded him not to be too hasty and to discuss the matter with "Uncle Frank," as the family affectionately referred to Frank Dailey. An appointment was arranged.

Seated comfortably in the elder man's office, he related his plan to go into politics. But Dailey quickly disillusioned him. "You are several kinds of a fool if you start out running for office. Of course you could be elected. But how long would you last? Maybe two terms! Your district is normally Republican, and the tide will soon turn against you. Then you would come back to Elwood and have nothing. In the interim you would have lost your chance to become a good lawyer." Instead of politics, Dailey advised him to take the opening he had secured for him at the Firestone Tire and Rubber Company at Akron. Considerably deflated, Willkie returned home. The following day he told an amazed Crittenberger that he declined the honor of running for Congress on the Democratic ticket. By the first of April he was on his way to Akron to become a "good lawyer," at a salary of $2,500 a year. His wife accepted cheerfully the decision to move to a new and strange community, although she was going to have a baby.

CHAPTER II

A Young Man
Founds His Career

WENDELL WILLKIE possessed the happy talent of identifying himself with the community in which he lived. As the young couple took up their abode in Akron, the city became to them the center of their interests, expectations and dreams. Because of Willkie's lively historical curiosity, he soon knew more of the city's background than most of the older inhabitants, while his compelling interest in men and affairs led him to master as many details of the industry, commerce and municipal government as were known to the secretary of the Akron Chamber of Commerce.

Akron in 1920 was a growing municipality of alert citizens, gigantic energy, and with a tradition that seemed to stem from the frontier west. It was the county seat of Summit County. Situated in a range of hills, surrounded by lakes and overlooking the Big and Little Cuyahoga rivers, it was thirty-five miles from its industrial rival, Cleveland. The city was a rail center of the Baltimore and Ohio Railroad, the Pennsylvania Railroad, the Erie, Canton and Youngstown Railroad, and the Northern Ohio Railroad.

The town had been settled in 1807, but its boom dated from the construction of the Ohio Canal in 1825. The surplus water used in lockage for the canals, collected by reservoirs in the hills, supplied power for large flour mills. The city, well located for diversified industries, was on the northern edge of the grain belt and the southern edge of the dairy section of Ohio. In the vicinity were deep beds of fire clay as well as coal mines. Industries rapidly increased and included the manufacture of tiles, ceramics, rubber goods, agricultural implements and household appliances.

The city itself deeply inspired Willkie. Yet his work in the legal department of the Firestone Tire and Rubber Company was routine, consisting largely of giving free legal aid to the employees. But Willkie aspired to practise corporation law.

With characteristic vigor, therefore, Willkie plunged into the forum of public opinion. Akron was in the isolationist belt of the United States and her citizens were only mildly interested in the bitter contest in the United States Senate over the League of Nations. Willkie had long been a disciple of Woodrow Wilson and shared his idealism for world co-operation. He looked upon internationalism as imperative, and he was shocked by the opposition to the League Covenant of Henry Cabot Lodge and Hiram Johnson. Eager to help arouse sentiment for the League, Willkie began making speeches in and around Akron. The fact that he had fought to make the world safe for democracy added strength to his arguments. He also became popular in the American Legion and, in 1920, was elected commander of the Summit County Post. Thereupon, Akron newspapers recorded his many appearances as a public speaker.

Established law firms, ever on the watch for smart young colleagues, were attracted by his growing publicity. Accordingly, in January, 1921, he received an offer from the distinguished firm of Mather and Nesbitt, at a salary of $3,500 per year.

Harvey Firestone made an attempt to hold the young lawyer with the tempting offer of $5,000. Willkie submitted the problem to his charming young wife. Despite their urgent need for funds, she encouraged him to accept the new offer. "The money really doesn't count, but insist that the firm adds your name to the door," she wisely counseled. This he did, and the law part-

ners agreed that if he made good, he would be received into the
partnership, a promise they fulfilled within the year. The firm
was counsel to railroads, utility companies, banks and other
business corporations. Thus, Willkie had a chance to practise a
wide diversity of corporation law. His career was now well
launched.

In later life, Wendell Willkie once remarked that all a man
needed to get up in the world was a powerful adversary. He had
two. In the thirties, it was to be Franklin D. Roosevelt. In the
twenties, it was Harvey Firestone. The opposition of the mighty
industrialist immediately gave Willkie a statewide reputation.
It grew out of a suit which Harvey Firestone brought against
William H. Kroeger in May, 1925. Kroeger retained Willkie.
The complaint was simple. Kroeger had long been employed as
general manager of the Coventry Land and Improvement Company, a subsidiary of Firestone Tire and Rubber Company.

The suit involved the ownership of fifty-seven shares of stock
of The Times Publishing Company, publisher of *The Akron
Times,* of which Firestone had been one of the founders. In
1925, the paper was sold to Roy Howard, of the Scripps-Howard
newspapers, for $710,000. The fifty-seven shares, amounting to
about $62,000, were in Kroeger's name. Firestone, contending
that the stock was held by Kroeger in trust, filed suit for an injunction to prevent Kroeger from disposing of the stock.
Kroeger contended that the stock had been assigned to him as
added compensation in lieu of a salary increase.

Willkie was thus pitted against the powerful Firestone. There
was intense interest in the suit. Although Firestone was an industrial giant, Kroeger was a man of excellent standing. Speculation arose as to how well Willkie could compete with the top
legal talent employed by Firestone. In addition to Amos C.
Miller, distinguished corporation lawyer of Chicago and vice-
president of the Firestone Company, there were half a dozen
other well-known attorneys. When the trial opened, Firestone
and his bevy of attorneys swept into the courtroom and spread
out at the counsel table. It was a formidable scene. Willkie
walked into the court alone, the only attorney for the defense.

The plaintiff began by asking that Kroeger be cited for contempt of court for failure to appear in court as summoned and

demanded he be summarily arrested and put in jail. As defense counsel, Willkie rose and faced the ten opposing lawyers. He explained to the Court that Kroeger had not been legally served with the writ of summons and thus was not subject to contempt proceedings. Casting his eye upon the group of attorneys confronting him, Willkie appealed dramatically to the Judge to "straighten them out on this point." The Court sustained Willkie and refused to issue the contempt order.

Willkie had kept Kroeger in seclusion until depositions could be taken from Firestone officials. Thus the plaintiffs were obliged to show their hand. Willkie's procedure proved effective, and the case was never tried. After numerous motions and demurrers had been filed, the matter was settled out of court, to the favor and satisfaction of Kroeger, in the summer of 1926.

The publicity of the Firestone case together with his more flexible schedule brought Willkie into greater participation in civic affairs. The American Legion provided him with a constant public forum to launch his ideas. At the same time, his commanding position within the Legion added prestige and strength to his political activity. Upon establishing his residence in Akron, he had identified himself with the Democratic Party and as he became well known in the community was enlisted in local campaigning. He especially participated in the activity for the re-election of Martin L. Davey to Congress. Because of his loyal party support he was selected as a delegate to the National Democratic Convention of 1924. In this hotly contested convention, which consumed eleven weary days and required 103 roll calls for the selection of a presidential candidate, Willkie opposed the nomination of William G. McAdoo because of the suspicion of support from the Ku Klux Klan. Willkie, like many Democrats, was an ardent admirer of the lovable Alfred E. Smith. On the first sixty-two ballots in the convention, the Ohio delegation cast forty-eight votes for James M. Cox, its "favorite son." For the next ten ballots, the Ohio delegation voted as a unit for Newton D. Baker, another "favorite son." On the seventy-fourth ballot, Willkie and some twenty other delegates, at last had the opportunity to vote for Al Smith. But after the decline in the drive for Smith, on the ninety-first ballot, Willkie joined the final movement for John W. Davis.

Willkie was one of the most vigorous opponents of the Ku Klux Klan at the New York Convention. He supported the resolution to denounce this un-American organization in the Democratic platform. Recognizing his leadership in this matter, the Klan in Akron sent him a telegram at the convention asking sarcastically when he had "joined the payroll of the Pope." As Willkie later related the story, finding himself short of funds, he simply telegraphed back the curt message: "The Klan can go to hell."

In the early post-war years, the Ku Klux Klan was a powerful organization in Ohio. It stood for ultraconservatism in domestic policy and isolation in foreign policy. The secret clique was part of the counter-clockwise movement that followed the Wilsonian reforms and the wartime restrictions. Willkie was one of the conspicuous leaders who finally broke the power of the Klan in Ohio.

In all these speeches and activities, Willkie was the crusader. He liked to call himself the champion of the common man. Yet there was also something of the actor in him. On numerous occasions, he had been known to jump down from the platform where he was speaking and stride down the aisle waving his long arms as he exhorted his listeners to a particular point of view. His interests were wide as his activities. He knew the problems of industry and the struggles of labor. He made speeches to all kinds of groups and defended all kinds of people. He was counsel for corporations, but he also defended truck-drivers and workers. Thus his reputation spread throughout the state.

Willkie was a man of great personal charm and easily attracted the attention of people wherever he went. As a result of the associations he made at the 1924 Convention, he received several interesting offers to go to New York. Perhaps the most flattering one came from James W. Gerard, former ambassador to Germany.

It was Bernard Capen Cobb, however, who finally induced him to leave Ohio. In 1929, Cobb had organized the billion-dollar utility company known as Commonwealth and Southern Corporation, which was a merger of 165 companies including the Northern Ohio Power and Light Company. It was as president of this company that Cobb first became acquainted with

Willkie, whose law firm handled the cases for the Northern Ohio Power and Light Company. Cobb was a genius of finance and one of the great empire-builders of American industry. He early recognized the need for a utility combination, honestly constructed, which would increase power service and decrease rates. The Commonwealth and Southern Corporation was the fulfillment of this objective. With the completion of this gigantic merger, Cobb needed a brilliant young man in the New York office. Accordingly, he urged Willkie to join the firm of Weadock and Weadock, legal counsel for C&S, as a partner at three times his Akron salary.

Willkie had now lived ten years in Akron and was a director of the Ohio State Bank and Trust Company, a director of the South Akron Savings Association, of which Kroeger was president, and a director of the Acme Mortgage Company. He was the youngest man on the board of the Northern Ohio Power and Light Company and he was president of the Akron Bar Association. For the departure of such a prominent citizen, there were many farewell banquets and toasts to his future success.

Exhilarated by the excitement of life in New York, Willkie increased his tempo of achievement. Not only was he most adaptable to the new environment, but he mastered in a few months the principles of the utility business. His colleagues soon recognized that the newcomer was a marked man. Indeed New York took kindly to this young man from Indiana. He made friends rapidly in all circles, including Thomas Lamont, of the House of Morgan, and Helen Reid (Mrs. Ogden Reid), vice-president of the *Herald Tribune*. Financiers, writers, artists, actors and scholars all accepted him warmly. His tramps across the country during summer vacations meeting all kinds of people had given him an easy manner so that he was as much at home in his lofty office on Pine Street, New York, discussing the market on bonds as he was sitting on a fence in Indiana, talking to a neighboring farmer about the crops.

Always affable, simple and spontaneous in his human relations, he was easy to like and easy to know. It was said that before he went into politics anyone could walk into his office for a conference. On several occasions his office staff attempted to sift the people whom he should see. When he learned about this, he gave instructions he wanted to see everybody.

His comfortable manner captivated his visitors. Sitting in his upholstered chair, he would twist himself into a half-lounging position with one leg swung over the chair arm. This lolling posture gave him the appearance of leisure. It also accounted for the crumpled suits he wore. Although he put on a pressed suit each morning, there was nothing left of its freshness by noonday. The tousled hair and the rumpled suit became characteristic of him, perhaps all the more so because they were unusual on Wall Street. And often, if Willkie put his feet on his desk, the visitor would behold mended shoes. Many homespun habits of his youth lingered with him always. Having the soles of his shoes repaired by a round patch was one of them. This complete disregard of appearance was frequently a source of embarrassment to some of the senior members of the firm who brought the great of Wall Street into his office to meet him. Yet he was a man of remarkably magnetic personality.

In appearance Willkie was strikingly handsome. His stature was imposing. He stood six feet one inch in height and weighed about two hundred pounds. For his habit of running his hand through his hair as he talked, there was usually a stray lock hanging over his forehead. The blackness of his hair enhanced the vivid blue of his eyes, eyes that always seemed to have a twinkle. He also had another unusual feature, a cleft chin. (Artists for some reason usually tried to sketch over this feature after he became famous.) Besides his appearance, it was his friendly, warm personality coupled with a fine sense of humor and quick repartee that made him a favorite among his wide circle of acquaintances.

But with all his popularity and marked ability he would not have advanced with such spectacular rapidity had he not won the esteem and confidence of Bernard Capen Cobb, one of the mystery men in the history of American utility enterprise, who modestly avoided the inquiries of the newsmen who chronicled, day by day, the process of Big Business.

Cobb was born in 1870 of old New England stock. He was educated at Phillips Andover Academy, after which he plunged into business activity.

At eighteen years of age he followed the popular nineteenth century trek westward and entered the employment of the Pennsylvania Railroad Company at Grand Rapids, Michigan. At this time, electric power and light and gas companies, established as separate units in municipalities, had begun the process of consolidation for the purpose of obtaining cheaper financing. Utilities were entering the phase of industrial development known as "Big Business."

Almost from the beginning, young Cobb participated in that miracle of modern business, mass production. In 1895 he left railroading and became an official in the construction department of the Grand Rapids Gas Light Company. Shortly after the turn of the century, he went to New York City to supervise more extensive projects. For fifteen years he operated, constructed, acquired, consolidated and financed utility properties.

In the 1920's he became associated with Landon Thorne and Alfred Loomis, investment bankers. Together, they undertook a series of public utility consolidations which culminated in 1929 when 165 companies were brought together in a billion-dollar holding company under the name of Commonwealth and Southern Corporation. On Wall Street, this achievement was hailed as one of the landmarks in utility financial history. The gigantic undertaking was accomplished without corporate chicanery such as characterized the manipulations of Samuel Insull and Howard C. Hopson. These buccaneers of finance were already bringing disrepute to the entire industry, by their matchless ingenuity of stock pyramiding and reckless system of interlocking holding companies.

The impending storm of government regulation was not apparent when Cobb consummated the formation of C&S. He had chosen Thomas W. Martin, head of the Alabama Power Company, a subsidiary, as president of C&S. Cobb became chairman of the board. In 1932, however, Cobb sent Martin back to the Alabama Power Company and himself took over the presidency while he searched for a successor.

Surveying the field of half a hundred available junior executives, he decided that Wendell Willkie was the most desirable and competent. Cobb liked his dash and verve, his quickness in seizing hold of intricate problems of management and

finance. Hence Cobb drew Willkie ever more closely into every
phase of the intricate management of the giant corporation.
Together they visited every operating plant in the vast system
and discussed all problems with the local management. Cobb
was pleased to see how easily Willkie won the confidence of
these staff officers and understood their technical difficulties.
Thus Cobb was ever more thoroughly convinced that Willkie
was the right man to carry on the operations of the financial
empire he had created.

In late 1932, ill health prompted Cobb to move Willkie more
rapidly into command of the Commonwealth and Southern
Corporation than he had previously planned. Suddenly, on the
evening of January 24, 1933, Cobb decided that the time had
come. The following morning, he telephoned to a member of
the board, requesting him to propose the name of Willkie as
president at the board meeting on that very day. Confirmation
was promptly made. In this simple way, Willkie was elevated
to one of the most spectacular and powerful positions on Wall
Street.

The following day witnessed a ripple of surprise on Wall
Street at the choice of Willkie as president of the mighty C&S.
Some observers felt that in view of his lack of real experience
in the operation of public utilities it was a mistake to place him
in such a responsible position of leadership. Certainly his competence was still to be tested.

Willkie had always been a man of vast energy. In his new
position he became a dynamo. No member of his staff could
match his pace. His rapid conduct of business left his associates
exhausted. It was not an uncommon occurrence for him to telephone a colleague at two o'clock in the morning or to arouse
him at sunrise to discuss some new phase of a problem which
had just occurred to him. These unusual calls were never
limited to a few minutes. They often were extended discussions
of a half hour or more. Such tactics were no doubt helpful to
Willkie in thinking through a problem, but they kept his staff
continually on edge.

A news ticker was installed in the Pine Street office and
closely watched for official statements, especially during the
struggle with the Tennessee Valley Authority. The comments

of President Roosevelt at his press conferences in the White House were anxiously awaited. When news was expected to break, Willkie asked his staff to remain at the office throughout the evening. At such times, he would munch a sandwich at his desk in order to avoid missing any important item. He even resented any desertion by his colleagues who sought more substantial food in near-by restaurants. When a derogatory statement appeared on the news ticker, the entire staff would work desperately to prepare the counter-statement for release to the press for the morning papers. In this way, the answer to the President's attack on Willkie and the utilities appeared in the same issue of the newspaper as the White House statement itself.

Cobb's health grew progressively worse until June, 1934, when he retired as chairman of the board of directors and from all active participation in the affairs of Commonwealth and Southern Corporation. Willkie now combined the office of chairman and president under his own direction. By the same arrangement, four directors resigned from the board in order to make room for the presidents of the four larger operating units of C&S, with the purpose of integrating more effectively the vast utility empire. Fate had now placed Willkie in a unique and powerful position on the eve of a political storm that was to shake the foundations of public utilities in this country. In November, 1932, Franklin D. Roosevelt had been elected President of the United States. During the presidential campaign, his sharp attack on public utilities had annoyed the executives of the industry, yet few had taken the New Deal candidate too seriously. Willkie was one of the few leaders of the industry who seemed to sense a foreshadowing of the approaching danger to private operations in America.

An era of American history, so to speak, separated the young Willkie and the most powerful figure in the utilities, Samuel Insull. The men were utterly unlike in their attitude toward government and business and the public morals of corporate wealth. Insull was typical of the "robber-barons" of the nineteenth century. Willkie represented the enlightened industrial leadership of the twentieth century. Insull and Willkie had one contact with each other which left them without admiration one for the other. It was a clash of the old and the new. They met at a meeting of utility executives in 1929 when Insull was at the height of his power. At that meeting Insull was bitter in his denouncement of agitators and radicals. He declared that there should be a way to silence the critics of Big Business. Then someone asked Willkie what he thought. Promptly and courageously the young man declared that he had always defended the right of the opposition to be heard. If his ideas were well founded, society would benefit thereby, and if they were not well founded the ideas would fall on barren soil to no one's hurt.

As Willkie concluded his little speech there was an awkward pause and a tense kind of silence. The arrogant Insull turned on the young man and said with devastating coldness: "Mr. Willkie, when you are older, you will know more!"

Clearly, Willkie believed in change and reforms. In fact he had long opposed the sort of industrial empire that Insull had created. To prevent such racketeering as the Mid-West Utilities Company, he advocated federal laws to regulate holding companies long before such a measure was introduced in Congress. In fact, Willkie went further. He believed there should be a national law for incorporation which would eliminate at the start many of the evils in holding companies. Likewise, he felt that government regulation of the New York Stock Exchange was needed. The entire field of public utilities would be improved, he thought, if the wolves in the industry were brought under control by proper legislation.

In his enlightened view of business he held that wealth was a public trust to be used wisely in the public interest. A well-organized business in which the interests of stockholders and consumers and workers were equally protected was a healthy enterprise for society. This concept was in sharp contrast to the policy of Insull who milked his subsidiary companies to the public hurt and who finally lost the confidence of the people in his enterprises.

The black depression of 1929 opened the flood-gates of criticism upon Big Business, especially utility companies. In its attack on President Hoover as the representative of Big Business, the Democratic Party was quick to seize upon this issue in the presidential campaign of 1932. When the ballots were counted, it was found that the Democrats had ridden into office committed to wide-sweeping reforms and regulatory laws for business enterprise. With this objective Willkie was in agreement. But even as a Democrat he was not prepared for the sudden and bitter attacks against all Big Business as soon as the victorious party was installed in Washington. Willkie had little more than got his office organized as the new president of C&S when the storm broke. For the next six years he spent most of his time defending free enterprise against the onslaughts of the New Deal.

CHAPTER III

The Attack on Government Monopoly

WENDELL WILLKIE had been president of Commonwealth and Southern Corporation scarcely three months when he was drawn into the spectacular controversy between the public utilities and the New Deal. At the outset, neither Willkie nor the utility magnates of New York and Chicago were aware of the seriousness of the New Deal challenge to the utility industry. Indeed, it was with some surprise that Willkie read the notable speech of the Democratic candidate delivered at Portland, Oregon, on September 21, 1932. As Governor of New York, Franklin D. Roosevelt had been a critic of public utilities, yet the Portland speech seemed to be unusually capricious and vindictive. Willkie was not particularly disturbed by the words: "The object of Government is the welfare of the people. When the interests of the many are concerned, the interests of the few must yield. . . . Those are the essential basic conditions under which Government can be of service." While these words suggested the welfare state, Willkie considered the speech as only the glittering promises of a political campaign. He took more seriously the New Deal candidate's charge that all public utili-

41

ties operated on the same low level of morality as the "Insull monstrosity" which had taken money from the people to the extent of over one-and-a-half billions of dollars and whose methods were wholly "contrary to every sound public policy." Willkie was further shocked to find that the Democratic candidate proposed to whip the utilities into line by the establishment of four great power developments by the Government, involving the St. Lawrence River in the Northeast, Muscle Shoals in the Southeast, Boulder Dam in the Southwest, and the Columbia River in the Northwest. "Each of these in each of the four quarters of the United States," Roosevelt promised, "will be forever a national yardstick to prevent extortion against the public and to encourage the wider use of that servant of the people—electric power."

Willkie was too shrewd an observer of political events to fail to observe that a momentous decision had been made by the Democratic candidate. Although Willkie had long been active in the Democratic Party and had even been a delegate to the National Convention of 1932, he cast his vote in this election with some misgivings. He had worked in the convention for Al Smith first, and Newton D. Baker second. Thus he was not won over to the Roosevelt candidacy. But he was still too good a Democrat to take a walk.

It was on April 11, 1933, shortly after the inauguration of Franklin D. Roosevelt as President of the United States that the Tennessee Valley Authority Bill was introduced in the new Congress by Senator George W. Norris. This bill, under the legislative name of S.1272, was later replaced by H.R.5081, which differed from it only in details. Willkie recognized that the proposed bill was a challenge to all his faith and beliefs in constitutional law of the United States and even in democracy itself.

Looking upon the projected Tennessee Valley Authority as public competition with private industry on the grand scale, Willkie felt that this policy would not only destroy his business but eventually would destroy free enterprise. Long before his associates, he perceived the implication of the welfare state. With high courage and rash audacity he launched an attack upon the New Deal. It was a spectacular performance. Opposi-

tion to government monopoly would be his greatest case. He
was to defend a system of philosophy which for one hundred
and fifty years had been the American way of life. The issue was
individualism as opposed to the welfare state. The entire nation
would be his courtroom in this great controversy. The battle
was waged in Congress, in the courts, and in the forum of public
opinion. In the end, his legal skill and sharp daring were to stir
a lethargic and confused country.

However, at no time did he discuss the relative soundness of
the Government's venture into such a project as TVA. Nor did
he ever discuss other features of TVA, such as navigation, flood
control and defense production of minerals. From this point
of view Willkie might have made quite a case out of the TVA
Bill, which the title called a flood control measure. Some engineers pointed out the problem of having both flood control
and power from the same dam since in the one, emphasis must
be on water storage which requires an empty reservoir, and in
the other emphasis must be on "firm power," which necessitates
a full reservoir. The two requirements are, therefore, frequently
opposed. In order to meet this problem the Government had
to construct, at an enormous cost, nine dams, so coördinated as
to provide for both power and flood control, and in addition, to
furnish optimum conditions for navigation.

The six operating companies of C&S in the South used steam
plants, which most engineers agreed was the modern way to
produce power and which easily provided firm power.

If the Government had been willing to contract its power at
the switch to C&S and other private companies, as had been
contemplated in New York State when Roosevelt was Governor
and the St. Lawrence hydro-electric plant was discussed, there
would have been no controversy. This might very well have
been possible if it had not been for the starry-eyed reformers
around the President who sought vengeance. In any event the
Government by March, 1951, was ready and willing to contract
its power at the switch to the Pacific Gas and Electric Company
from the great Shasta Dam in California.

But Willkie did not discuss such technical features of TVA.
In fact he never even questioned the production of electric
power from the government-owned dams. His only point of

opposition was that such public power should not be put on the market in direct competition with private companies who were efficiently producing power at a reasonable rate. No private company could hope to compete with a government-subsidized industry. The crux of the issue was whether the federal Government could enter into open market operations against private industry. If it could do so in the field of utilities, it could do so in countless other businesses, with disastrous effects on the system of free enterprise.

On Friday morning, April 14, 1933, Willkie sat at the long table facing the Military Affairs Committee of the House of Representatives. This young, handsome, dynamic executive presented a dramatic figure as he told his story. Justice was his plea, justice for 300,000 owners of securities in the six companies of the Commonwealth and Southern Corporation whose properties in the Tennessee Valley would be endangered by the TVA program as outlined in the pending bill. These stockholders and bondholders were not speculators, Willkie explained, but men and women who thought that they were putting their savings into safe high-grade securities. Local bankers had recommended such investments, because these utility issues had been approved by the public utility commission of the state in which each company operated. The investors, for the most part, were common people who lived in the Tennessee Valley and earned their living there. Indeed, their investments were relatively small and averaged no more than about four thousand dollars.

The distressed investors had besieged him, Willkie said, with thousands of letters since the day when Senator Norris had introduced the measure in Congress. They became more and more hysterical as they saw the value of their investments drop in the markets of the nation. Should they sell at once or should they wait for the rebound from the depressed value induced by the pending TVA Bill? To add to the panic of these investors, banking houses in New York had advised their customers to sell all utilities as soon as the Norris Bill was introduced.

In the name of justice, therefore, Willkie asked compensation for these unhappy investors. Pointing out that plans had already been made to compensate the real estate owners in the Tennessee Valley for their land which would be flooded by the TVA project, he asked that security holders be treated with equal consideration.

To cover in full the investments of the bondholders, preferred stockholders, and the common stockholders, Willkie asked for government compensation to the extent of $500,-000,000. This was considerably less, he pointed out, than the capital invested in the Tennessee Valley by his company, which amounted to $600,000,000. Commonwealth and Southern maintained the largest utility service in the Southeast and it provided sixty-four per cent of the power service in the Valley. If this market were destroyed, he said, the properties would be worth only their value as salvage. And the TVA Bill, with its proposed building of transmission lines, would destroy the C&S market.

He also offered an alternative plan, one which would save his companies a loss and also protect the investors. He proposed that all or any part of the electric current generated by the government plants be carried by C&S lines which were already established. In this way the Government would be spared the cost of building its own lines, and the C&S companies would be saved from ruinous competition. Whatever saving would result from the TVA production of power, he promised to pass on to the consumer. He made one stipulation. The contract would have to be from fifteen years to thirty years so as not to impair his company's long-term borrowing power.

Willkie's eloquence was fruitless. The TVA Bill (H.R.5081) became law with the President's signature on May 18, 1933. The vote in the House stood 306 to 92, with 34 not voting; and in the Senate it was 63 to 20, with 12 not voting. The public had not been greatly stirred by the debate.

Willkie recognized that the economic crisis facing the nation in the spring of 1933 had conspired to promote great public adventures such as the TVA. With widespread unemployment and the critical runs on the banks around the country, he had rejoiced in the noble courage of the President in his inaugural message that "the only thing we have to fear is fear itself." But then he beheld the President using this fear to drive through Congress legislation that had long been repugnant to American traditions. He felt that opinion of the Muscle Shoals development depended very largely upon whether one viewed it as an economic project, or as a relief program. In the face of a demoralized economy, with millions of unemployed workers walking the streets, the proposed TVA project meant jobs for thousands of men and women. Without the need for jobs, without the hysteria over deflation, he felt it was quite probable that the TVA Bill would have been defeated in May, 1933. Thus the real battle over TVA and the new philosophy it represented came upon the proposed amendment to the Act (H.R.6793), introduced in March, 1935. By this time the nature of TVA was more clearly understood, he believed, as the blackest clouds of the depression had lifted.

On the morning of April 3, 1935, the C&S president appeared before the Committee on Military Affairs to give his testimony on the measure. The bill contained three major proposals; to empower the Authority to dispose of real estate bought with federal funds and therefore federal property; to grant additional power to the board of TVA to purchase and operate transmission lines; and to authorize the TVA to issue $100,000,000 in bonds guaranteed by the United States Government for further development of the project.

Willkie adroitly passed over the issues of the first two points in the amendment, making only the passing comment that it had been the policy of the Government for a hundred years never to permit any of its independent agencies to dispose of real estate once acquired by the federal Government. Only Congress had been able to do that.

With his clear legal precision, Willkie limited his attack to the more vulnerable point of the $100,000,000 bond issue. He reminded the committee that, in the beginning, The New Dealers had explained to the public that the only reason the Government went into the power business was to set up a "yardstick rate." This new grant of money, however, was to expand the project. This was clearly a government subsidy far removed from the announced objective of a "yardstick." Moreover, the matter of interest rates was very important in any "yardstick" comparison. Willkie stated that if such a low interest rate could be extended to C&S he would be able to save $10,000,000 a year, and he added, with a smile, "I will give it all to the con-

sumer." His company had outstanding, he said, $500,000,000 at
an average interest rate of five per cent. But if he could use, as
a "yardstick" technique, the credit of the United States Government, if he had this kind of guarantee, C&S could issue bonds
for two per cent or even less. This very situation, he pointed out,
was inherently the reason why public competition would always
be disastrous to private industry.

As another reason why the bond issue made impossible any
comparison between private and public operations, Willkie explained the procedure of private borrowing. If one of their operating companies like the Tennessee Electric Power Company
wished to buy a $100,000,000 property it could only issue bonds
for one half the value of this proposed purchase, and the interest
rate of four or five per cent would be a fixed charge upon the
profit of the company. This is quite different from TVA, he
emphasized, which can float its own bonds for the full amount
of the purchase price because it is a government agency. In the
interest of fair play and a truly just "yardstick," he asked that
the TVA be required to issue its bonds upon its own ability to
pay. "I merely ask that these bonds that you authorize be required to be issued on the faith and credit of the TVA."

In this connection of a just "yardstick," Willkie asked that
two other changes be made in the law governing the finances of
TVA. One change was for a uniform accounting system. Neither
Congress nor the American people, he contended, could ever
know whether TVA actually operated more cheaply than private companies until both of them were subject to the same
accounting system. He therewith asked for an amendment to
Section 7, requiring that the board shall comply with the uniform system of accounting of the National Association of Public
Utility and Railroad Commissioners. This method of accounting was now universally required of public utilities. "What I
want is to make it mandatory that the TVA shall comply with
the same method of accounting that public utilities have to
comply with." This was an essential procedure, although complicated, as TVA would have to show allocations for flood control and navigation as well as power. Furthermore, it was
another reason why any comparison of costs was difficult to
ascertain. The utility companies had to charge all costs to

power, while TVA could make their kilowatt costs appear less by charging a larger portion to navigation or flood control.

The other change he asked for in the interest of a fair "yardstick" was that TVA be required to fix rates to return a fair profit upon the investment the same as private companies must do in order to survive. He told the committee that he welcomed a yardstick, but it should be a measurement whereby public as as well as private companies conform to the same rules. "If this yardstick could once be established on exactly the same basis, three years from now there would not be a public plant in the United States," he confidently predicted. Furthermore, he told a surprised committee: "Give private companies the same advantages. Pass a bill guaranteeing the obligations of Commonwealth and Southern system, and I will cut every rate in our companies 33⅓ per cent."

By his brilliant logic Willkie had presented a damaging argument against TVA, and some of the members of the committee were clearly impressed. His plea was for "simple justice." In the Congressional hearings on the original TVA Act, he had asked justice for his security holders. In the hearings on the amendment he asked justice for his corporation, the Commonwealth and Southern. He showed not only that the TVA Act was unfair to business but that all public competition with private industry must by its nature be unfair and destructive competition.

Turning from such inconsistencies as the "rubber yardstick" policy, Willkie attacked methods used in the establishment of the TVA and the procedure of squeezing out established private enterprise in the area. Faced with such ruinous competition, he was willing to sell any or all of his southern companies to TVA at a price which would protect his security holders. Therefore, Willkie asked for national legislation whereby utility companies in the area of public competition be promptly condemned so that a court of law might speedily determine a fair and equitable price of sale. This, he pointed out, was in the American tradition. What we are asking, said the eloquent president of C&S, is for you to require that if we cannot agree on price, an American court shall determine the price, according to the established rules of law. Just require them to condemn our properties, and eliminate every possible delay. "I do not ask you to take my price. I ask you not to take their price. . . . Require them to condemn it, and let happen what has happened since the beginning of the foundation of English justice."

Upon requests from members of the committee, he gave several examples of TVA tactics. There was the instance of the properties in Alcorn County, Alabama, which had cost $617,312, but for which the TVA offered $234,000. Nevertheless he decided to sell. In the background was the story of his discouraging negotiation with Lilienthal early in 1934. In his desire to co-operate with TVA in the establishment of a true yardstick, and at the same time wishing to preserve the territorial integrity of his C&S system in the South, he had entered into a contract with the Authority on January 4, 1934. This contract was for a period of five years, and provided for options to purchase electric properties in certain counties of Alabama, Mississippi and Tennessee, the sale of distribution systems to municipalities in these counties, restrictions on territorial expansion by the contracting parties, and the interchange of power. His purpose in making this contract, he declared, had been to limit the area in which the TVA would experiment with its so-called "yardstick." If the Authority merely wished to establish a basic rate, then a prescribed area was sufficient. By such geographical limitation, the utility business need not be disrupted by government competition in other areas.

With such a contract negotiated he had naively thought there would be protection for the operations of his company elsewhere in the southern area. But this proved a temporary truce. The Public Works Administration at once offered money to cities even in this restricted area of the contract on the basis of a thirty per cent grant in aid and a seventy per cent loan at four per cent without discount. "So," said Willkie, "these cities in the Alabama area began to go pell mell for municipal ownership and the PWA began to grant municipal loans." After protesting to Lilienthal about this matter, he related that he had received a letter dated April 6, 1934, in which Lilienthal said: "I see no alternative for me but to consider that our efforts to transfer these properties by purchase have encountered a stone wall. . . . and that I should do whatever I can to assist these communities in carrying their program forward by the alternative method of securing funds from the Public Works Administration." Dramatically, Willkie then said to the committee, "that was the reason I sold Alcorn County at the price I did. It is gently clothed but the fist is there." When he realized, he declared, that the strategy of the Authority was to use public funds contributed by the American taxpayer as a means of driving private industry out of a field in which the federal Government had chosen to enter as a competitor, he was dismayed. "I say to you that I lost more faith in American institutions during that period than I gained in the previous period of my life. When we are told, 'You sell at this price or federal money will compete against you,' industry has no alternative."

Willkie then pictured the impossibility of competition against government monopoly quite aside from the unfavorable economic aspect. There was government propaganda which could not be matched. Chattanooga, one of the largest consumers of the C&S system, had recently voted for municipal ownership. About six months previously, the Emergency Federal Housing Administration headquarters had moved to Chattanooga and brought with them a large number of employees. Three weeks before elections, plans were announced for building the Chickamauga Dam, twelve miles from the city, at a cost of about $15,000,000! The political influence of such an agency was incalculable. It brought a flurry of business activity to local markets and each employee was a salesman for public power. Furthermore, he declared, the announcement of a public project of this size so close to a small community was an inducement too good to be neglected.

Again there was Knoxville. The TVA Act provided that headquarters should be established at Muscle Shoals. But instead the Authority located at Knoxville, three hundred miles away. "Of course a municipal-ownership campaign resulted, with the new settlers leading the hue and cry," he said.

He also discussed what he considered was the more questionable activity of Director Lilienthal. Speaking in Memphis a couple of days before the election, Lilienthal had said, as Willkie recalled: "Gentlemen of this community, it is entirely up to you; but we only have so much power and it will be given to those cities that first apply. After they have voted for municipal ownership, they will get that power at these ridiculously low rates."

Continuing his story Willkie recited the facts concerning the Tennessee Electric Power Company, which was the largest subsidiary of Commwealth and Southern Corporation operating in the Tennessee Valley. The company had $99,000,000 worth of outstanding securities and all had been approved by the State Utility Commission of Tennessee after checking the company's books. Yet Lilienthal did not think the company was worth much more than $50,000,000 and that was his offer. Of course, declared Willkie, if Lilienthal could get the Tennessee Electric Power Company at that bargain price, he could reduce his rates even lower. At the Lilienthal price only the bondholders would receive full value of their investment, the preferred stockholders would get $15 a share ($100 par) and the common stockholders nothing.

Such was the strange story that Willkie presented to the Committee on Military Affairs concerning the workings of government monopoly. Willkie had made an intense and dramatic presentation, but his effort to secure modification of the Amendment Bill (H.R.6793) failed. A few Congressmen, however, now saw more clearly the pattern of the New Deal attack upon private enterprise.

Willkie was so sharp in his repartee and so vigorous in his comments that soon the public hearings were crowded with spectators whenever the word went round the Hill that he was to appear. The press, quick to sense the tense appeal in his testimony, gave him increasing coverage in the news columns. The Willkie rebuttal of the New Deal program offered a fine spectacle of the clash of opinion within the democratic process. Accordingly, an ever-increasing segment of public opinion came to doubt the wisdom of the government policy of punishing business indiscriminately. Many people wondered what could be gained by ruining thousands of honest investors in sound utility securities, approved by state regulatory boards, in order to establish a federal power system in the same area to provide the same facilities. Would any business henceforth be free from such bureaucratic interference? Moreover, there were those who looked askance at the spectacle in America of an honorable and successful young businessman representing an honorable and respectable corporation made the whipping boy of industry by such an inflamed group of bureaucrats.

Eagerly Willkie had welcomed the opportunity to testify in committee hearings, as they offered him the only opportunity to tell his story of public utilities to governmental officials and to the American people. For two years after the New Deal came to Washington, he had frequently traveled to the capital to talk with officeholders from the President down to clerks in the various bureaus. On all occasions he received a polite brush-off. Yet he clung to the belief that reason would prevail and that the men who held the power to destroy an industry would eventually find that the industry was worth preservation. It was through these hearings that Willkie began to arouse the people. Little did he realize the toughness of the assignment he had assumed in rallying the forces of free enterprise against the socialism of the New Deal and enlightening the people upon the true objectives of a welfare state.

Sometime after these hearings further light was to be thrown on Lilienthal's activities. In one instance, according to the testimony of Dr. Arthur E. Morgan in a congressional investigation in 1947, Lilienthal wrote a letter to Willkie in which he said: "Confirming our recent conversation you do not agree to co-operate with us except on the basis that you have a monopoly of power distribution in all the vast area of the four states in which you operate." Taking a copy of this letter to Dr. Morgan, then chairman of the TVA, he recommended that the board cancel the agreement between TVA and C&S (1934) not to raid each other's territory. Dr. Morgan, feeling dubious about such an autocratic procedure, called a meeting of the board and asked Willkie to attend. When Lilienthal heard of this action he immediately telephoned Willkie in New York saying that the letter was a mistake and not to come to the board meeting. But Willkie surmised something was wrong and went anyway.

When Morgan asked him at the meeting if the letter of confirmation sent by Lilienthal represented his views, Willkie stoutly denied that it did. He even stated that the conversation supposedly confirmed in that letter had never taken place.

Nevertheless, copies of that letter had been sent by the writer to President Roosevelt and a number of Senators.

Willkie's position was, as he stated it: "The Commonwealth and Southern will sell to TVA its whole system, or the system in any state, or any part of any system in any state. It will sell part of it now, and part of it later. The fact that some is bought now doesn't prevent other parts being bought later on." In short, Willkie was trying to stop the nibbling away of his utility properties in the South by the TVA. He was willing to sell at all times but wanted either a satisfactory negotiation as to price or public condemnation of his property with the Court fixing the value.

Another episode concerned a letter from Lilienthal's office to Bessemer, Alabama, which said: "We are estopped from pushing the extension of power while this agreement with the Commonwealth and Southern is on, but we can accomplish the same purpose in another way. If you will write us and ask us questions and ask us for help, we can't refuse those requests. And so long as the initiative comes from you, then we can get the same results without formally violating that agreement."

It was some time before Willkie was to understand the unusual combination of starry-eyed reformers who clustered around the White House, and who were contemptuously referred to as the "Palace Guards." How could any outsider understand the imponderable barricade of ideas which kept Roosevelt a prisoner of his own fancy? These men exploited the President's imagination for new ventures and excited his natural talent for experimentation, sometimes in dubious undertakings. Trusted advisers with understanding and balanced perspective were shunted into the background while a crew of eager young men with bright ideas captured the line to the White House. It was Raymond Moley, occupying a front seat in the Administration circles until the mid-thirties, who first recounted the amazing development of the "junta" and described its extensive power.

All the while Willkie was making his frequent trips to Washington for committee hearings, he was ignorant of the secret powers which were manipulating legislative proposals and launching press attacks upon business. He realized, of course, that he was not getting anywhere, and he often felt as if he were fighting a phantom. By the time Moley made his spectacular revelations in *After Seven Years* (1939) of the power behind the throne, Willkie realized from his own experience that he was up against an invisible wall of resistance because his opponents were constantly shielded by the concealment of their identity.

In the days of 1932-33, when Roosevelt had not yet wholly won the confidence of the American people, Adolph A. Berle and Raymond Moley were able to lead him to examine with skepticism every plan offered by the reformers. But after F.D.R. had gained his popular following and had tasted the heady wine of power, he lost, according to those close to him, some of his intellectual integrity. Thereafter, the President launched into planned economy without proper study. Throwing scientific scrutiny to the winds, F.D.R. seized one quack plan after another. After scuttling the World's Economic Conference as his enthusiasm for it waned, he adopted in October, 1933, the Warren monetary theory. This was a scheme to stabilize the market by linking commodity prices with the price of gold. He abandoned this project as a dismal failure three months later. There followed, in turn, the devaluation of the dollar, the soak-the-rich campaign, the effort to destroy confidence in business leadership, the unbalanced budget, and the attempt to purge the Democratic Party. Men like Moley could not abide this decline in political honesty. The early group of advisers was thus scattered by 1936.

The transition from the Brain Trust to the New Dealers was not a sudden affair. The forging of the new group, according to Moley, was chiefly the labor of that clever young lawyer, Tom Corcoran, whom Moley himself had welcomed into the Brain Trust, and to whom Moley was quite willing to surrender his mantle of leadership. Corcoran had come to Washington as a protégé of Felix Frankfurter, after his graduation from the Harvard Law School, and began his career as secretary to the distinguished Justice Oliver Wendell Holmes. From here he worked his way up to the Justice Department. But from the beginning Corcoran was the liaison between jobs in Washington and the promising students of Frankfurter at Harvard Law School.

After Roosevelt took office in March, 1933, there were many administrative posts to be filled. In his memoirs, Moley relates that he suggested a number of competent men in business and law who were eager to help the Administration either in or out of office. But the President was suspicious of their very success. This was not the case with the bright young lawyers recommended by Frankfurter, who inevitably received the enthusiastic approval of the President. In this way there was a continuing influx of the Frankfurter-Corcoran recruits into federal agencies. These radical young men who burned with the desire for reform became amazingly effective largely because of their unity, which was achieved partly by their devotion to F.D.R. and the New Deal, and partly by the tactics of Corcoran, who acted as their co-ordinator.

The inner circle of the New Dealers, according to Moley, included Robert Jackson, Leon Henderson, and, of course, Thomas Corcoran and Benjamin V. Cohen. Corcoran and Cohen usually worked together as a team. As special assistants to the Attorney-General they helped the Government in sustaining New Deal legislation that came before the Supreme Court for review.

From this spearhead of leaders, the Frankfurter-Corcoran appointees spread into all the major departments of the Government. Corcoran made it a point to place not less than two of the faithful in the same office so that they might take fire from one another. There were a large number of Corcoran employees in the Labor Department, in the Treasury, the Department of Justice, the Reconstruction Finance Corporation, the Securities and Exchange Commission, the Public Works Administration and the Works Progress Administration.

The New Dealers, Moley said, were connected with the White House through Harry L. Hopkins, who was the close personal friend of the President and who had once been a social worker. He had been appointed in 1933 Federal Administrator of Relief and in 1935 he was made head of the WPA. One of the first of the President's intimate advisers to recognize the merits of Corcoran, Hopkins soon came to rely upon the young lawyer both for errands and advice. Ickes was Secretary of the Interior, a frustrated reformer, Director of the PWA, but more important, chairman of the National Power Policy Committee. Cohen was associate general counsel of PWA and later general counsel to the National Power Policy Committee. This not only put both Hopkins and Ickes in a position to disperse large sums of federal money but it also brought Corcoran and Cohen into close association with each of them. Furthermore, Lilienthal was a member of the National Power Policy Committee.

This invincible network of government men, all in sympathy with the same ideas concerning the wickedness of the American economic system, had an able ally in James Lawrence Fly, general counsel of TVA. He was another of the Frankfurter boys and he worked closely with Lilienthal, Corcoran, Cohen, Hopkins and Ickes.

It was recorded that the philosophy of these New Dealers possessed a unique homogeneity. Part of it came from the classroom of Professor Frankfurter, who in turn received it from the distinguished jurist, Louis D. Brandeis. The appointment of Brandeis to the Supreme Court in 1916 had created a famous controversy in the Senate and throughout the nation. Father of the concept of the "Curse of Bigness" in American industry, Brandeis lacked the vision to see that only through mass production could the standard of living continue to rise. However, Brandeis was as much opposed to Big Government as he was to Big Business.

It was at this point that the New Dealers broke with the Brandeis philosophy. They ardently believed in a large and continuous flow of government spending. In fact they regarded anti-monopoly and government spending as interdependent. Raymond Moley recalled a conversation in which Corcoran seemed to believe money ought to be "shoveled out." In fact the best way might be to scatter it from airplanes. But the President expressed it more smoothly: An indispensable factor in prosperity was government investment great enough to lift the national income to a point which would make tax receipts cover the new national level of expenditure.

The well-integrated group, therefore, believed in a planned economy with the Government regulating society for the benefit of the people. They sought legislation which would discourage the bigness of business, redistribute wealth, and enlarge the control of Government over the economic life of the nation. This was the political background of TVA.

Willkie was fighting these tentacles of hidden power without knowing what they were. Many times he visited the White House to see the President with plans for some kind of a compromise, and would receive encouragement, but never were there any consequent "follow-throughs." There was nothing in the open with which he could come to grips. He felt baffled. The only channel available to him was the committee hearings, but behind these hearings was a blank space which he could not penetrate.

Yet the intricate web of concealed authority continued to tighten its hold upon New Deal policies. Its greatest strength was the secrecy in which it formulated policy. Willkie was to find his difficulties increasing as other attacks upon business were translated into bills by this powerful clique within the Government.

The next major assault upon the public utilities by the palace guard was to strike a severe blow at Commonwealth and Southern Corporation and arouse to higher pitch the fighting instincts of the Indiana boy who had risen to leadership on Wall Street.

CHAPTER IV

The Death Sentence

WILLKIE REFERRED to the thirties as the "Decade of Delusion" because of the bright young men in the federal government who essayed to reform the country but created chaos. The Public Utility Holding Company Act of 1935 (S. 2796) was one of the bills drafted by the eager reformers at the direction of President Roosevelt. This measure differed from the TVA Act in that it did not seek to establish government monopoly, but rather created an agency for choking the bigness out of big utility corporations. Newsmen dubbed the bill the "Death Sentence." To Willkie, the measure meant dissolution of his mighty company.

The struggle over the Utility Holding Company Act of 1935 marked the turning point in the development of the New Deal policy. The measure grew out of the deliberations of the National Power Policy Committee, under the direction of Harold L. Ickes, appointed by President Roosevelt in the summer of 1934.

The decision to inaugurate a drastic federal regulation of public utilities was made by Harold L. Ickes in the second year of the Roosevelt Administration. The studies of the National Power Policy Committee led him to conclude that the first step in federal regulation must begin with the holding companies, which had acquired control of the voting stock of hundreds of operating companies in many sections of the United States. The conclusion was in accord with the personal observations of Ickes during the past two decades. As an idealist and reformer he abhorred all forms of economic bigness and attempted to smear all public utilities with the Insull scandal.

After his decision to begin his attack upon holding companies, Ickes chose Benjamin V. Cohen, counsel for the committee, to draft the bill. Immediately he sought the assistance of his close friend, Thomas Corcoran, who had collaborated with him in the drafting of the Securities and Exchange Commission Act. When the drafting of the Utilities Holding Company Bill was completed, however, both Ickes and the National Power Policy Committee had lost their enthusiasm for the measure.

Willkie had accomplished a reversal of the presidential mind. Among his colleagues, Willkie was generally looked upon as the reform leader of the power industry. He had long advocated increased production of electric power, lower rates to consumers, and continual extension of distributing lines. But most of all, he advocated peace between business and Government. Moreover, he had a plan. He had secured from various utility executives an agreement to establish the "objective rate" which Willkie had tested out so successfully in C&S. (This meant a decrease of cost per kilowatt hour according to increased amount of power used.) He had proposed to F.D.R. that the President might announce this plan and even take full credit for it. In exchange, Roosevelt would agree that in areas where the new system was in effect, no TVA would be established.

Accompanied by Philip H. Gadsden, chairman of the Public Utility Executives, Willkie went to Washington to see the President and try to convince him of the mutual advantages of his proposal. His old friend, Oswald Ryan, of the Federal Power Commission, made the appointment with the President and accompanied Willkie and Gadsden to the White House. When Willkie was introduced, the President shook hands and said: "I am glad to meet you, Mr. Willkie, I am one of your customers." Recalling the fact that C&S supplied Warm Springs in Georgia with electric power, Willkie pointed a finger at the

President, and challenged, "We give you good service, don't we?" With this jocular comment the interview was well launched.

The President, impressed with Willkie and with his plan, turned the proposal over to the Federal Power Commission for study. This seemed fortunate, as the commission, though taking no official action, had advocated regulation but not extinction of the holding companies, and had so advised the President. The commission was highly favorable to the Willkie proposal.

But the presidential mind was to reverse itself again. On January 22, 1935, an announcement came from the White House that there was to be "no quarter with the utilities." The facts, unknown to Willkie and his colleagues, were as follows. Three weeks earlier, Corcoran and Cohen had been disappointed to find that Ickes was no longer interested in imposing a drastic curb upon public utilities. Determined not to miss this unique chance for revolution, they began to needle the Secretary of the Interior and to prod the members of the committee into action. Finally, their eager endeavor brought about a White House conference, with Ickes at last giving the measure his full support. Pressure was exerted upon the President during his visit to Warm Springs. Upon his return to Washington, he approved the proposal and made Corcoran and Cohen personally responsible for the passage of their bill. Another result of this momentous session with the Chief Executive was the fact that these two young men now found a permanent place in White House councils. It was only a few months later that Tom Corcoran won the presidential nickname, affectionately conferred, of "Tommy the Cork." In their preliminary skirmish with Willkie, Corcoran and Cohen had enjoyed the advantage of deploying their forces within the federal administration where they could act without publicity. Hereafter, in directing the campaign against public utilities, they sat next the President himself in planning the strategy in the bitter controversy.

Corcoran and Cohen accepted their new commission with unbounded zeal. The first step was to persuade Representative Sam Rayburn and Senator Burton K. Wheeler to substitute this newly drafted bill for the identical bills which Rayburn and Wheeler had already introduced in their respective Houses,

providing for restrictive regulation of holding companies. Two
months were consumed in winning these hardened politicians
to this switch, during which the young officials were frequently
summoned to the White House to report their progress directly
to the President. Their persistence won. After all, both Congressmen knew that the new bill would be called the Wheeler-
Rayburn Bill so that the two statesmen would receive credit
for its authorship.

Wheeler was chairman of the Senate Committee on Interstate
Commerce and Rayburn presided over the corresponding committee, the Interstate and Foreign Commerce Committee, in
the House of Representatives. Public hearings on the public
utilities bills were scheduled for April, 1935. Nevertheless, both
chairmen launched attacks upon the public utilities before the
hearings were held. Obviously, their minds were already satisfied concerning the guilt of all large public utilities regardless
of what the testimony might bring forth. Rayburn even opened
the battle in Congress with a violent personal attack on Wendell
Willkie. Thereupon, Philip H. Gadsden made a public defense
of his associate. He characterized Rayburn's action as showing
the "spirit of wanton destruction and ruthless vindictiveness in
which the legislation was conceived and was now pressed for
passage." He labeled the proposed Public Utility Holding Company Act a measure designed to annihilate the private operators
of utilities in order to make way for government ownership. It
was not, he contended, a holding company bill. It was a bill to
destroy an institution which had played an important role in
American economic history.

Again, it was Gadsden who took issue with Senator Wheeler
for a vicious radio attack upon utilities, on the night of April 3,
two weeks before the hearings of the Senate committee opened.
The Montana Senator charged the utility executives as the
"power gang." "Obviously," retorted Gadsden, "Wheeler is not
engaged in argument, but in vituperation." Few newspapers
of any character, outside the eastern seaboard, carried the
Gadsden reply. Despite Roosevelt's complaint that eighty per
cent of the American press was opposed to the New Deal,
Gadsden's able statements reached few readers.

In contradistinction to the Insull Empire, the Commonwealth and Southern Corporation had been described by a score of economists as one of the best public utility systems in the land. Professor James C. Bonbright, in a scathing attack upon some of the practices of holding companies in *The Holding Company,* published in 1932, had selected the Commonwealth and Southern Corporation as a model system which "offered the most practicable solution of the service charge—a solution that must sooner or later be adopted by all utility systems if they are to survive the growing resentment which their recent financial practices have aroused in the minds of the thinking public." Commonwealth and Southern Corporation was not itself an operating utility, but rather a holding company—a billion-dollar holding company. Both officers and stockholders were proud of the excellent services which it offered to the subsidiary companies, including the economy of large-scale production, centralized purchasing, mobility of the use of labor, more efficient engineering and accounting services, and more effective and courageous managerial leadership. But above all was the abundant and cheap financing which the holding company was able to furnish to its subsidiaries. For these benefits a fee was charged to the operating companies well within the ability of these companies to pay.

Critics of the holding companies pointed to the evils of some companies in pyramiding various layers of organizations between the holding company at the top and the operating company at the bottom, each with its separate issues of stocks and bonds. This was called "milking" the operating companies. The practice of operating scattered companies without regional integration or continuity was also condemned. And lastly, experts criticized with justification the evils growing out of the lack of state regulation of holding companies, although each operating company had long come under the strict scrutiny of state and federal regulatory commissions. Clearly there was need for federal legislation which would regulate holding companies to the same extent as operating companies.

But, instead of regulation, the bill prepared by Corcoran and Cohen was nothing less than a death sentence for a valuable economic device long sanctioned by law and custom. Section XI was considered the heart of the measure. It provided that by

January 1, 1940, every holding company must dispose of its securities and be dissolved unless it could show that its continuance was necessary for the operation of a geographically integrated system serving an economic district extending into two or more contiguous states. The authors of the bill believed that this requirement alone was sufficient to destroy the system of holding companies.

Willkie and his colleagues from Commonwealth and Southern Corporation went to the congressional hearings on this holding company bill like lambs to the slaughter. They knew the technique of legal procedure. But they were without proficiency in the Machiavellian tactics of a war of nerves or a battle of semantics on Capitol Hill. They were ignorant of the very existence of Thomas Corcoran or Benjamin V. Cohen.

As Willkie began his statement before the Senate committee, a C&S official, A. C. Watt, with accustomed nonchalance, sat down in one of the side seats among the news reporters. During an intermission, one of the newsmen said to him, "I see you choose nice company to sit with!"

"Yes, I like newspapermen," Watt affably replied.

"Don't you know you are sitting beside Ben Cohen?" snorted the incredulous reporter.

"Who is he?" naively inquired the financier from Wall Street.

"He is only the young man who drafted the bill to strangle the utilities" was the reply.

The Corcoran-Cohen team had a three-point method by which they successfully directed the hearings on the bill from seats on the side lines. They conducted a war of nerves; they timed their public blasts against the public utilities with unerring judgment; and they engaged in the use of words with new meanings. The war of nerves was conducted by the circulation of rumors they artfully originated. The C&S men were first told that Roosevelt was really after only a few holding companies, including the Associated Gas & Electric Company, which were considered the "bad boys" of the industry. C&S officials were jolted by the information that legislation was to be styled to destroy all holding companies, including the reputable ones. The associates of Willkie bitterly resented the attempt of the government men to bracket C&S with the Associated Gas &

Electric Company. It had one of the worst reputations in financial circles. It was headed by Howard C. Hopson, who had approached Willkie to co-operate in a campaign against the new bill, but the C&S president had rejected his proposal. Time finally caught up with Hopson, and in 1940 he was sent to the penitentiary. During the hearings of 1935, the behavior of the unscrupulous holding companies lost the utilities many friends both in and out of Congress.

Thus the continual emanation of rumors as to whom "the President was going to get next" was a disturbing factor of the hearings; no corporation knew quite how to defend itself, or what to expect under this barrage of rumors. The good companies were blamed with the bad ones.

In this respect another device was used which was both confusing and exasperating and which owed its origin to the intriguing nature of the two planners. Toward the end of a week, or before a holiday, C&S officials would be told that they would not be called for testimony until the following week. The men, eager to get home, would pack up their papers in preparation for their return to New York. Then, just as they were ready to leave the hotel, a telephone call would announce the fact that they would be called to testify within the hour. Frantically, they would unpack and try to arrange their papers in proper order again, and scramble for a cab to reach the committee rooms on Capitol Hill in time to appear for the hearing. Harassed and nervous, the C&S officials would not be at their best in giving testimony.

Another trick in this war of nerves was the smear campaign. Corcoran was able to induce certain Congressmen and federal officials to make bitter addresses attacking prominent industrial leaders. The New Dealers furnished these speakers with effective phrases for a rousing popular distrust against business executives. The "corporate earls" were pictured as throwing "corporate tentacles" around American industry and reducing it to "aristocratic anarchy." The smear campaign touched closely upon the fundamental philosophy of the New Deal. In the battle against Bigness in Business a wedge was driven to divide the people from business management and to foment distrust of executive leadership. If Big Business could be thoroughly discredited in the eyes of the nation, there would be a better chance to pass legislation for the redistribution of wealth and the more extensive control of Government over the economic life of the nation.

Senator George W. Norris delighted in referring to the utility companies on the floor of the Senate as the "spider-web of Wall Street." Willkie once called on Senator Norris to correct some of his errors, but Norris haughtily retorted: "Even if I have made a few mistakes, what of it? It is nothing compared to the mistakes of the utilities."

Willkie and his colleagues were also slow in comprehending the technique used by Corcoran and Cohen to manipulate publicity. The trick was to discredit all opposition to the Administration bill both in and out of Congress. Eleven A.M. was the deadline in most newspaper offices for the receipt of new stories for the evening edition. Watching the clock carefully, Corcoran would prompt Wheeler or some other committee member to ask a disconcerting question of a utility executive in the witness chair. Before the proper rebuttal, often lengthy in character, could be made, the newsmen were under necessity to dash to the telephones to relay their stories for the evening papers and thus missed the replies. In this way, the evening editions would carry the damaging question but with no adequate rebuttal, the implication being that the utility men had been so confused and disconcerted by the apt question that they were unable to make answer. By the time the answer was made in the afternoon session, the edge was off the news and the reply would be printed in one of the back pages of the morning papers.

Another trick used by the young strategists was to measure carefully the publicity space accorded to the hearings. If their press releases dropped to the second or third page in the newspapers they would have the committee subpoena another "big name" in the industry. There was always a good story concerning the appearance before the committee of any top power executive. This acted as the proverbial shot in the arm to give a fresh spurt to their propaganda campaign.

The amazing tactics of the two young bureaucrats did not go unnoticed in Congress. On several occasions, there were heated accusations against Corcoran and Cohen on the floor of both Houses, particularly in regard to their methods in attempting to influence the votes of members. A Democratic Congressman from Alabama for twenty years, George Huddleston, eloquently condemned their lobbying tactics on behalf of the Public Utility Holding Companies Act and castigated the pair as a "corrupt influence in the halls of Congress." During the final debate on the measure, he said: "Those two brain-trusters, those envoys extraordinary, those ambassadors and plenipotentiaries, this firm of Cohen and Corcoran, late of New York City, now operating in Washington, telling Congress what to do, pointing out to members of Congress what their functions and their duties are, they drew up this Bill."

Late in April, 1935, soon after the hearings on the TVA amendment, Willkie appeared before the Senate Committee on Interstate Commerce to testify against the Public Utility Holding Company Bill. The committee chairman was the sharp-tongued Burton Wheeler. In opposing the bill, Willkie attacked the fundamental assumption of the reformers, namely that public utilities had been grossly mismanaged. He admitted that there had been some abuses in some utility holding companies, but he contended that the electric business as a whole had made an excellent record which fully merited public confidence. The ethics, honesty and efficiency of the utility industry, he declared, was the equal of that in any other American business. In fact, he said, he would go even further and hold that the electric business was more worthy of confidence by the people than any other business enterprise in America. In support of this view he cited the steady reduction of electric rates charged to consumers during the past decade. His own company, he stated, had reduced rates every year since it was organized in 1929.

Obviously, Willkie was proud of the signal success of his leadership and the high ethical standard of his business relationships. With modest simplicity, he declared that most business executives conducted their enterprise on a high moral plane. "I do not put myself on a pedestal, and I do not want to claim to be superior to anybody else. There are many companies that pursue the same high standards of business practice."

Under sharp interrogation, Willkie undertook to explain to the Senators the intricate organization of the Commonwealth and Southern Corporation. It was an organization of six separate systems composed of eleven companies. The area of controversy with TVA included Tennessee, Alabama, Georgia, and parts of South Carolina, Mississippi and Florida. The operating companies of C&S in this area were Tennesse Electric Power Company, the Alabama Power Company, the Georgia Power Company, the Gulf Power Company, the Mississippi Power Company, and the South Carolina Power Company.

Commonwealth and Southern Corporation was in fact two corporations: one was incorporated under the laws of Delaware, and the other under the laws of New York. The former was strictly a holding company while the New York company was a service company. Willkie and the other officials served in the same capacity for each company. C&S of Delaware collected no fees from its subsidiary companies and it offered no management, no supervisory service of any kind. Its income was derived solely from the interest and dividends on securities which it owned. These were principally securities of operating companies forming the Commonwealth and Southern system. In fact it owned all the common stock of the subsidiary companies except two per cent of the Tennessee Electric Power Company. In addition it owned some bonds and preferred stock of certain of these same companies. In order to maintain the highly liquid position which its needs demanded, the company held government bonds, cash and other liquid assets to the amount of $72,000,000.

C&S of New York was a service company and had a contract with each of its subsidiaries to render assistance in such matters as accounting, rates, taxation, engineering, merchandising, inspection, insurance, purchasing, and traffic. These various services were rendered as requested by the officials of the company receiving them. Monthly bills were sent to the operating companies for these services on the basis of actual cost plus 1.15 per cent of the gross revenue of the operating company. Common-

wealth and Southern of New York received as further revenue
a fee of $150,000 a year from C&S of Delaware to cover officers'
salaries and certain other expenses.

The unique feature of this plan which had attracted such
favorable attention from the economists was that all of the
capital stock of C&S of New York (90,000 shares) was owned by
the operating companies in the ratio of the gross earnings of
each to the gross earnings of all. Any profit, therefore, which
C&S of New York earned was distributed as dividends among
the operating companies in proportion to their stock holdings.

As Willkie frequently told the congressional committees, the
process was the reverse of the "milking" which many Senators
had described as the ulterior end of all utility holding companies. Clearly the achievement of C&S had been to build up its
operating companies. This, of course, was a long-range self-
improvement policy, but it was sound financing and sound
management to the benefit of all concerned. Nevertheless, the
Committee on Interstate Commerce was suspicious. Senator
Fred H. Brown, of New Hampshire, called this procedure pure
selfishness. He refused to see any virtue in a policy of good management. Irritably, he interrupted Willkie to say: "You cannot
explain it to me. You have never helped anyone more than the
Commonwealth and Southern."

In this atmosphere of bitter antagonism to Big Business regardless of how well it operated, Willkie essayed to discuss
profits. He explained that utility companies, far from making
huge profits, often did not even earn a fair rate of return. Under
the law of the land, each operating company was entitled to a
"fair return" on the "fair value" of the properties devoted to
public service. This general principle had been laid down in
1898 by the Supreme Court in the famous case of Smyth v.
Ames. Further, the Supreme Court had held that a fair return
was six and one-half or seven per cent and in some cases even
eight per cent. Willkie boldly stated he did not think public
utilities should be expected to earn less than six and one-half
per cent because of the rate of obsolescence in equipment.

Certainly six and one-half per cent was a much smaller profit
than the average man in the street had been led to believe the
utilities made. The New Dealers had talked loudly of the

swollen profits made by the holding companies. But Commonwealth and Southern in the South made less than this modest figure because of the competition with the government project, the Tennessee Valley Authority. In the South, Willkie stated, his companies earned a profit of about four per cent. The sardonic chairman quipped: "If we quit the TVA, you would raise your rates, would you not?" This Willkie indignantly denied. He stated that every one of the C&S companies had reduced rates each year for the past ten years. Moreover, he pointed out that the power industry had been under the closest scrutiny for the past six years by the Federal Trade Commission. It had been combed completely and there had not been one scintilla of evidence produced to show that the creation of a holding company led to increased rates.

In further reply to the insinuations of Wheeler, Willkie denied that the TVA had forced the C&S companies in the South to lower their rates. The Alabama and Georgia companies, he declared, had cut rates every year before TVA as well as after. Furthermore, the companies in the North operated on even lower rates although with larger profits. Willkie also denied the New Deal contention that TVA had limited its sale of power to the demand for additional power in the South which the private companies were unable to supply. He pointed to the statement of David Lilienthal himself who declared on November 10, 1933, at Atlanta, Georgia, before any government installation had been made, that private companies in the Valley had the generating and transmission facilities to care for thirty per cent to forty per cent more power than demand required. This astounding announcement, Willkie explained, was a tacit admission that the Government was not only entering into competition with private companies but even was setting up a duplicate system.

Willkie exploded still another current falsehood. Government and TVA officials had widely publicized their view that the influence of the TVA legislation had not affected adversely the market value of utility securities. The Commonwealth and Southern executive now presented to the Senate committee two charts to show the damage of the Government's abrupt attack on utilities in the South. The first chart showed that the decline of industrials and utility stocks proceeded at about the same rate from 1929 to 1932. But, in 1933, industrial stocks began to rise, while utilities continued to drift lower. The second chart told a still more dramatic story. It showed that the securities of the holding companies declined because those of the operating companies declined. Yet the operating companies actually showed more recovery in business operations than any other major industry in the United States.

Carefully Willkie traced the fall of industrials, railroads and utilities. During the depression all of them moved down together, and all started the up-swing together. Then in 1933, came the government attack upon utilities. When the TVA Bill was assured of passing, the securities of those utility companies which had previously held up began to sag and finally bonds fell to the low point of twenty-four dollars. But when Judge W. I. Grubb, of the United States District Court of Northern Alabama, held that TVA had exceeded its power, the bonds made an immediate recovery and advanced up into the 90's.

To prove his point further, Willkie cited another illustration. From the passage of the TVA Bill until January 4, 1934, when Commonwealth and Southern made a contract with TVA to transmit government power, stocks of all operating companies in the southern area declined. But from the date of the contract, C&S preferred stock which was selling around twenty dollars per share doubled within two weeks. All of this showed, Willkie concluded, that the people had confidence in the management of the company, but feared the attacks of Government on business.

The atmosphere of the hearings of the Senate Committee on Interstate Commerce on S.1725 had for the most part been unfriendly. The chairman, Senator Wheeler, was clearly antagonistic to all representatives of Big Business. He assumed that there was something inherently wicked in mere bigness, something dark and unfathomable in large market operations. His hostility toward Willkie marked every step of the hearings and received unfavorable comment from the Washington newsmen who are ever alert to detect unscrupulous tactics of congressional investigations. The ill-temper of the chairman left Willkie undaunted. He was not intimated from speaking in glowing terms of the pioneer days of public utilities and of the men who had dared to enter a new field, risking all they had and all they could borrow from friends and relatives. On one occasion, Willkie spoke with admiration of W. P. Lay, of Alabama, a man who had a dream of water power. Willkie called him an idealist. At this point, Wheeler interrupted with biting sarcasm: "You started out that way, too, didn't you, as an idealist?" Unruffled by the sneer, Willkie replied, "And I hope I still am, Mr. Chairman, I still have my western views!"

CHAPTER V

Wings Over the
Supreme Court

DAZED BY their encounter with the national law-makers, Wendell Willkie and his colleagues now turned to the courts of justice. Although, on many occasions, Willkie had offered to sell to the federal Government the electric power plants with which governmental enterprise had entered into competition, his proposals were neither accepted nor rejected. By 1935, however, it was apparent to Willkie that the Administration expected to outbid the Share-the-Wealth propaganda of Huey Long with the Soak-the-Rich tax scheme of Tom Corcoran. The battle against monopoly, he surmised, was to be directed against bigness in business in every phase of the American scene. Uncertainty over the future of such solvent properties as the Tennessee Electric Power Company now induced Willkie to test the constitutionality of the legislation providing for the Tennessee Valley Authority and to test the authority of the federal Government to make gifts and loans to cities and villages with which to duplicate the existing power distribution systems.

Willkie was confident that his appeal to the courts would be successful and a vindication of honest business enterprise. His

72

legal education as well as his wide reading in history had led
him to look upon the Supreme Court as the bulwark of the
American heritage. In his law studies at Indiana University, the
treatise on *Constitutional Limitations* by Judge Cooley had
been a constant guide. This learned jurist had written ex-
haustively on the development of constitutional restrictions
placed on government. The paternal theory of government had
always been rejected in American constitutional theory. In the
words of Mr. Justice Brewer, the Fathers of the Constitution of
1787 had intended to give "the utmost possible liberty to the
individual, and the fullest protection to him and his property."

Willkie was aware that the Supreme Court harbored enemies
of American Big Business, but he had little apprehension that
hostility to free enterprise was an active influence in the Court.
Mr. Justice Louis D. Brandeis was chiefly known for his Curse
of Bigness. Not even Woodrow Wilson, to whom Brandeis owed
his appointment to the Court, had wholly accepted his thesis
that the concentration of economic wealth and the growth of
corporations was the "result of unwise, man-made, privilege-
creating law."

Willkie was disdainful of the Curse of Bigness doctrine on
the ground that it misrepresented the triumphs of American
industry in mass production. The full development of American resources required bigness in free enterprise. The record
showed that large manufacturing units reduced the cost of production and lowered the price for consumers. All of this had
resulted from the legal right of farseeing businessmen to apply
their executive genius to the production of wealth which in
turn benefited the workers, the consumers, the managers and
the bondholders and stockholders of the corporation. Big Business was as American as were the public schools, the two-party
system, the Bill of Rights or the Fourth of July.

Since the turn of the century it had been generally conceded
that public utilities, being in the nature of a monopoly, were
subject to governmental regulation. How far should this regulation extend? In 1898, the Supreme Court, in the case of
Smyth *v.* Ames, had held that regulation of rates by state commissions must not go so far as to deprive public utilities a fair
return on the investment. The Brandeis repudiation of the

doctrine of the "fair return" formula, which he had presented as a minority opinion in the Southwestern Bell Telephone case in 1923, struck at the very heart of the free enterprise system.

During the first three years of the New Deal, the Supreme Court included five "conservative" and four "liberal" justices. Thus, it was inevitable that the Court should invalidate some important New Deal legislation. In fact, several Administration measures went far beyond the horizon of the most "liberal" members of the Court. This fact was suddenly demonstrated in May, 1935, when in one day the Supreme Court ended the Blue Eagle (the National Industrial Recovery Act of 1933), invalidated a congressional act for the relief of farm debtors which had deprived creditors of all effective remedy, and finally repudiated the President's unwarranted use of the removal power.

If the Supreme Court voided New Deal legislation, the social revolution was doomed. At a press conference early in 1937, the President made an angry attack on the Court declaring that the decisions threw the country back to the "horse and buggy days." Shortly thereafter he laid before Congress a measure to pack the Supreme Court with appointees of his own selection. The "Nine Old Men" would thus be outvoted in all cases involving the constitutionality of New Deal legislation.

The broad and imaginative mind of Chief Justice Hughes recognizing the device of compromise, even in the solemn business of interpreting the fundamental law, assumed that the prestige of the Supreme Court could be saved by a dose of judicial co-operation. In a surprisingly short time, indeed in April, 1937, a "liberal" majority of the Court rendered the decision in the Jones and Laughlin case which upheld the National Labor Relations Act of 1935, and started the Court on a new road of interpretation that supported almost every measure of the New Deal. As a cynical commentator observed, "a switch in time saved nine."

The litigation of the public utilities seeking to protect the rights of the stockholders and bondholders was caught in the swing of the Supreme Court from the right to the left. Willkie had decided that the legal battle of the Commonwealth and Southern Corporation against the New Deal should begin on behalf of the small stockholder. Thus, the C&S espoused the suit of a citizen, George Ashwander, who considered his investment in the Alabama Power Company to have been jeopardized by the arrangements made by Commonwealth and Southern Corporation with the Tennessee Valley Authority, in the contract of 1934. Representing a minority group of stockholders, Ashwander had sought to test the constitutionality of the powers conferred by Congress upon the Tennessee Valley Authority.

The transmission lines of the Alabama Power Company reached into sixty-six counties of the state of Alabama. The transmission lines of the Authority, purchased from the Alabama Power Company (as provided for under the contract of 1934), extended from the Wilson Dam in northern Alabama into seven counties in the state, all within a radius of fifty miles. These lines served 190,000 customers, or about one tenth of the total number of patrons of the Alabama Company. The "friendly" suit of Ashwander v. Tennessee Valley Authority sought to enjoin performance under the contract, signed by Willkie on January 4, 1934, to determine the constitutionality of the contract, and to ask for a general declaratory decree concerning the powers of the Authority.

In view of the many obvious advantages to the entire nation that came out of the great TVA experiment, the historian may well ask why the shareholders and bondholders of a private utility company should attempt to thwart some of the activities of this governmental enterprise. No one could in good conscience object to the construction of dams to control floods, improve navigation and generate electric power for the manufacture of nitrates for national defense. To oppose the sale of surplus electric power to local distributing companies as a natural corollary of the project would also be unreasonable. All these activities were in the public interest. Unquestionably the increase of the electric power available in the Tennessee Valley contributed to raising the standard of living and increasing the happiness of the citizens in this region.

The unfortunate aspect of the TVA experiment was the deception practised regarding the "yardstick," the economic waste in duplicating power lines, and the ruthless disregard of property rights of existing utility corporations. To these grievances should be added the practices of various officers, in carrying on an extensive propaganda program of abuse against the local public utilities.

In the litigation of the next several years evidence concerning these practices prompted Mr. Justice Butler to say, in a memorable dissenting opinion written in 1939: "Pursuant to a plan promulgated in 1933, defendants are conducting a systematic campaign for the purpose of disrupting the established business relations between complainants and their customers, destroying the good will built up by complainants, seizing their markets and inciting the residents of communities served by them to co-operate with defendants [the Tennessee Valley Authority] in their scheme to develop an absolute monopoly. With full knowledge of the noncompensatory and confiscatory character of the 'yardstick' rates, they have represented to the inhabitants of communities served by complainants that these 'yardsticks' were fair measures of reasonable rates and have thereby attempted to incite the inhabitants to build publicly owned systems using power furnished by the Authority, to lead them to believe that they are being charged unreasonable rates, to stir up political agitation against privately owned utilities and to bring complainants into disrepute and disfavor."

The Ashwander case was heard in the first instance in the District Court of the United States for the Northern District of Alabama under the jurisdiction of Judge William I. Grubb. His decision, rendered on April 11, 1935, was favorable to the petitioner Ashwander. Judge Grubb ruled that Congress had no constitutional authority to authorize the Tennessee Valley Authority or any other federal agency to undertake the operation of a utility system for profit unrelated to governmental use. The program of the TVA, he held, was a service to various municipalities which clearly was based on a deliberate intention to generate electricity in excess of governmental use. Performance of the contract of January 4, 1934, would involve substantial loss and injury to the Alabama Power Company. He therefore annulled the contract in its entirety. While the Court gave no consideration to the prayer for a declaratory judgment concerning the powers of the Authority, this decision, of course, voided all similar contracts in the Tennessee Valley until ruled on by the Supreme Court.

Although the Willkie stockholders won the first round of the legal battle, the victory was destined to be short-lived. On appeal the case was taken to the United States Circuit Court which reversed the decision of Judge Grubb, and the case then went to the Supreme Court by writ of certiorari. Before this tribunal, the cause of the stockholders was brilliantly argued. Although Willkie had directed the legal strategy, he wisely left the court-room pleading to an able Birmingham lawyer, Forney Johnston, and a distinguished constitutional jurist, James M. Beck. The case was contested by Solicitor-General Stanley F. Reed (later to be elevated to the Supreme Court) and Attorney-General Cummings, assisted by a large number of attorneys from the Department of Justice.

On February 17, 1936, Chief Justice Charles Evans Hughes, ruling against the stockholders, reduced the issues before the Court to only two: one was the constitutional authority for the construction of Wilson Dam, and the other was the constitutionality of the distribution by the Government of electric energy generated at the dam. The Court held that the dam and the power plant connected with it had been installed for purposes of national defense and the improvement of navigation. As to the second question, the Court held that the United States acquired full title to the dam site with all riparian rights including the power generated therefrom. Under the Constitution the Government was expressly granted the authority to dispose of property legally acquired. Hence the Government possessed the authority to sell this power to consumers. Mr. Justice Brandeis contented himself with a concurring opinion replete with evidence of his hatred of Big Business, denying that the stockholders had standing in the Court.

To Willkie's mind the first part of the opinion of the Chief Justice ignored the express purpose of the suit, which was to determine the legality of governmental engagement in the power industry for profit. Counsel for the stockholders had shown that TVA was not merely a national project for defense and navigation, but that it was equally a project for the manufacture of power to sell to consumers. On the second count, Willkie also considered the Court astonishingly evasive. The stockholders had asked the Court: Did the Government have the authority to use public funds to compete with private business in the sale of a commodity? The question was important. It deserved an answer. But the Court dodged the issue, by a ruling: "The Court will not pass upon the constitutionality of legislation in a friendly, nonadversary proceeding, declining because to decide such questions is legitimate only in the last resort, and as a necessity in the determination of real, earnest and vital controversy between individuals. It was never thought that by means of a friendly suit, a party beaten in the legislature could transfer to the courts an inquiry as to the constitutionality of the legislative act."

Mr. Justice McReynolds made the only dissent from the decision of the Court. Citing the annual reports of the Tennessee Valley Authority, he asserted that the record left no room for reasonable doubt that the primary purpose of the Tennessee Valley Authority Act was to put the federal Government into the business of distributing and selling electric power throughout a large district, to expel the power companies which had long serviced these areas, and to control the market therein. This government instrumentality, he declared, had entered upon a pretentious scheme to provide a "yardstick" to determine the fairness of rates charged by private owners, and to attain "no less a goal than the electrification of America." In other words, the TVA plan as conceived and executed contemplated exclusive control over all power sites on the Tennessee River and tributaries. Concluding his dissenting opinion, Mr. Justice McReynolds made a profoundly prophetic remark: "If under their mask of disposing of property the United States can enter the business of generating, transmitting and selling power as, when and wherever some board may specify, with the definite design to accomplish ends wholly beyond the sphere marked out by the Constitution, an easy way had been found for breaking down the limitations heretofore supposed to guarantee protection against aggression."

Having fought first under the standard of the small stockholder, and lost, Willkie and his associates in the C&S determined to give battle a second time under the banner of the operating companies. Accordingly, Willkie advised the nineteen operating utilities in the Tennessee Valley to file suit to contest the constitutionality of the TVA. On May 29, 1936, therefore, the Tennessee Electric Power Company, with a number of other utilities in the area, brought suit in equity against the Tennessee Valley Authority to enjoin further construction of dams in the Valley. The operating companies which now appealed to the courts served more than a million customers in the Tennessee Valley and represented a billion dollars of capital owned by security holders all over the country. This capital investment paid fifteen million dollars a year in taxes to the state and federal governments.

After the filing of this suit, Willkie made routine business trips through the South. In an interview in Chattanooga on June 14, he expressed the hope that "the TVA would meet frankly and without legal technicalities the issues raised in the suit instigated recently by companies in the Valley in order to test the constitutionality of the act creating the TVA." Again, he declared: "With the filing of the law suit by the nineteen operating companies in this area to test the constitutionality of the act creating the Tennessee Valley Authority, there is afforded an excellent opportunity for the TVA to come into court and meet frankly the issues between the TVA and private utilities. If they will but do this, and not attempt to narrow the issues or escape on legal technicalities, the public will be able to learn the fallacy of their many claims."

There was little likelihood, however, that the directors of the Tennessee Valley Authority would meet the issue in the manner suggested. The control of TVA was already falling into the hands of an ambitious officeholder whom Willkie considered as a ruthless autocrat. David E. Lilienthal, according to the testimony of Dr. Arthur E. Morgan, was even at this time engaged in intrigues to succeed him as chairman of TVA. Indeed, Lilienthal, so addicted to maneuvers, would have little interest in assisting the courts to examine the real merits of the controversy.

Although the Tennessee Electric Power Company and its eighteen associates had originally filed suit in Chancery Court of Knox County in Tennessee, the directors of TVA removed the case to the United States District Court for Eastern Tennessee. A court of three judges was convened, which after a trial, on January 24, 1938, denied the injunction and dismissed the suit. Thereupon, fourteen of the complaining companies, on the advice of Willkie, appealed the decision. It was not until 1939 that the Supreme Court gave its opinion.

In the meanwhile, Willkie and his associates suffered stinging defeats in several other cases before the courts. One of these setbacks was the case of the Alabama Power Company *v.* Ickes. The Alabama Power Company, a subsidiary of C&S, had filed suit against Secretary of the Interior Harold L. Ickes as director of the Public Works Administration. The Alabama Power Company, as the holder of a non-exclusive franchise to operate electric distribution systems in several municipalities, sought to enjoin the loan and grant of federal money to municipalities for the construction of competing systems, alleging that the statute authorizing federal officials to take this action was invalid. Dismissal of the suit in the lower court was affirmed by the Supreme Court on the ground that the complainant had no standing as a taxpayer to question the expenditure of the federal funds. Furthermore, the complainant had no standing to question the lawful use of money by the Government even though it would result in competition with complainant's business. In fact, the complainant had no standing whatsoever in the Court.

As to the question of competition, the Court ruled that the director of PWA had made no attempt to regulate rates or even to foster municipal ownership of utilities. The PWA projects, moreover, were merely a part of the national program to relieve unemployment. The Alabama Power Company had only a non-exclusive franchise; so that anyone could compete with it who also secured a franchise. Hence the existing franchise of the Alabama Power Company could not be considered to exclude municipal competition even if subsidized from public funds.

To Willkie, the decision of the Supreme Court appeared as a denial of justice to honest businessmen. The *Harvard Law Review* commented that the Court did not provide a definitive answer to the real issue of the case, inasmuch as the Court insisted on viewing the question of loans and grants as completely separate from the question of competition. The legal question was whether or not Congress had authority to appropriate funds for creating public enterprises to compete with private business enterprises. This was the issue that the bureaucrats wished above all else to avoid. The growing "liberal" wing of the Supreme Court lent itself to the bureaucratic view.

A fourth important suit of the utilities in this long battle with the Government was the Electric Bond and Share Company *v.* Securities and Exchange Commission. Although Willkie was not the initiator of this suit, C&S intervened with a cross bill. The Electric Bond and Share Company, joined by fourteen associated utility companies, refused to register with the Securities and Exchange Commission before December 1, 1935, as provided by law, in order to test the constitutionality of the Public Utility Holding Company Act of 1935. The SEC, therefore, brought suit for injunction against these companies from using the mails or the facilities of interstate commerce. The Commonwealth and Southern Corporation then filed a cross bill praying for a declaratory judgment asking that the Act of 1935 be held void as being in excess of the power granted to Congress under Article I of the Constitution, and of the Fifth and Tenth Amendments, and that a permanent injunction be issued restraining John J. Morris, as United States Attorney for the District of Delaware, from attempting to compel compliance with the Public Utility Holding Company Act of 1935.

Nevertheless, the District Court sustained the validity of the Act and granted the injunction sought by SEC. The Court further held that the registration provisions were not inherently inseparable from the other provisions of the Act. Accordingly, the cross bill was dismissed for want of equity.

The case was finally argued before the Supreme Court in 1937 with a conspicuous array of legal talent. Four able lawyers appeared on the brief for the petitioners. The Government was represented by Attorney-General Cummings, Assistant Attorney-General Jackson, and other federal attorneys, including Benjamin V. Cohen and Thomas C. Corcoran. Mr. Chief Justice Hughes gave the majority opinion of the Court. Only Mr. Justice McReynolds dissented, while Justices Cardozo and Reed took no part.

The Supreme Court in 1938 sustained the lower court, which also meant that the bill of complaint filed by C&S was dismissed.

The Chief Justice brushed aside the argument that the intent of Congress had been to control public utility holding companies even to the point of their destruction. However, as soon as the Supreme Court rendered its decision in the case of Electric Bond and Share Company, the utility companies promptly filed with the SEC their notification of registration and the necessary documents pertaining thereto as required by law.

The lingering hope of Wendell Willkie for relief by the Supreme Court was ended on January 30, 1939, with the long-awaited final decision in the case of the Tennessee Electric Power Company v. Tennessee Valley Authority. It was a five-to-two decision. Counsel for the utility companies had again argued that the TVA Act had been a bold attempt, in the guise of exercising implied powers of the Constitution to improve streams for navigation, to exercise the further authority to manufacture a commodity and market it in direct competition with established business enterprise.

The majority opinion was read by Mr. Justice Roberts. Once more the majority of the Court evaded the real constitutional issue. The Court held that the Tennessee Electric Power Company and associated companies were without legal standing to challenge the validity of the TVA project. More than this, the Court rejected the claim of the power companies that their property was being destroyed by governmental competition. "The vice of the position," said Justice Roberts, "is that neither their charters nor their local franchises involve the grant of a monopoly or render competition illegal." The majority opinion agreed with the judgment of the District Court to the effect that the Tennessee Valley Authority was not guilty of coercion, duress, fraud, or misrepresentation in procuring contracts with municipalities, and that the Authority had not acted with any malicious motive.

The dissenting opinion in the case of the Tennessee Electric Power Company v. Tennessee Valley Authority has been quoted earlier in this chapter. It was written by Mr. Justice Butler and concurred in by Mr. Justice McReynolds. In clear and sharp words, the dissenting justices stated that the real purpose of TVA was obviously to authorize a large and indeterminate number of great works for the primary end of creating a vast supply of electric power. Any references in the TVA Act to navigation, they said, were mere pretense in order to achieve a federal object which, under the Constitution, had been reserved exclusively for the states. With the exception of the power generated at Wilson Dam, they stated that "the Act creates an outlet for power deliberately produced as a commercial enterprise to be sold in unlawful and destructive competition." The dissenting justices further stated that the rates of the Authority excluded the cost of the major part of the investment expenses and hence were "unreasonable and confiscatory as a measure of rates." Finally, the minority opinion accepted the validity of the charge that the directors of TVA harbored a policy to break the utilities in the Valley, and for this purpose the Authority had lobbied for bills in various state legislatures in order to provide municipal competition with the existing power lines.

Keen was the disappointment of Wendell Willkie and indeed of the entire business world over the failure of the Supreme Court to pass directly upon the constitutional question of the use of governmental funds to promote competition with private enterprise, and upon the legal question of governmental distribution of public power. It was the second occasion upon which the Court had avoided consideration of the real issue involved in the litigation. In the opinion of the *Southern California Law Review*, January, 1940, this decision, as well as the ruling of the Court in the Ashwander case, left open the question of the extent to which an agency of the Federal Government might enter into competition with private enterprise. Editorially, the *New York Times* commented that the decision was of such extensive import that the Federal Government was now free, if it chose, to compete with private enterprise in almost any field of business, even on terms that were obviously unfair to business.

Edwin F. Albertsworth, professor of constitutional law at Northwestern University, had said as early as 1935 that if the Supreme Court should sanction the policies of the New Deal as permanent and constitutional ventures of Government, then the American people would see the beginning of the end of private enterprise in this country and the inauguration of state and federal socialism. While perhaps this view was too gloomy, Willkie finally recognized that the New Deal had brought the American people face to face with absolute power.

A decade later, Roscoe Pound, Dean of the Harvard Law School and founder of the American school of sociological jurisprudence, described the legal procedure of the New Deal as follows: "For a generation the courts have leaned over backwards in an effort to facilitate the administration of social legislation. With the multiplication of the governmental agencies, the increasing subjection of every form of activity to administrative regulation and hostility of administrative agencies to all attempts to impose effective legal checks upon them, we have been coming in practice to a condition of what may well be called administrative absolutism." Another distinguished jurist, Walter F. Dodd, declared that the New Deal Supreme Court in ten years had removed substantially all previous restrictions on the powers granted to the national Government by the Constitution.

Willkie was loath to abandon faith in the Supreme Court. But conclusive evidence had been given of the Court's abandonment of the doctrine of free enterprise for the welfare state. The revolution had carried not only the presidency and Congress but even the highest tribunal. In these days of dark uncertainty, Willkie frequently declared: "If it's my baby that's hurt now, it may be your baby later. Our business simply happens to be the first target. But I have frequently said and I still maintain that you can take any business, and, in *ex parte* proceedings, with the backing of the senatorial committee, so picture it as to create public sentiment against it." Willkie sincerely believed that if the American people knew the facts they would not approve this gigantic change in governmental philosophy. He had appealed to Congress and lost. He had taken his cause to the courts and lost. Now he determined to appeal to the people.

Within several months of the TVA decision, therefore, Willkie wrote a devastating article entitled, "The Court Is Now His," which appeared in the *Saturday Evening Post*, March 9, 1940. In pungent words he described the attempt of the Chief Executive, in the spring of 1937, to secure the passage through

Congress of a Court Bill which would enable him to appoint an additional member to the Bench for every federal judge who did not retire at the age of seventy, provided that such appointments did not increase the membership of the Supreme Court to more than fifteen justices or increase the entire federal judiciary to more than fifty justices. The Court Bill was defeated.

Nevertheless, in the end, as Willkie explained, the President gained through a freak of fate what Congress had denied him by law. Deaths and retirements among the "Nine Old Men" had brought him victory. In rapid succession, he was able to name five justices to the high judiciary, including Hugo Black, Stanley Reed, William O. Douglas, Felix Frankfurter, and Frank Murphy. The Court *was* his! Instead of being the only President never privileged to nominate a member of the Court, as he had complained, he suddenly became the Chief Executive to appoint the most judges. And Willkie further pointed out that while only one justice was required to erase the five-four conservative complexion of the Court, the President had been able to appoint a clear majority on the Bench.

With brilliant logic, Willkie analyzed the significance of the change in the Supreme Court in relation to law, politics and business. The law as practised in the United States had been progressively built by the decision of cases which established a system of precedents. Over the generations, therefore, the Supreme Court had constructed its great body of constitutional interpretation. It had permitted an expansion of the powers necessary for the federal Government to fulfill its defined purposes and it preserved to the states the powers proper to their jurisdiction. These precedents of constitutional law, he declared, furnished many limitations on the powers of Congress which were effectively recognized by the Supreme Court prior to 1937. Today, "by a series of sweeping decisions," said Willkie, "the Court has not only annulled many of the precedents of four or five years ago, but it has uprooted and overturned some of the oldest guideposts of our constitutional law." In one sitting, on January 29, 1940, he said, the Court had over-ruled three previous decisions each one as recent as the year 1935.

While Willkie was quick to recognize that changing times might necessitate a new interpretation of the Constitution, he held it nothing less than revolutionary that a series of reversals of decisions were made in so brief a time on so important a subject as Government and Business. Since 1935, Willkie explained, the American people had received a number of major opinions from the Supreme Court which substantially changed their form of Government. He said: "I do not mean to say that even a Supreme Court precedent is sacrosanct. It is quite conceivable that from the point of view of one age the opinion of another is wrong. Or that a misguided interpretation made by one group of judges—who are, after all only human beings—might have been too readily accepted as infallible by successive groups of judges. In such cases, reinterpretation, however late, is to be welcomed. But when a series of reinterpretations overturning well-argued precedents are made in a brief time by a newly appointed group of judges, all tending to indicate the same basic disagreement with the established conception of government, the thoughtful observer can only conclude that something revolutionary is going on. And that is what has happened here."

Willkie's article was one of the first attacks upon the strange upheaval of the Court and its sudden reversal of a number of decisions. This break with precedence was not only disconcerting to businessmen, he explained, but it jeopardized the rights of Little Business as well as Big Business. He emphasized that basic principles of constitutional interpretation should not be changed in accordance with the clamor of the hour. The purpose of law was not only to regulate. It was also, and perhaps chiefly, to stabilize. Thus the persistent and wholly unpredictable changes in substantive law were demoralizing to the entire political and economic system. Much of the responsibility for the current unemployment and national debt, Willkie charged, was due to the revolutionary interpretations of the Court. If the situation continued it would be fatal to the economic life of the country. Wealth goes into hiding when capitalists become frightened, and, when capital is lacking, the employee is in danger of losing his position. And when production lags the consumer is ultimately faced with high prices.

Willkie ended his cogent article with the lively prediction: "From the point of view of the social philosopher, the underlying significance of the present Administration, as embodied in the present Supreme Court, is to be found in the creation of a vast, ineffectual, expensive, central authority. . . . The American public, on the other hand, has not yet tested all the whims, vagaries and caprices of a securely enthroned central government reaching into the daily lives of all the people. And the social philosopher may well speculate what that public's reaction will be when the tests have been made. If the present public is anything like its ancestors, I wager that when it does understand, it will mightily rebel."

The final defeat of the utilities in the case of the Tennessee Electric Power Company (1939) made Willkie all the more eager to sell this property to his privileged competitor, the Tennessee Valley Authority. Furthermore, a somewhat conciliatory attitude had become apparent on the part of the TVA directors, partly due to the influence of Harry Hopkins, who became Secretary of Commerce in 1938. Willkie now pressed TVA to purchase the Tennessee Power Company. He had offered to sell many times during the six long years of bitter strife with the TVA but Lilienthal had always set a price too low. Willkie had, therefore, maintained that he doubted if the Authority really wanted to buy his properties anyway and that he would never be convinced until he saw the money on the barrelhead.

Negotiations at last proved fruitful, and on August 15, 1939, Willkie finally saw the money on the barrelhead. The price that Willkie won for C&S by the sale of its prize operating unit, the Tennessee Electric Power Company, was some $78,000,000, part of which was paid by the Tennessee Valley Authority, and the balance by some thirty-five municipalities and co-operative companies. Although this sum was nearly thirty million dollars more than Lilienthal had once said he would pay for the company, it was a disappointment to many of the executives of C&S. Cobb, for one, felt that Willkie sold at too low a price, too low by some fifty millions. The selling price covered only the bondholders and the holders of preferred stocks.

As customary with Wall Street, the end of the negotiations for the sale of a large property was celebrated in a formal ceremony. On the occasion of the sale of the Tennessee Electric

Power Company, the formality was held in an assembly room of the First National Bank of the City of New York at 2 Wall Street. Two hundred and fifty persons witnessed the ceremony, including the Governor of Tennessee, officials of TVA, mayors of municipalities, executives of the utility companies, newsmen and photographers.

Willkie presided as chairman of the meeting. The occasion was perfect for his superb talents as a showman. He completely dominated the scene. As one eyewitness described it, the ceremony became a "one-man victory over the competitive inroads of the federal Government into the electric power business." Although virtually forced to sell a profitable corporation, Willkie had dramatized for the whole country the necessity for American business to question the objectives of the New Deal. His success in securing the additional purchase price became known on Wall Street as "Willkie's $30,000,000 shriek." As if overawed by the financial center of the world, Lilienthal was ill at ease, uncomfortable and sullen. The climax came when Lilienthal handed Willkie the certified check of the United States Government in the amount of $44,728,300. The director of TVA had nothing gracious to say. Willkie, good-naturedly, relieved the tension by replying: "Thanks, Dave. This is a lot of money for a couple of Indiana boys to be kicking around. For this I give you the deeds of the Tennessee Electric Power Company."

With the conclusion of the legal transaction, Willkie made a formal statement to the press. "The Tennessee Electric Power Company was started thirty-five years ago by a Chattanooga engineer who refused to believe that the Tennessee River could not be dammed. Since then thousands of employees and many thousands of investors from different states have participated in the remarkable development of this project. It has never received any gifts from the United States Treasury or from the PWA or from municipalities. On the contrary, it has made substantial tax payments to the federal and local governments, amounting to over $25,000,000 in the last ten years. From now on this business is in the hands of government agencies. Another business is removed from the tax rolls. While this sale does not represent the true value of this investment, at least we have received enough to make full payment to the owners of the bonds and preferred stocks. The common stockholders, principally the Commonwealth and Southern Corporation, are taking all the loss. But the loss of these properties will not be in vain if it serves to arouse the American people against government invasion of this business.

"In looking to the future, I plead with the Government for two principles, both of which are essential if the system of free economic enterprise is to be preserved. I ask first, as I have asked many times before, that the Government discontinue its competition with private business outside the Tennessee Valley. It now has its 'yardstick' area. It should be content with that, so in other areas of this nation the utility industry may make its vital contribution to American business recovery. Second, I ask that these government agencies should keep their books on a completely honest basis, so as not to mislead the American people from whom these commissions get their power."

Willkie now hoped for peace, but there was no peace. Commonwealth and Southern Corporation had sacrificed its prize operating company in the South—the Tennessee Electric Power Company—to the Authority. In consummating this deal Willkie believed that he had won protection for the other five southern companies of C&S. He gambled that Lilienthal would be content to follow a reasonable course with the remaining power companies, or else that an awakened public opinion would force the federal Government into a reasonable course. Two days after Lilienthal took title to the star utility of the South, Willkie signed a contract with TVA under which the Authority agreed to deliver at the switch between six and ten million kilowatt hours of energy weekly to the Alabama Power Company. Similar contracts were made between TVA and the other southern companies. Alabama Power Company adopted a program calling for the expenditure of $1,000,000 in 1940 on the construction of rural lines. Willkie believed that as soon as the investment market realized the extent of stabilization resulting from these agreements between TVA and his companies, he would be able to refinance their securities.

There was no peace. Willkie had underestimated the bureaucratic ambitions of Lilienthal and overestimated the promptness with which public opinion would rally to the defense of American business. The New Deal operations were militant to the end. On November 18, David Lilienthal made a public address at Lafayette, Alabama, bitterly attacking the Alabama Power Company, and urging rural co-operatives to build competing power lines. Charging that the company maintained a policy of antagonism and obstruction toward co-operative rural electrification, he expressed a hope for an end to "this dog-in-the-manger policy of fighting farm co-operatives." The day after Lilienthal's assault upon the Alabama Power Company, Willkie warned that the speech had jeopardized the plans of the Alabama Power Company to spend a million dollars on the construction of rural electrification. There could be no peace because free enterprise was built upon one economic pattern while the TVA and Government spending rested upon a totally different concept, the welfare state.

As the years passed, enthusiasm for the power experiment in the Tennessee Valley declined. The advantages of flood control and the creation of power for national defense were obvious, particularly during the Second World War. The stimulation of the experiment to community life in the Tennessee Valley was undeniable. But there were other features about TVA that were not so desirable. While the merits of the experiment were now almost universally admitted, the defects had become too conspicuous for even the Democratic Party to ignore.

In 1946, the General Accounting Office made a report to Congress which included the first audit of TVA other than audits made by its own staff. All previous audits, under an astonishingly loose practice, had been "inside" audits. The new report of the Comptroller-General revealed the fact that the Authority had drawn money from the public treasury each year of its existence and had made no repayment of these amounts. Furthermore, of the total sum of $718,000,000 of government money invested in TVA, more than one half of it, $400,000,000, had been spent on power facilities rather than control of floods. This colossal expenditure of federal funds had been devoted to the direct benefit of only 3.8 per cent of the population of the country.

The report of the Comptroller-General aroused sharp criticism of the TVA in Congress. A bill was hurriedly passed requiring the TVA to make full repayment of government funds within a period of forty years. This measure partly removed the dishonest feature of the "yardstick" which Willkie had strongly criticized. Senator Elmer Thomas, of Oklahoma, introduced a measure to place a curb on all public power projects. Senator Byrd, of Virginia, denounced the TVA because it continually raided the public treasury. As opposition mounted in heated debate, opinion crystallized against further expansion of government electric power systems. TVA was only the first such government project; there were seven smaller TVA's scattered throughout the country by the end of the Roosevelt Administration.

An indication that Congress was losing faith in public power projects was the reluctance of Congress in May, 1948, to approve some four million dollars for the TVA to extend its power operations by the construction of a steam-generating plant eventually to cost upwards of fifty million dollars. During the hearings in the thirties, Willkie had often tried to explain to the New Deal congressmen that water power had long been outmoded, partly because of the difficulty of securing firm power and partly because of the expense of installation. But New Dealers, in their deep hatred of Big Business, refused to listen to this advice. After fourteen years of water operation, however, the Authority wanted steam.

Congress, in 1948, showed its change in attitude toward TVA in another manner. It cut the President's recommendation for TVA in the 1949 fiscal budget by over seven million dollars. After much haggling, Congress finally approved a budget of $27,389,061 for the year. The debates accentuated the fact that during all the years in operation, TVA could not pay its own way, but had to depend upon an annual government subsidy. As Willkie had frequently said, a private industry cannot compete with a government enterprise. One enjoys a subsidy, and the other must pay interest on bonds and make a profit.

TVA received yet another setback from Congress. The House Appropriation Committee in reporting the Government Corporations Appropriation Bill in 1948 recommended that the town of Norris should be sold at auction unless it could be made "self-sustaining." The model town of Norris had been elaborately built by the TVA in 1933 in order to house workers on the Norris Dam, and was publicized as the ideal American community. The red-brick and white-frame houses, with landscaped gardens, were equipped with all modern conveniences and heated electrically. There were winding roads in the settlement, with parks and playgrounds at convenient locations, a modish shopping center well separated from the residential area, and "progressive" schools. Now a ghost town of only 350 families, it was finally sold on June 15, 1948, for some two million dollars.

An appraisal of the Public Utility Holding Company Act of 1935, a decade after its enactment, although showing many benefits, nevertheless indicated, as Willkie had predicted, great injury to investors in whose interests the measure was allegedly passed. Elisha M. Friedman, well-known consulting economist of New York, testified on November 15, 1945, before the Committee on Interstate and Foreign Commerce of the House of Representatives, regarding the setback that the Act of 1935 had inflicted upon public utilities in the United States. Friedman recommended several changes in the Act, the two most important ones being to limit the sweeping powers of the Securities and Exchange Commission, and to delete the section imposing the Death Sentence upon holding companies.

The Death Sentence was not essential to the Act and had been bitterly debated in Congress before passage. In fact this part of the Act had passed the Senate by only one vote. It was hasty legislation enacted in a state of emotionalism seldom surpassed in congressional history. At one stroke, as Willkie had declared, Congress placed a strait jacket on an industry that had evolved over three generations. Regulation of utilities and holding companies could have been effectively achieved through the SEC without this crippling clause. As the highly respected analyst, Elisha M. Friedman, pointed out, the public and the investor, as well as the utilities had been injured by the Death Sentence. The average amount of yearly construction for electric power from 1919 to 1932 had been $650,000,000. But, in the years 1934-35 and later when the utilities were under attack, new construction averaged only $150,000,000 per year. The difference was equivalent to a good-sized public works program. To express the effect of the Death Sentence on the public in different terms, said Friedman, there was a decline in the rate of growth of private generating capacity from an annual average of 5,700,000 kilowatts in the period 1920-33 to 1,600,000 kilowatts in the period of 1934-38.

The individual investor suffered severely by the Corcoran-Cohen campaign of hate against bigness. Eighty per cent of the investors in utilities owned less than 100 shares. After the Supreme Court upheld the Act, in 1938, the giant holding companies began to divest themselves of 521 subsidiaries having assets of $9,425,000,000. The threat of disintegration again reduced stock prices of utilities. Two million small stockholders were punished for the sins of a few speculators. Furthermore, the Act brought few benefits to the consumer. Residential rates had been reduced more rapidly before the passage of the Act than after. The holding companies had performed a service in the lowering of operating costs which was passed on to the consumer.

Willkie had pled with Congressmen in the various committee hearings to refrain from the abolition of holding companies. Regulate them, yes, but let them live because they serve a definite purpose in expert management, and in obtaining needed capital at lowest rates. Too late, even his enemies began to see that he was right. Senator Norris, on the floor of the Senate, on May 1, 1942, acknowledged that he had changed his views somewhat about utilities. The post-war world demanded a free and healthy utility industry, which would employ demobilized soldiers, and continue to produce steady power at ever lower costs, and increasing supply.

In 1939, Willkie could not even guess that the following decade would vindicate most of his views. Defeated by the Congress, rejected by the Supreme Court, Willkie turned to public opinion in an attempt to acquaint the voters with what was happening under the New Deal to individualism and free enterprise.

CHAPTER VI

The Appeal to Public Opinion

WILLKIE'S DRAMATIC pleas for justice had failed to impress the Democratic majority in the congressional Committee on Interstate and Foreign Commerce. His argument had even failed to find vigorous Republican support on the floor of either the Senate or the House. The measures which crippled American business had been passed with astonishing speed, against surprisingly weak opposition. Indeed, there was no competent defender of free enterprise among the leaders of either party.

Willkie at last recognized that while he believed in one theory of government, the Roosevelt Administration was committed to another. The rules of government had been quietly changed by the men of the New Deal. The American people, Willkie felt, did not understand the drastic alterations which were taking place both in the theory and the form of their Government. Few knew even the names of such men as Frankfurter, Brandeis, Corcoran and Cohen, much less the significance of the influence which they exerted on Government. Willkie believed that the majority of hard-working and hard-thinking Americans would not approve these subtle changes.

Disillusioned and frustrated by the sense of unfairness that he had met in Congress, Willkie resolved to take a direct appeal to the people of America, to acquaint them with the facts of the New Deal. He was convinced that the American people possessed the intelligence to distinguish between the freedom of free enterprise and the spurious "freedom from want" blithely promised by the New Deal. The hearings had given him a public reputation. By late 1935, business organizations in all fields of enterprise had begun to call upon him for addresses on Government and Business. Bond clubs, economic clubs, chambers of commerce and radio stations sought him. As his speeches began to have increasing news value because of his fearless attacks upon the New Deal, editors and publishers beseeched him for articles. A utility executive was winning a national audience. This businessman who had, like thousands of other Americans, risen from the bottom of the heap, was winning public attention. Voters who had been mesmerized by the charm and oratory of Franklin D. Roosevelt listened to Willkie and pondered. People who had been sore bereft in 1932 as a result of the economic debacle and who had been wonderstruck by the smooth promises of the Fireside Chats and the semantics of the Brain Trust now heard the other side of the story. Blind fear had driven many of them to a ready acceptance of the Rooseveltian revolution without much understanding of it. But the economic truths expounded by Willkie provoked a critical appraisal of the entire program.

His career as a publicist began with a speech at a joint meeting of the Economic Club of New York and the Harvard Business School on January 21, 1935. He faced a distinguished audience. James P. Warburg, president of the Bank of Manhattan, presided, and James B. Conant, president of Harvard University, was the guest of honor. The industrial and financial elite of the great metropolis were present to hear Willkie deliver an eloquent and impassioned speech on "Government and Public Utilities." At the end of his talk these distinguished men rose to their feet as one man in a cheering ovation which lasted some five minutes. Willkie suddenly became the man of the hour. Other addresses followed in rapid succession. Not before had there appeared such an attractive defense of American business nor such a devastating attack upon the New Deal. He became the recognized but unofficial spokesman against Rooseveltian policies.

Willkie attacked as a fallacy the theory of government spokesmen to the effect that all businessmen were "economic royalists" or "outmoded plutocrats of power." The people, he said, still had every reason to place their confidence in the business leaders of the country. Of course there had been men who had proved to be a discredit to business just as there had been men who were a discredit to religion or politics. But no sane person would lash at the church or condemn all ministers for the moral dereliction of a few. No one would condemn all government officials because dishonesty was sometimes found in high places, even in the cabinet and the legislature; and certainly few would advocate the abolition of Congress every time it passed an unwise law!

Again and again in various addresses Willkie stressed the significant gains in the American economy. This country paid the highest wages and possessed the highest standards of living. The costs of production and distribution had been continually reduced, which made for lower prices of commodity goods. As a result, good living had been spread to more than two-thirds of the people in the land. In all the statistical records it was shown that the American people enjoyed the highest standard of living of any people on the globe. All of this had been accomplished by the skill, the vision, and the daring of American business leaders who took full advantage of America's great natural resources.

He frankly recognized that in the lush years of the twenties certain abuses arose which led to wild speculation and manipulation of the stock market. Those abuses had to be curbed. But, Willkie added: "If the politicians had been content with that, if they had been content with safe regulation designed not to cripple all industry, but to correct malpractices, this country, in my judgment, by now would have surmounted most of its economic difficulties."

Willkie charged the politicians with shouting about abuses long since corrected and with lashing business leaders of America with an "undiscriminating whip." One of the most ridiculous of all accusations made against businessmen was that they had deliberately destroyed the prosperity of the country, destroyed the very house that they had built. The depression, he declared, was the result of the maladjustments resulting from the World War. The war itself had not been started by businessmen but rather by politicians. He laughed at the myth of the businessman conjured up by some politicians as a fat, white-vested individual with a top hat, sitting in a mahogany office inherited from his father, exercising some mysterious power over his fellow men. He recalled that his colleagues were for the most part men who started to work at wages less than the current relief payments to the unemployed. They had become business leaders because they worked hard enough and intelligently enough to rise to positions of responsibility and trust. Not only were they simple, sincere and ardently patriotic men, but also they were the most constructive force in America.

Willkie attacked the New Deal philosophy that profits were wrong. The politicians had continuously stressed social welfare. They ridiculed the desire for profits. He declared with some sarcasm that the dictionary signified *profit* as a desirable condition. The word meant any accession or increase of goods from the exertion of labor, comprehending the acquisition of anything valuable, intellectual or corporeal, temporal or spiritual. Profit had for ages been the hope of youth and the reward of age. It was the mainspring of all economic activity of mankind, and the dynamic force behind the progress of civilization.

Willkie attacked the politicians who loudly lamented the passing of the frontier and who so often repeated the comment that "gone were those incomparable opportunities of free land in the West." The great days of America are not yet done, he said. Only the borders of achievement have been touched. The frontiers of scientific exploration are unlimited and will bring millions of new jobs to workers and a higher standard of living to all. These frontiers of industry, he said, offer adventure and profit to the intellectually qualified beyond anything imagined by the pioneers of the nineteenth century struggling on a western homestead. The American economy has not yet fulfilled its destiny, he told the people. American leadership in mass production had been due to a simple faith in America. There was no reason to doubt that this faith would continue to create miracles. He called his creed the "faith that is America."

He attacked the economics of the clique who believed that the capitalistic system had dried up. This view had been succinctly expressed by Henry A. Wallace, then Secretary of Agriculture, at a speech in Atlantic City, February 28, 1935, who said: "The capitalism of the past will not endure indefinitely. Its emphasis on the individual, the survival of the fittest, and the free play of competitive forces is proving definitely destructive. Opportunities of the past are gone, and it is a mistake to educate children as if such opportunities were still there.

"The corporation of the past will not long endure. All stockholders are becoming increasingly interested only in dividends. If the choice were given them whether to improve working conditions or increase dividends, the chances are they would vote for the latter. Capitalism must collapse unless something is done to bring the individual under control. Capitalism, communism, and fascism are all of a piece—materialistic and godless. Perhaps instead of emphasizing liberty, rights and freedom, we should teach increasingly security, duty and responsibility— the things that hold people together rather than those that push them apart."

Willkie challenged this undue emphasis upon security at the sacrifice of the economic system as a shift in American philosophy which had rested from the days of the Founding Fathers upon the principle of freedom of opportunity.

Willkie pointed to the glorious accomplishment of free men which had produced a country possessing six per cent of the world's area, seven per cent of the world's population, but more than forty-five per cent of the world's wealth, with a standard of living almost double that of European countries. Americans had the highest wages, the shortest working hours, and the greatest percentage of home ownership on earth. All this had been accomplished because men in America were encouraged to take risks and to receive profits. He charged that business had become spiritless under the cudgeling of the New Deal. Willkie ascribed this melancholia in a naturally spirited people to the restrictive legislation passed by the New Deal Congress. This had discouraged the use of private capital for the development of industry and thereby prevented the investment of millions.

Willkie attacked the fallacy of the New Deal propaganda that businessmen had wilfully refused to co-operate with Government for the return of prosperity. Business was stymied because of the New Fear which gripped all business executives. Referring to the President's inaugural address in which he had said, "We have nothing to fear but fear itself," Willkie described the new fear which had paralyzed all business. The President had asked for the co-operation of business leaders. The executives had gladly given him that co-operation, only to meet indifference, contempt and neglect.

The utility president explained his own efforts at co-operation and the snub they had received. The attack upon the utilities had been so severe in 1933 and 1934 that he had offered a plan for regulation to eliminate all the alleged abuses. In addition, the plan proposed that utilities would spend for capital construction a minimum in the years of 1935 and 1936 of twice their anticipated requirements. It was estimated that this initiative would create in the first year a minimum of three and one half billion dollars of business. This was a sum equivalent to the entire national relief appropriation for the year 1935. A further advantage of the offer was that this large sum was private capital and hence did not come out of taxes or public funds. Such an expansion would have employed thousands of people directly and indirectly. It would have created great steel orders and a demand for freight cars. It would have administered an electric shock to business all along the line. No direct reply came from the Administration for his proferred co-operation. But the indirect answer was unmistakable. It was the Death Sentence.

Likewise Willkie related that he had offered several alternative plans of co-operation between business and the Tennessee Valley Authority. The whole TVA program with its vast expenditures of public money had subsidized the electric rates of a few hundred thousand people in a particular section of the country. This had greatly threatened the financial stability of all utility companies in the area. So he offered to buy all of TVA power at the switch and pass it on to the consumer at a

saving in rates. He offered the correction of all alleged abuses
in the utilities in the area and a guarantee to reduce even TVA
rates by more than 25 per cent if given the same gifts from the
federal Treasury as the TVA. But if this suggestion was unac-
ceptable, he then offered to sell out all of his properties in the
Valley if the properties were condemned outright and left for
the courts to fix an equitable price for them. No direct reply
to these offers ever was made. But again the retaliation was
unmistakable. It was an amendment to the TVA Act in 1935
to give greater power to the Authority so as to enable it to construct power houses, transmission lines, and to generate at all
dams the maximum amount of power. Thereupon, Willkie
concluded that the politicians were more interested in testing
out untried reforms than in the economic recovery of the American industrial system.

Not only were such offers of co-operation rejected, he declared, but also all efforts to amend these restrictive measures
so as to make them workable were met with punitive hostility.
Every week for two years drastic and defamatory statements
regarding public utilities and their holding companies had
emanated from government officials in Washington. The country had been fairly saturated with the tale of supposed abuses
committed by utilities. Every business executive knew that if
he criticized a government commission today, he and his company would suffer for it tomorrow. Reprisals were the coercive
whip used by the New Dealers. In all these public speeches,
therefore, Willkie emphasized the fact that it was not the lack
of co-operation on the part of business leaders with Government that had deepened and continued the years of depression.
Rather it was the renewed attacks upon business instigated by
the New Deal promoters and the campaign of personal abuse
against individuals entrusted with the operation of corporate
enterprise. All this had produced a lack of confidence in businessmen which acted as a restraint upon expansion of industry.
In addition to the drastic legislation that had crippled business,
there had been the constant threat of regimentation. In a radio
address, he pleaded that government co-operation should re-
place government hostility: "Public abuse and punishment
have failed to produce re-employment and economic rehabili-

tation. Isn't the elimination of the misery of the bread lines of greater importance to us than the attempted accomplishment of untried reforms?"

Willkie attacked the fallacy that the capitalistic system lacked inherent resilience for its own recovery. He charged that the Government was gradually taking over the functions of private enterprise. This conquest of business was being accomplished in three ways, all closely related to one another, namely by restrictive regulation of business, government competition, and unwise government spending. In 1929, the year before the depression, the excess reserves in Federal Reserve member banks averaged about $43,000,000. On April 26, 1939, the excess reserves reached an all-time height of $4,120,000,000, or about one hundred times the average amount of reserves of 1929, which had been the peak of prosperity. In other words, the greatest accumulation of reserves in our history was available to be used as a basis for credit expansion. But instead of being used by industry for normal expansion, it lay idle in the banks of the country. This was not the fault of the banks, for they have always been eager to put their deposits to work to earn yearly interest. Likewise, the investor wanted an income from his money. Was industry to blame? Emphatically no. Willkie cited the Brookings Institution's estimates of 1936 that between twenty-five and thirty billions of dollars would be needed for durable goods industries alone in order to make up the accumulated deficiencies because of postponed repairs and replacements. For the period since 1936, Willkie estimated, an additional fifteen billion dollars were needed for the construction of buildings and the manufacture of durable goods, including factory machinery and railroad equipment. At least forty billion dollars was needed by industry for immediate use.

If industry should begin to draw upon reserves in this fashion it would create employment directly for some three million men in operating plants and equipment, and for an additional six million men in service industries. Business could rapidly employ nine million men if given a chance by Government to rehabilitate itself. Willkie suggested that the possibility of employing nine million men out of the eleven million still walking the streets after six years of paralyzing experimentation was worthy of note by the Roosevelt Administration. Nothing was inherently wrong with the capitalistic system, he emphasized, except the danger of Big Government. Fear of this danger had almost paralyzed private enterprise.

It is capital that has made the free enterprise system operate, Willkie maintained. If capital from the great reservoir of savings into the channels of industry was stopped, then the whole democratic system as well as the free economic system would vanish in the chaos of national bankruptcy. A conspicuous phenomenon of American economy had been its ability to create capital rapidly. He emphasized that an economy cannot be called over-mature, or dried up, when it has the vitality to continue to create enormous amounts of capital.

Willkie attacked the fallacy that a nation could "spend its way to prosperity" as the New Dealers often claimed. The colossal expenditures of "priming the pump" were balanced by a colossal program to pay for it. This tax program had been a throttle to the free enterprise system, he explained, because it sterilized capital. Two evils resulted from government effort to spend its way into prosperity. One was the unbalanced national budget, and the other was the expulsion of private capital from industry. By 1939, the fiscal deficit amounted to twenty-seven billion dollars, with an estimated additional four billion dollar deficit for that year. These deficits meant higher taxes for the taxpayer for generations to come.

Willkie considered government spending as the most dangerous of the trio of governmental vices; business strangulation, government competition, and spending. It was more corrupting than over-regulation; it was more exhausting than direct government competition. Government spending, in order to promote employment, generally led to direct competition with business, and thus it was doubly vicious. All these evils had scared private investments into hiding. More than this, unbridled government spending had saddled the nation with an enormous public debt. There was a great difference between public debt and private debt. Public debt was created by the Government and not by the people who paid it. On the other hand, private debt was voluntarily created by individuals who expected to pay it off. Again, the New Deal public debt had been created primarily for non-productive purposes such as relief payments, unemployment insurance, military expenditures and public works projects. But the private commercial debt was incurred for purposes of industrial production, chiefly for production of durable goods. Thus during each year of depression, private debts had declined while the public debt increased. Furthermore, government property does not pay a tax. Hence, taxes on private property must be correspondingly increased. The TVA was an example. The Authority purchased all the properties of the Tennessee Electric Power Company with funds supplied by the Government, for which the taxpayers would have to pay a yearly interest rate on the borrowed cash. But, at the same time, the state and municipalities of Tennessee lost millions in taxes which could only be recovered by increasing the taxes on all citizens and all industries within the area. Thus government spending meant higher taxes, and higher taxes were a restraint upon the private investment of capital.

Willkie attacked the Government's tax policy further. The foolish spending of the New Deal had forced the taxing of new sources. It was not so much the severity of taxes that was dangerous to industrial production as it was the kind of tax imposed. There should be no tax on "venture capital." This is the money invested in common stock of new businesses and in which the investor took a risk on the success of the enterprise. It was the kind of capital that business must have; and it was the kind of capital which creates most of the new jobs. The personal income tax was a proper source of revenue, he believed, so long as the rates were not so high as to drive capital into tax-exempt securities. But far more to be criticized than an inordinately heavy income tax, according to Willkie, was the capital-gains tax and the undistributed corporate profit tax. The latter tax imposed a penalty on any corporation that built a new plant out of its earnings, inasmuch as the law required the corporation to pay a tax on all profits not distributed in dividends. In much the same category was the corporation income tax. All of this taxation, he explained, which dried up capital and thus prevented industrial expansion, constituted a fallacious tax system. And even worse, to his mind, was the proposal of the New Deal to use national taxation as a part of the social project to destroy private enterprise in the interest of the planned state.

Willkie also tried to make the people understand how impossible it was for business to operate under constantly changing rules. Wherever a new law was passed by Congress regulating industry, a commission was created to enforce its provisions, whose policies fluctuated as its personnel changed. Where there had been a score of these boards and commissions before the New Deal, there were now three score, he pointed out. The dictionary was exhausted for new names of new federal agencies. There was the Federal Housing Administration, the Securities and Exchange Commission, the Works Progress Administration, the Federal Emergency Administration of Public Works, the Commodity Credit Corporation, the Export-Import Bank, the Social Security Board, the Federal Communications Commission, the Rural Electrification Administration, the Federal Home Loan Bank Board, the Tennessee Valley Authority, the Oil Administration, the Agricultural Adjustment Administration, the National Labor Relations Board, and many more. All these boards and commissions possessed rule-making powers. It was extremely difficult for business to operate successfully under a commission form of government which might change its standards as it willed and dispense its favors in accordance with the economic or social predilictions of the members of the board. "Any poker player," Willkie said, "regardless of how skillful he may be, will get out of the game just as soon as somebody starts changing the rules." Some gifted officers in the Administration recognized the tragic defects of bureaucratic government then existing in Washington, but many rationalized the matter by saying the answer was in appointing "good men" to the commission. But this, said Willkie, was reminiscent of the theory that dictatorship is not bad so long as the dictator is himself a good man.

Willkie attacked the theory of a planned economy. He pointed out to the people that fixing wages and taxing payrolls had increased the costs of employment. That in turn reduced the number of employed. Unfortunately, when wage increases were arbitrarily set by law, they hurt the American laborer instead

of helping him. Wages are paid out of what industry receives for
its output. They are high if industry has confidence and ample
capital, and if there is an active market for its products. But if
wages are artificially raised beyond the level that industry could
meet out of its current operations, then a drop in employment
ensues. With deftness Willkie pointed out the error in the New
Deal thesis that wage increases were automatically desirable
because they always increased the laborer's purchasing power.

He used as an example the National Recovery Administration as the startling experiment of a planned economy with
arbitrary methods of fixing hours and wages. From March to
July, 1933, the period just preceding the NRA, industrial production had increased sixty-nine per cent. But under the NRA,
hours were shortened and wages arbitrarily raised. Labor costs
jumped, and there was a drop in industrial production of
twenty-five per cent from July to December. Further, because
of the minimum-wage provisions of the lumber codes, some
500,000 Negro workers in the South were on relief in 1934. To
Willkie, the economic disturbances in Puerto Rico as a result
of the minimum-wage standard there of twenty-five cents an
hour was significant. Although this was admittedly an absurdly
low scale by American standards, living costs in Puerto Rico
were correspondingly low. The result of the new law was that
100,000 persons lost their jobs in the needlework industry
alone. In Puerto Rico, as in the United States, whenever wages
were fixed by fiat, a real danger threatened to destroy the jobs
of the wage earners.

Likewise, he told his audience that a too rigid fixation of
hours was dangerous to employment. Hours in American industry had been steadily reduced without legislation, with the
result that the forty-hour week was now common. But in France,
the forty-hour week was established by law in 1937 and resulted
in widespread disruptions. One industry after another had to
be exempted from the forty-hour limit because each was lagging behind normal productive capacity. "When this happens,
fewer men are employed."

Willkie attacked the weakness in both the Securities Act of
1933 and the Securities Exchange Act of 1934. The fact that
both these Acts meritoriously remedied certain abuses in the

sale of securities to the public failed to justify the harmful aspects of the legislation. Abuses must be corrected, he said, but in a manner to preserve and promote that flow of private capital which is so vital for the orderly expansion of industry. The Acts in question had so completely restricted the market that businessmen, tangled in the red tape of governmental requirements, found it immensely more difficult to obtain the capital required for promotion. As a result, the workingman had fewer jobs.

In the spring of 1939, accordingly, seventeen spokesmen of the stock exchanges of the whole country submitted to the chairman of SEC, William O. Douglas, later a justice on the Supreme Court, a carefully drafted proposal for the amendment of the Acts. The report was lightly rejected by Chairman Douglas with the flip remark: "Throwing things out so that the boys in the Street can have another party isn't going to help recovery." To Willkie it was a matter of little concern whether or not the boys in the Street incidentally enjoyed a party as a result of these changes. The crucial question was whether or not such modification could provide American industry with the "life-giving flow of capital." Vices and virtues were equally annihilated by the Acts, and economic sterility resulted.

By such direct attacks upon the theories of the New Deal Willkie aroused the people to a fresh evaluation of the unwise policies instituted in Washington. He focused public opinion on the issues of profit versus security, and Free Enterprise as against a Planned Society. In strong and vigorous language he reminded the people of the vast accomplishments of industry and the high level of prosperity they enjoyed.

CHAPTER VII

Two Famous Debates

WILLKIE RELISHED forensics and verbal controversy. As a boy he had been brought up on debate. His father had encouraged him to present cases which the senior Willkie then proceded to tear apart. His best extracurricular activity in high school as well as college was debate. Thus by training as well as by natural talent he was brilliant in rebuttal and in spontaneous speaking. Such success reflected the keen enjoyment he felt in pitting mind against mind. Therefore he eagerly accepted the invitation of Town Hall to debate with Robert H. Jackson on the night of January 6, 1938. The question was: "How Can Government and Business Work Together."

Willkie had heard rumors that the President was fully aware of the seriousness of the 1937 depression and was now ready to end his quack experimentations and take the solid advice of his Secretary of the Treasury, Henry Morgenthau. Willkie believed these reports, especially after the Secretary's notable speech of late November, 1937, in which he promised a balanced budget and co-operation with business in a sound financial program. It was later said that the President vacillated between the stable financial advice of Morgenthau, Jesse Jones, Donald Richberg, and John W. Hanes on the one hand and the schemes of the Corcoran-Cohen-Hopkins-Ickes brigade on the other. In a quandary as to which way to jump, yet hoping he might juggle both plans, the President was persuaded to permit Corcoran and Cohen to launch a propaganda campaign to blame business for the 1937 recession and to renew the attacks against industrial leaders. The new goal was to be an expanded program of social security and government planning.

The key speakers chosen for this barrage were Robert H. Jackson and Harold L. Ickes. At this time Jackson was a young lawyer in the Justice Department and one of the Corcoran-Cohen circle, who was noted for his brilliant speaking. Ickes was selected because as a member of the Cabinet his name would add luster to the venture.

The first two speeches of Jackson's, given in early December, 1937, were so legalistic as to attract little attention from the press. Thereafter the Corcoran-Cohen team wrote the speeches themselves. As a result the third speech of Jackson's, given the night after Christmas, had plenty of punch. Radio listeners throughout the land heard an agent of the President throw all the blame for the economic recession upon business: "By profiteering, the monopolists and those so near monopoly as to control their prices have simply priced themselves out of the market, and priced themselves into a slump." Several nights later both Jackson and Ickes made speeches based on the spurious book by Ferdinand Lundberg, *America's Sixty Families* (1937). These three speeches received excellent press coverage which, of course, was their purpose.

In fact, the public was so aroused that the astute director of America's Town Meeting of the Air quickly perceived the drama of a Jackson-Willkie debate and hastily made plans for the event. The debate proved to be a landmark in national forensics. Ten million listeners in almost four million homes heard the champions join issue on this occasion. At last a spokesman for the businessmen of America faced on equal terms an official spokesman for planned economy. In the public hearings, before congressional committees, Willkie had been submitted to the inferior position which a witness giving testimony to a committee which controls the rules is compelled to assume. In New York, before the radio audience, both speakers met on terms of equality.

In the opening of the debate, Jackson bluntly declared that the word *business* meant something different to him from what it did to Willkie. To Jackson it meant small business enterprise, while to his colleague it meant corporate bigness. As a lawyer in private practice he devoted himself to the interest of small business. In government service he had continued to serve the interest of small business. It was his job now to use the "archaic anti-trust laws" to preserve small and independent business.

. He held that Big Business was at war on many fronts with Government. Why did business and Government oppose each other? First, business was expected to furnish steady jobs for all who wanted work. But industry had failed in its responsibility to the worker so that Government had to meet it for industry. "A man off the payroll is a man on the tax roll. And whether or not business liked this as a philosophy, it must face the fact," he said.

Second, while business loudly proclaimed that it could stand alone and hence resented any government interference, it could not in reality exist unaided by Government. Private enterprise had always operated under "concealed subsidies." In the nineteenth century it was public lands, and currently it was the Works Progress Administration. Hence, Government must fill in the gap of unemployment.

In the third place, Jackson declared that there was a silent conflict in the country between two kinds of industry, namely monopoly and competitive enterprise. Monopolies and trusts were committed to a policy of high price and low volume, while competitive business continually made its own price adjustments. He cited steel production, which had declined nearly ninety per cent of capacity without dropping its price a penny. If steel were a competitive industry, he maintained, this could not have happened. Other basic monopolies follow the same policy. Unfortunately much of competitive industry, he held, was largely dependent upon monopoly for its raw materials.

In the fourth place, he charged that the depression of 1937 was caused by lack of buying power. The Administration's underlying policy had been to sustain and promote purchasing power. He pointed to the desirability of a minimum wage law (Walsh-Healey Act, later written into the Fair Labor Standards

Act of 1938). The National Labor Relations Act, which guaranteed labor the right to bargain collectively for higher wages, and the farm bills and relief measures, which also aided the market, had all been opposed by Big Business.

In the fifth place, the American people do not want to see all business swallowed up by a few corporations. Congress had attempted to break down the concentration of power in business and would continue to do so as fast as the "imperialists of business" piled it up. Here was the point of difference between Mr. Willkie and the Government, he added. Mr. Willkie controls utility companies in six states through one holding company. It was the democratic instinct of our people which inspired the Public Utility Holding Company Act of 1935. The people would prefer that Mr. Willkie could control only two or three states rather than six, he added.

The address terminated with a smug eulogy of the New Dealers, which he termed "Men in Government." "Men in Government," he said, are faced with all kinds of problems and conditions. Everybody's business is their business. On the other hand, the businessman is preoccupied with a narrow section of the world. Here was to be found the fundamental difference in viewpoint underlying the conflict between Big Business and Government. "Men in Government," he concluded, having applied their superior wisdom to the problem of Business and Government, had found a solution. It was simple: Business must adopt a policy of large volume, low prices and a high wage scale.

With a keen sense of histrionic effect, Willkie began his reply in a somewhat different key from his opponent. "I wonder," he said, "if it seems strange to any of you tonight that we should be discussing the question of whether or not the Government should co-operate with American business." He thought that the Fathers of the Constitution who had founded the Government would also be puzzled by a town meeting which discussed the subject of whether or not Government should co-operate with American business. They might ask if it were not the function of Government always to encourage the development of private enterprise. As for the town meeting itself, the present program was being carried to listeners in all parts of the land by means of an instrument, the radio, which had been developed not by Government, but rather by Big Business in the short span of fifteen years. Large-scale production had cut prices of radio sets by three-fourths of the original figures, resulting in the sale of these instruments to nearly twenty-five million families in the United States.

He ridiculed the implication of Jackson that officeholders in Washington were endowed with special virtue, vision, and ability, while businessmen were ruthless dictators of sprawling industrial empires with no real ability except the talent for collecting money for themselves. He asked his audience to remember Joe or Tom or Dick who left the home town to go into business in the city, and others who had left to go into politics. On the basis of their own individual experiences of such home-town boys, he asked, which today wear the longer horns or the whiter wings: "I tell you quite frankly that I find no halo on the head of either." He thought Mr. Jackson might have difficulty in proving that governmental officials possessed a monopoly of virtue.

Willkie assailed Jackson's statement that Big Business and Small Business have different and opposing interests. Jackson had even warned against co-operation of Government with Big Business because Small Business required a different kind of co-operation. But actually, according to Willkie, Small Business and Big Business prosper under exactly the same conditions, while the conditions harmful to one are harmful to the other. In fact, Small Business suffered more acutely from such things as heavy taxation, governmental hostility, and timidity of investors, because it had fewer reserves with which to preserve itself in time of adversity. Big Business always supplied a market to Small Business not only by buying its products but by stimulating the general market. Furthermore, Big Business furnished Small Business with low cost materials and supplies. The two were dependent upon each other, and the prosperity of one was the prosperity of the other.

Moreover, a large corporation is simply a business divided among a great many small stockholders. If Government succeeds in destroying a large corporation, more people suffer—employees as well as stockholders. Every American worker knows that the highest wages and the best working conditions are found in large corporations. The effect of the Wages and Hours Bill would be trifling on American big corporations because their wage levels were already above the minimum stated in the bill.

It was ironical, he said, for government officials to be lecturing Big Business on the desirability of low prices and large volume, because that was the technique which had made possible the mass production and mass distribution which had won for American industry the admiration of the entire world.

Citing the oil industry as an example of what Jackson condemned, Willkie pointed to the system of service stations established by the industry, and now taken for granted in all parts of the country, but which could not be duplicated elsewhere in the world, as anyone who had traveled in Europe or Asia knew full well. Although nearly half the price of gasoline was a government tax, gasoline was cheaper in America than any other country, while the workers in American refineries were paid higher wages. In fact, the hourly wage rates in refineries had increased more than fifty per cent in the past fifteen years, while the gasoline price, excluding the tax, had declined by nearly the same amount.

Another case in point was the telephone industry. More than fifty per cent of all telephones in the world were in the United States, and they cost the user a smaller part of his income than in any other country. And still another illustration was the enviable record of the automobile industry. Between 1928 and 1932, the industry had lost eighty per cent of its business. In one year, the industry's net loss was half the cost of the Panama Canal. But during those bleak four years the industry produced a low-priced car which was better than the highest-priced car in 1926.

Turning to his own field, public utilities, he told of the accomplishments in electric power production. Since 1914, the cost of living had risen forty per cent, but the cost of electricity in this country had been cut by the same percentage. On an average, an American citizen paid nine cents a day for electricity, or less than the government tax on a package and a half of cigarettes. The American consumer paid a smaller part of his income for electricity than the consumer in any country in

Europe. It had been the big corporations in the utility field that had pioneered this constant reduction of cost. He cited the rates in Washington, D. C., where Mr. Jackson lived, as being one third lower than in the rural areas outside this city. Washington was serviced by the Great Northern American Holding Company system, while the neighboring territory was served by an independent company. The difference in rate meant to the homeowners in Washington a saving of one and a half million dollars per year in their electric bill. Similar comparisons could be made in almost any state.

Willkie declared that his Commonwealth and Southern companies operating in five states in the North and six in the South had an average rate that was lower than that of any other utility group in America. These companies were broadly scattered, a factor Mr. Jackson had highly condemned as pernicious to the economy. The billion-dollar holding company had effected such efficiency in management as to give the customers a continuously lower rate. He asked the logical question of his audience: Is mere size wrong even though it saves money for the people?

The blame for the depression of 1937 Jackson had attributed to business. That evening he had made much of monopoly prices which artificially held up the price level as in the steel industry. Furthermore, in recent speeches he had charged that there existed "a strike of capital against the Government." Willkie responded by saying such a castigation of business was absurd. Is it likely, he asked, that industrial leaders are willing, like Samson, to destroy themselves in order to pull down the house? Are the automobile companies deliberately trying to curtail the sale of cars? Are the steel companies purposely operating at only twenty per cent of capacity? Did they increase prices for no reason? Actually, the steel industry increased prices less than the increase in wages and costs of materials.

As to the strike of capital, if there be such a strike, Willkie declared, it came from the millions of small investors, not from the wealthy few. Because of the income tax laws, which took eighty-three per cent of a rich man's investment in private enterprise, most of them had been investing in tax-exempt government securities. It might be helpful to industry and to government revenues, he added, if Government removed these tax exemptions. However, that would not of itself solve the problem. The great cause of capital stagnation was fear of Government. For several years, the Government had taken definite action to show its hostility to business. It must now take definite action to demonstrate its sincere wish to co-operate. As an example, the utilities needed to spend several hundred million dollars for new construction each year; their only means for securing this fresh capital was by sale of securities. But the investor would buy the stocks and bonds of a corporation only in case he considered the investment safe and the return promising. When the Government competed with private industry as it was now doing in the Tennessee Valley by selling electricity at less than cost and then charging deficits to the federal Treasury, the investor lost confidence in private enterprise and kept his money in a bank. The investor knew that if the Government could compete in an area amounting to fifteen per cent of the United States, it could compete with any industry, anywhere. It was a question of confidence. Thus capital went on "strike."

Willkie freely admitted that there had been abuses in some industries and that these should be corrected. But, so also with Government. "Betrayals of trust have stained the record of public officials as well as businessmen," he said. The decade following the First World War displayed a notorious breakdown in public and private morals. For the first time in American history, a Cabinet official was sent to the penitentiary. Even some of the superintendents of veterans' hospitals were indicted for stealing supplies allocated for the care and comfort of the patients. Willkie referred to President Roosevelt's recent defense of the charges of fraud in the federal relief agencies, in which he said: "Every profession has its black sheep." If this be the attitude that the public should assume toward the mistakes of Government, then it should also be the attitude toward business.

The time had come to end the campaign of hate and hostility that the Roosevelt Administration had engendered against one segment of society. There should be an end to name-calling and glib catchwords such as "economic royalists," "Bourbons," "moneyed aristocrats" and "banker control," as well as all the nonsense about the "sixty ruling families."

Why did business and Government now stand so far apart? The cause was not only a difference in motives. It was also fundamentally psychological. Washington officials and business-men failed to understand each other. One spoke the language of politics and emotionalism, and the other the language of economics and realism. One thought economic forces could be controlled by politics while the other knew that economic forces were more powerful than either Government or business.

Willkie also was ready with a plan as a remedy of the present sorry mess. Both business and Government should put an end to the bitterness of recent years and sit down in conference like reasonable men with mutual tolerance and respect. Such a con-ference should not only deal with intelligent plans for the future, but also should review the Congressional laws hastily passed with a view to modifying them in such manner as to stimulate business activity without removing any of the ap-propriate social controls. Above all, such a conference must meet in a spirit of friendship and not hostility. "We are not enemies, but friends," he said, "we must not be enemies."

When Willkie finished his address, the applause of Town Hall amounted to an ovation. Willkie had spoken with dynamic effect, and the audience realized that it had just witnessed the skyrocketing of a man to national fame. The formal addresses were followed by questions from the floor. In this oral bout, Willkie proved to be particularly adept, while Jackson faltered.

A voice in the audience asked Jackson: "Do you think the fair way to get lower electric rates is to subsidize municipal competition with fifty per cent grants and free taxation?"

The spokesman of the New Deal answered: "I don't think the question of fairness enters into it. I don't know that it is necessarily unfair for two policemen to arrest one crook. But, if the Government of the United States is going to carry out its power policy by competitive methods, because we have seen the methods of regulation due to big holding companies' control break down, it must use the ordinary competitive methods."

The reply was received with a loud burst of condemnation from the excited audience. An American town meeting loves good sportsmanship. Jackson's castigation of utility executives as crooks, following upon Willkie's appeal to abandon the New

Deal practice of name-calling, struck the audience as a shabby trick. Even more significant, however, was the intimation that the underlying design of New Deal utility policy was to "break" the public utilities.

Likewise, Jackson won few friends by his flippant answer to the question about the difference in procedure between the Government's operations in the Tennessee Valley and the Insull operations. The questioner had pointed out that Insull and the Tennessee Valley Authority had presented to the public an incomplete balance sheet. With amazing irrelevance, Jackson replied: "I am not an accountant. I don't know the details of the accounting of the TVA and I don't know the details of the accounting of private utilities." To the alert radio audience, this confession of ignorance simply dodged the issue.

The "detail" of accounting, of course, as Willkie had so eloquently pointed out in his testimony before the congressional hearings, was fundamental to a comparison of public operation with private operation, or to an understanding of the advantages of public ownership as opposed to private ownership. Thus Jackson, the brilliant spokesman for the "well-integrated group," lost his case before a discerning audience when he disclaimed any knowledge of the very heart of the public utility question.

Among various interrogations, Willkie was asked two questions in particular which gave him an opportunity to reinforce his already convincing argument. The first was, "Why were the Canadian electric rates so much less than the rates of the utility companies on this side of Niagara?" He replied that the difference lay in the fact that American utility companies were paying up to twenty per cent of their gross revenue in taxes, while the public plants in Canada paid no taxes, except a small tax on real estate. The other question was whether it was not true that the rates of Commonwealth and Southern Corporation had been lowered because of the pressure from TVA. Willkie replied that in the eleven states in which his companies operated, the five in the North maintained a little lower rate than the six in the South. The question, however, gave Willkie the welcomed opportunity to point out some bitter facts. "The Tennessee Valley Authority was building competitive lines, and the federal Government was giving forty-five per cent capital absolutely free with which to duplicate existing utility systems in Tennessee. The average rate of the Tennessee Electric Power Company was less than three cents per kilowatt hour, which was twenty-five to thirty per cent below the national average, and private companies would be destroyed and the investors lose their money if this policy, which Mr. Jackson recognized had no element of fairness in it, was not discontinued."

The brilliance of his performance brought Willkie wide public acclaim. Editors of conservative journals were quick to exploit the sensational aspects of the meeting. They were unmerciful in exposing the weakness of Jackson's rebuttal.

Deep was the chagrin of the White House over the defeat of its spokesman in this debate. The President had even entertained plans for the young attorney as a vote-getter, and had directed Corcoran to explore the possibility of securing the Democratic nomination for governor of New York for him. The forensic defeat at the hands of Willkie, however, ended all hopes of winning an elective office for the fair-haired boy of the New Deal.

Willkie's second debate with New Dealers lacked much of the drama of the Town Hall Meeting of the Air. Nevertheless, he again pricked his opponents' arguments as if they were soap bubbles. The occasion was the eighth annual Forum of the *New York Herald Tribune,* on October 26, 1938, held at the Waldorf-Astoria Hotel. Among a distinguished panel of speakers, they were only two with whom Willkie was concerned: Thurman Arnold, Assistant United States Attorney-General, and William O. Douglas, chairman of the Securities and Exchange Commission.

Willkie was the last speaker on the afternoon's program, which gave him the advantage of rebuttal. Arnold's speech had been a little vague as he discussed the "established church" of the state, apparently equated with its "folk lore," which embodied the art of compromise and the reconciliation of spiritual values with material values. But lastly, he charged that all social reforms for the past hundred years had been opposed by the same forces using the same ideas and the same phrases.

Willkie replied that, since Mr. Arnold had substituted the

image and language of the church for the folklore of capitalism, the subtleties of his discourse were difficult to understand. "My faith," Willkie said, "is a more simple one." He stated that, assuming businessmen today did use the language of a hundred years ago, there were three basic fallacies in the conclusion drawn. First, that such criticism by what Arnold called the opposition had been only disgruntled croakings unworthy of serious consideration. The forebodings of this "opposition," he declared, had often proved to be accurate warnings of future disaster. Although Andrew Jackson's war on the United States Bank had been regarded by his supporters as the symbol of his triumph over capitalistic tyranny, the opposition had warned the irascible old President that smashing the Bank of the United States would leave the country without an adequate banking system. This warning went unheeded, he said, with the result that the panic of 1837 ensued while the nation suffered for the greater part of a century from a weakened financial structure. The violent fluctuations in our monetary values during the past one hundred years had been due to an inadequate credit system which stemmed back to Andrew Jackson. Undoubtedly, a more reasonable recognition of the merits of the opposition on the part of Jackson and his party would have led to a sounder solution. To President Jackson, Nicholas Biddle was an economic royalist, and thus Biddle was destroyed by a presidential policy guided by emotion rather than reason.

Willkie pointed to the Interstate Commerce Act of 1887 which, he said, was intended to regulate the railroads. Bitter opposition arose to this Act, the kind of opposition "which Mr. Arnold dislikes." Yet despite the abuses which the Act checked, it had not been wholly beneficial to railroad operations or the public. "May not the regimentation imposed upon the railroads with its multiple regulations covering everything from the speed of trains to the building of spur tracks, be partly responsible for making the railroads today the country's number one economic problem?" The opposition was sometimes right, Willkie declared, even though some of its members were "princes of privilege." Many times the cries of the opposition have proved to be all too accurately prophetic of the future.

A second fallacy was the assumption that opponents of reform had always been wholly ineffective. On the contrary, Willkie held, the opposition has frequently had influence in modifying measures which might otherwise have been far too drastic and destructive. The opposition to the New Deal in recent years, feeble though perhaps it was, had influence in eliminating some of the more dangerous and destructive provisions of the proposed legislation.

The third and worst fallacy, Willkie said, was that the protests of the opposition should be ignored and that the Administration program was inevitably right. Willkie admitted that the Roosevelt Administration had been statesmanlike in some of its social and economic proposals. Certainly, the industrial activities and social needs of the United States had outgrown regulations by the states alone. The increasing national and international operations of American business had created a need for federal economic laws, while the quest for security demanded social legislation on a national scale. But, he said with emphasis, enlightened industry also recognized these changes. The attitude of wise businessmen had come to be not "how can we fight this legislation?" but rather, "how can we make it workable?" Thus, those in Government should welcome this attitude and seek the co-operation of business. The name-calling, the loose accusations, the personal prejudices which hindered recovery should now end and be forgotten. Government and business should henceforth work together. "We shall be faithless to our generation and our time if we fail to consolidate the gains and remedy the losses, for there have been losses in the past five years. A blind faith in one's inevitable rightness is a fine quality for a crusade, but a dangerous one for the political administration of Government."

The other speaker with whom Willkie took issue was William O. Douglas, who spoke upon the great advantages of the system of administrative commissions, of which the Securities and Exchange Commission was one, and the need for increasing their discretionary powers.

Willkie was prompt to admit the cogency of the argument for administrative regulation of many phases of national life. But, Willkie countered, the men sitting on the various commissions who hold in their hands such extraordinary power must exercise it with such a fine sense of justice that all men subject to their jurisdiction would know and feel that their own political faith and their economic or political beliefs were not to be destroyed by agents of a tyrannical government. "For tyranny is but the exercise of discretionary power over the lives and fortunes of others," said Willkie. The experience with discretionary commissions had been that in the course of time they become either incompetent, tyrannical or corrupt, and frequently all three. But quite apart from these considerations, there was the more important fact that all this enlargement of administrative power presented an ideology different from the traditional democracy of this country. In America, this desire for greater security at all costs is the result of the depression which shook a too-blind faith in a too-blind industrial order. "We need more security and unquestionably we should take steps to attain it, but we must beware of its seductiveness," he said. A quick solution in order to solve temporary problems may only increase the problems of tomorrow. "A nation built for one generation is a nation built badly. From this standpoint many of us have found the planning of the New Deal alarming."

These debates helped to focus public attention upon the New Deal and its public ownership policy. The man who in five brief years could so sway public opinion and who could so dramatize himself and his philosophy, was bound to be attracted to politics. In fact, only by engaging in the electoral contest could he carry further his views to the people on free enterprise. The struggles with the Government during the years 1933-38, therefore, provided the background and the reason for his candidacy in 1940. The congressional committee hearings gave him a platform to oppose the government policy. His subsequent speeches ignited public interest. The debates with government spokesmen ranked him as the most powerful opponent of the New Dealers. The events of the year of 1939 were to make him a political figure.

CHAPTER VIII

He Becomes a Politician

SPRINGTIME ALWAYS reaches the District of Columbia a fortnight earlier than New York City. The year 1939 was no exception. It was April; the cherry blossoms along the Potomac Basin were in full bloom, and the warm, balmy air invited excursions along the white-bordered river of the beautiful city. Willkie and his associates in the Commonwealth and Southern Corporation, who had come to Washington for a conference with federal officials, had completed their discussions in the late afternoon. The New Yorkers were in a hurry to return to the financial metropolis. But Willkie lingered, pleading an appointment. Then he asked his friend, A. C. Oliphant, to drive with him along the banks of the Potomac River.

As the two men paused by the Lincoln Monument, Oliphant ventured to say: "Now that we are approaching conclusion of the Tennessee Valley controversy, with all the publicity that you have been receiving, you had better be careful or you will suddenly find yourself a candidate for the presidency."

"They will never drag me into anything like that," Willkie promptly replied.

The question brought to Willkie's mind a flood of memories concerning his brief venture into the political arena of Ohio. He had campaigned lustily, he told Oliphant, for Congressman

Martin L. Davey. This was the same Davey who was subse-
quently elected Governor of Ohio, but eventually ended his
career in public disgrace. At the outset of the campaign in 1922,
Willkie declared, the candidate had solemnly informed his loyal
workers that he intended to conduct an honest and straight-
forward fight. Each Tuesday morning, he held pep meetings
and reiterated again and again the honesty with which he was
conducting his effort for re-election. Willkie drove a wagon out
into the rural districts to talk to the farmers; he made, so he
thought, an honest effort to win their vote for an honest congressman. During the last week of the campaign, however, when
competition between the candidates was intense, Davey gave
final instructions which in Willkie's view lacked honesty and
straightforwardness. Willkie protested. The candidate explained: "This may be hedging a little, but you boys know that
you can't help people if you can't get elected!"

Willkie concluded his reverie by asserting that no politician
was honest and that he could not tolerate the risk of being
drawn into a vortex of deceit and chicanery.

Regardless of Willkie's own desires, the chain of events
which led directly to the nomination of the corporation lawyer
for the presidency of the United States by the Republican
National Convention of 1940 had already begun its rapid
progress.

The amazing aspect of his candidacy was not only the rapidity
with which his popularity developed, but also the fact that he
was the only leading candidate since the days of Horace Greeley
who had never held high state or federal office.

Where did the candidacy of this personality originate? The
answer requires a study of the sources. Where, indeed, is found
the first bubbling spring of the stream that grows into a mighty
river?

In an editorial column of the *New York Times,* on February
23, 1939, Arthur Krock broached the possibility of the Willkie
candidacy for President on the Republican ticket. The idea had
been developed in the mind of the distinguished columnist at
an evening of random discussion by political dopesters cele-
brating Washington's birthday. The evening had been spent

in the favorite American pastime of speculation on the availability of presidential candidates. All of Krock's companions had agreed that Dewey, Taft and Bricker were in the first line of favorites, and most of them also agreed that Senator Henry Cabot Lodge, Governor Leverett Saltonstall (Massachusetts), and Governor Arthur James (Pennsylvania), were in the second line of favorites.

Thereupon a Democrat exclaimed: "How about that utility executive Wendell Willkie? He managed to talk himself into a good agreement with the Tennessee Valley Authority."

A Republican volunteered: "Willkie owns two farms in Indiana which he actually farms. Being from Indiana and a lawyer, there can be no doubt that he is a presidential candidate. All Indiana lawyers are candidates."

A third member of the group said: "If Willkie is a Republican you can't count him out. He still has his hair cut in country style, and he will have a strong appeal to the folks back home."

If this penetrating observer of the folkways of the American people had possessed full knowledge of his subject he might also have added the information that Willkie wore old-fashioned long underwear, a fact which surely could be used as an asset for capturing the farm vote.

It was on the following day that Arthur Krock wrote his significant column, which gave the first conspicuous publicity to the Willkie candidacy.

Raymond Moley was also alert to the potentialities of the newcomer. At a dinner in the early spring of 1939 given by May Davie at the River House, Moley proposed the name of Willkie as a likely candidate. On the same occasion, Helen Rogers Reid, of the *New York Herald Tribune,* added her voice in praise of the utility executive.

Early in May, 1939, Samuel F. Pryor, Jr., a high-powered businessman, Connecticut politician, and church warden, invited Wendell Willkie to speak at a church dinner in Greenwich, Connecticut, held at the Greenwich Country Club in commemoration of the two hundredth anniversary of the founding of Christ Church. About seven hundred people attended. Willkie shared the platform with Raymond E. Baldwin, the governor of the state. The utility president, who spoke on national economy and production, completely overshadowed the fluent and personable Governor.

In the latter part of May, the shrewd Washington news analyst, David Lawrence, discussed the availability of Wendell Willkie as the Republican nominee in his column which was syndicated in hundreds of newspapers. "In Wendell Willkie," he said, "the Republicans would have an independent Democrat with a business ability and a leadership capacity which would fit the pattern that nine out of ten Republicans want but do not venture to ask for."

On all sides Willkie suddenly found himself being proposed as a presidential possibility. He was a frequent guest of Raoul E. Desvernine, a prominent lawyer interested in politics, who delighted to bring to his dinner table the leaders of New York finance, politics and the press. At one of these dinners in the fall of 1939, which included as guests, Alfred E. Smith, Herbert Hoover, Ernest T. Weir, Alfred P. Sloan and Raymond Moley, the former Governor of New York declared that he was too old for active politics and proposed to hand his mantle to the young and vigorous Willkie. Desvernine and Smith, as well as Willkie, had worked for Alfred Landon, the Republican candidate in 1936, under the mantle of Jeffersonian Democrats. The remainder of the evening, therefore, was spent in an evaluation of Willkie's "availability" by some of the shrewdest figures in American political life. Several weeks later, Moley ran an "availability" story in his column in *Newsweek*. Meanwhile, Ernest T. Weir, president of the National Steel Corporation, began a one-man campaign to raise funds for a Willkie boom.

Of all the loyalties that crisscross American politics, local patriotism is the most picturesque, especially as represented by any favorite-son movement. On the night of April 26, 1939, the Sons of Indiana had held an "Indiana Dinner" in New York City. Wendell Willkie and Homer E. Capehart were the speakers. During a pause in Willkie's dynamic address, Sumner Sternberg, a New York advertising executive, loudly exclaimed: "That's the kind of businessman we should have on the Republican ticket for President." Some six months later, on the night of November tenth, a second Hoosier dinner was held, on the eve of the Fordham-Indiana football game. Willkie was toastmaster. He was in high form and did credit to his alma mater. As the evening progressed and as his quips and charm enchanted the diners, whispers spread round the room: "Wouldn't he make an ideal candidate for the presidency on the Republican ticket!" A clever reporter whose story appeared in the Indianapolis papers described the sensational success of his performance and the sentiment of the Sons of Indiana in favor of Willkie for President.

At a luncheon of the Bond Club of New York on November twenty-first, Hugh Johnson declared that Wendell Willkie would make an excellent presidential candidate. Shortly afterwards, Johnson publicly bragged that he had been the first to launch the Willkie boom. But Arthur Krock had scooped him by nine months.

Despite such favorable signs of rising political fortune, the politicians had remained aloof, largely because it was generally believed that Willkie was a Democrat. About the middle of January, 1940, the *New York Sun* published a story that Willkie had voted for Alf Landon in 1936. It offered this evidence to prove that he was a good Republican and hence worthy to be the party's standard-bearer. "Mr. Willkie," said the *Sun,* "who beat the New Deal in a six-year battle over TVA, has changed his alliance from the Democratic to the Republican Party and is now registered here as a Republican."

On the train from his Greenwich home to his office in New York, Sam Pryor read the story with jubilation. Clutching a copy of the *Sun* in his hand, he hurried at once to Willkie's office to ask him if it were true that he was a Republican. Willkie replied that it was true because he could no longer stomach the Democratic creed. Then and there Pryor persuaded him to release a statement to this effect. Willkie reluctantly agreed, and Pryor telephoned the wire service and himself gave the story of Willkie's Republican adherence.

Willkie first took note of his candidacy in a public address on January 29, 1940, when speaking at Wooster College in Ohio. Here he told his audience that he had received several thousand letters urging him to run for the presidency. Later in the evening, in reply to questions by newsmen, he said: "I am not running for President. Of course, it is not going to happen, but if the nomination were given to me without strings, I would have to accept it. But I couldn't go out and seek delegates and make two-sided statements. I value my independence."

Early in February, Russell Davenport, editor of *Fortune,* interviewed Willkie for a story which appeared in the April issue of that magazine, together with an article by Willkie under the title of "We, the People." With Willkie's article was a box containing half a dozen paragraphs purporting to be a petition. It began: "Before the political platforms are written, we, the people, have a declaration and a petition to make." Each of the paragraphs which followed the preamble made a specific attack upon some phase of New Deal policies.

Harold E. Talbott, Wall Street capitalist, Long Island socialite, and polo-playing sportsman, met Willkie as a guest at a luncheon given for Willkie at the Ritz Carlton Hotel. Willkie spoke briefly at the luncheon, but it was enough for Talbott. The following week he called on Willkie at his office to ask what was being done to further his campaign. To Talbott's surprise the answer was: "Nothing." The potential candidate appeared to take all the political talk quite lightly. Talbott persisted. He wanted to know just who were the people actively supporting the candidacy. With a smile Willkie replied that the list was short. It consisted of Russell Davenport and Charlton MacVeagh. Thereupon Talbott gave a dinner party for the Willkies, the Davenports and the MacVeaghs in order to discuss politics. From then on, he was counted as one of the most active and important of the amateurs who sponsored the Willkie boom.

A twenty-nine year old lawyer, Oren Root, Jr., was attracted to the Willkie movement. Although he had never met the utility president, he liked all he had read about him. A grandnephew of the staunch Republican statesman, Elihu Root, young Root had joined the Republican Party as soon as he left Princeton University. He wondered how many other people felt as he did. Determined to find out, he printed about a thousand "declarations" which he mailed to a selected list of graduates of Princeton, Yale, and Harvard, in the age group of thirty to forty. The first of these were mailed on Tuesday night, April 9, 1940, and one was sent to Wendell Willkie. The title of the declaration was taken from Willkie's article, "We, the People." No party affiliation was listed. The paper called for the nomination of Willkie, and provided space for signatures. Returns were to be mailed to Root's home address.

The immediate response to these circulars was astonishing. The telephone in Root's law office was blocked for two days with calls about Willkie. Root decided to resign from his law practice and devote himself to the campaign. A small office was found at Sixty-third Street and Madison Avenue, and Root moved in. Here he set up the headquarters of the Associated Willkie Clubs of America.

Root was without funds. He inserted a ten-line classified advertisement in the *New York Herald Tribune* in April, asking for small contributions to promote a Willkie campaign. The name of Willkie proved to be magic: money, in small amounts, began to pour into the office. Talbott considered the Willkie Clubs an excellent idea and he frequently visited the headquarters, advising young Root and making temporary advances when the money ran low. A button was designed with "We the People" on it and a first order of twenty thousand was fearfully made. But the demand for buttons increased rapidly. Some days as many as fifty thousand were mailed out to local Willkie Clubs. By the time the convention opened some five million persons had signed the "declarations," half a million buttons had been distributed, and seven hundred Willkie Clubs had been organized.

All these various factors emphasized the growing awareness of Willkie as a political figure. Yet he steadfastly refused to make any public statement as to his plans. He did, however, take his brothers into his confidence in early March. His mother had died on March tenth; the children gathered at Elwood for the funeral. After the ceremony, as the four brothers sat talking, Wendell confided to them that he had decided to seek the presidential nomination at Philadelphia in the coming June.

In the meanwhile, Willkie continued to make speeches and write articles, but without posing as a candidate. He continued his attack upon the philosophy and policies of Big Government in the same manner as he had criticized the Roosevelt Administration since the year 1935. He castigated the past seven years as the "Age of Illusion." During this Age, he said, a false philosophy had flourished which taught that one man's gain was another man's loss. This was based on the fallacious idea that the American economy had become static, and that there was a limit to wealth, which in turn limited opportunity. According to such a philosophy, management could only gain at the expense of labor, or labor at the expense of management. But it was not the speeches which won him the hearts of America; it was, rather, a stunt radio performance.

Probably in no country in the world are quiz programs so popular as in the United States. By participation on such a program, called "Information Please," Willkie gave enormous momentum to his popularity. His friends advised him against such a foolhardy endeavor; partly because they considered it undignified and partly because there was a large risk of making himself ridiculous. But despite their words of caution, Willkie went on the air on the evening of April ninth. He surprised the experts, confounded his critics, delighted and thrilled his audience. Easy, fluent, and scintillating, he made an excellent showman.

Participating with him were Clifton Fadiman, the master of ceremonies, Christopher Morley, Franklin P. Adams, and John Kieran. The questions put to him which most thoroughly delighted the studio audience were those pertaining to government. With a mischievous twinkle, the master of ceremonies said: "The Constitution was adopted to promote what, Mr. Willkie?"

"To promote the public welfare," he answered, but was corrected to "general welfare."

"To insure what?"

Christopher Morley tried "tranquility," and Willkie supplied the missing word, "domestic tranquility."

"To provide what?"

"Wasn't that the blessings of liberty?" replied Willkie. And the studio audience applauded with relish and delight. The people were well aware of the single-handed fight he had made all during the thirties for the continued liberties of a free enterprise system.

To the question as how two bills might pass Congress, each

be unsigned by the President, yet one of them would become law and the other not, Willkie was the only one to raise his hand. Of course the simple answer was that a bill becomes law without the President's signature within ten days after being sent to his desk, unless in the meantime Congress should adjourn. After Willkie's explanation, Fadiman commented smoothly, "A pretty thing to know."

"I should know, I had to watch so many laws go through Congress," Willkie snapped back.

Millions of listeners followed every word with excitement. Call it radio personality or perhaps a casual, devil-may-care manner, but that night Willkie caught the imagination of the people. He had been natural, easy, spontaneous, and wholly charming. The following day, the country over, Willkie had suddenly become to the people a human personality. The simple quiz program gave the Willkie boom mass appeal.

Four days later the annual dinner of the Washington correspondents' Gridiron Club was held at the Willard Hotel in Washington, D. C. The elite of the capital's politicians and newsmen were present, as were the most imposing industrialists from Wall Street. Without benefit of professional guidance the Willkie boom had progressed to the point where the entire nation was aware of the man, Willkie. A paradox in American history had appeared. A presidential boom launched in Wall Street, the anathema of rural America, had won a welcomed response from every section of the United States. The boom had developed along unorthodox lines. His name had not even been entered in any state primary election, and no group of delegates had been pledged to his candidacy. These men of high influence clustered about in small groups talking about the sensation he had made on the Information Please program. That night Willkie's name was on every lip. Everyone was enthusiastic in their praise of his personality, his charm, his eloquence as a speaker, and his brilliance as a debater.

Another episode in the same month which promoted his reputation among local celebrities was the Willkie-Ickes debate on the third term issue. It was a highly humorous exchange and so unusual as to be talked about for weeks afterwards. The debate was before the Press Club in Washington, on April nineteenth.

Ickes refused to speak first, although he presented the affirmative side. To give the lighter touch, Willkie said he opposed the third term because there were available so many other good men. For example, there was Harold Ickes who would make an excellent presidential candidate. When Ickes arose to speak he only recited some doggerel poetry. In rebuttal, therefore, Willkie replied that "Mr. Ickes will have to write better poetry than that if he wants my vote."

By now there was another small group who had quietly begun to make plans. Frank Altschul was one of these. A member of Lazard Frères & Co., investment bankers, and a recent chairman of the Finance Committee of the Republican Party, he had been attracted to Willkie when he heard him debate with Jackson. Early in the spring of 1940, therefore, he asked Kenneth Simpson for luncheon. Simpson was New York County Chairman of the Republican Party and National Committeeman from New York. When Altschul told him that he had a presidential candidate for him, he asked, "Who?" without any show of interest. With pride the banker replied, "Wendell Willkie."

Simpson was unimpressed. He told Altschul, "You just don't understand politics! Damn it all! Just suppose I go to the boys and tell them I have a candidate by the name of Willkie. They would just laugh! Damn it all, you don't know what it takes for a presidential candidate!" Simpson went on explaining the intricacies of a political organization.

"You have to think of the workers in politics, the precinct captains and the ward committeemen. If I told them that Willkie is president of Commonwealth & Southern they would probably ask me where that railroad runs to. To tell them that C&S is a billion-dollar utility corporation would only make them laugh louder and say, 'So what?' You have got to understand politics, damn it! The man just won't pull the rank and file."

Unperturbed by the political wisdom marshaled by the practical politician, Altschul patiently and eloquently elaborated his arguments in favor of Wendell Willkie. To his own amazement, he ended by actually making a convert of the hard-headed committeeman. It was a brilliant conquest, for soon Simpson proved to be the most powerful supporter of Willkie in the "pivotal" Empire State. His support at the Philadelphia Convention in June, 1940, was to split the New York delegation, which gave Willkie a great advantage.

Altschul also interested Styles Bridges of New Hampshire in Willkie. Although Bridges was a favorite son of his own state for the presidential nomination, he had a marked admiration for the utility executive. He had become acquainted with Willkie during the TVA hearings and had watched with keen approval Willkie's spirited defense of free enterprise. So well disposed was the New Hampshire Senator toward the Willkie boom that he took a trip across the country early in the spring in order to estimate whether there was sufficient sentiment to make the nomination possible. In talking to politicians in state after state, Bridges used his own candidacy as a sort of blind to feel out the sentiment of western leaders towards the New York utility president. When Bridges returned to New York he was able to report to Altschul that Willkie was genuinely popular in the hinterland. More than this, he asserted his own readiness to pledge his support for the candidate at the Philadelphia Convention after the first ballot.

Another enthusiastic recruiter for Willkie was Charlton Mac-Veagh, littérateur and industrialist. He enlisted Russell Davenport to accompany him to Washington to see John D. M. Hamilton, the National Chairman of the Republican Party. MacVeagh was no mere acquaintance of the National Chairman. He had labored with Hamilton in the 1936 campaign and had written the great convention speech delivered by Hamilton. The National Chairman listened with more than his usual courtesy as MacVeagh discussed the political qualifications of Wendell Willkie. In fact, MacVeagh, a consummate master of the English language, presented his candidate to Hamilton in such convincing terms that the National Chairman therewith committed himself to the Willkie movement. This was another great triumph as Hamilton was not only National Chairman, but also the most influential personality in the upper echelon of Republican party leaders. Of course, no small influence in this decision was his respect and affection for Altschul. Hamilton was further impressed by a group of men he had recently met in the South who pledged themselves to raise more money than ever before if Willkie was to be the candidate of the party.

MacVeagh did much of the spade work for Willkie before the convention. He wrote nearly all of the early campaign literature, and indeed parts of Willkie's speeches. He was the channel of contact between the amateurs who labored for Willkie and the professional politicians like Pryor and Hamilton. He was also in constant touch with Talbott and Davenport.

Another original supporter of Willkie was Sinclair Weeks, of Boston. Weeks was a power in the financial world, and at the same time he possessed an enlightened concept of both industry and politics. He had inherited an interest in politics from his father, who had been Secretary of War in the Cabinet of President Harding. Through the influence of Joseph Martin, Republican boss of Massachusetts, Weeks had been appointed National Committeeman from the Commonwealth. Weeks first became acquainted with Willkie at a dinner of the National Association of Manufacturers in March of 1939. On this occasion, he sat next to Willkie, but had to ask the man on the other side of him the name of his unknown table companion. Their second meeting came six months later at another NAM banquet at which Willkie made the principal address. The concluding sentence of this speech impressed itself upon the Boston financier. Willkie had enumerated certain economic and political changes that should be made. "And if we do all these things life may begin in '40."

The next time that they met was in April, 1940, at the Gridiron dinner in Washington. Weeks greeted Willkie by saying, "I hear your name mentioned for the presidency." "What do you think I am, a God-damn fool?" replied the man who, on that evening, was the center of attention. He wanted no one to think he took such talk seriously. Only a few weeks after this encounter, Willkie telephoned Weeks for an appointment. In this conversation, Willkie frankly talked about politics and asked the millionaire Republican for his support. Without consulting Joe Martin, Weeks gave his pledge. Nor did he rue his prompt decision when several weeks later he was taken over the coals politically for this unilateral action.

Despite all this fanfare, Willkie made no political speeches until his speech in Saint Paul on May eleventh. He came to Minnesota on invitation from Governor Harold E. Stassen, who explained that at various times that spring, the party had brought Robert A. Taft, Thomas E. Dewey and Arthur H. Vandenberg face to face with the voters. Willkie eagerly accepted the invitation. This invitation in no way implied any support from either the Republican Party in Minnesota or from the Governor himself. The importance of the Saint Paul address, however, was the unique opportunity that it gave Willkie to launch his political career in a western state.

Before leaving for Saint Paul, Willkie discussed foreign policy with Raymond Moley. The distinguished political scientist discovered to his delight that Willkie was fully convinced that while the United States should stay out of the war, this country should afford the Allies the "brass knuckles" of war in order to carry on their defense against Hitler. In this respect Willkie anticipated the Rooseveltian lend-lease policy by seven months. He was a little vague about the details of this plan, Moley found, but at least he urged vigorous preparation for national defense in view of the eventuality that America might have to wage war against Nazi Germany without the aid of allies.

No one appreciated more than Moley the boldness of a candidate who would express such sentiments when seeking the nomination for the presidency from a party long wedded to isolation —a party that had blatantly rejected international co-operation and had fought every move of President Roosevelt to prepare the country for national defense. Moley was delighted with the courage of the new candidate. It remained to be seen how effectively he could perform at the hustings.

At Saint Paul, Willkie spoke for the first time as a Republican candidate to a Republican audience. "It is my deep conviction," he said, "as it is yours, that this recovery now can only be achieved by the election of a Republican Administration in this coming campaign." He added that as a Republican he did not speak in any sense of arrogance but because of the obvious fact that the country was not making progress under the Democratic Administration. In place of the principles of American free enterprise, a sprawling centralized government had been established which controlled the business activity of the people by non-elected commissioners. The New Deal had not only stifled initiative, but also had lowered the standard of living of the American people and had left more than nine million men without the opportunity to work.

He made an eloquent plea for international trade agreements, which was in effect an endorsement of the Hull reciprocal trade treaties. To secure peace, security, and spiritual values, America should give to the democracies assistance short of war, he said.

On the whole, the speech went off fairly well. Many western Republican politicians resented his support of the Hull reciprocity trade agreements, as well as his advocacy of international co-operation. The Midwest was still the center of American isolation. But the stark sincerity of the candidate captivated thousands of voters. Willkie made a good impression in Saint Paul and won some strong adherents.

From the standpoint of effectiveness, the St. Paul address showed some errors—the same kind of errors that later marked many of his addresses in the presidential campaign—particularly a misplaced emphasis. On May 10, the day before the St. Paul address, the Nazi Army had moved into the Low Countries and Winston Churchill had taken the place of the discredited Neville Chamberlain as Prime Minister of England. The critical situation abroad, therefore, made the discussion of foreign policy the most important portion of his speech and that should have been its crowning climax. Instead, Willkie ended the address with a discussion of the farm problem. Furthermore, he failed to build his lines on the foreign issue to a dramatic pitch, with the result that the applause came in the wrong place. He began the discussion of foreign policy with his big line: "There is no disagreement as to our determination to stay out of war. This country is resolved not to send its sons to fight on the battlefields of Europe." Immediately there was long and tempestuous applause. His concluding remarks on this issue ended with the platitude: "Whatever we can do to aid that faith [democracy] without jeopardizing peace for our own land, that we should be willing to do." This conclusion drew no applause.

Yet the speech did create considerable enthusiasm. The Willkie personality surmounted all technical flaws. One excited

Republican said: "It seems incredible, but maybe you can be nominated. If so, I'd better buy a little Commonwealth and Southern on a hunch." Willkie laughed. "Better try Pennsylvania Rail stock. If I ever get into the White House, there will be such an exodus of New Dealers as will jam their facilities!"

The Willkie pre-convention campaign was now fairly launched. The next strategic problem was the selection of the orator to present Willkie's name to the Republican Nominating Convention. This question had worried MacVeagh, and all the more so when he found old-line politicians skittish about committing themselves to a doubtful candidate. Hamilton urged that the nominating speech be made by a politician from Indiana, and suggested Charles A. Halleck as the logical man. Halleck was one of the new members in Congress, a young man of good appearance and fervent speech. Moreover Halleck and Willkie had known each other for some years as they had both gone to the same university, pledged the same fraternity. Ambitious but cautious, Halleck was dubious whether his nomination of Willkie would advance his own career in the Republican Party. Finally, Hamilton and Altschul persuaded him to take the risk.

Willkie hastened to make a public announcement of this decision before Halleck quite realized that he had committed himself. The occasion was an off-the-record talk at a luncheon of the National Press Club at Washington on June twelfth. About a thousand members and guests jammed the dining room. The off-hand way in which Willkie made the announcement produced a startling effect. He broke the thread of his speech to say: "People keep asking me if I am a candidate. Of course I am a candidate, and my good friend Charlie Halleck, Representative from Indiana, will place my name in nomination at the Republican Convention, and Representative Bruce Barton, from New York, will second it." To the newsmen who crowded around him upon the conclusion of the address, he predicted that his nomination would come quickly; probably on the sixth or seventh ballot.

To seasoned newspapermen, the Willkie campaign appeared refreshing but highly fantastic. Only a month ago he had delivered his first political speech. On the twelfth of June he now made his first formal declaration of presidential aspirations. The nominating convention would open in less than a fortnight, and yet Willkie did not possess the pledge of a single state delegation. Never had a candidate started so late to campaign. His candidacy, thus far, was just a puff of wind. If it was to be more than this, he must have a respectable showing of support on the first ballot. This was all too apparent to the ever-versatile Pryor, who now hastily arranged a rapid tour for Willkie through New England in a belated move to secure some delegates. He placed his private airplane at Willkie's disposal. The trip through Maine, New Hampshire, Vermont, Massachusetts, Rhode Island and Connecticut was completed in less than a week.

The invasion of New England was a prosperous enterprise. In New Hampshire, Senator Styles Bridges gave him a warm welcome. As a "favorite son," the Senator commanded the eight votes of New Hampshire, which he now openly promised to throw to Willkie after the first or second ballot. The arrangements for Willkie's speech in Boston had been made by Sinclair Weeks, before a luncheon meeting of the Massachusetts delegation, with Willkie as the only speaker. Willkie achieved a brilliant conquest of his select audience. It was afterwards said that Willkie "had sold the delegates a magnificent bill of goods." In any event he secured the promise of twenty-two out of thirty-four Massachusetts votes after the second ballot. In the evening Willkie spoke to a large public audience which applauded his remarks with genuine enthusiasm. This public approval deepened the conviction of the Massachusetts delegates that Willkie was the man for the Republican victory. On the following day, the Republican Governor of Rhode Island, William H. Vanderbilt, formally endorsed his candidacy at the Republican rally at Providence where Willkie spoke.

Governor Raymond Earl Baldwin was the "favorite son" of Connecticut, and had been pledged the support of the delegates of this state. Nevertheless, he welcomed Willkie in Connecticut. Pryor had made the speaking arrangement for Willkie in Connecticut although he did so with some trepidation as he had been urging Baldwin as the "favorite son" before knowing that Willkie was a Republican. He suddenly discovered that he had two candidates on his hands. Accordingly, he was much relieved when Willkie and Baldwin took an immense liking to each other. The New England tour furnished opportunity for a renewal of their earlier acquaintance at the church dinner in Greenwich. Baldwin was so deeply impressed with Willkie that he promised to release the sixteen Connecticut delegates after the first ballot to Willkie. On his side, Willkie was so captivated by the distinguished Governor that he promised to support him for the vice-presidential nomination.

The tour of New England brought encouragement to the Willkie's supporters. Everywhere there had been enthusiastic crowds. Moreover, the tour had netted him some seventy-four votes, to be received after the first or second ballot. He was still without any commitments for the first ballot, the significance of which he was just beginning to see. Nevertheless, he returned to New York highly pleased.

On June 18, Willkie made his first political speech to an audience in the state of New York. The occasion was a luncheon sponsored by the Young Republican Club of Brooklyn. The meeting had been arranged by Committeeman Simpson, who kept in mind the fact that Brooklyn contributed sixteen delegates out of the total of ninety-two for the entire state of New York. Willkie's candidacy in New York was hampered because New York already had two favorite sons, Thomas E. Dewey and Frank E. Gannett. But Willkie was dauntless.

The Brooklyn speech came the day after France had asked Nazi Germany for peace terms. Accordingly, it was a speech to stay out of war and it won applause. As the reporters crowded around him after the address, one asked, "What do you think of your chances of becoming President?"

"I feel very good," he replied, "and I am having a lot of fun."

A reporter, quick on the uptake, asked if he were in it for fun.

Willkie replied, "No, I wouldn't say that. I have a number of deep-seated beliefs and I have presented them to the public. Yes, I'd like to be President of the United States, wouldn't you?"

The time approached for the opening of the Republican National Convention. On Saturday morning, June 22, Willkie took the train for Philadelphia. On the eve of the convention, fortune again smiled on him. Hugh Johnson had been persuaded

to write an article about Willkie for the *Saturday Evening Post*.
This article became the lead in its issue of June 22. It was
excellent publicity. Most delegates going to the convention secured a copy of the *Post* to read on the train en route to Philadelphia. Johnson, who had an eye for the dramatic, began his
engaging article by quoting a Willkie statement: "I'm not running for anything and I'm not running away from anything.
But I would be a liar if I said I wouldn't like to be President
or wouldn't accept a nomination."

CHAPTER IX

Pre-Convention Campaign Strategy

AT TWO O'CLOCK on Saturday afternoon, June 22, a New York train arrived at the Thirtieth Street Station in Philadelphia. From it, Wendell Willkie stepped briskly to the platform. He was greeted by Representative Charles A. Halleck, Russell Davenport and half a dozen other Willkie supporters. A few newspaper reporters edged themselves forward into the group. As Willkie noticed the press men he said: "Ask me any damn thing in the world, and I'll answer it. Nothing is off the record. So shoot, ask anything you want."

"Where is your entourage, your secretaries and staff?" one reporter promptly inquired. He had never seen a major candidate arrive at a convention without a single companion.

"I haven't any," Willkie replied.

"Where are your headquarters?" persisted the reporter.

"Under my hat," the candidate blithely retorted.

When told of a rumored Dewey-Taft coalition to stop him, Willkie declared it was "a lot of bunk." He predicted that Philadelphia would witness a "wide-open convention" which would end in the nomination of a man named Willkie. His strength, he asserted, would increase rapidly after the first ballot. As to a suggestion that he might accept the vice-presidential nomination in a coalition of his own selection, he replied, "Politics isn't a career with me, and if I can't win the presidential nomination I would just as soon go back to my old job."

At the end of the frank, impromptu interview, Willkie and his friends crowded into an automobile which took them to the local headquarters of the Willkie Clubs in the Land Title Building. While he was inside the office a crowd of a hundred persons had rapidly gathered around the door. A passing pedestrian asked, "What's all the excitement?"

"The next President of the United States is in that building," replied an enthusiastic bystander. "That's all, just the next President of the United States."

When Willkie emerged from the building he received a spontaneous ovation. Ever the showman, he now took the middle of the street, while the crowd fell in behind him. At the head of this improvised parade, he continued along Broad Street towards the national headquarters of the Willkie Clubs at the corner of Locust Street. More and more spectators joined the noisy throng as Willkie continued on his way. As the procession passed the Union League club, members of this staid institution pressed to the open windows and gave the marchers a sedate cheer. It was a happy, uproarious parade, at times even rowdy and undignified. The crowd was pleased with Willkie, and Willkie was pleased with it.

At the Root headquarters, which was on the ground floor, Willkie stood on a chair and waved his hat. The crowd cheered, the photographers' cameras flashed, and more people congregated. As the candidate left the headquarters, the crowd once again surged behind him and merrily continued back along Broad Street to the convention headquarters at the Bellevue-Stratford Hotel.

The street was decorated with flags, waving from every window and from every lamp post. Here and there perched a symbolic elephant of gaudy pasteboard. The City of Brotherly Love had been transformed into a city of Grand Old Party elephants. At convention headquarters, a large sign stretched across the street with giant letters, reading:

HEADQUARTERS REPUBLICAN NATIONAL CONVENTION, JUNE 24th, WELCOME

And below these words, there floated in midair another majestic elephant.

The jubilation of the paraders increased as the crowd neared its destination. A loud burst of final hurrahs and cheers filled the air, as Willkie disappeared into the hotel. As soon as he stepped inside the crowded lobby he was recognized and given a resounding ovation. But without stopping, he proceeded straight towards the barroom. Willkie had no inhibitions about drinking even if he was a candidate for the presidency of the United States. In the language of a Texas cowboy, "He bellied right up to the bar and said he would take a whiskey and soda." Bystanders swarmed after him into the bar, and soon a jostling crowd milled back and forth within the barroom. The crowd pressed close but Willkie, with his stalwart frame, stood his stance without budging despite the shoving of eager admirers for a stand-in at the same bar. He drank his highball with relish. He wisecracked, drank another round, and wisecracked some more. Everybody who could get near the bar also drank, and laughed, and drank some more.

Finally Willkie shook hands all around. Eager hands were thrust into his powerful grasp. Then the candidate left. In the lobby again, he was quickly surrounded. The chairman of the Oregon delegation, Walter Tooze, who was a Taft supporter, accosted him. A rough-and-tumble debate ensued, unique in convention history.

"You answer all questions, Wendell," Tooze began, "so tell me what are your views on reciprocal trade treaties. They are poison to the voters of the Northwest."

While the crowd pushed and justled from all sides, Willkie explained that he believed after World War II every effort should be made to enlarge the area of American trade, but that for the present, the war had made the reciprocal trade treaties academic.

As Tooze turned away he half muttered that he had been given a run-around. Willkie wheeled at once and reached out through the crowd to grab hold of his challenger. Spinning him around, the candidate sternly exclaimed: "You said I gave you the run-around. I never gave anybody the run-around. I answered your question, but if I didn't satisfy you, I'll repeat."

After the second explanation, Tooze remarked: "I didn't get the answer I wanted, but I've got to hand it to you, you're not afraid to talk up and say what you think."

While Willkie was leaving the hotel, he was caught in a jam near the entrance. Someone asked what was his attitude towards aid to the Allies in their struggle with Hitler. Willkie replied that he favored all possible aid to the Allies without involving the United States. Amid cheers in response to this declaration, he made his way from the hotel.

He then went up and down Broad Street, talking and shaking hands with everyone he met. Wherever he went he created a stir of excitement.

For the most part the delegates had come to Philadelphia without enthusiasm. Listlessly, they stood around hotel lobbies. A heavy gloom pervaded the air. Even the skies were gray. The sober tones of the pre-convention scene was increased by the gloom of events in Europe. There was now no suspicion that Hitler's aggression was a "phony war" as William E. Borah had predicted. Denmark and Norway had been brought under Nazi occupation. Holland and Belgium had been invaded. The prosperous city of Rotterdam was ruthlessly annihilated by artillery and bombs. The remnants of the defeated British Army was evacuated from Dunkirk under heavy gunfire. France had capitulated.

Those tragic facts made isolation, long espoused by the Republican opposition, suddenly appear hopeless. Furthermore, every Republican knew that Franklin Delano Roosevelt would be the Democratic nominee. Defeatism, dullness and lethargy were noticeable in all the convention haunts. Then Wendell Willkie arrived in Philadelphia. Immediately, his personality won the city. The quiet calm was gone. A sparkling new hero had appeared, and the air became charged with his glowing vitality. He was spectacular, dramatic and compelling. Within twenty-four hours Willkie jokes were being told on every street corner and by every cab driver. He was the most talked-about man in town. The Taft headquarters was transformed overnight from a center of supreme confidence to one of obvious anxiety. The Willkie sentiment had assumed alarming proportions.

During the course of the evening Willkie circled back to the Bellevue-Stratford Hotel. He saw James Watson, former Senator from Indiana, John D. M. Hamilton, and several other bigwigs sitting together in the foyer. He barged into the group with complete assurance and said to Watson: "I understand you are not supporting me."

"No," said Watson, "I am not!"

"Well, as we are both from Indiana, I had hoped you would," Willkie replied with his broad, friendly smile.

"I will tell you why," said the Senator with a stony glare. "You have been a Democrat all your life. I don't mind the church converting a whore, but I don't like her to lead the choir the first night!"

Even Willkie was taken back by this expression of distrust and contempt.

It was close to midnight on this boisterous Saturday before the inexhaustible Indianian was ready to seek seclusion in his hotel. He had spent a part of the evening in the small Willkie headquarters located in the Benjamin Franklin Hotel. His wife had joined him, and she was now extremely fatigued. As the Willkies were leaving the hotel, Arthur Krock and Turner Catledge, of the *New York Times,* were about to enter. These distinguished newsmen had spent most of the evening at the National Committee headquarters and were now on their way to call upon Alf Landon, hoping to learn from the Kansas politician to whom he might eventually swing his support. Willkie loudly called out to the newsmen to come along to his hotel. They readily accepted. When they arrived, they could hardly conceal their surprise. They had been perplexed earlier in the evening by the meagre and amateurish character of the Willkie headquarters in the Benjamin Franklin Hotel. The living quarters of the candidate appeared no less unpretentious. The Willkie suite consisted of two small rooms. Mrs. Willkie at once sought rest. The men, in the outer room, mixed iceless drinks and began to talk. Krock asked the usual question as to how everything was going. Naively, Willkie replied that everything was going fine and that he had even received offers of unexpected support. But to the direct question as to the choice of his floor leader, Willkie looked blank. Did he need a floor leader? he asked. What was such a person supposed to do?

Krock attempted to enlighten his host. A candidate must have a floor leader supported by a committee on strategy. The committee must work on the floor and off the floor among the delegates to win their votes. As the strength of top men like Dewey and Taft began to wane, then the Willkie strategists must capture their votes. There were a number of "favorite sons" of various states who would release their delegates after the first or second ballot. His strategy committee must consist of alert and skillful party men who would know when such releases would come and be prepared to garner as many of the released votes as possible. These "accession" votes must come along on each new ballot. Furthermore, members of the strategy committee must act as political floorwalkers, roaming among the various delegations "plumping for Willkie." They must create a "bandwagon movement." Krock explained that the other contenders had been closely organized for months, with liaison men and women in every delegation. Even on the opening day of the convention, a profusion of undercover agents would be working on the floor for each of the leading candidates.

Willkie sat amazed. He had no idea that nominations were handled in this fashion. His preparation for the convention had been limited to securing Charles A. Halleck to nominate him in the convention, and another Congressman, Bruce Barton, of New York, to second it. In his ignorance, he had felt confident that was enough. But as Krock and Catledge pointed out, Halleck was on the Resolutions Committee, which would engage all his attention during the early days of the convention. Moreover, one man could not possibly handle the task of winning the nomination for a candidate. Only a strategy committee and a floor leader in addition to Halleck could accomplish the undertaking.

No false pride kept Willkie from learning of the ways of politicians from these astute newspapermen. Who, he asked, would make a good floor leader? Krock suggested that the ideal man would be Governor Raymond E. Baldwin, of Connecticut, himself a favorite son, and one of the most highly respected poli-

ticians at the convention. It was a lucky suggestion, as Willkie
had already been promised Governor Baldwin's support. He
readily saw the advantage of Krock's suggestion and immediately
declared he would ask Baldwin to select a strategy committee.
Then Willkie asked about Harold Stassen. The *Times* men
explained that inasmuch as he would be temporary chairman of
the convention he could not engage in partisan politics until
after he had fulfilled this conspicuous duty.

It was now two o'clock in the morning. Catledge and Krock
briefed the Wall Street candidate on a few other routine matters
of politics and then departed. To Catledge, as the two newsmen
left the hotel, Krock likened Willkie to a man who had set out
on a mule to defeat a German panzer division, confident of his
star, expecting that he needed nothing more than destiny to
defeat the mechanized forces against him. Both men were doubtful whether so naive and unprepared a candidate could capture
any considerable strength from the old-time leaders. On the
other hand, both of them agreed that the very simplicity of
Willkie might in the end operate to his advantage, especially
if his candidacy should take on the character of a crusade. But
whatever the outcome, the two newsmen agreed that Willkie
was the most unusual politician on the Philadelphia scene.

On the other hand, Willkie was not quite so unprepared as
the newsmen suspected. Among the men committed to him were
Hamilton, Pryor, Weeks, Weir, Simpson, Altschul, Talbott,
Bridges, Vanderbilt and Baldwin. It was true, however, that no
Willkie organization had been formed. Most observers blamed
Halleck for this neglect. Some even surmised that the Hoosier
Congressman had no intention of carrying the Willkie cam-
paign to a finish.

In the choice of headquarters and accommodations, presidential candidates have seldom tended to be modest. The most pretentious quarters are thought to lend the impression to voters,
newsmen and delegates that millions of citizens are clamoring
to support the claims of the candidate. John D. M. Hamilton,
the National Chairman, had taken the fifth floor of the Bellevue-
Stratford Hotel as official headquarters for the National Committee. The supporters of Thomas E. Dewey secured seventy-
eight rooms at the Hotel Walton, and floated a large blue flag

in front of the hotel with his name in white letters. The committee for Senator Taft found adequate quarters in a collection of one hundred and two rooms at the Benjamin Franklin Hotel. The committee for Senator Vandenberg engaged forty-eight rooms, most of them at the Adelphia Hotel.

At the last moment, Wendell Willkie had secured two small rooms on the sixteenth floor of the Benjamin Franklin Hotel. While the other candidates had their personal rooms adjoining or close to their headquarters, there was no space in the Willkie headquarters for his personal use. Russell Davenport had the idea that Willkie, in order to lessen the Wall Street stigma, should appear at the convention as a "poor man." So he had reserved the limited accommodations for his candidate at the Chancellor Hall.

Harold Talbott and Charlton MacVeagh quietly secured from Samuel Pryor, chairman on Arrangements, the release of a beautiful suite of rooms at the Warwick Hotel. When Talbott arrived in Philadelphia on Sunday, June 23, he took upon himself, in the absence of both Edith and Wendell Willkie, the task of packing their belongings, including nightgowns, pajamas, toothbrushes, linen and clothing, and forthwith moved their lodgings into the Hotel Warwick. This incident, small and homely, was the beginning of a long series of disagreements between Talbott and Davenport. In fact, by the end of the campaign, there were few of the inner circle around Willkie who were on speaking terms with the brilliant Davenport. His ideas, in the opinion of his colleagues, were poetic but rarely politic. On his side, with equal vigor, Davenport resented what he considered as the lack of vision on the part of his colleagues.

On Sunday afternoon Willkie was the recipient of an almost undeserved stroke of fortune. In estimating the number of votes that Willkie would probably receive on the first ballot, Sam Pryor could discover no more than twenty-six, and among these there was not an entire delegation of any one state. Thus, he would trail behind not only Dewey, Taft and Vandenberg, but also behind almost every "favorite son." Pryor was convinced that Willkie could not move forward on the second and third ballots unless he showed greater strength on the opening ballot. To his mind, some "favorite son" must make the sacrifice for the good of the Grand Old Party, and no candidate could more easily do this than his friend, Governor Baldwin. The Connecticut Governor kindly consented to withdraw in favor of Willkie and immediately released the sixteen delegates from their pledge to himself. As a result, Connecticut voted as a unit for Willkie on the first ballot.

In the meanwhile, Hamilton was concerned over the lack of organization on behalf of the Willkie candidacy and felt that Halleck had been inept in this matter. As chairman of the Republican National Committee, Hamilton was barred from active participation in the campaign of any candidate. Nevertheless, to secure at the eleventh hour some organization for Willkie, Hamilton arranged a meeting of key Republicans in his private suite in the Bellevue-Stratford Hotel early Sunday evening. It was necessary of course for Hamilton to be discreetly absent from this conclave. The guests at this unusual meeting included Sinclair Weeks, Kenneth Simpson, Governor Baldwin, Representative Halleck, who was expected to make the nomination speech for Willkie, Representative Bruce Barton, Walter Hallanan, of West Virginia, and Rolland B. Marvin, the vigorous Mayor of Syracuse, who had been won to the support of Willkie scarcely an hour before the meeting. MacVeagh and Davenport were invited to represent the amateur politicans who favored Willkie.

This group agreed to serve as the strategy committee for Willkie. Accordingly, late on Sunday night, with pride and exultation, Willkie telephoned to Krock to inform him that he had won the support of Governor Baldwin and the Connecticut delegation and that a strategy committee had begun its task. Krock was not told, however, that Baldwin had been promised the vice-presidency.

About midnight after this historic Sunday evening conclave, Hamilton routed Halleck out of bed and summoned the young Congressman to his official drawing room. Although Halleck had agreed to make the nominating speech, he had appeared so pessimistic about it that Hamilton wished to ease his mind about the probable success of his commitment. He sat Halleck down at a typewriter while he proceeded to break down delegate-voting strength, indicating the weaknesses of Taft, Dewey and Vandenberg and the growing strength of Willkie. At the end of this devastating analysis, Halleck was reassured that Willkie would sweep the convention on the third or fourth ballot.

Important support began early to swing to the candidate. By Monday morning it was announced to the press that Governor Ralph L. Carr, of Colorado, had agreed to serve as one of Willkie's floor leaders. He was an important addition to the working forces of the candidate because of his western influence. Governor Vanderbilt, of Rhode Island, had already openly endorsed the candidate. Thus Willkie at the outset had enlisted three Republican governors on his strategy committee, each of them a responsible party leader.

Willkie was also hopeful of securing the personable Harold Stassen on his team. The young Governor of Minnesota turned over the gavel of the convention to the permanent chairman, Joseph W. Martin, early on Tuesday afternoon. He was thereafter free for any partisan activity he might choose. Up to this time, Stassen had made no formal commitment. However, in the ways of politics there had been a tacit understanding. The naming of the keynoter for the convention has long been considered the prerogative of the National Chairman, and Hamilton chose Stassen. Although there was no outright commitment at the time of this appointment it was generally known to insiders that Hamilton was for Willkie, so that the implications were clear.

On Tuesday evening, therefore, after surrendering the gavel to the permanent chairman, Stassen made his perfunctory call upon Dewey and asked for his clarification on foreign issues, and then he made a similar call on Willkie. This gave him his opening for a statement. On Wednesday morning he called in the press and announced that he was supporting Wendell Willkie because of his clear views on foreign matters. Within the hour Willkie telephoned the Governor expressing his appreciation and formally asked him to be his floor manager. It was now Wednesday noon. From then on until after the Willkie nomination in the early dawn of Friday morning, Stassen gave all his attention to the Willkie campaign.

Stassen secured a little office off the second-floor balcony of

Convention Hall where the floor leaders could conveniently meet to co-ordinate their plans. This sanctuary was arranged by Samuel Pryor. Stassen chose twelve floor leaders. Among these were Governors Baldwin, Carr and Vanderbilt, Charles Halleck, Walter Hallanan and Sinclair Weeks. These twelve leaders fanned out into an organization of forty-eight members, one for each state. A state floor leader was not in all cases a member of that delegation. Stassen was compelled to use many of his own Minnesota delegates as floor leaders for states in which there was no available Willkie worker.

Sam Pryor was not a floor leader inasmuch as he had become chairman of the Committee on Arrangements upon the sudden death of Ralph E. Williams, of Oregon, six days before the convention opened. Immediately after the keynote speech, however, Pryor felt himself released from a position of neutrality and thereupon openly declared himself a supporter of Willkie.

Senator Styles Bridges had his own unique way of helping the Willkie boom. Circulating among the New England delegates, the New Hampshire Senator extolled the virtues of Wendell Willkie. Rounding up a dozen delegates at one time, he would bring them to meet the new candidate. Willkie greeted these small contingents of possible supporters with all the warmth of his generous personality. On these occasions he never disappointed either Bridges or the delegates. Willkie was always at his best in small groups of politically-minded men and women. If the delegates wanted a speech, he gave them an engaging summary of his views from atop a chair. If they wished to ask questions, he responded with frank and comprehensive answers. This process of personal talks to groups of delegates, which began before the convention opened, continued throughout the sessions. Furthermore, by his scouting expedition early in the spring, Bridges had learned of key leaders throughout the West who were sympathetic to the Willkie candidacy. This information proved of great help at the convention to the Weeks-Bridges-Simpson-Pryor team in soliciting western support.

The most spectacular feature of the Willkie boom and one which was criticized by some professional politicians, was the deluge of letters and telegrams received by the delegates. It had never happened before. Early in June, Talbott had suggested to Oren Root that the Willkie Clubs be instructed to have their members send letters and telegrams to the delegates at the convention demanding the nomination of Willkie. This maneuver brought five hundred thousand telegrams and letters to the delegates.

Moreover, the amateurs at Philadelphia were also helpful in this matter. Talbott, Davenport and MacVeagh were joined by Harold J. Gallagher, a distinguished New York attorney. Gallagher's activity in the American Bar Association gave him an acquaintance with the leaders in state and local bar associations. To these people he telephoned asking them to get telegrams from their membership to the convention delegates urging the nomination of Willkie.

Talbott himself sat for long hours at the telephone talking to businessmen he knew in all parts of the country asking them to get their employees to write and wire delegates concerning the Willkie candidacy. Every businessman he met in Philadelphia he persuaded to do likewise.

As a result, all the wires came from real persons and real places. It was all a simple stratagem. But the result was fantastic. Telegrams, letters, post cards, and petitions, were delivered by tens of thousands to the delegates. The messages reached them at Convention Hall, at their hotels, and at their headquarters. It was estimated that between Saturday and Tuesday night a million messages from all sections of the country, including those from the Willkie Clubs, had been received by the delegates in Philadelphia. The influence of these messages was enhanced by the fact that the senders were frequently recognized as friends and neighbors as well as financial and industrial leaders in the home towns of the delegates.

Like other delegates, Kenneth Simpson was amazed by the magnitude of his mail. He reported receiving more than one hundred thousand telegrams, letters and post cards. The letters varied from penciled scrawls on cheap paper to engraved letterheads. "The sentiment in New York," he declared, "was overwhelmingly for Willkie." William F. Bleakley, county chairman of Westchester and head of the New York delegation said, "I have never seen anything like this. I have received thousands of letters, telegrams and petitions asking me to vote for the nomination of Willkie."

By the time the convention doors swung open, three thousand members of the Willkie Clubs from around the country had arrived to watch the proceedings from the gallery and cheer their idol. Root made good use of them and hastily organized a battalion of young salesmen to "sell" Willkie to the delegates. They were instructed to interview as many of the delegates as possible, extolling the merits of their candidate. There was never a dull moment after that. Between sessions they were beseiging delegates and during the proceedings they took every opportunity to chant, in college style, "We Want Willkie. We Want Willkie." All of this proved to be a devastating performance, because it dramatized the import of the thousands of letters, telegrams, and petitions that the delegates were receiving. The "Willkie Chorus" began at the first night session and continued throughout all the sessions. The remarkable demonstration from the galleries that Talbott, Gallagher and Root prepared gave tremendous help to the strategy committee. This vast enthusiasm was expertly channeled by the professionals. They had to translate this aroused public opinion into delegates' votes. Conspicuously missing from the little group was Frank Altschul. Davenport had informed the banker it would be best if he returned to New York immediately, as his presence would only jeopardize Willkie's chance of nomination. Because Altschul was from Wall Street, Davenport feared the financier might elicit some bad publicity from the press. So Altschul obligingly left.

The opposition was enraged when they beheld the growing success of the Willkie boom. The leading contenders and their vanguards had reassured each other that he lacked even a chance. He was an amateur. Now, before their eyes, they saw the incredible happen. A Willkie strategy committee had developed overnight, composed of some of the most influential men in the convention. They saw delegates with popping eyes and stifled breath pore over the huge pile of mail asking for the Willkie nomination. Such proceedings were not to go unchallenged.

The Taft and Dewey forces took bitter exception to the

Willkie demonstrations. Each had worked for many months to develop well-knit organizations. The Taft forces struck with a vengeance. Colonel R. B. Creager, the Taft floor leader, National Committeeman from Texas, and a member of the Committee on Arrangements, charged that the galleries were packed with Willkie supporters who led his demonstrations. He demanded an investigation. Creager now accused Samuel Pryor, the chairman of the Committee on Arrangements and in charge of tickets, as being responsible for the packed galleries. Pryor, he declared, had perpetrated an outrage on the Republican Party, and he had done it for the purpose of aiding the nomination of his candidate, Wendell Willkie.

Pryor was too busy at the convention to make the obvious explanation. Tickets to the balconies were guarded as carefully as though they were crown jewels. The Committee on Arrangements had received the largest demand for tickets of any convention in history. All boxes had been removed so that "everybody would have the same kind of seats." Balcony seats were numbered. These were distributed to state delegations on a quota basis.

Under such a system of quotas there could be no juggling of tickets. They were all apportioned to the states according to a definite plan. But the galleries were something different. There had been so little interest in recent years in Republican conventions that the galleries had for the most part been vacant. It was the plan of Pryor, therefore, to fill them up. Accordingly he gave orders to keep the doors to the galleries open until the safety capacity had been reached.

David S. Ingalls, campaign manager for Taft, jibed at Willkie by saying that the next President should be a "Republican" as well as one experienced in the science of government. Meanwhile, delegates had received through the mail and from an anonymous source, photostatic copies of election data purporting to show that Willkie was a registered Democrat in the years 1934 to 1939.

But the most organized effort to stop Willkie came from a group of Congressmen. A caucus was held on the opening day of the convention to draft an appeal to the delegates to oppose the Willkie candidacy. Among those who attended the meeting were Representatives Brewster of Maine, Harold Knutson of Minnesota, B. Carroll Reece of Tennessee, John Robinson of Kentucky, Leo E. Allen of Illinois, Leonard Hall of New York, Frank Keefe of Wisconsin, Cliff Clevenger of Ohio, Arthur Jenks of New Hampshire, and Senators John Thomas of Idaho, and Charles McNary of Oregon. .

Senator Thomas declared that the nomination of Willkie would be fatal to the Republican Party and that he himself would not be a candidate for re-election as Senator if this New Yorker were nominated. Senator McNary stated that the declaration of these Congressmen represented the views of many Republicans of the West. He predicted that the Willkie star would go down as rapidly as it had risen once the convention began to ballot. "The West," he declared, "will go against us if Willkie heads the ticket." Representative Stephen Bolles of Wisconsin remarked that if Willkie were the nominee, Wisconsin would be lost to the Republicans by a majority of one hundred thousand votes. The particular point at issue with these Congressmen was Willkie's support of the Hull reciprocal tariff and aid to European democracies in the war against Hitler. They were all high-tariff men. They were all isolationists. This movement of western Congressmen lost some of its sting by the prompt replies of Governor Ralph L. Carr of Colorado and other western Republicans who denied the existence of a western revolt against Willkie.

By Monday morning, Willkie's little headquarters in the Benjamin Franklin Hotel was swarming with pretty girls from the social world to answer the telephone, take messages, and run errands for delegates. Quite unprofessional, but effective! Every stunt was a new surprise which left the delegates gaping. Was this an old-time political convention or was it something new? What would happen next? Then the delegates began to find that suits received from the hotel valet had Willkie campaign literature in every pocket. One delegate found a Willkie brochure in his pajama pocket. Laundry packages were returned with "Vote for Willkie" stickers. All these devices conveyed the thought that he was a people's candidate.

Such were the currents and cross currents of this strange political convention as it met on the twenty-fourth of June.

William Allen White, with long years of political experience, observed it was a convention run "hog-wild." The reason for this was twofold. One was the peculiar antics of Willkie, which turned the convention topsy-turvy; the other was the indecision of the delegates on foreign policy. White stated that about seventy per cent of the delegates favored giving aid to Britain and the Allies.

Thus the convention was torn apart by the divergent views on the issue of war and peace. It was generally conceded by the press that the appointment by President Roosevelt, June 20, of two distinguished Republicans to his Cabinet, Henry L. Stimson and Frank Knox as Secretary of War and Secretary of the Navy, emphasized the seriousness of the foreign situation. This strengthened the boom for Willkie. Yet the platform-makers were endeavoring to make the Republican Party the "peace party." Those who favored aid to the Allies were beginning to turn to Willkie; those who put their faith in isolationism were continuing to support Dewey or Taft. Furthermore, the collapse of France and the heartbreaking accounts of Dunkirk had made many delegates feel that the hour of crisis was at hand.

CHAPTER X

The Philadelphia Convention of 1940

AMERICAN DEMOCRACY includes many curious traditions. Not the least curious is the procedure of nominating candidates for President. In the age of George Washington, the Presidential Electors met in the state capitols to select the man who in their opinion had the best qualifications for the office. Today, in June or July of every fourth year, each of the two major political parties, in a huge convention of some one thousand delegates and an equal number of alternates, with an audience of ten to twenty thousand noisy spectators, amidst speeches, songs, marching, rowdy demonstrations, and secret conferences in hotel rooms, nominates a candidate who will thereupon become one of the two men between whom the American people will make their choice in the November elections. But even the election is obscured by legal fictions. Instead of voting for a President directly, the voters are compelled to vote for lists of Presidential Electors who are pledged to cast their ballots for this or that candidate, without any constitutional redress in case the Electors violate their pledge.

The process is democratic and autocratic. It contradicts itself.

155

It baffles reason. It defies logic. It invites the criticism of philosophers. It confuses European observers. It seems the negation of systematic representation. Nevertheless, it is American democracy.

The twenty-second convention of the Republican Party met in Philadelphia on Monday morning, June 24, 1940. The two thousand delegates and alternates and the fifteen thousand spectators sitting in Convention Hall made an impressive sight. All of the delegates and most of the spectators were aware of the historic importance of the meeting. The excitement was intense. The air was full of great expectations. The urge for action was impelling.

Banging his gavel with vigorous strokes, handsome John Hamilton, Chairman of the Republican National Committee, declared the convention in session. The vast audience arose for the impressive singing of the hymn "America." The Reverend Dr. Albert Joseph McCartney, pastor of the Covenant-First Presbyterian Church, of Washington, D.C., then gave the invocation. After the "Call for the Convention" was read, there was the election of temporary officers. In accordance with custom the temporary chairman is considered "patronage" of the national chairman of the party, so that election is merely a confirmation of his choice. The selection of Harold E. Stassen had been arranged some weeks earlier and now he was chosen by acclamation. The brief second session which convened at four-thirty o'clock was significant chiefly because of the address given by Chairman John Hamilton on "Americanism and Patriotism."

The decorations of the hall created a unique and impressive atmosphere. Flags of the nation and flags of the states hung from the roof of the hall in a glowing mixture of red, yellow, green and blue. Around the balcony were the colorful shields of the states with large gold spread eagles spaced between them. These emblems shone and glistened in a soft, indirect light. On the floor were the standards of the delegations each bearing the name of the state. Atop each standard was a gray elephant with an American flag in his rolled-up trunk.

The dramatic third session of the convention came on Monday night when the gavel sounded at ten o'clock. Samuel Pryor had planned the staging of the evening program to achieve a cathedral-like effect. The states' shields around the balcony stood out almost like stained glass. As soon as Chairman Hamilton called the convention to order, the lights were dimmed, and a blue spotlight flodded the platform.

Into that blue light stepped His Eminence, Cardinal Dougherty. The scarlet robes of the Prince of the Church reflected the blue light so that he stood there as if enveloped in an aura. A hush fell over the vast audience, while the Cardinal invoked divine guidance for the convention: "Inspire the Assembly to a high resolve to perpetuate the blessings of liberty, based on equal justice and right."

The spirit thus created was continued by a cantata, the "Ballad for Americans." The Philadelphia Orchestra played the score, and the Lynn Murray Chorus from New York sang the parts with Ray Middleton as baritone soloist. The theme of the musical epic was liberty, based upon four peaks in American history: the Revolution, the growth of the Union, the Civil War, and the Machine Age. Through the cantata ran the "Voice of America."

Question:

"Did they all believe in Liberty in those days?"

Answer:

"Nobody who was anybody believed it.
Everybody who was anybody—
    They doubted it.
Nobody had faith,
Nobody, nobody but Washington, Tom Paine, Benjamin
    Franklin, and Lafayette."*

This stirring chorus, first sung over the Columbia Broadcasting System in November, 1939, and written by John Latouche with music by Earl Robinson, created a sensation in Convention Hall. The rendition took fifteen minutes and was given at a cost of eight thousand dollars. It was money well spent. The

* *Ballad for Americans,* Text by John Latouche, Music by Earl Robinson. Copyright 1940 Robbins Music Corporation. Used by Special Permission Copyright Proprietor.

cantata keyed the audience to a high pitch of patriotic fervor. In the midst of this spiritualized setting, Governor Stassen was now escorted to the platform, where he was received by Chairman Hamilton. Presented to the delegates as the temporary chairman, he at once began his keynote address, developing the theme of liberty in the Latouche aria: "Our forefathers created here a great lighthouse of liberty. They showed a new way for men to live." Although Willkie's name was never mentioned, the speech was well calculated to extol the kind of liberty that Willkie epitomized. Indeed, the staging of the convention had been built around Willkie and his spectacular battle for liberty, freedom, and individualism. Hamilton and Pryor, working together, had produced the atmosphere for the Willkie nomination. Stassen now carried the campaign forward with his effective keynote address.

It was not until Wednesday afternoon that the convention adopted the party platform and was ready to turn to the supreme event for which it had been called—the nomination of a candidate for the presidency. In time-honored fashion, the secretary of the convention called the roll of the states in alphabetical order.

"Alabama," intoned the secretary.

"Alabama by a vote of seven to six yields to the State of New York," cried the chairman of the Alabama delegation in a jerky voice, barely heard by the galleries.

"Arizona," again intoned the secretary.

"Arizona yields to New York," responded the chairman of the Arizona delegation.

"Arkansas," continued the secretary with the rollcall.

"Arkansas by unanimous vote yields to Ohio," declared the chairman.

The roll call thus proceeded to Wisconsin and Wyoming at the end. By courtesy of Alabama in yielding to New York, Thomas E. Dewey was the first candidate to be nominated, followed by Frank E. Gannett and Robert A. Taft. The intervening states of the roll prior to Indiana passed, which made Willkie fourth in the order of nomination.

Until the last moment, no one really knew who was going to place Willkie's name in nomination. Since the meeting with

Hamilton Sunday night, Halleck had wavered again. He had been so uncertain whether he would or would not make the nomination speech that no one had any confidence in what might happen. Riding to Convention Hall that evening with John B. Hollister, of Cincinnati, a law partner of Robert A. Taft, Halleck was extremely nervous and doubtful as to what he should do. If Willkie turned out to be an unpopular candidate in the convention, Halleck wanted no part of his nomination. Even Hollister did not know what his companion would do when the hour struck. All Willkie men were filled with gloomy foreboding when, in the rollcall of states for presidential nominations, Indiana passed. But at the conclusion of the rollcall, the chairman of the state delegation arose to say: "Indiana wishes to change her pass in order at the appropriate time to place in nomination the name of Wendell Willkie." It was not, however, until they saw Halleck step onto the platform that Willkie's supporters had any assurance that he would go through with the nomination.

When Chairman Martin introduced Halleck to make the nominating speech, some of the delegates began to boo. At this moment occurred a simple stage device that saved the day for Willkie. Chairman Martin quickly put an arm around Halleck, and raised the other arm for silence. It was a kind and lovable act which seemed to say: "He is one of my boys, now be good to him!" The boos stopped. The beginning of the speech was not auspicious. The address had been prepared by Russell Davenport, and, although it was well read, it fell flat. But the worst was yet to come. Halleck had made no arrangement with the Indiana delegation for a demonstration following the nominating speech.

At the end of a nominating speech it is customary for the delegation of the home state of the nominee to raise its banners and to start a procession around the convention hall. Other delegations as well as delegates and alternates from divided delegations, then join the parade. This demonstration, which will sometimes continue for fifteen, twenty or even thirty minutes, is supposed to indicate the degree of popularity of the nominee.

Halleck concluded his nominating speech at 10:20 that evening. Thereupon, wild cheering poured down from the galleries upon the impassive delegates. But, on the floor of the convention, no one moved. Not even the Indiana delegation lifted its banner to honor the boy from Elwood. Then suddenly the New York state banner was seen violently to wave back and forth. The attention of the vast auditorium was attracted to the scene. Spectators beheld a strange sight. The 220-pound figure of the Mayor of Syracuse, Rolland B. Marvin, was engaged in a struggle to wrest the New York banner from five Dewey men who were desperately clutching it. Marvin seemed about to be overpowered when Senator Frederic R. Coudert, Jr., and several other Willkie delegates jumped to his assistance. A general scuffle ensued. Twenty thousand people excitedly watched the outcome. Then Marvin, like a fullback breaking through the scrimmage line, burst clear of his adversaries and started the Willkie parade around Convention Hall.

Senator Coudert and a few other New Yorkers followed. The huge organ struck up. The banners of a dozen delegations now belatedly began to move, and almost timidly fell into line with the paraders. Thirteen times Marvin passed in front of the New York delegation, and each time a fight ensued as the Deweyites, who constituted a strong majority of the delegation, attempted to recapture the New York standard. But the husky Marvin was more than a match for them. For twenty minutes the demonstration continued. Then as the paraders subsided, Mayor Marvin dutifully and carefully returned the banner to its standard at the head of the New York delegation.

The heavy banging of the gavel by Chairman Martin had continued during the demonstration. As the paraders took their seats, the galleries slowly subsided. The chair was ready to recognize delegates for seconding speeches. Four speeches were permitted. Willkie had arranged for only two. Stassen wisely chose a third, a woman from his own delegation. This selection recognized the women voters and again gave emphasis to the Middle West. The seconding speakers followed in rapid succession: Bruce Barton, of New York; Miss Ann Stuart, of Minnesota, and Governor Raymond Baldwin, of Connecticut. This ended the third day. Motion for adjournment came quickly. The delegates left the hall with the Willkie cheers of the galleries ringing in their ears.

The balloting upon the candidates began late Thursday afternoon. Although the floor leaders of other candidates had been at work for months before the convention convened, none possessed in the same degree the nimble ability of Stassen to find a few votes here and there with which to swell the total for his candidate. The well-timed accession of votes as the "favorite sons" began to release their delegations, and the final triumphant pyramiding of votes on the fourth and fifth ballots, were largely due to the superb leadership of the young Governor.

Nomination required a majority vote of the 1,000 delegates, or 501 votes. On the first ballot, Dewey received, as had been expected, the largest number of votes, although considerably less than the number he had repeatedly claimed. His vote was 360. Taft scored second with 189 votes, Willkie third with 105. The next closest was Vandenberg with 76. On the first ballot, Connecticut was the only state to cast her entire strength for Willkie, and it was also the only state to cast as many as 16 votes for him. The balance of the 105 Willkie votes came mostly in dribbling ones, twos and threes from individual delegates who had bolted from their delegations.

Stassen's technique was first to deflect votes from Dewey regardless of where they were accredited, and then to show an increase for his candidate on each ballot. For this purpose he held in reserve some twenty to thirty votes on the first five ballots. He well knew that the psychological effect of loss of strength on any ballot is demoralizing. It suggests that one's boom had passed the peak and that one's candidacy is now finished. On the other hand a steady accession of votes creates a bandwagon effect. One of the startling surprises of the Philadelphia Convention was the ease with which the Taft and Willkie forces made raids on the Dewey delegates. After the first ballot, the strength of the New York delegation was greatly reduced, and the Dewey organization collapsed. If Dewey had promptly released his delegation to Taft, the victory would have gone to the Ohioan. But Dewey delayed and did not send word to Taft of his support until after the third ballot. By this time the bandwagon movement for Willkie was already started.

As each roll call of states was taken, the Willkie floor leaders scurried among the delegates endeavoring to persuade wavering

VOTES FOR WILLKIE ON EACH BALLOT

	Number of Votes	1st	2nd	3rd	4th	5th
Alabama	13	..	..	1	1	5
Arizona	6	..	..	6	6	6
Arkansas	12	2	2	2	2	2
California	44	7	9	8	10	9
Colorado	12	3	4	2	3	4
Connecticut	16	16	16	16	16	16
Delaware	6	3	4	6	6	6
Florida	12	..	..	..	..	7
Georgia	14	..	..	1	2	6
Idaho	8	..	..	..	..	..
Illinois	58	4	5	7	10	17
Indiana	28	9	12	14	15	20
Iowa	22	..	..	..	..	7
Kansas	18	..	..	4	5	18
Kentucky	22	..	..	..	..	..
Louisiana	12	..	..	..	..	..
Maine	13	..	9	9	9	13
Maryland	16	..	4	10	14	14
Massachusetts	34	1	8	28	28	28
Michigan	38	..	..	..	..	..
Minnesota	22	6	6	8	9	9
Mississippi	11	..	..	..	..	..
Missouri	30	6	13	16	18	21
Montana	8	..	..	2	2	4
Nebraska	14	..	2	3	5	5
Nevada	6	2	3	4	4	4
New Hampshire	8	..	..	4	4	6
New Jersey	32	12	17	19	23	26
New Mexico	6	2	3	4	4	4
New York	92	8	13	27	35	75
North Carolina	23	2	6	7	9	12
North Dakota	8	1	3	3	3	4
Ohio	52	..	..	..	..	..
Oklahoma	22	..	..	..	3	4
Oregon	10	..	..	..	1	1
Pennsylvania	72	1	5	15	19	21
Rhode Island	8	3	4	4	4	4
South Carolina	10	..	..	..	2	9
South Dakota	8	..	..	..	..	1
Tennessee	18	2	5	5	5	6
Texas	26	..	..	..	..	..
Utah	8	1	..	1	1	5
Vermont	9	3	4	5	5	6
Virginia	18	5	5	8	11	11
Washington	16	..	..	..	..	..
West Virginia	16	3	6	7	7	6
Wisconsin	24	..	..	..	..	..
Wyoming	6	2	2	1	1	3
Alaska	3	..	..	..	1	..
Dist. of Columbia	3	..	..	1	2	2
Hawaii	3	..	..	..	..	1
Philippine Islands	2	1	1	1	1	1
Puerto Rico	2	..	..	..	..	..
TOTALS	1000	105	171	259	306	429

delegates to deliver their votes to Willkie. This was a grueling assignment, but these lieutenants were faithful to their task as the long evening hours wore on. Illinois was one of the first delegations to respond to the Willkie strategists, in spite of the opposition of Robert R. McCormick of the *Chicago Tribune.*

After the third ballot, Governor Baldwin went to Joseph N. Pew, Jr., boss of the 72 votes of Pennsylvania, seeking to engage his support. Pew was not unfavorable to Willkie but he was committed to Governor Arthur H. James, the "favorite son" of his state. James clung tenaciously to the hope that Dewey, Taft, and Willkie would deadlock the convention, in which case he might become the compromise candidate. Baldwin told Pew that James had no chance whatsoever and that the present moment was the time to support Willkie. But shipbuilder Pew was a man of tough fibre and remained loyal to his hopeless commitment. When Baldwin reported the situation to the strategy committee as the members met in a huddle in the little office, Willkie exploded in disgust and said impetuously, "Pew be damned!"

On the fourth ballot, the Willkie victory was within reach. Success seemed assured when Kansas then shifted to the Willkie column. Chairman of the Kansas delegation was Alfred M. Landon, who had met Willkie and Pryor at Greenwich in the latter part of May. Although the Kansas vote was placed on Capper on the early ballots, Landon was known to be friendly towards Willkie. Stassen had been talking to Landon off and on and he made his final plea just before the fifth ballot. There was so much noise on the floor of the convention that Stassen tried to find a quiet place to talk. Finally, in exasperation, he chose the freight elevator. Stationing policemen at the top and bottom doors, he and Landon rode undisturbed, up and down. Finally, Landon agreed to cast the entire 18 votes of Kansas for Willkie. Whether the decision was due to the persuasive logic of Stassen or to the monotony of riding the freight elevator neither participant disclosed.

On the fifth ballot, Vandenberg of Michigan dropped to 42 votes. At the conclusion of the count, the word spread that Vandenberg was going to release his delegation without instructions. Thus, as the roll call of states began for the sixth ballot, the Michigan delegation was in caucus. The Willkie floor leaders had anticipated such a move and had long been in contact with various Michigan delegates. Stassen now realized that he must stall the roll call long enough to give Michigan the opportunity to complete her poll of delegates before she was called on to cast her ballot. Therefore, he sent word to Leo E. Anderson, leader of the California delegation and one of Stassen's twelve floor leaders, to delay proceedings by the time-honored trick of calling for a poll of his delegation. Thus, when the secretary of the convention called, "California," Charles H. Segerstrom addressed the chair and asked that the California delegation be polled. Amid the grumbling of many delegates and the surprise of the California delegation, the chairman so ordered. There were forty-four delegates. By the time the poll had been completed, Michigan had completed her caucus.

TOTAL BALLOT OF THE FOUR LEADING CANDIDATES

	1st	2nd	3rd	4th	5th
Dewey	360	338	315	250	57
Taft	189	203	212	254	377
Vandenberg	76	73	72	61	42
Willkie	105	171	259	306	429

In the meantime much had happened. Hamilton, as National Chairman, and Pryor, as chairman in charge of Arrangements, had desks on the speakers' platform not far from each other, which were also connected by telephone. The signal of these telephones was not the usual bell, but a small electric light. The two men were thus able to keep in constant touch without anyone's realizing that they were in conversation. Hamilton knew better than his colleagues which delegates might switch votes and about when each was ready to "break." During the early rounds of balloting, Hamilton was frequently instructing Pryor to go to the floor to see such-and-such a person as he believed him to be weakening and ready to be persuaded for the Willkie switch. Thus did Hamilton and Pryor give Stassen invaluable support in his floor strategy.

The real break in the line-up of candidates came from Michigan, which had been well groomed to turn to Taft. Hamilton, by his quick strategy, prevented such a turn of events. The episode was eloquent proof of the adage that political bosses never forget a political obligation. During the 1936 campaign Frank McKay, of Michigan, had asked Hamilton to do something about the bad publicity he was receiving from the Hearst newspapers. When Hamilton actually accomplished this feat, he earned the gratitude of the Michigan boss. Therewith, McKay promised to give aid when called upon. "You have a large credit in my bank," he told Hamilton. Now after the third ballot, in the 1940 Convention, Hamilton decided it was time to make use of this credit, and so he sought out McKay and told him he wanted the Michigan votes for Willkie as soon as Vandenberg released the delegation. "But," replied the Michigan politician, "I am in a hell of a fix. Mrs. Vandenberg has just sent me a note saying to turn the votes over to Bob Taft."

"Well," said Hamilton, "that is just too bad. But I have to have those votes. You owe me a great deal more than you owe the Senator's wife."

The reminder of a political obligation was effective. McKay agreed to deliver the votes. Hamilton next went to his friend, Joseph N. Pew, Jr. He asked for a switch to Willkie on the next ballot. "The limb will be sawed off behind you if you don't come in on the next vote," he predicted.

"Tell that to Governor James," said Pew dourly. So Hamilton sought out James and asked that he release his delegation at once. But the little Welsh Governor stubbornly refused. "Well," snapped Hamilton, "you are putting the best friend you ever had through the wringer." In this, of course, he referred to Pew who was keeping his word to support James until released. It was generally known that Pew was for Willkie after his initial support to the "favorite son" of Pennsylvania.

Back on the platform, Hamilton was surprised to find that McKay was awaiting him with two of the local bosses. Time was running out too rapidly for McKay to be loitering. However, they wanted to know whether in case the Michigan delegation swung to Willkie the Republican organization could name the federal judges in the state or if the Willkie Clubs would have this patronage. "That," said Hamilton, "I could not answer. Only Willkie himself could make that pledge." So he took the three Michigan boys to Pryor's desk, requesting him to telephone Willkie at his hotel room. To the amazement of Hamilton, Willkie readily agreed that McKay and the Republican state leaders should choose the judges. This promise clinched the Michigan vote. Although an experienced politician, Hamilton was shocked that any candidate would bargain with the federal judgeships. In the mad rush of convention business, he had little time or disposition for reflection. But even so, the suggestion came to mind that Willkie's inexperience in politics was responsible for this extraordinary commitment to the Michigan bosses.

Thus, when the secretary of the convention read the name "Michigan," Governor Dickinson of that state, arose to ask that one of his delegates, Howard C. Lawrence, be permitted to go to the platform to make an announcement. From the rostrum, Lawrence announced that Senator Vandenberg had authorized the release of his delegates and that after taking a caucus, the Michigan vote stood, Hoover 1, Taft 2 and Willkie 35. A great roar of mingled delight and disgust greeted this announcement. After Kansas and Michigan had swung to Willkie, Stassen sent word to his floor leaders to report all votes on the sixth ballot as he was ready for the grand slam.

Meanwhile, the galleries had resumed the chant: "We Want Willkie! We Want Willkie! We Want Willkie!" After the fifth ballot they were wild with glee. At this point a slender and graceful woman wearing dark glasses and a large hat slipped quietly out of her seat in the gallery and left the seething auditorium unobserved. It was Edith Willkie. Confident that the long hours of uncertainty were over, she decided to return to the Warwick Hotel. All during the balloting she had sat there unnoticed, taut and nervous, as she witnessed the excitement about her. The atmosphere was vibrant with the demand of the galleries for Willkie. She was now confident that her husband would win the unanimous vote of the convention.

She returned to the Hotel Warwick and found her husband alone. One brief spontaneous moment of embrace they had in joyous recognition that the victory was won. In a few seconds, a crowd of news reporters had closed around them. The press had taken for granted that the next ballot would decide the nomination and the newsmen were anxious to get a statement for the early editions of their papers.

With the departure of the press to make the morning head-lines, the Willkies settled down comfortably to await the con-gratulatory visits of their friends. To their chagrin, no one came. Well after midnight, they telephoned a few of their close friends to ask a little wistfully: "Aren't you coming over to see us?" Only then did they learn the amazing truth. The police and the hotel employees had established a line of protection around the Willkie suite. No visitor was able to get past that line. The most important bigwig, the most ardent personal friend, as well as the merely curious, had all been turned away. The faithful police who had been assigned to "guard" the Willkie apartment interpreted their orders to mean "solitary seclusion."

Meanwhile, at the Convention Hall, the roll of states was in progress for the sixth ballot. The voting led to a tumultuous victory. After the Michigan announcement, as the swing towards Willkie became increasingly apparent, state after state "hopped on the bandwagon." One such state was Pennsylvania with her big block of 72 votes. On the sixth ballot, the spokesman for the delegation announced, "Pennsylvania passes temporarily." By the time the clerk read the name of Virginia which declared 16 of her 18 votes for Willkie, David A. Reed, of Pennsylvania, successfully interrupted the roll call and secured recognition. His voice, zooming through the hall over the floor microphone, was heard to announce: "Mr. Chairman, Pennsylvania casts her seventy-two votes for Wendell Willkie." It was a dramatic state-ment. The galleries exploded with enthusiastic shouts. The chairman banged his gavel for order, but order was slow in returning.

At last, Governor Bricker, of Ohio, gained recognition and moved that the nomination of Wendell Willkie for President be made unanimous. Again, great applause and hilarious cries of jubilation spread through the auditorium. With difficulty, the chairman restored order. He immediately ruled that he was unable to recognize Governor Bricker at that time for such a motion, but would do so after the roll call had been completed. The Governor, however, could change Ohio's vote for 52 for Taft to 52 for Willkie, the chairman explained. Governor

Bricker sat down. The chairman then directed the secretary to continue the roll call of the states.

A few minutes later, several states followed the example of Pennsylvania by casting a unanimous vote for Willkie. Maine and Nebraska had passed, but now were ready to declare their vote. Colonel Creager, of Texas, the same leader who several days earlier had led the fiery attack upon the Willkie forces for "packing the galleries," announced that Texas wished to change her 26 votes from Taft to Willkie. This was followed by the spokesman of the Washington delegation who declared that his state cast all 16 votes for Willkie.

The great landslide of votes came at the conclusion of the roll call when twenty-five states with a total of 570 votes announced in rapid succession a unanimous vote of their delegation for Willkie. Not all of these votes were additional votes inasmuch as many of the delegations, on previous ballots, had given a portion of their votes to Willkie. For example, New York had given him 75 votes on the fifth ballot; the state delegation now cast its entire 92 votes for the man of the hour. It was a thrilling scene. The men who had fought him bitterly, the men who had held their delegations under rigid control, suddenly announced support for Wendell Willkie. It was a rolling, omnipotent tide of sentiment that swept away all opposition. The final result of the sixth ballot was 998 for Willkie with two delegates absent.

Great and prolonged cheering broke out. The galleries had waited anxious hours for this moment of victory. They would not be stilled. Again and again, the chairman pounded his gavel for order. The shouting continued. Thousands of spectators had come to Philadelphia to see Willkie nominated. They intended to enjoy to the full this magnificent vindication of their confidence in a new leader. It was their show. Each Willkie fan felt that somehow he had contributed to this final triumph, and each wanted to share in the crowning glory of his nomination.

Finally, with a semblance of quiet restored, the chairman recognized Governor Bricker. With a smile, the Ohioan said: "The motion I desired to make, now seems to be in order, but unnecessary. At any rate, Ohio moves that the nomination of Wendell Willkie for President be made unanimous." The mo-

tion was promptly seconded by Russell Sprague on behalf of
the Dewey Republicans of New York. Several others also made
short seconding speeches, among them Governor James, of
Pennsylvania. The chairman put the question for a unanimous
nomination, and as there was no dissenting voice, he declared it
a vote.

A generous message from Herbert Hoover to Willkie was read
to the convention by the chairman: "My congratulations," said
the former Republican President. "The result of a free convention of a free people will carry you to victory." This was followed by the announcement of a telephone message from Willkie expressing his appreciation of the loyalty and support of the
delegates to his candidacy. The hour was now 1:57 on Friday
morning. It was a frazzled and exhausted convention. Stassen,
probably the most exhausted man in all Philadelphia, moved a
recess until the following afternoon.

The nomination of Wendell Willkie was acclaimed by the
press as the most revolutionary action in Republican politics
since Lincoln was chosen in 1860. A vivid new personality had
swept aside the experienced leadership in the convention of such
men as Taft, Dewey, and Vandenberg. It was a most spectacular
legerdemain. There has never been anything like it before and
as Harold Stassen said there would never be another like it again.
That Willkie should catch the popular imagination was not surprising, but that he could translate a sudden "grass roots" movement into the hard reality of delegates' votes seemed sheer
fantasy. It was one of those episodes which lend glamour if not
logic to American politics. Yet the nomination was highly
prophetic. It forecast the future program of the Republican
Party. It reversed the Republican policy of isolationism. It con-
noted aid to the Allies and especially succor to England for
the Battle of Britain. It meant Republican support for foreign
trade and lowering of the tariff barriers. It also meant a reinterpretation by the Republican Party of the meaning of free
enterprise. It was the Republicans' answer to the New Deal.

The triumph of Willkie at the convention was an amazing
synchronization of the efforts of the amateur and the professional
politician. It was unfortunate for both groups, however, that
many of the amateurs discounted the performance of the ex-

perienced floor workers. As soon as the nomination was won, most of these newcomers to politics took to themselves all the glory of the victory. They seemed to think that they had out-smarted the convention, that they had shouted the delegates into a stampede. The dramatic fanfare of popular support was exceedingly helpful, but by itself it would have been dissipated like summer clouds. To accelerate the vote, ballot by ballot, required the most careful strategy by experienced manipulators of political events. The cockiness of the amateurs boded ill for the future. With the nomination assured, intoxicated with their success, they believed themselves to be possessed of more political wisdom than the professional politicians.

The hours following the adjournment of the convention early Friday morning, with the rush of politicians to the Willkie suite after the barricade was broken, gave the candidate little time for reflection. Although utterly weary, Willkie was compelled to hold a conference on the selection of the Republican candidate for Vice-President. According to time-honored custom, the nominee for President is usually consulted on the question of the candidates for the vice-presidency. Advisers of Willkie now declared that Baldwin to whom Willkie was pledged would draw little support to the national ticket and might even do it harm. In the public mind, they said, Willkie was identified with New York, rather than Indiana. Accordingly, his ticket would be immeasurably strengthened by securing a running-mate like Senator Charles L. McNary, of Oregon, who came from a state almost as far from Wall Street as a state could possibly be.

Willkie admitted the cogency of their arguments. Perhaps he could secure release from his commitment to Baldwin. Sam Pryor had just fallen asleep after returning to his room from the all-night nominating session. Willkie telephoned him to come to his room immediately. Perplexed as to the sudden urgency, Pryor hurriedly dressed and came. Willkie explained the pressure now placed upon him to choose a running-mate from the West. He said he recognized his commitment to Baldwin but that he "just couldn't hold to it." Therefore, he asked Pryor to see Baldwin and explain the situation to him.

"No," said Pryor emphatically, "I won't do that. But I am

certain that if you put the matter straight to Baldwin, as you have to me, he will withdraw of his own accord. He is just that kind of a man." Pryor urged that Willkie telephone Baldwin at once and ask him to come to the hotel. When Baldwin arrived, a few minutes later, Willkie explained in honest and eloquent fashion, of which he was a master, his predicament. The stalwart Baldwin took this major disappointment in stride, and promptly replied that he would not only withdraw his name, but also would make the nominating speech for the man selected. This was the second time that Baldwin had been sacrificed for Willkie. On both occasions he withdrew with a smile and with no recriminations.

After Baldwin departed, Willkie canvassed with Pryor the advantages and disadvantages of selecting Senator McNary as his running-mate. The Senator from Oregon was leader of the Republican Party in the upper house of Congress. His nomination would appeal to the agricultural West and would also cement cordial relations with the isolationist Republicans in the Senate. Furthermore, it would effectively dissolve the initial opposition to Willkie of which McNary had been a part. Pryor agreed to the choice, although with misgivings. Other loyal supporters, such as Styles Bridges, likewise felt that this selection was unfortunate.

The next question was to decide who should ask McNary. Pryor suggested Joe Martin. Another telephone call aroused another sleeping politician. When the situation was explained to him, he readily agreed to telephone McNary, who had returned to Washington. In view of McNary's slashing attacks upon Willkie only a few days previously, there was considerable doubt among the three whether he would accept; he held diametrically opposed views to those of Willkie on the two biggest issues of the campaign. But Willkie and his friends need not have been concerned. Martin had hardly put the question to the Senator before he replied: "Yes, yes, indeed, I will accept the nomination!"

This was the first blunder of the campaign, in which there were to be so many. Thoughtful voters were highly critical of such a team as Willkie and McNary. It was an obvious trick, to appeal to internationalists and to isolationists at the same time, to those who believed in the free enterprise system and those who relished at least a little government planning. At the same time, the choice was a laudable effort to heal the breach between Willkie and the congressional leaders.

Friday, June 28, marked the beginning of the political career of Wendell Willkie. In the American tradition, that career included his wife as well as himself. Edith Willkie was not a woman to shirk her responsibility. On that very morning she held her first press conference in the Blue Room of the Hotel Warwick. The shy Indiana girl who only the day before had successfully disguised herself and sat alone in the gallery of Convention Hall in order to elude the press, now accepted the inevitable with poise and dignity. Amid the clicking flash of the photographers, she calmly answered the barrage of questions put to her by the reporters. How did she like to be surrounded by police guards and secret service men? "Not at all," she replied, "I'm much too independent to enjoy being followed everywhere."

Another reporter asked if she thought the First Lady should hold press conferences, write a column, and generally take part in public affairs. Here was an opportunity to play upon the prejudice entertained by millions of voters against the manifold activities of Eleanor Roosevelt. Edith Willkie refused the political gambit. She answered simply, "Yes I do, if she is able to do it." This generous answer offered a magnificent rebuke to the narrow-minded Republicans who had condemned the First Lady for her speeches and other public activities.

Asked her preference among all the White House ladies, she responded without hesitation that she would feel herself highly successful if she could equal the popularity of Mrs. Coolidge. "So many of them were very fine. I only hope I can be as gracious."

At 4:35 the same afternoon, Mr. and Mrs. Willkie walked down the center aisle of Convention Hall to the platform amid the cheering welcome of the delegates and visitors. Hats were tossed in the air, handkerchiefs and flags waved from all over the floor as well as the galleries, the organ thundered and the delegates hurrahed. The handsome nominee bowed to the left and to the right down the long walk to the rostrum. The presentation of Wendell Willkie and his wife to the delegates was the concluding ceremony of the convention. Earlier that afternoon, Charles L. McNary had been nominated as vice-presidential candidate.

Chairman Martin presented Wendell Willkie, the candidate, for a word of greeting. Old party leaders like Pew waited anxiously and critically for the speech. To their surprise, he did very well on the first few paragraphs of his brief remarks. As the nominee of the people, he said, he expected to conduct a fighting campaign to bring unity to America, unity to labor, capital, agriculture and manufacture, and unity to all classes for the preservation of freedom. He invited all of them to join him in "this great crusade." Only forty-eight days ago, he recounted, he had begun to preach this doctrine of unity to the American people, and it was evident that this simple doctrine had made a wide appeal.

Up to this point all the party leaders heartily applauded. Then they were chilled by his concluding remarks: "And so, you Republicans, I call upon you to join me, help me. The cause is great. We must win. We cannot fail if we stand in one united fight." Men like Pew and Hamilton were piqued. He had called them "YOU Republicans." There had been much ado about Willkie's earlier Democratic affiliations. His concluding sentence, thoughtlessly uttered, might well have gone unnoticed if made by Hoover or some other "old-line" Republican. But when spoken by the newcomer to the field, it aroused doubts and suspicions all over again. It marked a decided decline from the high plane of enthusiasm of the night before when the delegates had chosen him leader because his cause was just. Upon this note of doubt the convention adjourned.

Was the fervor for Willkie which developed to such lofty heights at the convention to be permitted to dissipate itself? Could it be recaptured and retained? A clever strategist would have advised an immediate acceptance speech—a strong fighting speech. The word of "greeting" that Willkie had given at the convention had been ineffectual and inadequate. It was Russell Davenport who had advised against the immediate acceptance speech. He proposed that Willkie give his acceptance speech from the steps of the high school in Elwood. Furthermore, the National Chairman should have been named at once to the end that he might bind the workers together before they dispersed from Philadelphia. This, of course, was the traditional procedure. But Willkie wanted to think it over before giving his decision, and the party managers respected his desire.

Saturday afternoon, the twenty-ninth of June, the Willkies left the convention city in triumph aboard the yacht *Jamaroy*, owned by Roy W. Howard, newspaper publisher. This short cruise gave the nominee two days of rest, most of which he spent in sound sleep. Russell Davenport was the only other guest aboard the yacht. On Monday morning, the *Jamaroy* docked at Pier Twenty-six, New York City. Reporters eagerly awaited the arrival of the Republican presidential candidate. The campaign had begun.

CHAPTER XI

The Acceptance Speech

WHEN WILLKIE reached his office Monday morning from the Philadelphia Convention, he found that his son Philip, a Princeton student, had made an appointment through his secretary to see him. Somewhat amused by the formality of the young man, he awaited with interest to learn the nature of the interview. His son, it developed, had been worried over the nomination and he had come to have a man-to-man talk with his father. "You see, Dad, you may not win," he explained in all seriousness. "You are giving up a good job, a sure thing. If you lose the campaign, perhaps you couldn't find another position of $75,000 a year, and I just wondered if you had considered all this." Willkie was thoroughly delighted with the boy's point of view, but he assured him that even if he should lose the election, the family finances would not suffer. As a matter of fact, Willkie had planned to resign from Commonwealth and Southern if he had not been nominated, so as to go into general legal practice again. He had delayed his resignation that spring because of the presidential boom as he felt that his political enemies would make capital of it by saying he was quitting utilities in order to win votes.

There were other callers waiting to see the candidate although none with such a keen personal interest in his future.

The matter of greatest importance which confronted Willkie was the choosing of a national chairman. Most of the National Republican Committee favored Hamilton, except Alf Landon. Willkie did not like him either but he had a commitment to Hamilton. So Willkie conceived of a compromise plan; to make Hamilton the National Chairman for fund-raising, and then create an executive committee to guide the campaign. No one seemed pleased with this suggestion, certainly not Hamilton.

Therefore, Willkie sought advice from Raymond Moley about his ingenious plan for a board to direct the campaign. Although Moley was unimpressed by such a scheme, he suggested getting advice from an expert. Accordingly, he telephoned Will H. Hays, chairman of the National Republican Committee in 1918-21. By this time it was past ten o'clock at night and pouring rain, but Hays responded loyally to the call and visited Moley at the St. Regis Hotel. Hays listened patiently as Willkie explained his novel idea. Smiling kindly, he explained: "You have to remember the millions of little people in a campaign. They like to look clear down the lane to a great political leader." With reluctance, Willkie gave up his idea of a board.

Hamilton now came to New York for a conference with Willkie. But after a two-hour session, he left the Pine Street office of the famous executive in the knowledge that he would not be the one to direct the forthcoming campaign.

Many of the party leaders were highly incensed over the treatment of Hamilton inasmuch as they considered him to be the greatest organizer and strategist since Mark Hanna. In 1937, he had gone to England to make a study of the Conservative Party which had remained out of power for years and still maintained its vitality. It was Hamilton, therefore, who had seen the necessity for a permanent national party headquarters and who had been instrumental in establishing it. The idea was to maintain a regular staff with continuing chairmen so as to establish constant contact with the local party leaders. Between 1937 and 1940, he set the pattern by making trips to all parts of the country, talking to county chairmen and city bosses. Between visits, he kept in touch with them by long distance telephone calls. In this way he reconstructed the party morale among the workers in the field.

Before the National Convention, definite commitments had been made by all the major candidates to the retention of Hamilton as National Chairman. Hamilton had not only organized the party on a firm basis, but had raised the money to pay off the three and a half million dollars' debt after the 1936 campaign. The men who had contributed most of this money had each of them individually asked Willkie and the other candidates for a personal pledge, if nominated, to the continuation of Hamilton as National Chairman. All the candidates, including Willkie, gave this pledge. These financial backers wanted to be assured a stable structure and a solvent party.

Moreover, many Republicans resented this Hamilton episode as showing a callous disregard by the candidate of the influence used on his behalf at the convention by the National Chairman. They knew that the one man above all others responsible for the Willkie nomination at the Philadelphia Convention was John Hamilton. He had appointed as chairman of Arrangements, Samuel Pryor. Just as easily he could have appointed Colonel R. B. Creager of Texas, the outspoken opponent of Willkie who was loyal to Taft. He had chosen Stassen to keynote the convention. But that was not all. Hamilton had worked actively on the floor and used his wide acquaintance and prestige to garner votes for Willkie. The brutal treatment of Hamilton, therefore, aroused bitter resentment by the men at the core of the party's activities. This unhappy episode lived throughout the campaign. Pew most vividly described it when he said, "Willkie carved the heart out of John Hamilton."

Willkie was never a politician. Neither by training nor academic study had he ever learned the structure or function of political parties. He looked upon the party as something unclean. This was revealed by his comment to Justin Whiting, who succeeded him as President of C.&S. Immediately after the convention, swarms of people, party members, came to see him, to get his nod. They were kept waiting as he received each in rotation. So Justin Whiting, recognizing the serious and awkward situation, tried to smooth out the snarl by suggesting to Willkie that he should secure a trained political secretary who would recognize the distinguished people lining up in his office and who would know the courteous way to handle them. Willkie had taken a young woman from the company's secretarial pool who was known for her painstaking work but who was wholly untrained to meet the public. He chose also a young man efficient as a secretary, but again without any political experience. But to Whiting's kindly suggestion, Willkie replied sharply: "Justin, you do not seem to understand that the importance of my campaign is that it is a spontaneous reaction of the people. I do not want an organization of politically trained people in my office."

Willkie had been able to rationalize his participation in politics only by establishing new standards. He intended to carry on the campaign by new rules and he wanted as little to do with the career politicians as possible. He looked upon his campaign as a crusade. He announced to the press that party labels would mean little in the November election. The people, regardless of party affiliations, would either support or oppose the New Deal. Such views were considered heresy by the party leaders. Indeed, it would be a denial of the purpose of the party system and of the principle of party responsibility.

Another unorthodox view which Willkie announced was that he would not accept any contributions from a corporation, or any cash contributions in excess of ten dollars. "This is the people's movement and I am going to keep it that way," he declared. This remark annoyed Weir, who was the National Treasurer of the party. In flaming anger, he read the statement in the press and promptly telephoned Willkie. "If any more such statements are issued without my knowledge, I will resign," he said, and demanded that hereafter there should be the closest co-operation on all matters relating to contributions. The earlier feeling of good fellowship was breached.

Not a few of the friends around Willkie recognized the necessity for making peace with the political leaders. Even a people's movement needed organization and direction. Harold Talbott was one who urged greater organization. He had labored brilliantly for Willkie at Philadelphia but he had expected that as soon as the nomination was secured, the experienced party men would take over guidance of the campaign. Accordingly, he hurried to Washington and engaged a large suite of rooms at the Willard Hotel. This was to be the setting for those important party conferences to bring peace and co-operation within the Republican ranks and to allay the acrimony, bitterness and dissension which developed at the convention. But Willkie stayed in Washington just twenty-two hours. He arrived by plane from New York at 2:45 on Monday, and was met at the airport by a delegation of congressmen headed by Representative Halleck of Indiana. In the evening, he attended a dinner given by Joe Martin and Halleck. Taft, Vandenberg and Bridges were among the guests, and each in the best traditional manner pledged his loyalty to the candidate.

The following morning Willkie announced to a waiting press his decision for the national chairman and the rest of his official family. Joseph W. Martin, chairman of the recent National Convention and Minority Leader of the House was to serve as the Republican National Chairman and campaign manager. The honesty and fairness of Martin during the convention and his loyalty during the McNary episode had completely won the affection of Willkie. There was the further reason that Martin provided another link with Congress, as he was the most popular Republican in the House of Representatives. Owing to his congressional obligations, however, Martin had been loath to accept the campaign assignment. Nevertheless, Willkie had been persistent and proudly made the announcement: "Like a member of the famed Northwest Mounted Police, 'I've got my man!' " Probably no one realized better than Martin the seriousness of the mistake of his appointment. It was in fact the second major blunder of the campaign.

Martin was to serve as chairman without remuneration. As a member of Congress he could not accept a second salary. To soothe Hamilton, Willkie named him "Executive Director" in charge of the western campaign with headquarters in Chicago. He was to retain his salary of $25,000 a year. When Hamilton was acquainted with this proposal, he promptly rejected it. He said, "I will pass out literature, I will help in any way that I can, but I cannot step down in rank." Pew and Weeks at once rallied around him and urged "harmony" and the good of the party. So Hamilton in a superb display of good humor entered upon his curtailed duties.

Samuel Pryor was made vice-chairman in charge of the campaign in the East with headquarters in New York. Willkie had first asked Pryor to be his manager, but Pryor had definitely refused because of business duties, and out of loyalty to John Hamilton. In addition to these two chairmen, Willkie established an executive committee of some twenty-five members from diverse parts of the country under the direction of Governor Stassen. This committee, however, was never active as a group. Russell Davenport was named personal representative of Willkie, which meant that everything must clear through him before it reached the nominee.

With little accomplished in Washington, Willkie and his party embarked on a chartered plane for Colorado Springs, Tuesday afternoon. A number of Republicans made no effort to conceal their delight at his departure. In the meantime, a concerted move had developed among Democratic Senators to discredit the Republican nominee because of the avalanche of telegrams received by the delegates at Philadelphia. Senator James F. Byrnes of South Carolina, Democratic chairman of the Committee on Appropriations, asked for an investigation and declared: "I feel that anything as comprehensive as that high-pressured campaign is of enough public interest so that the voters ought to have the facts for such weight as they may attach to them." Senator Guy Gillette of Iowa, chairman of the Investigating Committee, was not loath to push the inquiry. Nevertheless, the attempt to show that the telegrams were synthetic was doomed to failure. The correspondents and the politicians at Philadelphia knew that the telegrams were genuine.

Some of the Democrats resorted to name-calling in an effort to ridicule the Republican candidate. Senator Alben Barkley referred to the Philadelphia Convention as the "second charge of the light brigade in the heroic battle of kilowatts." Mayor Edward J. Kelly, of Chicago, described the candidate as "Morganized." Maury Maverick, Mayor of San Antonio, Texas, called Willkie only a "flash-in-the-pan" and a candidate who catered to the "Hate-Roosevelts, to the Fascists, and to the Communists." Harold Ickes told his press conference that Wendell Willkie and his friends had become a holding company for the Republican Party. Senator Tom Connally said: "The Republicans have nominated Wendell Willkie who has an electric background, an electric personality and an electric campaign chest. However, he had better prepare for a blackout in November." Senator James M. Mead, of New York, contributed the phrase that Willkie was the "Pied Piper of the Utilities."

A far more serious effort to smear the candidate was started when Speaker of the House William B. Bankhead said that the Republicans in nominating Willkie were trying "to place the Executive in control of forces foreign to our American way of life." This was a touch-off for a whispering campaign that Willkie was a Nazi. The President himself on July 5 warned Americans against the desire of a large number of persons to surrender freedom to the interests of efficiency under a "corporate government." The word "corporate" was a term Roosevelt had not previously used, as the press hastened to point out. It carried a double meaning. The totalitarian government of Italy was frequently spoken of as a "corporate state." Willkie, on the other hand, had been the head of a huge American corporation. The "corporation" of fascism was a cycle of production, such as the electrical industry, operating within the planned economy of the Fascist Government. In the United States, however, a "corporation" was an individual business within the orbit of the free enterprise system. The two "corporations" were as different as chalk and cheese.

Resenting Willkie's appeal to the people, the New Dealers questioned his patriotism. He was ridiculed as the representative of Wall Street, a pawn of the capitalists, and one sympathetic with the Fascists of Europe. Edward J. Flynn, chairman of the Democratic National Committee, declared that Willkie had been chosen as the candidate of the "public utility party." The Democratic boss of Tennessee, Edward H. Crump, charged that "Willkie's whole life had been a fight against the people—defending high electric light rates and watered stock." Willkie, as the representative of the "economic royalist," was pictured as a danger to the American system of government, while the faithful Democrats conveniently forgot the President's attempt in 1938 to purge the party of all those who opposed him.

As to the Willkie family background, there had never been any secret about it. In his speeches, Willkie had frequently spoken of his grandparents who fled the Prussian Government to seek liberty in America. His paternal grandparents later visited their native land and there his father was born. But at the age of two, he was brought back to this country by the grandparents who then remained permanently in America. His mother was born here. Both his mother and father grew up and were educated in this land of the free. Such were the simple facts twisted by the opposition to discredit Willkie as a dangerous and disloyal citizen.

Another effective weapon used to detract from Willkie was his stand on public power. The New Dealers were emphatic that if the Republicans should be elected, this inherent right of the people, to secure electric power, at lowest possible cost, would come to an end. Although Willkie was opposed to public power projects because he believed all trends towards a planned economy were limitations of the freedom of the people, he had declared as early as June 14 that "you can't turn the clock back on TVA." He termed it "unrealistic" for any President to try to give TVA back to the utilities. Although the establishment of TVA was ruthless, he explained, the dams had been built, and distribution systems had ben acquired. Thus before the nominating convention Willkie had advocated a five-year test for TVA to see what benefits might accrue.

Meanwhile, the Democratic National Convention in Chicago had a sour ending. The third term issue alienated many faithful Democrats, as well as Roosevelt's demand that Henry Wallace be nominated as Vice-President. But as a further blow to the confidence of a large number of loyal party members was the resignation as National Chairman of that beloved leader, Jim Farley. This sharply emphasized the irregularity of the third term nomination. The high and mighty action of the Corcoran-Cohen crowd caused sober party members anxious reflections. And furthermore, many responsible members of the Democratic Party criticized the whispering campaign directed against Willkie concerning his German ancestry. Accordingly the *Fortune* poll for August recorded a drop in the Roosevelt popularity.

	July	*August*
Roosevelt	49.0%	44.3%
Willkie	31.4%	40.8%

As a result of all this dissatisfaction many prominent Democrats announced support of the Republican candidate. Among these were Vance C. McCormick, National Democratic Chairman in 1916; Ex-Governor William H. (Alfalfa Bill) Murray of Oklahoma; Stephen F. Chadwick, former National Commander of the American Legion; Hamilton Holt, president of Rollins College, and Irvin S. Cobb, humorist. During the month of August, Alfred E. Smith, former Democratic nominee for President, publicly announced his support of Willkie, as did Judge Samuel Seabury. Then, in rapid succession, came public declarations in favor of the Republican candidate from Justice Joseph M. Proskauer, formerly of the New York State Supreme Court and one-time consultant of Roosevelt, Stanley High, former editor of the *Christian Herald*, O. M. W. Sprague, Harvard economist who had advised the New Deal in 1933, Ewing Y. Mitchell, former Assistant Secretary of Commerce under Roosevelt, and Young B. Smith, Dean of Columbia Law School.

Perhaps the most important of these insurgent Democrats were John W. Hanes and Lewis W. Douglas. Former high officials of the Administration, the Under-Secretary of the Treasury and the Director of the Budget, respectively, their support had great significance and far-reaching influence. They wired Willkie proposing to enlist the Democrats who believed that loyalty to country took precedent over loyalty to party. This telegram came to the attention of Harold Talbott who was handling Willkie's correspondence at Colorado Springs. Quick to perceive the advantage of such an organization, Talbott urged Willkie to telephone Hanes an immediate acceptance.

Thus was born the Democrats-for-Willkie organization. Talbott suggested that Alan Valentine, president of the University of Rochester, and a Democrat, be included. As events worked out, it was Hanes, Talbott, and Valentine who did most of the work. Although Talbott was not a Democrat, he was the liaison man between the Democrats-for-Willkie organization and the Willkie headquarters. Hanes and Talbott collected the money which made the Democrats-for-Willkie so highly effective. In addition the Hanes committee put on a publicity campaign, sent out speakers, bought radio time, and carried on a full program of political activity. These Willkie Democrats prided themselves that the Republicans even borrowed their talent from time to time. The Hanes committee set up an organization in every state in the Union, although they did not get started until August.

There was little doubt of Roosevelt's chagrin that some of the stalwarts of his party deserted to the Willkie camp. When press correspondents asked the President what he thought of Hanes and Douglas coming out for Willkie, he replied with sarcasm that they had always been more interested in dollars than in humanity. In acknowledging the Alfred E. Smith support, therefore, Willkie slapped back by declaring: "I hope that nobody suggests that the warm-hearted Alfred E. Smith is one of those persons who is actuated by love of money rather than love of humanity."

Rarely had a candidate been so favored by the quality of the support accorded him as was Willkie. He touched the man at the top and the man at the bottom, the industrialist and the banker as well as the shopkeeper and the man of small business. Economists and scholars had confidence in him as did the rank and file. The directors of big business and the small share-holders believed in his honesty and ability. The broad people's movement behind him was no mirage, no propaganda trick. It was real. No better proof of this could be presented than the story of the Willkie Clubs, with their large number of non-partisan members eagerly working for a Willkie victory.

The Democrats-for-Willkie and the Willkie Clubs influenced Willkie regarding the pattern of his campaign. He took it for granted that the Republicans would vote for him. Thus he determined to direct his appeal to the Democrats and the independent voters. To newsmen he said: "I do not know of any reason why Democrats who subscribed to the Democratic platform of 1932 or who believe in the historic principles of the Democratic Party, or [one] who was a Woodrow Wilson Democrat should not vote for me in preference to the President."

Among the reasons for support listed in the numerous telegrams from Democrats which Willkie received while in Colorado Springs were: opposition to the third term as a menace to the free functioning of democracy, opposition to the continuous centralization of power in the federal Government and most especially in the office of the presidency itself, opposition to the whole philosophy of scarcity economics which limited production and which had decreased the nation's standard of living, and opposition to a class-conscious government by men instead of a government by law giving equal opportunity for all.

To woo these discontented Democrats became the chief focus of the campaign. The Republican Party was subordinated. All Willkie wanted from the Republicans were their votes. His neglect of party officials, however, brought sharp complaints. As criticism increased, Willkie invited a group of important Republicans to visit him in Colorado Springs. This was an attempt to pacify the turbulent feelings of his party leaders. When Root suddenly heard that the politicians were going to fly out to see Willkie he was greatly disturbed. Accordingly, he telephoned Willkie, and the candidate loyally asked him to come out at once. In this way young Root arrived before the politicians, much to his satisfaction. He happily stood beside Willkie as the plane carrying the Republican leaders rolled onto the runway at the airport. By this quick maneuver he was able to entrench his control over the clubs he had organized.

This powwow of the Republican high command and independent leaders resulted in a momentous decision that three separate organizations were to run the campaign: The Associated Willkie Clubs were to continue under Oren Root, Jr., as Executive Director. The Democrats-for-Willkie organization would be left under the leadership of John W. Hanes. Lastly, the Republican Party would function under Joseph Martin. Each organization was wholly independent of the other and accountable directly to Willkie.

This was the beginning of the comedy of errors, as Raymond Moley characterized the ensuing campaign. It was a threefold authority with the supreme command lodged in an amateur, Russell Davenport. Annoyed Republican leaders posed the question: "Whose party is it anyway?"

However, the candidate admitted that the Willkie Clubs had become a questionable asset. Their constant quarreling with the regular Republican organization lessened the effectiveness of both. Several days after the convention, therefore, he had asked John B. Hollister to act as special adviser to Oren Root and his Willkie Clubs. Hollister was well known throughout New England. He had gone to Yale and kept up his associations in the East, although long associated with the legal firm of Taft, Stettinius and Hollister, of Cincinnati. He fulfilled this difficult task of keeping a semblance of order and peace within the ranks of the Willkie Clubs with supreme skill until he was assigned by Joe Martin to the Willkie special train for the campaign tour.

Meanwhile, the weeks at Colorado became more and more chaotic. There was no over-all direction and the politicians and the amateurs seemed to be working at cross-purposes. The former tried to swing the political organization into action and the amateurs tried as hard to prevent it. This was to be a people's movement and the politicians, therefore, would only contaminate it. Each group felt resentment towards the other. The situation was aggravated as one Republican leader after another who came to Colorado was snubbed. Two of the most notable cases were Herbert Hoover and Henry Fletcher, general counsel to the Republican Party. Hoover was kept waiting while Willkie chatted amicably with Elliott Roosevelt about his vacation, although Hoover had flown in from a fishing trip upon the request of the candidate. It was an unthinking slight to the former President, but resented by all Republicans.

Henry Fletcher came out to Colorado to discuss the effect of the Hatch Act, which Congress had just passed, limiting campaign expenditures to three million dollars. The question at issue was the reporting of the expenditures of the Willkie Clubs and other independent groups. He presented a fourteen-page legal brief which had taken days to prepare and much learning of the law. But unfortunately, he did not know that this was a sensitive point with the candidate from Wall Street. Willkie had already established a policy for scrupulous and exact accounting of all expenditures. Verbally, he showed Fletcher the door. As it worked out, the Republicans spent only $2,242,-742 in the 1940 campaign, which was a record of economy.

Amid all the strain and jangled nerves there were lighter moments from time to time that relieved the tension. Willkie was always an early riser. It was his custom to sit down to break-

fast in Colorado about six o'clock. He had it served on a private
veranda off his suite. Frequently he telephoned across the hall
to Talbott or Davenport to join him for a quiet talk. The freshness of the mountain air, the dew still on the shrubs and
flowers, and the early stillness of the morning were an invitation
to friendly banter.

Each morning after breakfast, the day began with a press
conference. Even the President has no more than two press conferences a week. The news runs a little thin when a statement
must be made each day. Yet this was the pace Willkie set for
himself. Instead of commenting only upon important issues,
he was giving his views on anything and everything. This of
course opened him to needless attack. Republican leaders criticized him for talking too much.

Frayed nerves, small irritations, contradictions, and confusion
were constant, with such ordinary matters as photographs getting out of hand. Photographers were insatiable. They always
wanted another picture. On one particular morning several of
the photographers decided that a colored picture of his wife
would be nice. Accordingly, Mrs. Willkie was requested after
breakfast that morning, to get ready for a colored photograph
in the rose garden. This time she rebelled. There had been so
many pictures and she hated all the publicity and fanfare of
politics, anyway. Quite clearly she would have been happier
living quietly in her apartment on Fifth Avenue with her two
men, Wendell and Philip. But her husband had chosen politics
and dutifully she tried to do all that was expected of a candidate's wife. She had been simple and charming to all. The newsmen unanimously praised her. But taut nerves sometimes snap.

On this morning she had no desire to be photographed even
in the rose garden. In the hall outside the Willkie suite the
argument took place. The photographers were present and
ready for the occasion. The publicity director was there too.
In her determination not to be photographed she had summoned several of her husband's aides. They settled the matter
very neatly. "If you don't want to be photographed, don't be.
You are not compelled to go to the rose garden." Oh, but she
was, spoke up the young publicity director! Then someone
fetched her husband to the scene. He was nettled by being called

to the squabble. Summarily he directed his wife to go into the apartment and make ready for the photograph. Smarting from this public rebuke, she marched into the suite with her stubborn little head high. She went straight to the bathroom and filled the basin with water and plunged her head into it. Three minutes later, the door opened and she stuck her head out dripping wet!

Meanwhile Russell Davenport was working away on the acceptance speech, which nobody liked. Willkie had invited Raoul Desvernine to Colorado for the one purpose of appraising this important speech. They had discussed many political talks together in the old days during the thirties when they both were engaged in effective attacks upon the New Deal. So when Willkie asked for an opinion of the speech Desvernine was frank: "It is the lousiest political speech I have ever read." Consequently, Desvernine suggested that an experienced political speech writer be secured to produce a worthy acceptance speech, and mentioned Raymond Moley who certainly had the experience. Willkie had sought advice from Moley on numerous occasions and, moreover, Moley had become one of his most enthusiastic column writers. But Willkie replied, "No, it would be embarrassing to have Moley because of his former connection with Roosevelt." Such statements usually found their way back to the person involved to prick his vanity and corrode a friendship. Desvernine then added the names of Ralph Robey, Hugh Johnson, and George E. Sokolsky. He told Willkie these men were all for him and each would accept the assignment. All Willkie had to do was to telephone them. But he never did. Moley wrote one speech on foreign policy which Davenport disposed of. Thus the important acceptance speech was left in the hands of the poet, in whom Willkie continued to have confidence.

It was generally conceded that up to the time of the acceptance speech, Willkie was elected. But those who visited Colorado Springs, and witnessed the lack of organization there, began to wonder. The National Chairman, Representative Martin, was busy on the floor of the House, although he tried to keep in touch with the candidate by telephone and even spent some time in Colorado in conference with the candidate.

On the fifteenth of August, the Willkie entourage left for Indianapolis in two chartered planes. Fifty-five thousand persons shouted a welcome to him on his arrival at the airport. From Indianapolis, Willkie, accompanied by his wife, motored with a police escort to Rushville. Groups of people in villages and towns along the route stood waiting for the cavalcade to pass. Much of the time Willkie stood in the car waving to the people although he and his wife both were tired and worn. Hence it was close to midnight when the party arrived in the village, but the entire population of six thousand persons were on the streets to greet their hero. Perhaps the people of Elwood were hostile to him, but there was no doubt that the citizens of Rushville loved him. Placards all over town boasted, "Willkie is a successful Rush County farmer." A picture inscribed "The Pride of Rushville" adorned the front window of his mother-in-law's house, where the Willkies remained overnight.

Saturday morning Willkie entrained for the fifty-five-mile ride to Elwood for the acceptance speech. But in typical Willkie fashion he forgot his manuscript. A hurried wire to Rushville, and the precious document was rushed to him by motorcycle police. Only a few minutes before time for delivery, therefore, did Chairman Martin have an opportunity to read the lines. He was amazed to find that it was a plain typewritten speech. Willkie did not know that political speakers always have their speeches typed in capital letters with lines three spaces apart so that they can easily look up and down from the manuscript. He did not know that experienced politicians never give an important address without carefully and quietly going over it with half a dozen colleagues. A campaigner like Thomas Dewey never gave a speech that he had not gone over aloud some ten or twelve times with seasoned henchmen. There had been no consultation on this speech with the experienced men of the party.

The acceptance speech was given at Elwood. This was another major blunder. The town was too small to have the necessary facilities to handle the huge crowd for such an occasion. However, a valiant attempt was made to overcome this disadvantage. As soon as Joe Martin was chosen national chairman of the

Republican Party, he appointed Homer E. Capehart, of Indianapolis, to take complete charge of the arrangements.

Capehart, who several years later was elected senator, was an experienced politician and a successful businessman. He had achieved national prominence in the summer of 1938 when he revived the Republican Party in the state by holding a "Corn Field Conference," on his own farm at his own expense. Fifty thousand people came including such bigwigs of the party as John Hamilton, Joe Martin, Senator Jim Watson and Governor Clifford Townsend.

As soon as Capehart received the assignment he went to Elwood and stayed there until after the ceremony. The task before him was colossal. He estimated there would be about two hundred thousand people coming to the ceremonies, as the candidate was the most spectacular Republican the party had had since the days of the gaunt rail-splitter from Illinois. The first problem was how to get all those people into and out of such a small town with only four roads. Capehart induced a reluctant council to pass special traffic regulations making these roads one-way thoroughfares for the day of August 17. Before the ceremony all cars moved only into the city, and afterwards all cars moved only out of the city.

The next problem was to arrange a place for the ceremony itself. There was a small City Park, sometimes called Callaway Park, at the edge of the town. But a stage had to be built. Electricity, water, telephones, a public address system, and broadcasting apparatus had to be installed. Concession stands had to be erected to provide the multitude with cold drinks and sandwiches. In addition, comfort stations and an emergency first aid room had to be constructed. All this had to be done in a little over a month's time.

There were other problems. The matter of parking space was one. In fact the park itself was not large enough for the anticipated crowd and additional pasture land had to be rented for the occasion. As the ground was owned by a Democrat active in state politics, and one who was an open enemy of the candidate as well, the price was fantastic, $12,000. Parking space for forty thousand cars had to be provided. Congestion was cut to the minimum by dividing the parking space into four sections, one section for each of the four roads leading into town.

The road leading to the park was a dirt road. This had to be oiled to lay the dust, or no one would have been able either to see or breathe. It was but another item of expense in the gigantic preparation for an event too big for the size of the town. Thirty thousand chairs were secured to be set up in the center of the park. This was done not so much to provide seats as to keep the crowd spread out so that they would not crush each other to death in an effort to get near the platform.

All this preparation was difficult enough. But the candidate then had a sentimental urge to stop at his old high school to say a few words. Capehart tried to discourage this feature of the day's events, but to no avail. The difficulty was twofold. The street was narrow, making it difficult to get in and out of the schoolyard even with a few hundred people present. Capehart feared total congestion if not several bad accidents. To add to the difficulties were the half dozen large trees in the school grounds. These had to be removed. The school board was not favorable to this action but finally agreed on the condition the trees should be carefully lifted out of their places and later replanted. This little procedure cost $2,500. Finally a small platform was built over the steps, but the space and position made it difficult to erect a secure structure. It would hold with safety the candidate and two or three others. But if the crowd should break loose and start climbing on the platform, it would collapse. Capehart almost collapsed himself, thinking of the dread possibility. The schoolhouse episode added a clear $10,000 to the total cost of the day in Elwood.

In addition to all the physical handicaps to be surmounted, there was the hostility of the people towards a Willkie. They didn't want him to come back. They took no civic pride in the fame he had brought the community. All they could think of was that he had ignored Elwood for twenty-three years. When he bought farm property, it was in Rushville. Now that he had suddenly turned to politics, they felt, he wished to brush the dust of Wall Street from his boots, and be just a small-town boy again. Moreover, the townsfolk usually voted Democratic. Willkie's recent conversion to the Republican Party was an added point of grievance. And, anyway, the people didn't like all the fuss and inconvenience of the preparation for the event. No group or organization was particularly helpful, and frequently it seemed as if these people actually were making arrangements more difficult.

The amount of money contributed by individuals and commercial firms in Elwood was almost negligible. The whole affair cost about $75,000, most of which was secured by Capehart himself. On the other hand, the merchants of Elwood were eager to make all they could out of the unwelcome event. Reporters and others of the advance guard on arrangements were living at the small hotel in the town at a rate of three dollars a day. On August 14, the rate was suddenly hiked to ten dollars a day, and three days' guarantee required. Several of the men tried to reason with the manager on patriotic grounds but this was wasted oratory. It took the suavest of politicians to quiet the press and prevent the story being spread in the press from coast to coast. Then the restaurants and food stores stocked up with large supplies thinking they would have a rushing day of business, but all the cars zoomed right through the town to the park and there the people bought what they wanted from the concession stands. Many people brought a hamper of food with them. So instead of being enriched by a few extra dollars, these merchants lost money. Furious about that, they promptly blamed it on Willkie. Another cause for resentment was the removal of the Republican headquarters immediately after the ceremony to Rushville, where Willkie stayed until the start of his campaign tour.

In the midst of such unfriendliness, it was not surprising that black rumors were spread far and wide. Letters and postcards were circulated, making malicious charges. It was said that Willkie let his mother die in poverty and that she had been buried in a potter's field. All lies, but damaging to people who did not know the truth. Some half a dozen persons threatened violence if Willkie ever came to Elwood. Special detectives, therefore, were assigned to watch this little band. But no disturbance occurred. The only unseemly action which must have made visitors wonder a little was the number of Democratic banners displayed at the park while Willkie was speaking.

Willkie arrived from Rushville by special train about 12:30 on Saturday, the seventeenth. Sharply at one o'clock, the University of Indiana band struck up and the parade began. The men of Summit Post of the American Legion in Ohio, of which Willkie had once been the commander, came as a unit to march in the parade as an honor guard. There was to be a stop at the schoolhouse. Capehart had given careful instructions to the driver of Willkie's car to leave the police escort when they arrived at the high school and circle inside the grounds. But the driver forgot and followed the police chief's car into the street, stopping in front of the steps. At once the crowd surged forward and the candidate was trapped in the middle of the street. Capehart called together twelve husky police officers and, forming a V-shape wedge with himself at the point, lunged through the crowd knocking people down, and bruising others, but finally reached the car. Willkie, his wife, his mother-in-law and son were pushed into the V-wedge guarded by police on both sides as they all struggled through the mob to reach the platform. It was a very hot day with temperature near a hundred and the sun shining with a torrid glare. By the time they were clear of the packed crowd, they were all crumpled and exhausted. Willkie spoke briefly but his freshness and sparkle had been lost in the tussle to get from the car to the platform. And the main event of the day was ahead.

Meanwhile, several hundred thousand people had gathered at Callaway Park. They had begun to arrive at dawn. By four o'clock in the morning ten thousand people had come. Some of them were asleep in trailer-cars, others were lying on the ground. They had come from all parts of the country. Many drove shiny new cars, but most of them came in vehicles that had seen considerable use. The people had rallied as for a crusade. There had never been anything like it before in American politics. Never had so large a crowd gathered for an acceptance speech and in such heat. Indiana was scorched by a drought that summer. And the town was no attraction in itself. But despite the temperature, and the exhaustion from traffic congestion, these people were joyous and enthusiastic when they saw Willkie step onto the platform shortly before three o'clock.

Here was a man the nation acclaimed. All major newspapers in the country sent reporters to cover the event, all radio networks were hooked up for the broadcast. Congress had adjourned for the week-end so that Republican members could go to Elwood. Ten million people sat before their radios from Wall Street to Main Street.

"We are here today," the strong voice of Willkie began, "to represent a sacred cause—the preservation of American democracy. . . . We go into our campaign as into a crusade." He told how precious liberty was to all his family since the time his grandparents fled Prussia to find freedom in America. When the war came in 1917 three of the four boys in the family enlisted in the United States Army within one month after the declaration of hostilities, to preserve those same precious American traditions. "I cannot ask the American people to put faith in me, without recording my conviction that some form of selective service is the only democratic way in which to secure the trained and competent manpower we need for national defense."

On foreign issues, Willkie charged the President had "courted a war for which the country is hopelessly unprepared." His economic creed, he declared, was the restoration of full production and re-employment by private enterprise in America. The true test of a good reform must always be whether it has encouraged industries to produce, and whether it has opened up new opportunities for the youth of the land. "Will it increase our standard of living? Will it encourage us to open up a new and bigger world? . . . It is from weakness that people reach for dictators and concentrated government power. Only the strong can be free. And only the productive can be strong."

The policy of taxation under the New Deal, he said, had produced inevitable results. The investor has been afraid to invest his capital. The businessman has been afraid to expand his operations. "For the first time in our history, American industry has remained stationary for a decade."

In conclusion, Willkie made the most daring proposal ever

offered in an acceptance speech. It was repeated, next morning, in the front-page headlines of the metropolitan dailies throughout the nation: "I propose," he said, "that during the next two and a half months, the President and I appear together on public platforms in various parts of the country, to debate the fundamental issues of this campaign."

Late in the afternoon, as the cavalcade of thousands of automobiles carried the weary spectators in four directions from Elwood, many people were speculating as to whether Willkie would get his opportunity to meet the "Champ."

CHAPTER XII

The Campaign of Amateurs

RUMORS THAT the Old Guard politicians believed the Willkie campaign to have gone sour reached the ears of Justin Whiting, the new president of Commonwealth and Southern Corporation. Accordingly, from New York he telephoned Willkie at his home in Rushville to which the candidate had returned immediately after the Elwood ceremony. Whiting frankly told his former colleague that he was creating needless animosity by his brusque treatment of Republican politicians. "Call up headquarters from time to time," he suggested, "and ask the party officers how you are doing." The dead silence at the Rushville end of the telephone line clearly indicated that the friendly advice was not only ·rejected but also bitterly resented.

The politicians had indeed become discouraged with the performance of the Republican candidate at Colorado Springs. For nine weeks they had given him loyalty and co-operation, only to be ignored. They had offered their services and made suggestions, only to be snubbed. They had found it difficult even to obtain interviews with the candidate, while the amateurs, regardless of competence or experience, were received with open arms. The party leaders had been denied any consultation on the acceptance speech and many of them could not suppress a smile when it proved to be a disappointment.

Contradictions within the party ranks became distressing. Congressman Joseph W. Martin had pleaded with the candidate not to declare himself in favor of the military draft inasmuch as Republicans in Congress almost unanimously opposed the measure. But Willkie, impelled by his devotion to the truth, allotted a conspicuous section of his acceptance speech to support of compulsory military service. The patriotism and statesmanship of Willkie rose above any petty maneuvers of expediency. In taking his stand on the side of the President on this issue, Willkie undoubtedly contributed to Roosevelt's campaign. But his countrymen received the benefit of his forthrightness.

Such tactics of the Republican candidate, however, placed Martin in an embarrassing predicament. When the conscription bill was being drafted, Martin was absent from Washington. When the vote was taken, Martin surprised anti-conscriptionists by voting in favor of the bill; however, a majority of his Republican colleagues voted 112 to 51 against it. As for Willkie, he was too contemptuous of the Old Guard to come to Washington to make a personal appeal to Republican Congressmen to reverse a program of opposition which was detrimental to the country. Disturbed by the confusion of the campaign, Martin complained to Talbott: "I am not a rich man, but I will pay you ten thousand dollars if you will get me out of this task of chairman."

By the end of August, 1940, Joseph N. Pew, Jr., considered the Willkie campaign already lost. Dewey Short, Republican Representative from Missouri, with equal cynicism, croaked in the cloakrooms of the Capitol: "Roosevelt is not running against Willkie, he is running against Adolf Hitler." Thus Willkie's contempt for the political bosses led in turn to defection and even disloyalty on the part of the professional politicians whose support was indispensable for his victory at the November polls.

One of the amazing mysteries regarding Wendell Willkie was his lack of a sense of reality in American politics. His platonic idealism and his repugnance to political trading impelled him to disregard or belittle the place of political parties in American government. His hatred of dishonest bosses and shifty candidates warped his understanding of political leadership in modern democracy. "The fact that I got the nomination at Philadelphia proves the clumsiness of the politicians. I'm a different kind of an egg than the professionals have ever met and they just don't know what to make of it," he frequently boasted. Yet men like Stassen and Baldwin well recognized that it may be fine language to speak of a mass movement or of a spontaneous people's party, but the organization of political activities is an essential element for victory at the polls.

The humble party worker who knocks at the doors of all residents in his precinct, the precinct captain who directs and encourages the labors of the party workers, the ward chairman who supervises the precinct captains, the county committeeman who directs the ward bosses, the state committeeman who inspires the county committeemen to greater efforts, the chairman of the National Committee who vitalizes the state committees, together with the numerous workers at party headquarters scattered throughout the country—this army of thirty to forty thousand men and women are just as important in winning elections as is the candidate himself, and probably more so. Politicians agree that in American democracy, there is no such thing as a people's party. The so-called vote of the masses is a myth. The party is built upon the precinct worker who has the task of knowing every voter in his precinct and who gets the voters out to the polls on election day, rain or shine, to cast their ballots for the party's candidates. Politics is built on organization from the bottom up.

There were loyal friends of many years' standing who could have pointed out the pitfalls of Willkie's dangerous course. Among them was Raoul E. Desvernine, who was shocked at the ineptitude of the Willkie amateurs. On September 3, he drafted a long letter to the candidate, vividly describing the errors of the campaign and calling for a reform of strategy. The letter was never mailed. When the missive was completed, Desvernine became convinced that advice to Willkie was futile. Today, however, this document serves as a criticism of the campaign by a personal friend whose comments were based on an uncanny perception of events.

Desvernine sought first to say that the candidate was talking himself to defeat. "Stop shadow-boxing," urged Desvernine, "and concentrate on a few, simple fundamental issues." He advised Willkie to "personalize" a limited number of problems before the country. He proposed a maximum of four issues, namely: constitutional democracy, free enterprise, individual liberty versus totalitarianism, and American capitalism in opposition to the socialism of the New Deal. The second criticism was directed towards the lack of harmony within the party as to principles and policy. "Of course, unanimity is impossible, but the impression of unified opposition on fundamentals must exist," said Desvernine. "It is just good politics."

Lastly, Desvernine suggested a staff of researchers to provide the necessary facts in order to avoid the numerous errors which delighted the enemies of the Republican candidate. For instance, in Willkie's statement on the Property Condemnation Amendment to the Selective Service and Training Bill, the candidate failed to include any reference to the National Defense Act of 1916 and other legislation already on the statute books. Indeed, his statement seemed to imply that such legislation was entirely lacking, but an alert research staff, he said, would have avoided this blunder.

Perhaps it was unfortunate that Desvernine never sent his wise letter of advice, because Willkie might have harkened to an old friend in whom he had long had much confidence. Instead of such sympathetic counsel there were the carping attacks from the press and the sniping from party members. Irked by this constant criticism, Willkie made a concession to the politicians. He invited eighty party members from twenty-two eastern and midwestern states to come to Rushville for a one-day conference. Willkie had rented a large brick house on North Harrison Street with a shady lawn to serve as his home until the campaign caravan should begin its tour of the United States. On the fifth of September came the trek to Rushville, including Sinclair Weeks of Massachusetts, Samuel Pryor of Connecticut, James F. Torrence of Pennsylvania, David Ingalls of Ohio, and Harold Stassen of Minnesota. Homer Capehart, residing only a few miles away in Indianapolis, was not invited.

The Rushville conference was calculated to preserve the

"country-town spirit." A two-hour luncheon was served by the women of the Eastern Star, a fraternal organization. Then they all gathered on the Willkies' lawn, to listen to an informal and effective talk by the candidate. He urged his guests to take to heart the fact that he really was a Republican and indeed supported the entire Republican ticket. Again, he stressed that the campaign was a "crusade" against the New Deal philosophy which threatened to undermine the traditions of American democracy.

As usual, Willkie made an excellent impression upon his audience, but it accomplished little in ending the feud between the professional politicians and the amateurs. Nothing could placate the Republicans except the elimination of the amateurs from key positions on Willkie's staff. On his part, Willkie had been pricked by the cool response of the Republican leaders to his acceptance speech. This cleavage between Willkie and his party at the outset of the campaign foreshadowed trouble.

At Rushville, furthermore, Willkie began to ponder the failure of the press to acclaim his acceptance speech. He recalled that Desvernine had suggested, while in Colorado, a professional speech writer. Smarting under the criticism of his own associates, he decided to try out a political writer. But he rejected the well-known names that Desvernine had proposed. Whether it was doubt as to their ability or whether it was a desire to be more independent in his selection is a moot point. The thing he actually did was so naive as to be almost unbelievable. Willkie wrote to Carol Hill, a literary agent in New York City, asking her to procure for him an expert political writer. This was an unusual request for her to handle, so she telegraphed Raymond Moley, who was then vacationing in California, for advice.

Despite his amusement and perhaps even some irritation at this round-about approach for his help, Moley promptly recommended Elliott V. Bell, staff writer for the *New York Times*. Bell had drafted a number of speeches for Thomas E. Dewey when Dewey was District Attorney. When Moley returned to New York City on September 8, he found a distressed Bell awaiting him. Six precious weeks had slipped by, Bell pointed out, and it was almost time for the final speaking campaign to open. How could he take such an assignment? Moley tried to comfort him. Certainly he could do better than anyone else in the circumstances, Moley said. But Bell was not cheered. After an unsatisfactory long distance telephone call, Davenport hastened to New York to convince Bell that he was the one person Willkie wanted for this work. Finally Bell relented and agreed to join the Willkie campaign special train. But quite frankly he told Davenport that it was all useless, that it was too late to begin the writing of speeches, and that in his estimation the campaign was already lost. Certainly this was not an auspicious beginning for the Willkie-Bell-Davenport team.

In accord with traditional tactics in presidential campaigns, Willkie and his staff planned for a "swing around the country" in a special railroad train carrying the candidate and his wife and family, his staff of advisers and writers, local politicians who would board the train as it passed through their states, and finally a whole coterie of newspapermen and photographers. Stops would be made in principal cities for prepared speeches, but there were to be a large number of station stops also for a "few words" from the back end of the train.

On September 12, the campaign cavalcade of fourteen cars called "The Pioneer" left Rushville. As Willkie stepped aboard the train, he shouted to reporters: "I am opposed by the most ruthless gang of buccaneers in history."

In Chicago, the Willkie Special was met by a large delegation of Republicans including John Hamilton (chairman of the western campaign), Mrs. Bertha Baur (National Committeewoman for Illinois), Dwight Green (Illinois gubernatorial candidate), C. Wayland Brooks (senatorial candidate) and Werner Schroeder (National Committeeman). On this memorable Friday, the thirteenth, Willkie made four appearances.

The first stop was at the Union Stock Yards, where three thousand persons were lined up waiting for a look at Willkie. They were stolid and silent men who listened respectfully but without enthusiasm. Many of the workmen had come to the speech directly from the slaughter-houses wearing their soiled and blood-stained aprons. Despite the stench and surroundings, Willkie made an earnest plea. It was obvious, however, that he made few converts in the district of Chicago whose grimness had been pictured thirty years earlier in the novels of Upton Sinclair.

Leaving the stockyards, Willkie was taken to the Wilson Packing Company plant where about a thousand workers greeted him. He told these men that if he were elected President he would "create jobs instead of spinach." Referring to the European situation, he said that he had been a soldier and thus, if elected, he would see to it that no American boy would be sent to the "shambles of a European trench." This was a match for Roosevelt's "again and again and again" pledge that he would never send American boys to fight in foreign wars.

At his third stop, an audience of thirty thousand awaited him. This was at the Western Electric Company, located just outside Chicago in the town of Cicero. Willkie started his speech bravely. He began: "Now that we're in Chicago—" He got no further. Some rowdy in the crowd yelled out, "Not Chicago, this is Cicero." Willkie grinned. "All right," he replied. "To hell with Chicago!" Within twenty-four hours, the unfortunate language, intended in humor, appeared on the front page of almost every newspaper in the United States. Chicagoans who viewed Cicero as a town of gangsters were piqued, religious persons everywhere were shocked, and conservatives were rendered apprehensive of a candidate who would indulge in such reckless expressions. Newsmen accounted this episode as one of the worst blunders of the campaign.

Thereafter his associates on the Special listened to every speech in cold dread of what he might say. To a man like Willkie who was used to extemporaneous speaking and who even had a reputation for sparkling repartee from the platform, strict conformity to a script proved to be practically impossible.

Later in the day he addressed an audience of eight thousand Negroes assembled at the American Giants Baseball Park on Chicago's South Side. He promised them that, if elected, he would labor to eliminate discrimination of race and religion. The colored audience showed little enthusiasm. Indeed, the only ovation of the day occurred when Willkie passed through the financial section of the city on LaSalle Street. A blizzard of ticker-tape showered down upon him as he stood in his open automobile. Men and women, leaning out of tall buildings, yelled to him a tumultuous welcome. The "white collar" denizens of Chicago had become ardent supporters of the new Republican leader.

That evening, as the Willkie Special moved out of Chicago, the candidate's voice was husky. The first day of the campaign tour had been a long, fatiguing strain. He had refused to use a microphone as he was unused to the instrument and considered it an obstruction to his method of speaking. The next principal objective was Coffeyville in Kansas, with train speeches along the way at Joliet, Ottawa, LaSalle, Peoria, Rock Island, and Davenport. With each back-platform speech, Willkie's voice became more strained until by the time he reached Rock Island he could only whisper to the crowd: "The spirit is willing but the voice is weak."

At Peoria, Willkie again departed from script. He tried to reply to a jibe made by Henry A. Wallace that the Republican Party was "the party of appeasement." In his excitement he said: "Roosevelt is the great appeaser. At Munich what was Franklin Roosevelt doing? Was he standing up, fighting for democracy? Oh, no! He was telephoning Hitler and Mussolini and Chamberlain, urging them to sell Czechoslovakia down the river." The charge was, of course, not warranted. Roosevelt had made a bid for peace—an inconsequential bid, for he had nothing tangible to offer in the way of a threat. But in no sense could it be characterized as a proposal to dismember Czechoslovakia. Elliott Bell and Raymond Leslie Buell who was on the train as the adviser on foreign affairs, were frantic. They hastened to issue a statement to explain that what Willkie really meant was that Roosevelt had urged a settlement at Munich but that the Munich Pact actually had "sold Czechoslovakia down the river." To prevent the recurrence of such errors, Bell prepared notes for Willkie to use for his platform speeches. Never once did the candidate use these briefs. He would ad-lib from what he could remember of previous speeches or even the punch-lines of the next major address. On one occasion Willkie told a wayside audience that the American people were paying money into social security as into a bankrupt insurance company. When Bell took issue with him over such a reckless statement, the candidate replied: "I just can't get my ideas across if I go into all the ramifications of what I mean." Yet such mistakes brought charges from the Democrats that Willkie was addicted to careless and inaccurate statements.

As his throat condition became worse, so did the anxiety among his associates on the Willkie Special. They pleaded with him not to speak to the crowds that gathered at the railway stations, but merely to wave them a greeting. Willkie protested that the people had come to hear him talk and he did not want to disappoint them. Meanwhile, a telegram had been sent to Dr. Harold D. Barnard, a Hollywood throat specialist, who was flown from California by Robert Montgomery, the movie star and a warm friend of the candidate, and who met the train on Sunday at Kansas City. When the eminent physician confronted the patient he was greeted by a cold glare.

"Lean back and open your mouth," said Dr. Barnard.

"Go to hell and take your tools with you," growled Willkie in a rispy whisper.

Dr. Barnard looked at him a moment and said calmly, "Personally, I don't give a damn. But that throat of yours right now is the only way some twenty million Americans can express themselves. Lean back!"

Willkie looked at the doctor, suddenly grinned, and opened his mouth. Dr. Barnard relieved anxiety on the Willkie Special by his announcement that there was no throat infection but only some badly strained vocal chords. He ordered the patient not to speak again until he reached Coffeyville. That evening as the train left Kansas City, Willkie bumped his way forward to the press car. He sat down with the reporters and rasped: "Anybody here got a cigarette? They won't let me have one back there." He explained there was really nothing wrong with him, he was just a little hoarse. Apparently he was the only one on the train who was not concerned over his condition and the possibility that the entire campaign tour might have to be canceled. One reporter described him as every bit as cocky as "an unbroken college freshman."

The speech at Coffeyville on Monday afternoon, the sixteenth speech on the tour, was to be the first big speech of the campaign, with a national radio hookup. Coffeyville had been selected by Russell Davenport because Willkie had once taught there. Notwithstanding the experience at Elwood, he still wanted to dramatize the American small town. Coffeyville, therefore, was to be a symbol of all towns. Furthermore, it was planned to show how the New Deal had injured this fine little community in the Midwest, by its public power program. Then it was discovered that Coffeyville had a very successful municipal electric system, and from its profits had paid the entire cost of street paving.

This discovery required that the pattern of the speech be quickly changed. Instead of talking about public utilities, Willkie shifted to a discussion of dictatorship. From miles around, people came to hear him. Fifty thousand countryfolk jammed the ball park, now called Willkie Park, to listen to the Wizard of Wall Street. On this occasion, he made no departure from his script. Moreover, his voice had greatly improved by the rest and treatment of the past twenty-four hours. He gave a fine performance. In fact, his delivery was much better than at Elwood.

On Monday evening, Willkie spoke at Tulsa, Oklahoma. A crowd of forty thousand whooped and hollered a welcome to him. Willkie made a special appeal here to Democrats to vote for him. "For the life of me," he said, "I cannot see why any real Democrat would vote against me. Every Democrat ought to applaud me for this crusade, for upholding the two term tradition. Surely, no Democrat will vote against me who believed in the 1932 Democratic platform. I believed in it then. I voted for it. I still believe in it."

Traveling on the Willkie Special was a corps of top-ranking newspapermen, a research staff, and a secretarial staff. There was a valet-barber, a radio coach, and the throat specialist. The top echelon advisers were Russell Davenport and Raymond Buell. Unhappily, Buell took ill with pneumonia and left the train a few days out of Chicago. He was replaced by Brooks Emeny. The second group of advisers included Elliott V. Bell, Pierce Butler, Jr., and John B. Hollister. Butler was one of the Democrats-for-Willkie leaders. He wrote a few speeches but mostly handled the wire stories. The routing of the tour was the work of Harold J. Gallagher. Only two regular Republicans were on the train: Hollister and Halleck. Hollister had been assigned to the Willkie Special as the official representative of the National Republican Committee.

The candidate's family included his wife Edith, his son Philip, and two brothers, Edward and Fred. Fred was on the Special only for a few days. Mrs. Willkie became a favorite with the crowds that met the train for platform speeches. Frequently she was called for by the crowd before it was quite time to present her. Although she never spoke a word, her gracious smile and friendly manner were highly satisfying. Edward was the official greeter of visitors aboard the Willkie Special when the candidate was otherwise occupied.

Practically all speeches were written on the train. Bell had explained when he first joined the Willkie Special that the proper way to write campaign speeches was for several writers to sit down with the candidate, discuss their ideas, and then separate to write drafts which the candidate must then go over to make appropriate changes. There must be continual discussion between writer and candidate that each might understand the views and objectives of the other. During the entire six weeks' tour, Bell talked with Willkie only five times, and then never under the conditions that he had proposed.

Accordingly, the staff wrote speeches based on the writer's own surmises of what the candidate wanted to say. Immediately after completion, all speeches were delivered to Davenport who sought to "improve" them. After the poet had partly ruined half a dozen good speeches by his fine writing, Pierce Butler upbraided Davenport and beseeched him to let the speeches alone. Davenport was highly offended.

Bell was attempting to write one speech after another. Occasionally he received some relief from Bartley Crum, of San Francisco, or Pierce Butler. On one occasion, after Roosevelt had attacked Willkie, the candidate announced that a reply would be made the following day at ten o'clock over a national hookup. So close was the margin of time that Bell was still writing the speech and rushing the pages to the microphone as Willkie was talking.

The candidate continued to improvise, and thereby often ruined the sequence of ideas in an otherwise good speech. Rarely did Willkie read an address aloud before giving it. This was partly due to the lack of time and the general confusion; and partly because he failed to understand the need for rehearsal. As a result, he frequently placed the emphasis in the wrong place, with the result that his audience would often cheer the wrong sentiments.

From Tulsa, the cavalcade proceeded towards the Southwest, through New Mexico and Arizona to California. Three principal speeches were scheduled for California; San Diego on September 18, Los Angeles on the following evening, and San Francisco on the twenty-first. Between these engagements were numerous short speeches often delivered from an automobile. California had been termed a "doubtful state."

Thirty thousand spectators gathered at Lane Field Baseball Park, San Diego. As Willkie stood on the platform ready to speak, a single voice sang out, "We want Roosevelt!" Instantly, Willkie flashed back: "There you are, one in a hundred thousand and they are growing fewer every day." The crowd was delighted and responded with prolonged cheering. California gave Willkie the largest crowds and the loudest cheers thus far received on the tour. The warmth, the acclaim, and the homage were beyond expectations. To observers it looked as if all the handsome candidate had to do to win the state was to ride through the towns and villages in an open car waving his hand to the welcoming throngs.

At Los Angeles, Willkie was met with exuberant enthusiasm. On Wednesday evening, seventy thousand people filled the Coliseum. A Hollywood entrance had been arranged for the candidate. His car was held at the mouth of the tunnel leading directly onto the field. When he was introduced as the "next President of the United States," the candidate and Mrs. Willkie rode into the dark arena with spotlights illuminating the car as it crossed the field. The crowd rose and began to chant, "We want Willkie." The band of the Hollywood Legion Post played, "California Here I Come" and "Back Home in Indiana." When he mounted the platform, the band played, "Hail, Hail, the Gang's All Here," with the crowd joyously singing the chorus. The press declared it was the greatest ovation ever received at any time by any candidate in Los Angeles.

Willkie discussed business and taxes. It was not what this

cheering, gay, ebullient audience wanted. They were in the mood for gag-lines and slam-bang oratory. After ten minutes, the audience began to trickle away. The speech, unfortunately, was not in tune with the theatrical setting.

More successful was the speech delivered at San Francisco on the twenty-first. Willkie quoted the powerful words of Winston Churchill spoken in 1937: "There is one way above all others in which the United States can aid the European democracies. Let her regain and maintain her normal prosperity."

Meanwhile, confusion on the Willkie Special increased. The jealous conflict between the amateurs and the politicians reached its height in California. Members of the Willkie Clubs vied with the politicians for preferment even in boarding the train and riding the fifty or hundred mile stretch allotted to local leaders. Although the Willkie Clubs had been a unique and powerful agency before the Philadelphia Convention, they had since become an increasing liability. One of the experienced Democrats-for-Willkie plainly told the candidate that they had become a vicious influence in the campaign. They lacked the discipline and responsibility of the party organization. Sometimes even, a discontented party member who had been booted out of the Republican organization gained control of a local Willkie Club. On one occasion, the head of a Willkie Club forced out a Republican Party member who thereupon devoted his time to the election of the Governor. This candidate won the election by a majority of one hundred thousand votes while Willkie lost the state by some twenty thousand.

It had been expected by the politicians that these clubs would be co-ordinated under Republican leadership during the campaign. But Oren Root resisted all such attempts, and in loyalty to him, Willkie allowed his campaign to be injured while the clubs continued to function as an amateur organization.

So great, indeed, was the confusion that Elliott Bell considered the campaign hopeless and in San Francisco explained to Davenport that he was leaving the train to return to New York. He had been grinding out speeches day and night since leaving Rushville, yet he rarely had a moment with the candidate to discuss ideas or policies. He felt he was caught in a stultifying position. Davenport was distressed. He urged Bell to remain to the end of the campaign, as otherwise gossip would say that he left in a pique. Reluctantly Bell agreed but inwardly he writhed in indignation over the chaotic situation under which he had to work.

From California, the Willkie Special rolled on to Portland, where another major speech was scheduled. This was the territory of Willkie's running mate, Senator Charles L. McNary. It was also the section containing the Grand Coulee Dam project which had proved extremely popular in the Northwest. The speech writers decided that the locale required an address on public utilities. Accordingly, the candidate delivered a speech which was regarded in some quarters as an abandonment of his former position on public utilities. He said: "The people in the area affected should determine whether this power is distributed through private or publicly owned local utilities."

It was also in Portland that Willkie began the reckless series of promises for which he was castigated by the press. The Gallup polls showed that he was losing the campaign. Therefore he was urged to make specific commitments. As a consequence, he promised to maintain the Wagner Labor Relations Act under whose rigid clauses all industry was suffering. Willkie promised to expand social security. He promised to combine soil conservation, commodity loans, rural electrification, farm credit and crop insurance. He promised to give a place in the Cabinet to the Northwest. He promised to call a national conference of farmers, labor and industry to plan national prosperity. He promised to revise and make more equitable the tax laws. He promised to maintain for the people the gains made in public power. Lastly, he promised to provide jobs for every man and woman in the United States willing to work and to continue public relief to those who could not work.

In addition to such specific pledges, he promised that his crusade would culminate in building a new America with higher standards of life than "we have ever dreamed of before." Finally at Yonkers, New York, he said: "I pledge a new world." As one of his disappointed Wall Street friends said: "He suddenly tried to out-promise Roosevelt, and that was like trying to out-Santa-Claus Santa Claus."

From Portland, the Willkie Special stopped only at Seattle

before turning eastward with scheduled speeches in Omaha, Madison and Yonkers. The address at Madison was considered by correspondents as the best of the tour. The amateurs had failed, however, to have it radioed to the nation. The address was delivered at the Field House on the campus of the University of Wisconsin where the candidate was awaited by a heckling, howling mob of students and townspeople. At the outset, he captivated his young listeners by referring to the early evening broadcast of the Democratic Party which made two serious charges against him: first, that he frequently split his infinitives, and second, that Katharine Hepburn opposed him. "I plead guilty," he said, "to the charge of splitting infinitives. I also have occasional trouble with the accusative case. As for the charge that Miss Hepburn is against me, I can only say that Mary Pickford, Robert Montgomery and Walter O'Keefe are on my side." The students loudly cheered. Willkie always made a special appeal to young people, and his speech this evening had been especially geared to suit their temperament. They loved it. He ended the tumult and the jeering almost with his first sentence. From then on the audience was his.

He enjoyed historical references. In the afternoon of the same day, he delighted a mid-western audience with a summary of celebrated Democrats who undoubtedly would give him their blessing. Jefferson opposed the grant of far-reaching powers to the federal Government, he said. At the same time, Jefferson strongly believed that the presidential office should be limited to two terms. On these grounds Willkie claimed the support of all Jeffersonian Democrats. "As for Andrew Jackson," continued Willkie, "he balanced the budget, and even eliminated the national debt. Surely all Andrew Jackson Democrats should vote for me." Governor Grover Cleveland was opposed to centralization of power in Washington and he refused to run for a third term. Consequently "No Cleveland Democrat should vote against me," said Willkie. William Jennings Bryan was opposed to concentration of federal power. "No Bryan Democrat should vote against me," added Willkie. Woodrow Wilson held that the function of the state in the governing of men was

to see that they did not prey upon each other. Accordingly,
"No Woodrow Wilson Democrat should vote against me."

Willkie had telephoned Hamilton at his headquarters in
Chicago to meet him in Madison and to continue with the
Willkie Special to New York. This Hamilton did. Shortly after
the train left Madison, therefore, Willkie sent for him to come
back to his Pullman car. Stretching out on the bed for a little
rest, Willkie opened the conversation. He asked Hamilton to
take back the full chairmanship of the National Committee,
because, he said, Joe Martin had double-crossed him.

Hamilton refused even to consider the resumption of the
chairmanship. The pattern of the campaign was already set, he
explained. If it were successful, Martin should get the credit,
and, if a failure, Hamilton should not take the blame. Moreover,
Willkie was in error in his belief that Martin had betrayed
him, he said. His appointment as national chairman in the first
place, said Hamilton, had been a mistake. No man should be
asked to run a campaign who had to maintain his own voting
record. Martin's ambition was aimed at securing the speakership
of the House of Representatives. Thus, Martin's first loyalty
was to his own constituency rather than to Willkie. On the
other hand, Hamilton told him, it would be foolhardy from a
personal standpoint to turn Martin out at this time. If Willkie
should be elected President, said Hamilton, Martin would
become Speaker of the House. How much co-operation would
he then receive from Martin?

"Well," said Willkie, "the organization is disloyal to me."
Again Hamilton scoffed. They were not disloyal to him, he
explained. A leader receives from party workers the loyalty he
himself exhibits. "They will work for you and they will vote
for you. But your lack of confidence in them will cost you six
hours of work on election day," he chided. When a precinct
captain is enthusiastic about his candidate, he works from six
until six. But if he is not enthusiastic he does only poll duty.
The result in this case would be the loss of from five to seven
votes per precinct, which may cost the election, Hamilton
predicted.

"But why," persisted Willkie, "is the organization so opposed

to me? Herbert Hoover used amateurs in his campaign of 1928."
Patiently Hamilton explained the wide difference. The amateurs in the Hoover campaign tied in with the regular organization. When an old-timer went into the headquarters and
began to look around, feeling strange, an experienced party man
suddenly appeared from nowhere and greeted him with a warm
handshake and taking him by the arm whispered in his ear that
he would find "the boys" over at the Mayflower Hotel. Thus
the regular party men were made to feel welcome. But Willkie
seemed unable or unwilling to grasp the political angle of such
an arrangement.

Although the hour was now late, Willkie wanted to discuss
Pew. What should be done about the arrogant Pennsylvania
boss who had quit the campaign to go on a fishing trip at his
summer home in New Brunswick? Hamilton advised him either
to make peace with Pew or to denounce him openly. "In the
case of Pew, you only told reporters you didn't like him. Thus
you are not getting his support, and, at the same time, you are
not winning the support of his enemies."

Willkie agreed that it was the best policy to make peace with
Pew. "But what shall I do?" he asked. Hamilton suggested sending Pew a telegram. "All right," said Willkie, "you send him
a telegram and tell him I will be at the Commodore Hotel
[Republican headquarters] this week-end. He can sneak up the
back way and no one will see him."

Hamilton slowly shook his head. That was hardly the way to
do it. He reminded the candidate that when he kicked Pew
aside on Tuesday following the convention, the act was performed before reporters at a press conference. Pew could hardly
be expected to come back at this date except by an open invitation from Willkie himself, said Hamilton. As a result of this
conversation, Pew was given an invitation to board the Willkie
Special when it reached New York. Pew accepted and, as he
ostentatiously passed through the corridor of Grand Central
Station to join Willkie, he saw to it that newspaper reporters
followed his triumphal approach to the Republican candidate.

The first leg of the swing around the country was scheduled
to end with a speech on September twenty-eighth at the Empire
City Race Track at Yonkers in New York. On the eastward

journey, the Willkie Special had been slowed down by engine trouble so that Willkie left the train at Syracuse, and flew to Yonkers. The state Republican Convention had convened in that city, and forty-five thousand good Republicans waited impatiently for his arrival. His car drove into the floodlights of the race track at four minutes to nine o'clock, the appointed hour of his speech. The crowd recognized him and yelled their welcome. When he finished speaking, the delighted throng would not let him leave the platform but called him back four times for encore speeches.

After the Yonkers meeting, Willkie drove to the town apartment of Samuel Pryor. Here John L. Lewis awaited the candidate. The bristling president of the United Mine Workers of America and founder of the Congress of Industrial Organization had exhausted the bounty of Roosevelt and now was eager for personal revenge. Willkie was not adverse to winning the support of the angry labor czar. It would be folly to reject the labor support which Lewis might swing to the Republican ticket, he thought. After listening to an astonishing tirade on F.D.R. by the labor leader, Willkie hastened to make his own position clear. He would not surrender to any group in either labor or management, or favor one side against the other as had Roosevelt during the past eight years. While he stood for governmental impartiality as between labor and management, he would seek to correct the discrimination then existing in the National Labor Relations Board against management. In turn, he would always maintain the right of collective bargaining as one of the pillars of American economic freedom, and he agreed that a large part of the Wagner Act could properly be viewed as a fundamental charter of labor.

The hours ticked by. Conversation droned on till early morning. Pryor dozed in his chair. Finally, Lewis leaned forward, and, with a note of finality, declared: "If you will say publicly what you have said to me now, I will support you."

Willkie promptly replied: "Where do you want me to say it?"

"In your Pittsburgh speech," the shrewd Lewis replied.

"Agreed," said the candidate.

Willkie was enthusiastic over the sudden conversion of Lewis. He thought Lewis could swing him the CIO labor vote. On the other hand, Willkie's advisers could muster small interest in the accession of Lewis and some of them were plainly distraught. Hamilton, who had remained in New York for several days, was much concerned over the matter. He told the candidate that it would be disastrous to have Lewis speak, as it would offend the American Federation of Labor. Furthermore, three Republican governors had recently been elected because of their opposition to left-wing labor. If ever a man went down on his knees, Hamilton later disclosed, he did at this time in an effort to dissuade Willkie from association with Lewis. Thereafter, Governor John W. Bricker cooled perceptibly towards the campaign. Many other leading Republicans were exasperated. Governor Arthur James of Pennsylvania never made another speech for Willkie.

Lewis demanded opportunity to make an hour's address on a national radio hookup which would cost $45,000 in radio fees, while he refused to speak under the sponsorship of the Republican National Committee. The Democrats-for-Willkie were reluctant to sponsor Lewis and to accept the financial burden. Eventually, the argument that Lewis might swing four million votes to the Republican side won the day and they agreed to pay for radio time. It was settled that Lewis should speak from Washington on October 25.

On the following day, Willkie again boarded his special train for Detroit, Grand Rapids, Cleveland, and finally Pittsburgh, where he was scheduled to give his labor speech on October 3. A motor tour through Pontiac, Kalamazoo and Grand Rapids impressed Willkie as never before with the bitterness of the class hatred which had developed in America in seven short years. Workmen leaned out of the factory windows as his car passed by to boo defiance at him. At Pontiac he spoke in the town square to an audience that listened in a sullen mood. As he finished speaking, hoodlums began to throw eggs at him. One struck Willkie in the face and another spattered Edith Willkie as she was to enter the car. Willkie swung around fiercely to see from whence it came. He had taken in stride the missiles thrown at him, but his anger flared when the rowdies aimed at Mrs. Willkie. There was a tense moment. But Edith smiled and began to hand out roses from the large bouquet in her arms to the small boys near by. The newsmen, who adored her, had started to close in to protect her, but now relaxed. One of them voiced the opinion of all when he said: "There's a little champion."

Willkie rejoined his special train at Grand Rapids. As the train pulled out of the siding, a rock was hurled through a window. For the first time in more than a generation, an election campaign had become a matter of physical assault. Edward J. Flynn spoke for the Democratic Party when he said that he hoped the guilty persons would be punished. Congress passed a resolution in condemnation of such rowdyism, and President Roosevelt himself denounced as reprehensible the action of persons who threw missiles at the Republican candidate. At the same time, it was soon evident that every egg and every stone thrown at Willkie meant thousands of votes for the Republican candidates.

While in Michigan, Willkie took occasion to reply to a speech made by Governor Herbert H. Lehman, of New York, on September thirtieth, before the Democratic State Convention. The Governor had declared that nothing could give greater satisfaction to Hitler, Mussolini, Stalin and the Japanese militarists than the defeat of Roosevelt by Willkie. In reply, Willkie charged Lehman with false, malicious and subversive innuendo. Resort to such language in the present world crisis, he contended, threatened the safety of all Americans. If the President's party branded all opponents as Nazis and Fascists, it would be but another step for the President to prohibit the existence of any political opposition in the United States as inimical to the Government in office.

The Governor made no apology or retraction. Other members of the Democratic Party were less subtle in their efforts to link Willkie to the Hitler menace. A short time later, Henry A. Wallace, candidate for the vice-presidency, declared in a public address: "The Nazi support of Wendell Willkie is part of Adolf Hitler's plan to weaken and eventually conquer the United States. A Republican victory in November is a necessity for the dictator's plans to overthrow our peace and our liberties." On the eve of the election, Chairman Edward J. Flynn released a statement to the press stating that "Every Nazi and Fascist organization in the United States is for the Republican presidential candidate." Dorothy Thompson announced over the Columbia Broadcasting System that "A vote for Wendell Willkie is a vote for fascism."

Never, since the campaign of 1860, when the Southern Democrats flung the grossest libels against Abraham Lincoln, had American presidential politics sunk to such a low level. This "smear" was the more reprehensible inasmuch as the Republican candidate had refused to take advantage of the unpopularity of the President's position on foreign policy. The Selective Training and Service Act was most unpopular. But Willkie gave full support to the draft. The President had strained his constitutional powers by his military aid to Great Britain in the transfer of fifty American destroyers. Willkie raised no point of criticism. A less patriotic candidate would have unleashed the fury of the isolationism of the Midwest against an Administration committed to such explosive issues.

On the way to Cleveland, the Willkie Special stopped at Toledo, Ohio. Willkie detrained at Sylvania and drove into the city through the industrial area. Here he found the same expressions of hostility that had been exhibited by the workers in the factory towns in Michigan. As his car passed along the streets, men in their soiled work-clothes and women in greasy slacks shook their firsts at him and bellowed epithets. Crudely lettered signs were held aloft, saying: "Roosevelt Forever," "Win What with Willkie?" and "To Hell with Willkie." Through the long line of mocking hecklers, Willkie maintained a stiff set smile. He believed that he could win these men if only he could talk to them as man to man. In his Toledo speeches as well as in Michigan he pleaded with the unruly toilers to lend him their ears and to open their minds to his words. "Please listen to me on the radio, please listen to me before you decide," he implored. "If we go down this New Deal road, democracy will disappear. Please listen to me. Don't let them lead you like cattle to the shambles. Boos don't hurt me. All I ask is a square shake."

At Cleveland, a more receptive audience awaited him. There were enormous crowds, hysterical ovations and frantic applause. But, too frequently now, Willkie had wasted his energies on addresses to small audiences of workmen and was tired and exhausted when he appeared before large and responsive audiences. His fatigue showed itself in his voice. He hurried one sentence on top of another; he slurred his words so that the sense was sometimes lost. The Cleveland address was intended to be his most important speech on foreign policy. Yet its delivery was almost a failure. Today, the speech reads far better than it sounded in Cleveland.

An audience of thirty thousand had gathered in Forbes Field in Pittsburgh to hear him. In Washington, John L. Lewis awaited the speech before making his declaration of support. Willkie chose the text of his address from the words of Abraham Lincoln: " 'Labor is prior to and independent of capital. Capital is only the fruit of labor, could never have existed if labor had not first existed. Labor is, therefore, the superior of capital and deserves much higher consideration.' " Then he declared, "I stand with Abraham Lincoln. I have earned my bread by the sweat of my brow and I know, as well as any man, the strong bond that unites those who labor. But this bond should not lead to war on business, or upon property. Because, as Lincoln also said: 'Property is the fruit of labor; property is desirable; it is a positive good in the world. Let not him who is houseless pull down the house of another but let him work diligently and build one for himself, thus by example, assuring that his own will be safe when built.' "

On this thesis Willkie proceeded to extend his own position. "I stand," he said, "for a democratic society resting on the Bill of Rights and a system of private property with full rights for labor. I subscribe without reservation to the principle of collective bargaining by representatives of labor's own free choice. I stand for maximum wages and minimum hours and for legislation to enforce them. I stand for social security benefits and I believe that they should be extended to other groups." He declared his labor program included a conciliation service under the federal Government, labor representation in the councils of the Government, enforcement of a minimum wage in the South, extension of legislation to regulate maximum hours, and decentralized activities of the federal Government. But he also admonished labor leaders that they must eliminate the racketeer from the unions and that labor must work with management for a cooling-off period in all company contracts. The program was a moderate plan of labor-management relations. But it probably gained few votes for Willkie. It satisfied neither labor nor business.

The Lewis speech, which soon followed, was a great disappointment to Willkie and more especially to the professional politicians. Too obviously his support of the Republican candidate was based entirely on his spleen towards the President. His pettish threat to resign as president of the CIO in case Roosevelt were re-elected was castigated by labor leaders in every section of the country. Newsmen thought that the speech actually injured the Republican campaign. Hamilton was certain that it did. He was in New York when the speech was made and heard it over the radio in his room at the Waldorf-Astoria. As he was leaving his room immediately afterwards to return to western headquarters, a telegram was delivered to him. It was from a prominent labor leader and read: "After tonight I cannot do anything to help your boy."

Ever and constantly the advice of the regular politician was spurned and the advice of the amateur accepted. Old friends, neutral observers of the trend, tried to warn Willkie that he was courting disaster, but to no avail. As one wag expressed it, "Trying to give Willkie advice is just as effective as giving castor oil to the Sphinx!"

Moreover, there were numerous slights to leading Republicans in every state through which the Willkie Special passed. On one such occasion, a particularly important man came aboard the train. Hamilton had labored strenuously to interest him in the Republican Party and had finally succeeded in getting him to accept the chairmanship of the Finance Committee of the Republican Party in his state. The man, furthermore, had contributed liberally to the national as well as to the state chest. One day Hamilton received a sharp telephone call from this man. He had been on the Willkie Special for two days and two nights and had not yet met the candidate. He was quitting the train therefore, and he was going to resign as finance chairman, too. Hamilton conciliated him and said there had been some mistake, and that he would clear everything up in an hour. He then telephoned Davenport and explained the situation to him. "Oh," replied Davenport, "Willkie is too busy to be bothered with shaking hands with all those people!"

Even Sam Pryor, his good friend and eastern manager, was given the brush-off. Early in the campaign, Pryor sent Willkie a telegram on behalf of Bruce Barton and several other party leaders saying that Barton felt further assistance should be given to the preparation of speeches. From Flint, Michigan, came the fiery reply. The candidate telegraphed that he would appreciate it very much if all supporters in New York would concentrate on building the organization in the East rather than giving so much concern to speeches. "Apparently Bruce Barton did not think my speech at the Republican Convention was any good. I thought his speech was lousy, but I was too courteous to tell him so. We can win if the organization will concentrate on organization and let me concentrate on the campaign."

In Detroit, the Republican Party boss called at the hotel to see Willkie. Later, when his boys gathered around him to ask, "What kind of a guy is Willkie?" he had to answer, "Sorry, I didn't get to meet him!" Matters of this kind are most important to politicians. As John Hamilton so well knew: "It's the stuff that unites and binds the party together." It is what builds party morale.

Halleck quit the train when it arrived in New York after the Yonkers speech in anger and humiliation. He complained that he and his wife had not once been invited to the rear end of the train where the Willkie private headquarters were located. And never was his advice sought, or any of his suggestions acted upon.

The trip to New England became something of a riot. J. Wells Farley, a distinguished attorney in Boston, and a member of the Board of Overseers of Harvard University, arranged an auto-caravan tour through Massachusetts. Being a very methodical person, he had worked out a time schedule to the minute. But immediately after the Providence speech (October 10), Willkie was so exhausted that he asked Sinclair Weeks to telephone Farley and cancel the entire itinerary except the major speech at Boston on the following evening. As a result, Farley sat up all night telephoning local leaders saying that Willkie would not be able to come, but he appreciated all their wonderful help and support!

Quite early the following morning Willkie changed his mind again. He sent for Sinclair Weeks and told him to telephone Farley he would come after all. When Weeks relayed the message, Farley exploded. "Where are you now," he barked, "Well, stay right there until I arrive. I will be there in less than one hour!" The train followed along with the automobile caravan and was used as headquarters for the candidate and his entourage. When Farley arrived at the train, Willkie was not yet dressed. As Farley waited in the back-end lounge of the Willkie suite, he impatiently beat a nervous tap with his foot. Pierce Butler wandered through the car and came upon him. "Will you tell me what goes on here?" asked Farley. "I will tell you," said the learned son of the former distinguished Supreme Court Justice. "This place is like a whore-house on a Saturday night when the madam is out, and all the girls are running around dropping nickels in the juke boxes!"

The Willkie tour had been replete with political melodrama as well as amateur bungling. In the farm sections and the financial centers the candidate was greeted by swarming crowds and fanatical enthusiasm. The inspirational quality of Willkie was an innovation in politics. The other side of the picture showed the candidate facing hostile audiences in the slums and factory districts, where even physical violence broke out, and where, in almost humble terms, he pleaded for a fair hearing. In all this there was a touch of revivalist fervor. The tour was in fact a crusade, and like all crusades there was an emotional ecstasy, a slay-the-dragon complex.

Harold Gallagher ecstatically cried that "Willkie is God's gift to America." There were thousands who felt the same way. Strong, successful businessmen would come up to the candidate after a speech and ask to shake his hand. "You don't know what it means to me, Mr. Willkie, just to touch you," some would say. By such admirers he was looked upon as the bearer of the sacred torch, the prophet sent to lead the people.

The final speech was at Madison Square Garden in New York City. This is the traditional ending to a presidential campaign.

The occasion demands a dramatic and scintillating speech. Moreover Willkie was especially desirous of a high-sounding speech. So in writing the speech, Bell put peroration first and persuasion second.

Early Friday evening as the Special was speeding eastward for this last engagement, Bell read the finished speech to the small inner circle, Hollister, Butler, Davenport, and Willkie. As usual, at its conclusion, Davenport thought the speech needed a little touching up to improve it here and there. After the little conclave broke up, Butler went to the "Chief" and urged him not to let Davenport spoil this excellent speech as he had so many others. He asked Willkie to release the speech to the press at once.

The candidate seemed convinced but decided first to talk to Bell and Davenport, alone. In this interview Willkie almost pleaded with Davenport to let well enough alone and not to make any changes. However, Bell was most generous and said that Davenport with his special touch might very well improve the speech as it was really the first draft anyway. Thereupon, Willkie slid out of the awkward situation by saying that the two of them should work it out together.

When the two men sat down in the quiet of Bell's drawing room to talk over revision, Davenport suddenly jumped up exclaiming that he could not work that way. So he left Bell, taking the manscript with him. All night long he fiddled over the speech. When the train pulled into New York City the following morning (Saturday) Davenport had finished it. But there was no time for any further revision or changes. It had to be released to the press immediately. It began: "This is the battle of America. The drums of victory are rolling, rolling, rolling. The thunderous drums of an aroused electorate are beating in the nation tonight. Victory, victory is on the march. . . . A free people now arise to write a single word across the vast American sky: Liberty, Liberty, Liberty!"

However, as the *New York Times* wrote, it mattered little what the candidate said that night anyway because the vast uproarious crowd gave him an ovation at every pause. His voice was painfully hoarse, the candidate was fatigued, but the crowd was happy and enthusiastic. The people had begun to come to the Garden by four o'clock, some six hours before the candidate was scheduled to speak. When he arrived, punctually at 10:15, the great throng broke into one vast yelling, screaming, flag-waving body. For fifteen minutes as the precious radio time slowly slipped away, they cheered and would not be quieted by the chairman, Kenneth Simpson. It was a magnificent demonstration.

The speech carried a refrain every few paragraphs: "This is the method of the New Deal. It is not the method of democracy." The crowd soon caught the reiteration and took up the chant with him. It was, indeed, a wild, tumultuous, gay audience, thoroughly with the candidate in everything he said.

The campaign was over. No other candidate had ever attempted to spread his message over so extensive a territory. It was the longest continuous campaign tour on record. Willkie had averaged six to ten speeches a day and sometimes as many as fifteen, and he had traveled thirty thousand miles.

Willkie's glowing devotion to the cause of freedom did not prevent contradictions in his political creed. He had long advocated governmental economy. But at Los Angeles he approved an increase in old-age pensions. This city was the home of the Townsend Plan and of the Ham and Egg Movement, and some critics said that while campaigning in California Willkie had found it opportune to surrender to the crackpots. Willkie had repeatedly favored maximum aid to Britain and China in their heroic struggle against totalitarian aggressors, but at San Bernardino, he paid a glowing tribute to Hiram Johnson, long known for his isolationism, while the St. Louis speech was considered by many observers as an appeal to the isolationist sentiment of the Middle West. For seven years he had fought public electric power, but at the Republican National Convention in Philadelphia he accepted as his candidate for Vice-President, Charles McNary, who had loudly demanded public power projects for the Northwest. In the thirties, he had opposed wages and hours legislation as an interference with the laws of economics; in a free economic system, he had contended, the market determines such matters as wages and conditions of labor. In the campaign of 1940, however, he accepted both proposals.

Many of his old friends who had been his most ardent boosters before the Philadelphia Convention began to lose faith. His abrupt swings to the left disturbed them. It meant that the issues of the campaign were blurred. There was indeed a sharp difference between Willkie and the New Deal, but unhappily he never made it crystal clear to the voters. Willkie believed that a free economy was the most competent system to provide more jobs and a higher standard of living for all citizens of the United States. He believed that democracy and private enterprise were indispensable to each other and that both were imperiled by the New Deal experiments with collectivism. Free enterprise could not long survive either in a government atmosphere of hostility or under domination of federal control. Federal regulation yes, but not strangulation. Among economists, it was generally recognized that the Tennessee Valley Authority, the Social Security Act, the National Labor Relations Act, and the Corporate-Surplus Tax were all part of a program for a controlled economy.

Another issue of the campaign was the constitutional question of the third term, which, however, Willkie failed to exploit to the full. The Jeffersonian Democrats and the Democrats-for-Willkie supported Willkie primarily on the issue of the third term. Foreign policy was not an issue in the campaign. With the highest of patriotic motives, Willkie kept the questions of national defense and of aid to Great Britain out of the contest.

The campaign had been waged under unusual difficulties. The imminence of war made many Americans loath to "change horses in midstream." Moreover, the party lacked funds. The distrust of Willkie by the professional politicians closed many sources of revenue and the strict interpretation of the Hatch Act was a severe handicap. Finally, there was the dissension within the Willkie organization. It was Gallagher who routed the campaign train across the country and who sent out the tickets for the visitors on the Willkie Special. Neither Hamilton, nor Pryor, nor any of the state Republican chairmen were ever consulted. The men who best knew the situation were never asked for advice or suggestions. In fact Hamilton learned about the campaign schedule for the West from the newspapers.

Willkie was never an organization man. He was a star, a lone performer. Possessed of a dogged determination, he had a passionate zeal and a lustrous flame and enthusiasm for any undertaking. But he lacked the understanding of group co-operation.

His detachment from his party was a fatal blunder. He spent much time trying to convice the people that his policies and objectives were very different from those of the Republican Party as represented in Congress. This lack of agreement and unity between Republicans in Congress and the presidential candidate presented a sorry spectacle. He was attempting to reform the party and change its policy at the same time he was running a campaign. Even this he might have accomplished if he had taken some of the party's leaders into his confidence and worked through them. This, of course, he refused to do because he thought all politicians were tainted persons who had lost the confidence of the people. In effect he was asking the voter to believe in him and not in his party. Hence his emphasis upon the amateurs and the subordination of party men.

Election day came on Tuesday, November fifth. After casting his ballot in the morning, Willkie spent most of the day in his suite on the fourteenth floor of the Commodore Hotel. The Commodore had been Republican Headquarters for the eastern division. In an adjacent suite, two news tickers were installed for the use of statisticians in compiling the election returns. As evening came on, the candidate secluded himself in one room of his suite with his brother Edward and John Hollister. From time to time, Mrs. Willkie and Philip would look in. But most of the evening the three men sat alone. In the room was a radio and a television set. While Willkie slumped in a chair with his feet propped on another chair, Edward fiddled with the television set, and Hollister made his own computations. Occasionally, the candidate arose, stretched himself, and stomped around the room, ran his hand through his hair, and lighted another cigarette. As the returns began to come in, he looked more and more grim.

About eight o'clock, Hollister telephoned Robert Taft to see how the returns from Ohio were going. Hollister considered Ohio as a reliable barometer because that state was well organized as a Republican stronghold. It it were going to Roosevelt, there would be little hope of carrying New York, Pennsylvania,

Michigan or Illinois. To be successful, Willkie had to carry four out of five of these states. The Taft report was gloomy: the early returns indicated the state would go Democratic by 100,000 votes. Hollister reported this to Willkie and urged him to concede the election at once. This Willkie stubbornly refused to do. "I can still win statistically," he argued.

At eleven o'clock, the now unhappy Willkie heard Elmer Davis announce that Franklin Roosevelt "appears to have been re-elected." Willkie suddenly looked haggard. Shortly afterwards, he heard on the radio that Senator McNary, across the continent in Oregon, had conceded the election. For a moment Willkie looked stunned, but said nothing. He continued to cling grimly to the hope that late returns from the rural areas would overcome the Roosevelt lead.

A few callers, in evening clothes, came to the Willkie suite. Among these were Tom Dewey, Russell Davenport and Roy Howard. Amidst the election gloom, Edith Willkie maintained her gracious poise and high spirits. Defeat did not frighten her. When the returns indicated clearly a Democratic victory she was heard to remark: "I wish Wendell would now get ready to go home."

Shortly after midnight, Willkie left his suite to enter the Grand Ball Room where the campaign workers had gathered to listen to the returns. Earlier in the evening some five thousand party workers and visitors had waited patiently, but the number had now dwindled to barely fifteen hundred. The candidate made a brief speech. He thanked his "fellow workers" for their loyalty and congratulated them on being part of the greatest crusade of the century. With head high he announced that he was neither afraid nor discouraged. Yet he refused to concede defeat. At one-thirty he announced to the press that he was going to bed and would make no statement until after breakfast.

Late on Wednesday morning, Willkie sent the overdue congratulatory telegram to Franklin Roosevelt at Hyde Park: "Congratulations on your re-election as President of the United States. I know that we are both gratified that so many American citizens participated in the election. I wish you all personal health and happiness. Cordially yours, Wendell Willkie."

Election returns gave Roosevelt 27,243,466 and Willkie 22,304,755 popular votes. The victory in the Electoral College was decisive. Roosevelt won thirty-eight states and Willkie only ten states. This gave F.D.R. 449 Presidential Electors, and Willkie 82. Willkie had polled the largest popular vote ever given a defeated candidate, or any Republican candidate. It was larger than the Hoover victory of 1928 by nearly one million votes. He carried only eight western states. He failed to carry New York, but he had the satisfaction of carrying Indiana. Of the ten million independent votes in the United States, however, Willkie secured but four million.

The campaign was ended, but the crusade would go on. There was nothing faint-hearted about Willkie. He was a gallant figure defending proudly the ideas he believed right.

He once told his good friend Roscoe Drummond: "If I could write my own epitaph I would choose, 'Here lies one who contributed to saving freedom at a moment of great peril.' " The presidency was secondary.

CHAPTER XIII

The Leader of the Loyal Opposition

THE MORNING after election night Willkie sat alone at his desk in the deserted Republican headquarters in the Commodore Hotel. The noise and excitement which had filled the crowded rooms during the past three months had abruptly ended at midnight. Now, in the cold atmosphere of the new day, Willkie wearily resigned himself to the bitterness of defeat. He was pondering the role that the rejected candidate should play in the national scene, when suddenly the door was pushed open and there, smiling, stood Sam Pryor. He had come to the headquarters because he guessed that the candidate would be alone with his dreary thoughts. Hiding his own disappointment, Pryor had arrived to offer good cheer. Yet he could not refrain from a little chiding. With his friendly broad grin, he said: "I shall never say this again, but you could have been President if you had worked with the party organization."

After a pause he continued: "I have a small cottage on an island off the coast of Florida, I am going down there for a vacation."

Willkie's eyes lighted with interest. "How big is your place? Big enough to include Edith and me?" he eagerly asked.

"Big enough for the four of us," replied the warm-hearted Pryor.

Two days later, Wendell and Edith were traveling with their hosts southward by airplane to Pryor's sunlighted retreat. The following days were decisive in the career of Wendell Willkie. Far from the scene of his struggle for the presidency, he found peace of mind. More than this, he was able to appraise his spiritual losses and gains, to review his seven-year battle against the New Deal, and to chart his course in the future.

In retrospect, his contest with Franklin D. Roosevelt over the Tennessee Valley Authority now assumed a more significant role than the events of the past several months devoted to the presidential election. The struggle of free enterprise against planned economy had been a battle of giants. In his island sanctuary, Willkie reviewed every detail of the contest. He was justly proud of his part in this bitter struggle. He re-examined the principles on which he had waged his war with the New Deal and found them sound. He had won a partial victory in the struggle with the Roosevelt bureaucracy against great odds. He had shown the country that the dangers of Big Government were as serious as those of Big Business. Then, he had plunged into the exhausting presidential campaign. His nomination, he sincerely believed, was the manifestation of a popular movement. He was still leader of an irresistible public cause. He was convinced that the European war had warped the domestic problems out of their true perspective. The British evacuation at Dunkirk and the ensuing Battle of Britain had thoroughly alarmed the American people. He felt therefore that the election was not a vote for the New Deal program of the welfare state.

This conclusion brought Willkie great peace of mind, together with an intense eagerness to renew the struggle against the New Deal. Although a defeated candidate, he possessed by tradition a claim to the leadership of the Republican Party. He now determined to assert that claim and at the same time to chart a fresh political program. Immediately after the election, thousands of letters from voters in all parts of the country had come to him urging that he continue the crusade for freedom and calling upon him to declare immediately his leadership of the Republican Party. These sincere citizens deserved a public answer. Willkie now decided to give a radio address on Armistice night. The National Broadcasting Company, the Columbia Broadcasting System and the Mutual Broadcasting System eagerly donated their time for a nation-wide outlet for his speech to the American people.

With Sam Pryor, the now refreshed Willkie returned by airplane to New York. On the evening of November 11, a small group of friends gathered in the familiar suite on the eighth floor of the Hotel Commodore, where a broadcasting room had been set up. At ten o'clock the announcer spoke his lines. In a few seconds, the voice of Wendell Willkie reached an audience in every section of the country. Although he still spoke with a slight huskiness in his throat, his words were distinct and carried a vibrant message to all listeners. It was the greatest speech of his career. It has become one of the landmarks in American history.

Constitutional government had been suppressed in almost a quarter of the globe, he said, but the men and women of the United States had preserved it here, in this country. Although it was a fundamental principle of this democratic system that the majority should rule, the American people should not forget that the function of the minority was equally fundamental. Only by maintaining a strong and alert opposition could the delicate balance of the constitutional system be maintained.

Willkie charged his twenty-two million constituents—the men and women who had voted for him in the November election—with the task of debating at all times the policies of the Administration and of expressing themselves freely to their representatives in Congress. But he warned his followers that their opposition must be a program in which loyalty to their country remained the first principle. He proposed a Loyal Opposition rather than mere obstruction. The platform of this Loyal Opposition must be positive in character. It must stand for a strong America, which meant a productive America: "For only the productive can be strong and only the strong can be free."

The radio address awakened an enthusiastic response in every state in the Union. It particularly impressed such men as Henry L. Stimson and Frank Knox, two patriotic Republicans who had braved the wrath of their own party to enter the Roosevelt Cabinet as secretaries of War and the Navy. The address, however, had small immediate effect on the White House. Inadvertently, Edward J. Flynn, chairman of the Democratic National Committee, disclosed the fact that the President had not listened to the Willkie address. This indifference incited a stinging rebuke from Arthur Krock in the *New York Times,* advising the President to read the text of Willkie's address and to ponder it well.

The role of the Loyal Opposition, as expressed by Wendell Willkie, was something new in American politics. It meant responsibility as well as criticism of the party in office. Critics of the Willkie speech attempted to draw a distinction between the twenty-two million citizens who voted the Republican ticket and the minority members in Congress. The Loyal Opposition, they contended, was purely a British term, defining the largest party out of office in the British Parliament, and including only the parliamentary leaders and their followers who actually held seats in Parliament. Accordingly, many Republican Congressmen maintained that leadership in the drafting of legislative programs was the function of the members of Congress rather than of party leaders outside Congress. Representative Joseph W. Martin hastened to declare that while there was no disposition to deprive Willkie of his voice in party councils, the members of Congress and the Republican governors would be viewed as the principal source of direction on political and legislative policies. Senator Taft, as Republican leader in the Senate, added that the position of the Republican Party on various issues must be determined at a later time. To him party leadership always signified control of the party in Congress.

One of the few Republicans who commented favorably on the Loyal Opposition speech was Kenneth F. Simpson, of New York, who promptly declared: "It was a magnificent challenge to America. I will be proud to continue to fight under his leadership until we achieve final victory with Wendell Willkie in 1944."

Seldom in American political life had the weight of a minority public opinion been so much needed as after the election of 1940. Almost half of the electorate opposed the radical social policies of the New Deal. The Democrats in the House of Representatives, however, commanding a majority of about a hundred members, rendered the minority party powerless to moderate the legislative program of the White House. All three branches of government—the Executive, Congress and the Courts—moved in the harmony of a single philosophy of government.

Immediately after the Armistice Day broadcast, Willkie returned with Pryor to Jupiter Island to remain until after the Christmas season. The Pryor children and Philip joined their parents for the Christmas vacation. The relaxation originally planned for only a few days now lengthened into a merry winter holiday. Willkie found pleasure in bicycling about the island when he was not ensconced with a book in some comfortable nook by the sea. In the midst of these occupations, Willkie reached the decision to visit war-blitzed England. He had begun to write an article on the question of American aid to the Allies, when he suddenly realized that he knew little about the needs of Britain. Why not go to England and see for himself? He would then be in a better position to report to the American people.

As soon as he returned to New York, Willkie telephoned Secretary of State Cordell Hull for a passport and government approval of the trip. Hull was unable to give an immediate answer as wartime clearance had to come through President Roosevelt himself. Several hours later, the Secretary telephoned approval but asked that Willkie come to Washington for a conference with him and the President.

Before Willkie had opportunity to see the President and his Secretary of State, he proved himself eminently worthy as leader of the Loyal Opposition. On the tenth of January, 1941, the Lend-Lease Bill proposed by the President had been introduced in Congress. It provided that the Executive be empowered in the interest of national defense to sell, transfer, exchange, lease, lend, or otherwise dispose of munitions and implements of war to any government engaged in battle with the enemies of democracy. It was a device to make America the "arsenal of democracy."

Many Republicans launched a torrent of abuse against the Lend-Lease Bill. Alfred M. Landon, in a speech at Tulsa, Oklahoma, branded the bill as a war measure and as a "slick scheme to fool American taxpayers." Senator Burton K. Wheeler poured upon the measure his usual invective, declaring that the Aid-to-Britain bill was merely another "New Deal triple A foreign policy to plow under the ground every fourth American boy." General Robert E. Wood, chairman of the America First Committee, branding the bill as totalitarian, called upon the local chapters of his organization to flood Congress with protests.

As titular leader of the Republican Party, Willkie released a statement on January 13, 1941, taking issue with the isolationist blast of Governor Landon. The statement was a great declaration of policy and ranks in historical importance with his Armistice Day address. It was a pledge of unity for national defense.

Willkie declared that he had examined the Lend-Lease Bill in the light of the current emergency, and had come to the conclusion that with a few modifications, it should be promptly passed by Congress. Eloquently, he described the situation as one of the critical moments in history. "The United States is not a belligerent, and we hope we shall not be. Our problem, however, is not alone to keep America out of war, but to keep war out of America." It sometimes becomes necessary in a democracy, he explained, to grant extraordinary powers to the elected Executive. "Democracy cannot hope to defend itself from aggression in any other way." Hence, all parties should unite in delegating sufficient power during the emergency to the Roosevelt Administration.

In a direct challenge to Landon, he declared, "It makes a vital difference to the United States which side prevails in the present conflict. I refute the statement that our national security is not involved in a British defeat. The difference between a British defeat or victory is not only military but economic." A German victory would close the free markets of the world to American trade. As a result the economy of this country, already weakened by New Deal legislation, would be forced into regimentation. "We shall be driven back to a controlled economy as to both foreign and domestic trade," he concluded.

Addressing himself to the Republican members of Congress, Willkie admonished them to refrain from opposition to the Administration merely because it was the Democratic Administration. Although everyone could wish that the Administration loved power less, the executive powers required by the emergency must not be denied. He pleaded with Republican members in Congress to forego the cheap satisfaction of debating the Lend-Lease Bill as a partisan measure. "The Republicans," said Willkie, "will gain much in public esteem if they ignore this confusion of partisanship with patriotism." Debate should be confined to the merits of the measure.

While defending the Lend-Lease Bill, Willkie did counsel the President that his program for the American national defense was lagging. The New Deal had sadly depressed American industry, he warned. Production of all goods could be greatly increased if the Government would cease its attacks on business and allow confidence in American economy to return.

The Willkie statement on the Lend-Lease Bill was a unique public paper. It marked a new kind of politics and a new kind of patriotism. It was indeed the forerunner of the bipartisan policy which, in 1945, insured the ratification of the Charter of the United Nations in the United States Senate. Walter Lippmann, writing in the *New York Herald Tribune,* said that it was not too optimistic to hope that under the leadership of a man like Wendell Willkie the opposition would yet turn from barren obstruction to the real business of holding the New Deal Administration accountable for the effective execution of the national defense policy. William Allen White, the Kansas sage, wrote in the *Emporia Gazette:* "Again Wendell Willkie has revealed his statesmanship. Mr. Willkie is not the leader of Congress, but he is the leader of 20,000,000 Republicans, and both the President and the Congressional leaders must reckon with him. He has taken a position to which he can summon his party." White commended the proposed trip to England as a means to dramatize the question before Congress as nothing else could do. It was, he said, a great service to his country.

On the eighteenth of January, two days before the inauguration, Willkie went to Washington for his passport and official conferences. He called on Secretary of State Cordell Hull at the Carlton Hotel. By the time the two men were ready to leave for the White House, a crowd of several hundred had gathered to cheer Willkie. The friendly mob closed in so thickly that hotel attendants were compelled to clear a path to the street. It was a spontaneous recognition of his gallant statesmanship by Washingtonians accustomed to the sight of political celebrities.

Arriving at the Executive Mansion, Willkie and Hull were immediately ushered into the Oval Study, where the President was preparing his third inaugural address. After a warm handshake, the Republican leader declared, "I won't be long. I know what it is to be interrupted while laboring on a speech."

"I wish you were going to have to stand out on that cold inaugural platform tomorrow instead of me," said the President with a chuckle.

"Well, when I get to London, Mr. President, you would want to change places with me again," responded the defeated but smiling candidate.

When Willkie left the White House a short time later, he carried with him a letter in the scrawling handwriting of F.D.R. addressed: "To a Certain Naval Person, kindness of Wendell Willkie." The letter began, "Dear Churchill," and it introduced the bearer to the British Prime Minister as one who had tried to keep politics out of the controversy over aid to Britain. It was a gracious gesture by the New Deal President. Yet Willkie, leader of the Loyal Opposition, traveled to Britain at his own expense on a private plane. Many Republicans bitterly resented his visit to England and especially the fact that he carried a letter to Churchill. They believed Willkie possessed sufficient distinction to meet any British statesman without a letter of introduction.

On the twenty-second of January, the *Yankee Clipper* zoomed off the runway at La Guardia Field for its flight across the Atlantic, with immediate destination at Lisbon, Portugal. In the cabin of the airship was Wendell Willkie on the first leg of his flight to Great Britain. With him were several editors, including John Cowles of the *Minneapolis Star Journal* and *Tribune*, and an old friend, L. K. Thorne, who had formerly been on the board of directors of the Commonwealth and Southern Corporation.

On Sunday afternoon, four days after the take-off in New York, Willkie arrived at the London airport. As he saw the landing field, he became so excited that he impetuously unfastened his seat belt, and with the exclamation, "What is the need of it?" jumped up from his seat intending to secure a better view of the crowd that had gathered to greet him. At that moment, the pilot slipped the plane and he was thrown violently on his face, breaking a small bone in his nose, and smearing himself with blood. Scrambling to his feet, he hastily explained that he never felt better in his life. Nevertheless, the London *Times* reported that his appearance fulfilled expectations. His necktie was awry, his famous unruly lock of black hair was straggling over his forehead, and his clothes were crumpled. He was met at the airport by Herschel V. Johnson, United States Counselor of Embassy at the Court of St. James's, and other embassy officials.

As he shook hands with those around him, Willkie radiated a spirit of friendliness. Confronted with a microphone, he said good-naturedly, "I am very glad to be in England, for whose cause I have the utmost sympathy, and for whose cause I am attempting to do all I can to unite the United States to give England all the assistance it possibly can in her struggle for free men all over the world." To the news reporters who crowded around him, he declared that he had little to say except that he had enjoyed a fine flight over the Atlantic.

Willkie was eager to discover the reactions of the common men and women of England towards the war. His interrogation of individuals began with the chambermaid in his hotel room.

"How's the war going?" he asked.

"Of course we are going to win, but I think we'd like a little more help from America," she replied.

At breakfast he questioned the waiters in the same vein and received much the same answer. Everywhere he found tenseness and hope.

On Monday morning he promptly sallied forth to call on

Anthony Eden, at the Foreign Office, and later to have luncheon with the Prime Minister at No. 10 Downing Street. On this occasion, he delivered to Churchill the President's note. In the afternoon he called on Ernest Bevin, Minister of Labour, and Duff Cooper, Minister of Information. Then he toured the devastated sections of the city. Witnessing the débris of Paternoster Row, the street of book publishers, he observed, "They have destroyed the place where the truth is told." The first busy day in London ended in a gay dinner party at the residence of Lord and Lady Josiah Stamp.

The succeeding days were filled with interviews, inspections, and visits to air-raid shelters, hospitals, factories and chemical works. He even went on bus rides so that he could talk to the passengers and get a cross-section of English views. He called at the Office of the Admiralty and conversed with the First Lord, A. V. Alexander. He visited the Inns of Court and discussed legal procedure with the Lord Chancellor, Viscount Simon. Other conversations took place with Montagu Norman (Governor of the Bank of England), Arthur Cardinal Hinsley (Primate of the Roman Catholic Church in Great Britain), Clement Attlee (Lord Privy Seal), Arthur Greenwood (Labour M. P.), Sir Kingsley Wood (Chancellor of the Exchequer) and Lord Beaverbrook (Minister of Aircraft Production).

Willkie later confided to friends that he was tremendously impressed by Winston Churchill. He considered him the most intellectually alert statesman in England and greatly admired his abilty, his strength, his intellectual dexterity and his grace. Contrariwise, he was keenly disappointed with Ernest Bevin. He had looked forward with intense interest to meeting this powerful leader of the Labour Party. But in his account to intimates he disclosed that he found Bevin heavy, brusque and somewhat dull.

Shortly after his arrival in England, Willkie received the sad news of the death of his loyal friend, Kenneth Simpson. Willkie's supporters in New York assured him they could secure his nomination to take Simpson's seat in Congress if he desired. He promptly sent a cable declining. Although his friends were disappointed in this reply, it would have been awkward for him to take a seat in the House of Representatives. Here he would have been contesting with Joseph Martin, his own campaign manager, for the leadership of the minority party. Furthermore, Willkie realized that was not the road to the White House.

Perforce he continued with his mission. Disregarding all personal danger, he made a trip to Dover and the Southeast coast to view the front line defenses of the British Isles. Twice he saw the anti-aircraft guns open fire on a German *Dornier*. His inspection of the bombed ruins of Coventry and Birmingham brought an enthusiastic response from the plucky citizens of these historic cities. On this occasion, he told British newsmen that nothing had been published in America to describe adequately the damage which the Nazi Luftwaffe had inflicted upon these regions. A short plane trip was made to Ireland for a talk with President De Valera. On his return to London he called on the exiled King Haakon of Norway. As the official climax of his visit, he was duly received by the King and Queen of England at Buckingham Palace.

One of the simple events of his stay in London was his visit to quaint old Shepherd's Market in Mayfair, where he entered a pub and drank beer. A group of soldiers strolled in and he promptly ordered beer for all, and then joined them for a game of darts. The licensee of the shop was so delighted with the performance that he produced a half-bottle of champagne which he had been keeping for Armistice Day and declared that the visit of Willkie was as worthy of celebration as that devoutly expected event. The American and the Englishman drank to "That Day."

The letter Willkie had taken to the Prime Minister was given a dramatic public reply. Addressing the House of Commons, a few days after the Willkie-Churchill interview, the British Prime Minister declared: "The other day, President Roosevelt gave his opponent in the late presidential election a letter of introduction to me, and in it he wrote out a verse in his own handwriting from Longfellow which he said 'applies to you people as it does to us.' Here is the verse:

> Sail on, O Ship of State!
> Sail on, O Union, strong and great!
> Humanity with all its fears,
> With all the hopes of future years,
> Is hanging breathless on thy fate!

"What is the answer that I shall give in your name to this great man, the thrice-chosen head of a nation of 130,000,000? Here is the answer which I will give to President Roosevelt. Put your confidence in us. Give us your faith and your blessing, and under Providence all will be well. We shall not fail or falter. We shall not weaken or tire. Neither the sudden shock of battle nor the long-drawn trials of vigilance and exertion will wear us down. Give us the tools and we will finish the job." The episode furnished another example of the fact that Churchill was a master not only of words, but of political expediency. The President's note provided him the opportunity for a strong and colorful plea for Lend-Lease aid at the very time that debate in the American Congress was at its peak.

Willkie's inspection of Britain was cut short by a cablegram from Secretary Hull requesting his early return in order to testify before the Senate Committee on Foreign Relations on behalf of the Lend-Lease Bill. The opponents of the bill had recruited Colonel Charles A. Lindbergh, described as the "world's greatest aviation expert," General Hugh S. Johnson (newspaper columnist), Joseph P. Kennedy (former Ambassador to Great Britain), Alfred Landon (Republican presidential candidate in 1936), Norman Thomas (chairman of the Socialist Party), James S. Kemper (president of the Chamber of Commerce of the United States), and General Robert E. Wood (national chairman of the America First Committee). Both Roosevelt and Hull were worried. William Allen White, lately convinced that Lend-Lease might lead to war, had deserted the cause of all-out aid to Britain. Now Willkie, and only Willkie, could supply the dramatic effect to offset the strength of the isolationist opposition. With his usual generosity, Willkie gave prompt compliance. On February 5, he left England for the United States.

It was with genuine regret that the people of Britain learned of Willkie's sudden departure from their island fortress. The semi-official London *Times* pronounced him the most interesting personality in American public life in the past thirty years, with the exception, as it added with a sense of official loyalty, of President Roosevelt. While in England, Willkie had sought out men, women and children in every class in the social scale.

The homeward flight was facilitated by Juan L. Trippe, president of Pan American Airways. Trippe had planned to fly the hydroplane *Dixie Clipper* on a new route from Europe to the United States, which would skirt the coast of Portuguese Guinea in West Africa. The mapping of the new route required a stop at the island Bolama, lying 360 miles south of Dakar. Arriving at Bolama, the crew of the *Dixie Clipper* proposed as a few hours' diversion an excursion inland to hunt lions on the edge of the jungle. This jungle hunting expedition, however, saw no big game and bagged only some wild ducks. Along the way they stopped at several native villages. The largest of these was the seat of the tribe of the Bijagos.

Willkie was taken to the hut of the chief of the Bijagos, who, surrounded by many of his wives, children and faithful clansmen, awaited him. Through the interpreter, Willkie and the chief carried on an animated conversation. The chief had twenty-seven wives, but only fourteen of them were present. Twelve of them were working in the fields, while one wife with her daughter was bathing in the river. The Willkie party had passed the mother and her daughter on its way to the village. When the distinguished visitor asked the chief how he could support so many wives, he explained that the answer was simple inasmuch as each wife meant the acquisition of a new field worker. Willkie then asked the chief about the mother and daughter he had seen bathing. Members of the party who were acquainted with native customs were shocked at Willkie's mention of the chieftain's daughter. By mentioning the girl to her father, he had violated the tribal code prohibiting all mention of daughters except in connection with a marriage contract. As a consequence, he had actually incurred the obligation to take the girl as his wife in return for the customary price of twelve silver dollars.

Towards dusk, the Willkie party returned to the *Dixie Clipper*. Early the next morning, the crew was busy with the plane in preparation for the takeoff. Suddenly they heard a ripple in the water and, looking up, beheld the young native bride. Draped in white, demurely sitting in the canoe with her mother, she was borne rapidly towards the *Clipper* by the skillful paddling of several retainers. Some quick-thinking members of the crew stepped into the small collapsible boat carried by the *Clipper* and met the bride a few yards from the hydroplane. They explained as best they could that there was no room on the *Clipper* on this trip for the bride, but that the purchase money would be paid immediately. Thereupon, they laid twelve silver dollars in the hands of the mother. Willkie did not learn of the predicament until well over the Atlantic. Not amused, he reimbursed the young pilots who had paid twelve dollars for his would-be bride. The story was well kept and never reached the press.

The *Dixie Clipper* came to a perfect landing in the choppy water off LaGuardia Airport in New York Harbor. Wendell Willkie alighted, a worn and weary traveler but happily flourishing the native saber given him at Bolama by the Governor of Portuguese Guinea. He promptly told newsmen that he was returning from the most stimulating experience in his life. Certainly, he had completed one of the strangest journeys in American history. Compared to it, the leisurely world tour of President Ulysses S. Grant in 1880 was far from spectacular and the European tour of President Theodore Roosevelt in 1910 was unproductive of political achievement. Willkie had lacked the prestige of exalted office, and he had traveled as a private citizen at his own expense. But his journey had taken him into and out of a beseiged fortress. He had brought cheer and comfort to a gallant people whose heroic resistance saved Europe from the domination of the Nazi empire. Mark Sullivan wrote in his column: "Those nineteen days were more crowded with incidents, some significant, some colorful; were more noticed by agencies of publicity, were more stirring to national interest, than any journey ever taken by any other American in public life. Decidedly Mr. Willkie has political 'it'!" Willkie now returned to the United States to tell the American people that the defense of Britain was linked to the defense of their own country. His arrival turned the tide of the struggle over the Lend-Lease Bill from defeat to victory.

Willkie was, as he phrased it, walking through history. When he had left New York nearly three weeks earlier, the headlines of the newspapers had announced the fall of Tobruk in North Africa and riots in Rumania. On his return, the papers carried dispatches regarding the British naval bombardment of Genoa, the capture of Bengazi by General Wavell and the advance of the British Army towards Tripoli. When Willkie had left America, debate on Lend-Lease had just begun in the House of Representatives. There was strident opposition to the measure, although the Willkie press statement of January 13 had done much to weaken the foes of the bill in the Republican Party. On his return, the measure had passed the House by a wide margin of 260 votes to 165. Its fate in the Senate, however, was a matter of conjecture. The isolationists in the Senate were spearheaded by Senators Hiram Johnson, who had been a leading figure in the defeat of the Covenant of the League of Nations in 1920.

The hearings were held in the Senate caucus chamber, which normally holds about five hundred persons. On the morning of Willkie's appearance, unparalleled crowds jammed the Senate Office Building to gain admittance for the Willkie testimony. Spectators began to gather at six o'clock in the morning, although the hearings did not begin until ten. The first to be admitted were visitors with Senators' cards. By the time all of these persons were in the room, there was little space left for the hundreds who had been waiting long hours. The crowd was so great that any effort to maintain seating arrangements was quickly given up. The wife of Vice-President Wallace pushed her way through the crowd to a place behind the committee table. Without a seat, she had to stand during the entire session. Eighteen hundred people jostled into the room, and more were standing outside hoping that some of those inside might leave.

The day was a triumph for the leader of the Loyal Opposition. Aside from government officials, the majority of the witnesses who had appeared before the committee had been isolationists. The Roosevelt Administration had been unable to enlist any spectacular witnesses save Mayor Fiorello LaGuardia, and even he had proved ineffective because of his bellicose talk and his lack of precise information. The White House now depended upon Willkie to save the day. He was well aware of the strangeness of this situation that he should be the one to save from defeat a measure sponsored by the New Deal President whom he had opposed for seven years.

Willkie gave his testimony at the last session of the public hearings on the Lend-Lease Bill, February 11. When he arrived at the Senate caucus room, he was escorted to the witness table with great difficulty because of the crowds. Then in typical Willkie fashion, he discovered that he had left his prepared statement in his hotel room. A wait of three-quarters of an hour ensued while the document was retrieved.

When the manuscript finally arrived, Willkie proceeded to read it. Because of the delay, he read with haste, thereby impairing the effectiveness of his statement. Even so, however, it was an able presentation of the thesis that Nazi Germany would win the Battle of Britain if Britain were left without help from America. In this event, the totalitarian powers would soon control the world and eventually demoralize the economic system of the United States. Willkie repeated his confidence that England would survive in case aid came from America. He proposed that the United States give effective aid to Britain by sending five to ten destroyers a month to her as well as making available patrol bombers. He concluded his statement by asking for three revisions of the Lend-Lease Bill: (1) fixing a time limit on the powers granted to the Executive; (2) retention of authority to terminate by concurrent resolution the powers granted; and (3) apportioning the amount of money usable under the Lend-Lease Bill from current appropriations.

Questioning of the witness by the committee members was sharp and at times bitter. Especially vitriolic was Bennett Champ Clark, Democratic Senator of Missouri. He attempted to trap Willkie into saying that if the United States sent all the supplies he recommended to Britain and she were defeated, then this country would be too weak to fight Germany. Willkie, however, insisted that every plane and every ship sent to Britain weakened Germany by so much. The longer England remained fighting, the more time this country had to prepare her defense. The Senator became so flustered in his questioning that he suddenly turned towards Willkie and yelled, "Mr. President, Mr. President." On the Senate floor, members so address the presiding officer; and in his anger and confusion, he momentarily forgot that he was not on the floor but in a committee hearing. Everyone, however, laughed and applauded. And Willkie, fully master of the situation, said: "Senator, you merely speak of what should have been." Again there was applause from the spectators. Senator Walter F. George, chairman, pounded his gavel and warned: "There must be no applause"; then he smiled and added, "but you may laugh!"

One of the most widely discussed episodes that developed in the questioning period concerned itself with what Willkie called "campaign oratory." The interrogation developed in this manner:

SENATOR NYE: One more assertion of yours, that of October 30; namely, "On the basis of his [Roosevelt's] past performance with pledges to the people, you may expect we will be at war by April, 1941, if he is elected."

MR. WILLKIE: You ask me whether or not I said that?

SENATOR NYE: Do you still agree that might be the case?

MR. WILLKIE: It might be. It was a bit of campaign oratory. (Laughter.) I am very glad you read my speeches, because the President said he did not. (Laughter.)

The witty, off-hand reply made headline news. Immediately the enemies of Willkie attacked him as having admitted that all his criticism on the conduct of American foreign policy was "campaign oratory"; and that his doubts concerning the President's efforts to maintain the peace were buncombe. Neither of these accusations was true; Willkie had made clear statements on both questions earlier in the cross-examination. The garbled accounts rendered by his opponents were designed to make him appear as an insincere candidate who had flung reckless charges against his opponent in the presidential campaign. But his brilliant defense of Lend-Lease far outweighed in the public mind the rash statement so distorted by his enemies.

Upon the conclusion of the hearings, the crowd surged around Willkie. He was widely congratulated. The opinion of the audience in the caucus room was well expressed by the *New York Sun,* which called Willkie's conduct an "extraordinary example of self-sacrifice and courage." His performance caught the imagination of the nation. The metropolitan newspapers spread the story of his testimony on the first page. It provided a sensational conclusion to the hearings. The White House, which had ignored his Armistice Day radio address, studied every word of his testimony and was highly pleased by the popular response. Willkie had made the Battle of Britain real to the people of the United States.

After four weeks of angry debate in the Senate, the upper chamber passed the Lend-Lease Act on March eighth, by a vote of 60 to 31. An amendment added by the Senate was approved by the House of Representatives, three days later, by a vote of 317 to 71. When the President signed the Lend-Lease Act on March 11, 1941, American history broke in halves. For one hundred and fifty years, American foreign policy had vacillated between isolation and temporary adventures into the field of international co-operation. At long last, Lend-Lease identified the American people with the defense of democracy against aggressions of dictatorships in every quarter of the globe. It made America truly the "arsenal of democracy." During the remaining years of the Second World War, Lend-Lease logically led to American leadership in the creation of the United Nations and, after the war, to the negotiation of the Charter of the United Nations. On the side of the Government, the victory for Lend-Lease had been won by means of the superb leadership of President Roosevelt and Secretary Hull. On the side of public opinion, a not less remarkable leadership was achieved by Wendell Willkie. The victory over isolation was secured with the support of the Loyal Opposition, which developed from the magnanimous statesmanship of a defeated presidential candidate.

CHAPTER XIV

Origin of the
Bipartisan Policy

WENDELL WILLKIE was always more conscious of issues in the public forum than he was of party strategy. This had been true even in the campaign, when he had supported the draft, eliminating it as a campaign issue. As a result of his vigorous support of this measure, the extension of the Selective Service and Training Act had been passed by a narrow margin in Congress, although the majority of the Republicans and many Democrats had voted against it.

The Act was amazingly unpoplar. Worst of all, the morale of the young men drafted under it was very low. There was widespread talk among the draftees that if they were not released from service at the expiration of the one-year induction, October, 1941, they would desert. On walls and billboards everywhere, there appeared almost overnight the mysterious letters "OHO" written by young recruits in an effort to intimidate Congress. It meant that regardless of any Act of Congress they would go "Over the Hill in October."

In view of this antagonism to the draft the President hesitated to ask Congress for its extension. Willkie insisted that it was the paramount duty of the President to do so. The military also urged that the issue be squarely faced. The debate in the Senate was acrimonious. Willkie was blamed by isolationist Senators as bitterly as were Roosevelt and the Army. Nevertheless, on August 7, the resolution to extend the service of enlisted men, selectees and the National Guardsmen and reserve officers to thirty months was passed by a vote of 45 to 30. Debate in the House of Representatives continued while the President was out of the country, engaged in discussions with Winston Churchill on the SS *Augusta* off the coast of Labrador. The isolationists rallied for a last stand. A New York Republican declared that the draft extension authorized the War Department to "order four million death tags for American boys." Hamilton Fish denounced the bill as a part of the Roosevelt-Willkie conspiracy to drag the country into war. In spite of this opposition, the bill finally passed, but only by the narrow margin of 203 to 202. Sixty-five Democrats deserted their party to oppose the bill while only twenty-one Republicans voted for it. Without Willkie's strong leadership to encourage his party members it would have been defeated.

While the President might be able to hold the Democratic Party behind his foreign policy, the future of any program of world co-operation required a reform of Republican thinking. Willkie's agile mind had already begun to speculate upon various phases of a bipartisan foreign policy. In time of international emergency, he felt this must be the only sound procedure. More than this, it was obvious to him that a consistent bipartisan foreign policy must rest upon a certain degree of parallelism of foreign policy within the two major parties. Even in the gravest emergency, a party wedded to a policy of prairie isolation would find it difficult to co-operate with a party devoted to dogmatic internationalism. Willkie believed that the immediate need, demanding all of his talents for dramatization, was converting his party from isolationism to a permanent policy of international co-operation.

By his press release of January 13, he had launched singlehanded a campaign to drive isolationism from the Republican Party. But that was only the beginning. The day after Willkie's spectacular testimony before the Senate Committee on Foreign

Relations was Lincoln's birthday, the twelfth of February, and he spoke before the National Republican Club of New York at the Waldorf-Astoria Hotel. His address disclosed his firm determination to scourge isolationism from the Republican Party. Challenging his party to seek a higher destiny than "negation and failure and death," he reminded his listeners of the fact that the old Federalist and Whig parties had collapsed because they were unable to change with the needs of the times. If the Republican Party could do no better than merely to find fault with the way the Democrats ran the Government, it would meet the same fate as the Federalists and Whigs.

He presented his audience with further lessons from American history. Party government in this country, he said, had always followed a simple pattern. Parties are born and die in times of great crisis and struggle—perhaps sometimes they are reborn in such periods. When the Whig Party failed to understand the great moral issue of the day and resorted to compromise with local prejudices, it passed away. The Republican Party, he declared, was founded to preserve freedom, and if it remembered that, the party would not fail. "But if we become like the Whig Party, merely the party of negation . . . merely those who find fault, and who in one of the critical moments of history find nothing nobler to do than compromise, this great party will pass from the scene. I am here to speak to you tonight to challenge you to a higher destiny. . . ."

Alsop and Kintner commented that a similar situation existed when Stephen A. Douglas told his party to stand behind Lincoln and the Union. The *New York Herald Tribune* editorially commended the patriotic plea to seek unlimited support for Lend-Lease. "In the end we shall earnestly hope that the high ideal of national unity which Mr. Willkie upheld—and in his personal attitude symbolized—will prevail. If such can be the case the effect upon the totalitarians . . . will be the equivalent of many guns. And the defense of America will have been profoundly strengthened."

Willkie's prompt and dramatic endorsement of the Lend-Lease Bill had encouraged a few Republican leaders to stand with him. Echoing the Willkie press release of January 13, Governor Baldwin of Connecticut asked for an enlightened concept of opposition and urged his fellow Republicans to refuse to be "against something just because the Administration is for it." Thomas E. Dewey, ever alert to political issues that gave promise of popular support, astounded his isolationist audience at the Mayflower Hotel, in Washington, D. C., by reversing his earlier opposition and declaring himself in favor of Lend-Lease to the Allies. Within the week, Herbert Hoover asserted that the United States at last had a national duty to aid the Allies. And William Allen White, returning to his original point of view, declared: "Willkie is just dead right on foreign policy."

On the other hand, the Lincoln Day celebrations were employed by the isolationist leadership in the Republican Party to brand Willkie as a menace to the party and a danger to American peace. Robert A. Taft, speaking at a rally at Harrisonburg, Virginia, caustically remarked that the 1940 nominee "does not speak and cannot speak for the Republican Party." Gerald P. Nye branded Willkie as the "betrayer" of the party. Already Alf Landon had castigated Willkie for his policy of all-out aid to England as a deliberate risk of war. Dewey Short, Congressman from Missouri, called him a Trojan horse seeking to split the Republican Party.

The revival of the challenge to the leadership of Willkie brought confusion among the party members in Congress. Since 1939, Joseph W. Martin had served as minority leader in the House of Representatives. After the 1938 elections, he had been able to develop party discipline and to establish a somewhat united party in opposition to such Administration measures as Roosevelt's Re-organization Bill and the dollar devaluation program. With the advent of Willkie, party discipline was suddenly shattered. The real tug-of-war between the two factions came on the twenty-fourth of March, 1941, when the Republican National Committee met in Washington to choose a national chairman and to re-establish the Republican battle line. The skillful strategy of Joe Martin was barely sufficient to keep the revolt from splitting the party wide open.

Shortly after the election of 1940, Martin had announced that he would resign as national chairman. The reason for this decision was that the burden of the chairmanship was too heavy, in view of his responsibility as minority floor leader of the House of Representatives. The proposed resignation, however, opened the flood-gates of dissension as to the new leadership of the Republican Party. The Old Guard was avid to bar all Willkie influence. Even the Young Republicans raised hostile voices at a conference in February at Des Moines, Iowa. Although many of them had been members of the Willkie Clubs, they now were bitter in their denunciation of their former leader. Resolutions had been drafted which condemned Willkie's trip to England and repudiated him as spokesman for Republican foreign policy. Joe Martin immediately countered this anti-Willkie demonstration with a statement from party headquarters in Washington, declaring that he would "regret it" if the Young Republican National Federation meeting in Des Moines "seriously considered" any resolution attacking Wendell Willkie. The rebuke from the capital stopped any formal action, although the delegates seethed in rebellion.

Several days later, Republicans from sixteen midwestern states met in Omaha. Without delay, Martin dispatched his secretary, Robert McIvaine, in an effort to curb any discussion either of Lend-Lease or of Willkie. Nevertheless, Gilbert E. Carpenter, National Committeeman from Nebraska, told newsmen that "a lot of the boys are angry!" Ben L. Berve, Illinois State Chairman of the Republican Party, openly chafed against what he called the "gag rule" from Washington. The conference finally took mild vengeance upon Willkie by adopting resolutions of confidence in Martin and McNary, leaders of the minority party in the House and Senate respectively, while ignoring the existence of Willkie as a national leader. The conference also voiced the demand that the new National Chairman of the party should be chosen from the Middle West, where, in a burst of pride, they declared that "the Republicans had won the presidential election."

At the midwestern political rally at Indianapolis on March 21, Martin appeared in person, having heard that the isolationists planned to make a public repudiation of their defeated candidate. In a brilliant defense of Willkie as the only party leader who then held the devotion of the rank and file of the GOP, the chairman beat down the incipient rebellion.

Nevertheless, Martin was still determined to resign as chairman of the Republican National Committee. The bitter clash of personalities and the appalling lack of unity upon national issues had proved to be an intolerable burden. But Willkie repeatedly urged Martin to retain the key post if only for one more year. Twelve Republican governors demanded he remain at the helm. Even McNary, Landon and Dewey joined the petition. Joe Martin, possessed of a more pressing party conscience than most of his associates, agreed to remain as chairman until after the 1942 elections.

This turn of events was fortunate for Willkie. The retention of the chairmanship by Joe Martin brought some peace to the Republican Party. Then also, Martin reiterated his view that Willkie was still to be considered as the head of the party, which encouraged others to voice their acceptance of the Willkie leadership. Cyrus McCormick, National Committeeman from New Mexico, was one who promptly spoke out: "Nobody can deny the fact that Willkie was our last nominee and that as such he is boss of the Republicans."

The pressure of events on the international scene did not wait while the Republican Party debated. In the struggle of the democracies against Hitler the passage of the Lend-Lease Act had come none too soon. The Nazi armies had invaded Bulgaria and breached the frontiers of Greece. The entire Balkans were about the fall into the orbit of Berlin. In occupied France, a new Vichy Cabinet agreed to deliver cattle and other produce to Nazi Germany, and Marshal Pétain declared that France would willingly participate in the New Order in Europe created by the Axis Powers. The Battle of Britain had continued throughout the winter of 1941 with nightly raids by Goering's Luftwaffe on London, Plymouth and English industrial centers, while frightened people gathered in air-raid shelters bravely sang, "There will always be an England."

Amidst this disaster, Lend-Lease brought cheer to the weary citizens of Britain. In their minds Wendell Willkie shared equally with the President the responsibility for this victory. But even as they rejoiced, a new fear confronted the democracies. This was the submarine danger. Shipments of war supplies purchased in the United States and other American republics were seriously menaced by Nazi submarines, sea raiders and the

Luftwaffe. The Battle of the Atlantic had reached a high tempo with the increase of shipping to Britain as a result of the Lend-Lease Act. Lloyd's in London listed British, Allied and neutral shipping losses for the first eighteen months of the war as 1,245 ships of 4,962,257 tons, or half a million tons more than the losses in the first two and a half years of the First World War. During March, the Allies lost 437,730 tons of shipping.

Willkie's visit to the British Isles had led him to see the necessity for American co-operation to protect the highways of the Atlantic long before most Americans were aware of this dire need. It had become of the most critical urgency that every cargo of American war supplies safely reach the British ports. On his return to the United States, therefore, he was convinced that American battleship convoys were as necessary for the defeat of Hitler as was Lend-Lease itself. But his awareness of public opinion prompted him to follow the discreet course of allowing the issue of convoys to rest until the battle for Lend-Lease had been won. It was on April 25, in an eloquent plea before a large audience in Pittsburgh, that Willkie first demanded convoys to protect Lend-Lease supplies crossing the Atlantic. He chided the Administration for not taking the American people into its confidence and for not giving the people the full facts on the sinking of American war supplies en route to Britain. By this time, Willkie was far in advance of the President. Even on the day of the Pittsburgh address, F.D.R. declared in a press conference that while the United States Navy would extend its neutrality patrol to the seven seas if necessary for the protection of the Western Hemisphere, convoys would not be employed as protection for ships carrying aid to Britain.

Two days after Willkie's Pittsburgh address, the Committee to Defend America by Aiding the Allies announced in a Chicago radio broadcast that the time had come for the United States to use convoys. On the same day, in New York, Lewis W. Douglas, chairman of the committee's policy board, released a similar statement in favor of convoys. On May 2, support for the Willkie program came from an unexpected source. The national executive committee of the American Legion, meeting in Indianapolis, adopted a resolution urging the use of American gunboats to deliver war materials to Britain.

Willkie was now the leader in the forum of public opinion.

This advanced position forced him into the role of answering Colonel Charles A. Lindbergh, the most eloquent foe of the Administration's foreign policy.

In a rally of the America First Committee in Chicago, on April 17, 1941, Lindbergh told an audience of twenty thousand persons that the European war was lost by Britain and France and that the United States was powerless to win alone. A few days later, before a New York audience, he said that the British Government had hatched a desperate plot to drag the United States into the war as a belligerent. For such utterances the President contemptuously called him a "Copperhead," which Willkie thought was unfortunate as he always disapproved of name-calling. Lindbergh promptly resigned his commission as colonel in the Air Corps, conferred upon him in 1927 after his Paris flight. But he kept on talking.

In a remarkably eloquent address before an audience of fifteen thousand persons in St. Louis, on May 3, Lindbergh confidently declared that no matter how many planes the United States built for Great Britain, she would never match Nazi Germany in air power. A week later, before a large audience in Minneapolis, he attacked the Roosevelt Administration for concealing its foreign policy from the American people. At a rally in Philadelphia in the last week in May, Lindbergh made a personal attack upon President Roosevelt, declaring that the American Executive and not Hitler "advocated world domination," and he called for a change in American leadership.

Willkie replied with an effective rebuke to the young hero on June 6 before an All-Chicago Citizens' Rally, composed of twenty-two thousand people, declaring that in the present emergency appeals for a "new leader" were reckless and mis-guided, while charges that F.D.R. was more of an aggressor than Adolf Hitler were nothing short of outrageous. But on September 11, at an America First rally in Des Moines, Iowa, Lind-bergh made the fatal mistake of charging three groups with a plot to drag the United States into the war: the British Govern-ment, the Roosevelt Administration, and the Jews. Immediately, angry retorts were made by Hadassah, the Committee for a Jew-ish Army, the *Protestant Digest* and the White House. Willkie waited two days for passions to subside, and then without rancor but with firmness declared that Colonel Lindbergh's remarks were un-American. The eclipse of the popular hero was abrupt.

In his public addresses, Willkie now sought to mold a public opinion that would compel the President to take a more drastic action to protect the flow of Lend-Lease supplies to Britain. Events in Europe were moving rapidly. Germany had extended her war zone westward to within three miles of the shores of Greenland. The United States acted immediately by signing an agreement with the Danish Minister in Washington to place Greenland under the protection of this country. This at once brought up the question of Iceland.

Because Denmark was now under Nazi occupation and so unable to protect her outposts in the North Atlantic, President Roosevelt proposed the occupation of Iceland also. This created frantic opposition in Congress, led on the Republican side by Arthur Vanderberg of Michigan and on the Democratic side by Burton Wheeler of Montana.

On July eighth, Willkie promptly declared: "My feeling is strong that we must get aid to Britain, and for that purpose a base in Iceland is necessary. It will not only protect the sea lanes, but also it will now be possible for the British forces to be released for duty elsewhere."

The President had finally grasped the full significance of the Loyal Opposition. He now began to invite Willkie to luncheon conferences at the White House. These conferences were the beginning of those consultations with the Loyal Opposition which soon were to develop into the famous bipartisan foreign policy. Such a conference was held on July ninth concerning the establishment of bases in Iceland. Willkie assured the President of his full support and that of the overwhelming number of the Republican rank and file on the occupation of this important station along the North Atlantic sea route to England.

Willkie made three suggestions to the President: that he should now continue his aggressive leadership in an effort to deliver more effective aid to Great Britain; that he should take steps at once to co-ordinate under one head the defense production of the United States; and that he should cause his associates to desist from actions and statements which were contributing to the disunity of the country.

The following day, Willkie released a statement to the press again defending the proposed occupation of Iceland and demanding the establishment of American air bases in northern Ireland and Scotland. "There is no use just giving lip-service to Britain," he said. Arthur Krock observed in the *New York Times* that after the Willkie luncheon there were no trial balloons to ascertain public opinion, which had so long been the custom of the White House. Instead, with the support of the leader of the Loyal Opposition, the President as Commander-in-Chief gave the military order for the occupation of Iceland.

Bitter denunciation of Willkie increased day by day. The Nazi-controlled press in Germany shrieked that Willkie was a foul betrayer of civilization, while the isolationist press in the United States branded him as a warmonger. The American Friends of Irish Neutrality denounced the "outrageous proposal" advanced by the repudiated presidential nominee for air bases in northern Ireland and branded him as an aggressor against friendly Ireland. Senator Wheeler, in the Senate, charged that "Willkie and his little clique of Wall Street bankers, together with the motion picture industry, are trying to stir up sentiment to take us into war."

Willkie's campaign for more vigorous aid to the enemies of Hitler was furthered by his own popularity, while in turn his esteem with the public was increased by the growing importance of the cause which he had espoused. Willkie had captured the hearts of the American people. A Gallup poll, published on March 2, 1941, showed that his popularity with the voters was on the increase. In September, another Gallup poll reported that in a nation-wide survey, Willkie had received the highest number of votes of all favorites as "presidential timber" for the 1944 election, with Secretary of State Cordell Hull in the second place and District Attorney Thomas E. Dewey as third. He had even won the respect and gratitude of Roosevelt, as reported by Robert E. Sherwood, for his persistent battle against isolationism in the Republican Party.

On a number of occasions, furthermore, Willkie immeasurably assisted the Administration by suggesting modifications of policy that brought the emergency legislation more nearly in line with American traditions of democracy. Notably in June,

1941, he induced the President to effect a modification of the Property Seizure Bill drafted by Under-Secretary of War Robert P. Patterson. This controversial measure had been couched in language which inevitably raised suspicion that the free enterprise system was vulnerable. Under Willkie's advice, the War Department itself offered the amendment which removed from the bill the dictatorial power to draft every man's property for federal use. With this amendment, the Property Seizure Act was passed by Congress.

At White House conferences, however, Willkie was not so successful in persuading the President to his point of view on the convoy question. This divergence highlighted the difference in the political philosophies of the two great Americans. To Willkie, the indirect methods of F.D.R. were little better than hypocrisy—an attempt to deceive not only Hitler but also the American people. Arthur Krock well understood Willkie's views, and with increasing bitterness, in his column in the *New York Times,* charged the President with lack of intellectual honesty.

In mid-July at a mammoth "Beat Hitler" rally in New York, Willkie again called for convoys. On July 23, in another mass meeting in the Hollywood Bowl in Los Angeles, Willkie appealed to voters to demand that their Congressmen act more promptly in establishing the first line of American defense.

Again events ran ahead of the debaters in the forum of public opinion. On September 4, the United States destroyer *Greer,* on patrol duty to Iceland, reported to the Navy Department that an unidentified submarine, presumably a German U-boat, had attacked the patrol ship by firing torpedoes, which fortunately missed their mark. The *Greer* immediately counterattacked with depth charges. Once more, Wheeler, Nye and the isolationist press scored Willkie as well as the President. Willkie replied, in an address commemorating Yugoslav liberty, by urging the President to meet the Nazi threat openly by resorting to convoy.

It was not until September 11, several days after the State Department had reported that the United States government-owned steamship *Sessa* had been torpedoed and sunk without warning on August 17, that President Roosevelt broadcast his order to the Navy "to shoot on sight." Isolationists denounced the order as an "unauthorized declaration of war." Willkie immediately applauded the decision, adding: "This is the time for all Americans to rally to the President's support."

By the end of August, Willkie had enough information to lead him to believe that the patrol of the sea lanes by the Navy had practically been developed into a convoy system. The forthright Secretary of the Navy, Frank Knox, finally admitted that convoying was under way, when, on September 15, he told the American Legion Convention in Milwaukee that on the morrow the Navy would provide protection for ships of every flag carrying Lend-Lease supplies to Iceland. Obviously the British Navy had convoyed vessels from Iceland to the British Isles from the beginning of this operation. From April to September Willkie had constantly urged the convoy system. The final result, therefore, was both a vindication and a victory for his views.

Public opinion polls began to show more strongly than ever before that Willkie's campaign for aid to Britain had captured the public mind. A Gallup poll taken in April at the time that Willkie first advocated convoys indicated that forty-one per cent of the voters who were questioned favored the use of American convoys. Another poll, announced on May 20, indicated that fifty-two per cent demanded convoys. By early June the percentage of voters for convoys, recorded by the Gallup poll, had risen to fifty-five. A poll on the occupation of Iceland, reported in mid-July, gave sixty-one per cent in support. Still another poll on October 2 showed that sixty-one per cent of the voters who were questioned supported the shoot-on-sight convoy orders.

A heavy handicap upon American protection of the sea lanes had been the Neutrality Act of 1939. Ever since the passage of Lend-Lease, Willkie had stood for repeal of the entire Neutrality Act. By the end of the summer of 1941, he felt that the campaign of internationalism might well concentrate on this objective. On October 6, in an address before the National Republican Club in New York, he branded the Act as "a piece of hypocrisy and a deliberate self-deception by which we tried to lull ourselves into a sense of safety." He made the audacious assertion that the Republicans should take the lead in the repeal of this Act: "I recommend that the Republican Party, through its membership in Congress, forthwith and forthrightly, candidly and courageously, take the leadership in the repeal of the Neutrality Law." He reminded his audience that neither the extension of the Selective Service Act nor the Lend-Lease Bill could have been passed without the "courageous votes of some members of the minority party."

The President was at last spurred to action. In the spirit of the Loyal Opposition, he took the unusual procedure of calling a bipartisan conference of congressional leaders to discuss the measure. Eight persons were invited to the White House, three of whom were Republicans. The minority party was represented by Senators Charles McNary of Oregon, Warren Austin of Vermont, and Representative Charles A. Eaton of New Jersey. Of the three, only McNary had expressed himself as unfavorable to repeal. The following day the President held a second bipartisan conference and added on the Republican side Representative Joseph Martin of Massachusetts, who opposed the repeal, and Representative James W. Wadsworth of New York, who favored it. Accordingly on October 9, three days after Willkie's New York speech, the President sent a message to Congress asking for repeal of section 6 of the Neutrality Act of 1939, which prohibited the arming of merchant vessels so that henceforth American ships under the protection of their own guns might increase the flow of material aid to nations resisting Axis aggression.

It was felt at the White House conference that with the strong opposition in Congress probably no more than this could be secured. There were those who humorously referred to the proposal as a "policy of scuttle and run instead of cash and carry." Nevertheless, a few days later the House approved the President's request by a vote of 259 to 138. But the real struggle came in the Senate, where an effort was made for stronger action.

Relying upon Styles Bridges of New Hampshire, Willkie sought to rally the Republicans in the upper house to support outright repeal. The young New England Senator found his colleagues apathetic and in some cases hostile. Three of them, however, stood firmly together: Bridges, Warren Austin, and

Chan Gurney of South Dakota. This little group which dared to lead the fight had to endure the slurs and sneers of their fellow Republicans. Each day as they came on the floor someone would jibe, "Good morning, Wendell," or "Have you got your orders from Willkie today?" David A. Reed, former Senator from Pennsylvania, snapped: "Willkie is just a stooge for President Roosevelt. He and the Republicans with him are completely out of step with the majority of the party."

Among Republican Senators who took a strong opposition stand were Arthur Vandenberg of Michigan, Hiram Johnson of California, Robert Taft of Ohio, Gerald P. Nye of North Dakota, Charles Tobey of New Hampshire, and the Progressive, Robert LaFollette of Wisconsin. While most of these men later proudly accepted the bipartisan foreign policy, they had not yet become internationally minded. Strangely enough, it was Arthur Vandenberg who, four years later as the ranking minority member of the Foreign Relations Committee, was to assume the leadership of a bipartisan foreign program and to make it part of the Republican policy as announced in the report, "Accomplishments of the Republican Congress," released on July 1, 1948. In fact, one of the most impassioned speeches against the measure was made by Vandenberg on October 27, 1941, in which he said that repeal of the Neutrality Act would "needlessly and unwisely ask for war." He even proposed that an effort be made for a negotiated peace with Hitler and the Axis Powers. The Democratic opposition was led by Burton Wheeler and Bennett Champ Clark. In the cloakrooms, Wheeler whipped the Republicans into a fury of resentment by his insulting comments about the "Wall Street boss of the Republican Party." In protest at the repeal of the Neutrality Act, Wheeler arranged a rally at Madison Square Garden on the evening of October 29 with Charles Lindbergh as the principal speaker. This meeting had little influence either on public opinion or on congressional voting. It was, moreover, the last large audience that the flier addressed in his opposition to aid to the Allies.

In the meantime, Willkie worked desperately to bolster his little group of supporters in Congress and to keep alive that small flame of the Loyal Opposition. He wrote a message to

Bridges, signed by one hundred prominent Republicans from forty states including six governors and twenty-four national committeemen, asking for repeal of the Neutrality Act. This encouragement from the party ranks outside of Congress was not easy to obtain in so short a time, but it was most effective in strengthening the position of his few loyal defenders in the Senate. With this show of confidence, the Willkie Republicans now made a surprise move by introducing a resolution for outright repeal. Their opponents immediately dubbed it the Willkie Amendment. Although it was defeated by 78 to 12, it did point the way for a bolder action on repeal. The *New York Times* commented: "It is the opinion of many in Washington that had not Willkie Republicans grabbed the ball and had not the former Republican nominee followed with the petition of 100 outstanding party leaders for repeal of the remnants of the law, Administration leaders would have let the armed-ship resolution go its route and waited until later to attempt to repeal the other sections."

At the end of October, the sinking of the U.S. destroyer *Reuben James* off the coast of Iceland while on convoy duty made a profound impression on public opinion. The further announcement by the Navy that thirteen American-owned merchant ships had been sunk by Nazi torpedoes within the past six months, with a loss of seventy-one lives, strengthened the growing feeling for action. The Willkie forces received another unexpected boost from the Gallup poll released in the *New York Times* on November 5.

"Should the Neutrality Act be changed to permit American merchantmen to be armed?"

ALL VOTERS

	Yes	No	Undecided
Mid-October	72%	21%	7%
Today	81%	14%	5%

REPUBLICAN VOTERS

	Yes	No	Undecided
Mid-October	49%	44%	7%
Today	59%	34%	7%

These statistics supported Willkie's statement that the majority of the rank-and-file Republicans approved his stand for repeal.

It was not, however, until November 7 that the bitter debate in the Senate ended and the vote was taken: 50 for the amendment and 37 opposed. The resolution for amendment of the Neutrality Act was for repeal of sections 2, 3 and 6, which was more than the President had asked for in his message of October 9. Repeal of sections 2 and 3 removed the restrictions from merchant ships entering combat zones and belligerent ports, and repeal of section 6 permitted the arming of merchant ships. Six brave Republicans voted for the measure: Bridges, Austin, Ball, Gurney, White, and Barbour. Among the prominent Republicans who voted against it were Vandenberg, Tobey, Taft, Nye, Brewster, and Hiram Johnson. Because this resolution differed from the one passed by the House in mid-October it had to be returned to the lower chamber for approval. Within a few days the House passed the measure by the slender margin of eighteen votes. The tally was 212 to 194. Twenty-two Republicans supported the bill or it would have lost. Again an important Administration measure had been saved by the strong direction of the leader of the Loyal Opposition. The astounding part of this success was that Willkie had to work from outside the legislative halls and against a formidable wall of opposition of the party from within. Turner Catledge, writing in the *New York Times* of October 12, said: "The Republicans in Congress are a straggling, leaderless minority each hoping to save his own skin." To attempt some kind of organized leadership under conditions of such obvious confusion and bitterness would have seemed hopeless to one less dauntless than Willkie.

Such men as Tobey and Vandenberg were slow to accept the broader concept of responsible opposition. But as soon as the bipartisan foreign policy caught the imagination of the people, there were a number of Republicans and even Democrats who hastened to claim the credit for it. In later years, Senator Vandenberg admitted in a private conversation that Willkie had in fact paved the way for the bipartisan foreign policy. He even conceded that the Loyal Opposition of Willkie was the very spirit of the agreement between the two parties that saved the Charter of the United Nations in 1945 from the fate of the Covenant of the League of Nations in the United States Senate a quarter century earlier. It was regrettable that Cordell Hull ever maintained his hostility to the Republican leader and steadfastly refused to give Willkie this recognition. When writing his *Memoirs,* Hull declined to accept the suggestion of a friend to give at least honorable mention to Willkie in the origin of the bipartisan foreign policy. Indeed, the Secretary liked to feel that he alone originated what he called the "Nonpartisan Foreign Policy."

Of course, the burden of such a policy must rest with the minority party. It is this party which must agree to co-operate with the Administration. The party in power cannot make this decision. It is true that the majority party has to show a willingness to confer with the opposition to achieve this support, but the burden of effective response logically comes from the party out of power. It was Willkie who pointed the way to co-operation on foreign policy and who at great hazard to his political fortunes won some Republicans to this viewpoint. It was he who broke the solid phalanx of isolationism within his party which in fact made co-operation tenable. It should also be remembered that this speech on the Loyal Opposition was made in November, 1940. It was not until 1945 that the Vandenberg-Hull agreement for a bipartisan foreign policy was achieved.

Events which were edging the United States towards the catastrophe of the Second World War were beginning to fit into a pattern. On June 22, the Führer astonished the world by declaring war on Soviet Russia. While Kiev and other Russian cities were bombed by German warplanes, columns of the Wehrmacht crossed the Russian borders. So sudden was the attack that only a few days earlier Communist Party members had picketed the White House in Washington, decrying aid to Britain. On order from the Politburo in Moscow, they learned that the party line had changed overnight. The same Communists now praised aid to Britain and begged for similar aid for Soviet Russia.

In November came the long negotiations with the Japanese Ambassador Nomura for an understanding with Japan. A special envoy, Saburo Kurusu, arrived from Tokyo to aid in the discussions. Finally on November 26, after infinite patience, the Secretary of State handed the Japanese diplomats a historic paper. It was not an ultimatum. It stated simply that trade relations between the two countries could not be resumed until the invading armies of Japan should be withdrawn from China.

On Sunday afternoon, December 7, 1941, Willkie received the news of the Japanese sneak attack on Pearl Harbor. He was shocked but not surprised. Willkie had publicly shown far more suspicion of the Japanese militarists than had the President. As early as September, 1940, in his San Francisco address, he had called upon the President to pursue a more vigorous policy towards the Japanese Government than F.D.R. was willing to undertake. Now, however, Willkie had no recriminations. During the past twelve months, the foreign policy advocated by Willkie had been almost parallel with that of the President. As a conscientious leader of the Loyal Opposition, he felt as much responsible for the results of that policy as the President himself. Indeed, he was even more ready than the President to deny the vindictive charge of Senator Gerald P. Nye that this policy had led the Japanese to attack Hawaii.

The Imperial Japanese Government had declared war on the United States a few minutes before the bombs fell upon Pearl Harbor. On the following day, President Roosevelt appeared before Congress and asked for a declaration of war. The resolution was voted with one dissenting vote, which occurred in the House of Representatives. On December 11, Germany and Italy (Axis partners of Japan) declared war on the United States. Congress immediately replied with unanimous declarations of war.

After his victory for a bipartisan foreign policy in Congress, Willkie endeavored to secure formal recognition of this program by the Republican National Committee. Therefore, at the meeting of the National Committee at Chicago, on April 20, 1942, representatives of Willkie offered a resolution. Although it was strongly opposed by Taft, it was approved and read: "We realize that after this war the responsibility of the nation will not be circumscribed within the territorial limits of the United States; that our nation has an obligation to assist in bringing about an understanding, comity and co-operation among the nations of the world in order that our own liberty may be preserved, and the blighting and destructive processes of war may not again be forced upon us and upon the free and peace-loving peoples of the earth." The passage of the resolution was another of the great achievements of Willkie.

Throughout the country, the press generally commended the resolution of the Republican National Committee as the strongest statement on foreign policy made by the party since its defeat in 1932. Said the *New York Times,* "The resolution adopted by the Republican National Committee at its Chicago meeting cuts cleanly away from those influences within the party which still counseled a 'defensive' war, a war of limited liability. . . ." It was indeed a great step away from the policy of many Republicans in Congress who sought to oppose every constructive proposal that was presented to them by the Administration extending from Secretary Hull's reciprocal tariff agreements in 1934 to the President's Lend-Lease Bill in 1941.

The success that Willkie achieved with the adoption of his resolution on foreign policy by the National Committee was quickly followed by his declaration of support to those members of Congress seeking re-election in 1942 who opposed isolation. "I want to see men elected," he said, "who will see that barriers to international trade are broken down." He proposed to give his approval to the candidacy of those Republicans who subscribed to an international program. To be specific, in regard to the Illinois election, he frankly declared that if he were a citizen of that state he would not vote for Stephen A. Day, an unrepentant isolationist Republican candidate for representative-at-large.

Nevertheless, the bipartisan policy in foreign affairs which Willkie so ably initiated cost him dearly in party support. After the congressional elections in 1942, Joseph W. Martin resigned as national chairman. A special meeting of the National Republican Committee was called early in December in St. Louis. Ever the political amateur, Willkie was slow to select a candidate. Not until after the *Chicago Tribune* gave support to Werner W. Schroeder, an isolationist Chicago lawyer, did Willkie instruct his friends as to his nominee. John Hamilton supported a young politician from Washington by the name of Fred E. Baker. To the surprise of political forecasters, Baker tied with Schroeder on the first ballot and took the lead on the second ballot.

Then followed a curious incident. Joe Martin offered a motion for a recess. Thereupon one of the Baker men sitting in the front row jumped up to see how many members were going to vote for a recess. The other Baker men thought that this was a signal for all of them to rise. The vote for recess was thus an overwhelming majority. Obviously, there was no advantage for Baker in such a procedure—on the next vote he probably would have been elected. By such small margins of chance are political careers sometimes made.

During the intermission, the Old Guard talked party harmony, and prevailed upon both candidates to withdraw their names. As the meeting reconvened, Schroeder and Baker walked down the center aisle together arm-in-arm. Thereupon Harrison E. Spangler, of Iowa, was promptly elected. To newsmen, Willkie commented: "Not victory, perhaps, but averted catastrophe. My fight was to prevent the masthead of the *Chicago Tribune* from being imprinted on the Republican Party. Mr. Spangler has a great opportunity for progressive service."

In the prosecution of the war, the leader of the Loyal Opposition was to prove as useful to the nation as he had been in the confused twelve months preceding America's entrance into the war. All of his eloquence was spent on sustaining the efforts of the Administration in the efficient prosecution of the war. In a radio address from New York on December 20, on the eve of the arrival of Prime Minister Churchill in Washington to plan grand strategy with the Administration, Willkie declared that the war would be won or lost "as we do or do not outproduce the Axis powers." He urged the Administration to cut non-defense expenditures to the bare minimum and called for an immediate end of bickering between labor and capital. After a much-publicized luncheon with F.D.R. on December 15, at the White House, a persistent rumor prevailed to the effect that Willkie had accepted membership in a Roosevelt war council. The rumor was incorrect. Both Willkie and F.D.R. knew that Willkie was of far greater service to his country in the prosecution of the war as leader of the Loyal Opposition than as a federal officeholder.

In the war years, Willkie gave spectacular service also in arousing popular approval of American leadership in forging an international organization to maintain the peace at the end of the war. In this connection he persisted in carrying on his efforts to purge the Republican Party of any isolationist leadership. In all these endeavors Willkie was to continue to lay the foundation for the famous bipartisan policy which in 1945 saved the American Senate from repeating the folly of 1919 when the Covenant of the League of Nations was wantonly destroyed.

CHAPTER XV

One World

IN THE late summer of 1942 Willkie set forth upon his spectacular tour of a war-torn world in forty-nine days. He traveled thirty-one thousand miles, visiting South America, Africa, the Middle East, Russia, and China. This voyage by air made him almost as well known as Winston Churchill or Franklin Roosevelt in the lands he visited. In the course of his journey, he discussed the problems of the war and the peace with King Farouk, General Sir Harold R. L. G. Alexander, General Sir Bernard L. Montgomery, General Charles de Gaulle, General Georges Catroux, Marshal Joseph Stalin and Generalissimo Chiang Kai-shek. His daring flight around the globe in time of war was an act of outstanding courage. Coming at a time before American troops had invaded Africa, when Hitler's armies dominated Central Europe and Marshal Rommel held North Africa, it dramatized the unity of the peoples allied in the great struggle against the Axis Powers. It warned the dictators of Germany, Italy and Japan that America was devoted to her allies and would prosecute the war to the very end. It was a unique and historic flight.

The idea of an expedition to all the nations in conflict with the Axis Powers began to formulate in Willkie's mind when he was in London in the winter of 1941. At that time, the Chinese

Ambassador approached him to inquire if he had any intention of visiting China. In that case, the Chinese Government would be happy to welcome him. After his return to the United States, evidence that there was still doubt in certain parts of the world as to the sincerity of the American people in the support of President Roosevelt's prosecution of the war strengthened his resolution to make the spectacular journey. Who would be better prepared to dissipate doubts regarding the unity of the American people in carrying the war to an allied victory than the leader of the Loyal Opposition in the United States?

Accordingly, the President agreed to sponsor the flight, arrangements being made by the White House, rather than by the Department of State which ordinarily would have taken charge of the mission. Transportation was provided by the Army Air Transport. Traveling as an emissary of the President, Willkie held diplomatic rank. In fact, he took precedence over the duly accredited American Ambassador in each country visited.

The Department of State looked askance at the venture. Through long experience, career diplomats were aware that the average American knew little about the function of the Foreign Service. All too frequently, officials were looked upon as mere agents to further private affairs. If an illustrious person decided to visit a foreign country, he invariably expected the Embassy or Legation to act in his personal behalf. This placed an additional burden upon the already heavily laden Foreign Service staff.

Every citizen leaving on a mission to a foreign country should know that the function of the Foreign Service is to carry out the policy of the Government as it is formulated by the President, the Secretary of State and the Congress. Typical of his countrymen, Willkie lacked the understanding of the organization of the Foreign Service, the protocol of the service or even its place in the pattern of Government. In diplomacy he was to prove himself as amateurish as he was in politics. He had been given no briefing as to his conduct, nor as to his personal relationship with the American embassies and legations in the countries which he visited. For this mistake, the White House was chiefly responsible. Removing arrangements for the flight from the State Department to the Chief Executive pre-

cluded directions from the career officers that might have
avoided some of the mistakes that later occurred. It would be a
distortion, however, to magnify these mistakes. The world flight
of Wendell Willkie performed a great service to the cause of
the allies banded together under the Atlantic Charter to defeat
Hitler. The spectacular success of the flight was in the field of
publicity, not of diplomacy.

Willkie left Mitchel Field on the twenty-sixth of August,
1942, in a four-engined Consolidated bomber, christened the
Gulliver. His companions were the publisher, Gardner Cowles,
and Joseph Barnes, former correspondent of the *New York
Herald Tribune* in Soviet Russia and later deputy director of
the Overseas Operations of the Office of War Information. This
choice of companions did not ease the anxiety of the State Department. Neither Cowles nor Barnes was a specialist in foreign
affairs nor did they understand diplomatic protocol.

The principal African stop of Willkie's world flight was Cairo.
When the *Gulliver* left New York, the plucky British Eighth
Army still faced the Afrika Korps of Marshal Rommel at El
Alamein. There was intense anxiety whether the victorious Nazi
desert fighters would break through the British lines and seize
Cairo and the Suez Canal, the life-line between Britain and the
Orient. Willkie thus took the risk of capture by the German Fox
of North Africa. There was a sense of relief to find on landing
in Cairo that the flag of Britain still floated over the military
base. Yet rumors and alarms so filled the streets and cafés that
frightened Egyptians were packing cars for flight southward.

Fearless of personal danger, Willkie asked to visit the front.
Accordingly, he was taken to the firing line at El Alamein, where
he was received by General Bernard L. Montgomery and General Harold R. L. G. Alexander (commander of all British forces
in the Middle East). Montgomery and Alexander informed him
confidentially of their belief that the Nazi Marshal had been
stopped, at least temporarily, in his headlong drive towards the
Suez Canal.

So enthusiastic was Willkie over this secret information that
he forgot all wartime caution and with reckless excitement reported to the press upon his return to Cairo that Alexander and
Montgomery had assured him that the "battle is over and Egypt

is saved." With apologies to the American Office of War Information, the British censor deleted this statement from the news releases of the Willkie interview.

The audience with King Farouk was well reported in the Egyptian newspapers. But of even greater news value was the interest Willkie aroused among the Egyptian people. They liked his informality in appearing on the streets, in the shops and cafés, and about the town. His very presence attracted attention to his country and the Allied war effort. So well was he received, in fact, that the Axis radio attacked his visit as British propaganda designed to entice Egypt into the war.

From Cairo, Willkie flew to Beirut, Ankara, Bagdad, Teheran, and then Kuibyshev in Soviet Russia. He was met at the airport in Beirut by Georges Catroux, Commander-in-Chief of the Fighting French in the Levant, with a French guard of honor. General de Gaulle was then in Beirut, and received Willkie in his Residence des Pins. In the starlit gardens of this house, De Gaulle and Willkie talked far into the night. Willkie, like F.D.R. on a later occasion, found the Frenchman arrogant, defiant and unbending. He urged De Gaulle to retire from Syria and renounce the French Empire. It was not a successful meeting. In Cairo, the British had warned Willkie against showing any friendliness to the Fighting French in Lebanon. American officials, therefore, were a little worried that his visit with De Gaulle might prove embarrassing. The American Embassy, however, reported: "There is every reason to believe that, from the propaganda point of view, the visit was extremely successful."

From Bagdad, the American Embassy in Irak reported that Willkie's visit had an electrifying effect upon the Arabic population. His simple American manner, especially his casual visits to Arab coffee shops and his presence on sightseeing trips, had delighted the people. In a café at Teheran, a Royal Air Force officer recognized him and asked him to autograph a dollar bill. That started a long line of requests for autographs. Everywhere he appeared there was excitement.

All along the way, at every stop, the staff of the American Legation or Embassy had been present when the great bomber circled the field and came to a landing. Every courtesy of the

Foreign Service was extended to Willkie. But nowhere were the American diplomats so eager to receive their distinguished countryman as they were at Kuibyshev, the war capital of Soviet Russia, some five hundred miles north of the Caspian Sea on the Volga River. The Ambassador, Rear Admiral William H. Standley, had long admired Willkie and felt delighted and proud to welcome him. At the flying field to greet Willkie was a delegation from the American Embassy. But, from the moment of his arrival, there began slow disillusionment. Career officers who were eager to respect and serve Willkie were appalled by his discourtesy to them.

With impatience, Willkie waved aside the staff officers who had left busy desks to honor him. "Why do I have to waste my time with all these diplomats?" he said. "Where are the American newsmen? I want to see the newsmen." It so happened that the newspaper correspondents were then in Moscow. The career officers from the Embassy were chilled. The brusqueness of Willkie was occasioned by the advice of his companion, Joseph Barnes, as well as his own lack of understanding of the line-service of American diplomacy. Barnes had urged Willkie to pay no attention to the American diplomats, as they were not liked by the Russians. If he ignored the Embassy, said Barnes, he would win favor with the Soviet officials. Willkie seemed to feel that Barnes had a better understanding of the Kremlin than did the American diplomats.

The error was stupendous. Although Barnes had served as a newspaperman in Soviet Russia, he knew little of the problems of the Embassy nor did he understand the task of government officials. The Embassy is merely the channel through which the State Department carries out its relations with foreign governments. All policies are determined in Washington. Barnes's advice to Willkie, therefore, was not only embarrassing to the diplomatic corps but it brought merited contempt from Soviet officials. The embassy staff felt that it was fantastically naive for Barnes to expect that Willkie could establish better relations with the Russians in two short weeks than the duly accredited diplomatic agency in its permanent capacity.

A cordial smile and a warm handshake could not dispose of the deep-seated problems which existed between the two nations. The story of these difficulties has since been well told by General John R. Deane, head of the American staff stationed in Soviet Russia for Lend-Lease, in his graphic account of the war years called *Strange Alliance*. The Kremlin officials, although eager to acquire the billions of dollars' worth of food and war equipment which the United States unstintedly sent to Soviet Russia, nevertheless treated the American officers as enemy spies and stubbornly refused to divulge any helpful information concerning Nazi Germany.

Barnes had counseled Willkie against placing any confidence in the Ambassador, Admiral Standley, although he was the official representative of the American Government to the Union of Socialist Soviet Republics, the appointee of the President. Willkie enjoyed the role of personal emissary of the President merely as a courtesy so that he might possess a degree of prestige and recognition in the countries he visited. But his temporary rank did not invest him with diplomatic authority.

At the villa on the Volga River which the Soviet Government had provided for Willkie, the American Ambassador promptly called to acquaint him with the political situation in Russia. But Willkie showed clearly by his aloofness that he was not interested in this briefing. As a result he never obtained a clear understanding of the intricate situation which existed between the Soviet Union and the United States. It was Barnes who gave him his information about this strange land.

The Ambassador arranged a reception for Willkie and his companions. At first Willkie refused to go. But Admiral Standley insisted that he must attend, as all the invitations had been sent and the diplomats of other countries were expecting to meet him. Somewhat irritably, Willkie consented. But he was an ungracious guest. He talked only to a few persons secluded in one corner of the room, and left the Embassy after a short stay. This was an open discourtesy to the American Ambassador and a disappointment to the distinguished guests.

Andrei Vishinsky, Deputy Minister of Foreign Affairs, gave a dinner for Willkie. Only Americans and Russians were present. It was on this occasion that Willkie lost the confidence of Soviet officials. In reply to the toast given by his host, Willkie said: "Please help me to see everything in Russia. I want to see the churchmen and the people in every phase of activity. Please help me. I won't report anything that I don't like. I want to improve American-Soviet understanding. I will tell the American people only the good things I see."

The American guests were embarrassed over this display of obvious bad faith. They perceived that the point was not lost on their Russian colleagues. "I have a lot of friends in America. Twenty-two million people voted for me. They will believe what I tell them!" The shrewd and callous Vishinsky was amazed that any prominent American would utter words with such an implied meaning. Then Willkie went further. Imperialism was dead, he declared. After the war, there would be only two great powers, the United States and Russia. Thus these two nations should trust each other. Therewith, he proposed a toast to Soviet Russia and the United States. At once, the clever Vishinsky arose and replied: "To the Allies, the United States, Great Britain, and Russia." Willkie's indirect criticism of Great Britain soon reached the ears of the British Embassy and was resented. Nor did he improve the situation in Kuibyshev by his careful effort to avoid the English diplomats.

As Willkie had expressed a desire to see one of the large farms, the Embassy made the necessary arrangements. They took him to one of the model farms up the Volga a short distance from the war capital. Willkie concluded that it was a cooperative farm. It was, in fact, a state farm. By this time no one felt disposed to explain such differences to him.

The excursion to the state farm was a gala occasion. The Soviet Government placed a beautiful new boat at his disposal for the trip. The captain of the boat allowed Willkie to take the wheel. While the captain's back was turned, Willkie almost wrecked the craft. With his lack of dexterity and the strong current of the river, he came close to running the craft on the bank. Again the American diplomats who accompanied Willkie were embarrassed.

The Embassy arranged with a local hotel for several of their best-looking servant girls to prepare and serve a lunch. Such delicacies had been procured as sturgeon, caviar and wine. The food was packed in baskets and taken below decks. Upon arriving, the Russian girls proceeded with their baskets to one of the farm buildings in order to prepare the luncheon. They had at no time been conspicuous, and thus moved unobserved by the Willkie party. Meanwhile, Willkie was conducted on an inspection of the state farm.

When the party returned from its inspection tour, Willkie looked over the table spread with the fine food and expressed amazement. "Where did such choice food come from?" he innocently asked. This was too much for a mischievous member of the embassy staff. With serene countenance, he replied that it had been produced on the farm. "And the pretty girls, too?" he asked. "Yes," was the reply, "they belong to the farm, too!" No one ever revealed the truth to him. They felt that he would not appreciate the humor of it. But the story brought much merriment around the Embassy.

The American career officers who accompanied Willkie, disciplined by diplomatic protocol, were shocked at his constant desire for publicity. They resented his insistence on taking the newsmen with him wherever he went. They resented the poses he assumed, particularly a picture in which he had his arm around the neck of a cow. Of course, the entire trip was actually based on publicity in order to shape public opinion abroad and in America. From Willkie's viewpoint, therefore, the newsmen were essential.

At Kuibyshev occurred the most distressing episode of the entire flight. One evening, the Embassy entertained Willkie with a box-party at the ballet. The box was situated just off the stage, in fact it even projected over the stage. As the dance was performed, Willkie suddenly decided he should present a bouquet of flowers to the ballerina. So he whispered to an aide from the Embassy to rush out and procure a bouquet. The distressed young man explained that there were no flower shops open in Kuibyshev so late at night. Willkie insisted that he find flowers somewhere. The official left the theatre bewildered, but an idea occurred to him. He hastened to a park near by and picked a large bunch of blossoms. They were faded and frost-bitten, but nevertheless flowers. He tied them together with string, and returned to the opera box.

At the conclusion of the performance, to the consternation of the audience, Willkie climbed over the railing of the box and onto the stage. He tripped over an electric light cord and almost fell, but managed to regain his balance by wildly pawing the air. The audience sat stunned. The NKVD tensed for action. This sort of thing was not done in Russia. The Americans in the box sat embarrassed and helpless as they watched him move clumsily across the stage and up to the dancer. He presented her with the tawdry bunch of flowers and then kissed her. The awkward situation was saved by one quick-witted member of the Embassy sitting in the audience. He began to applaud, indicating it was a kindly gesture. Other Americans promptly did likewise. The audience relaxed. They understood. It was a queer American custom.

From Kuibyshev Willkie and his entourage went to Moscow to meet Stalin. Despite all the snubs, the ever-courteous Standley accompanied the Willkie party in order to make the necessary arrangements for the interview. The stay in Moscow went off somewhat better than the visit to Kuibyshev. Here Willkie actually went out of his way to associate with the British diplomats whom he had called "imperialists" while in Kuibyshev. This change of conduct was not lost on the Soviet officials and further increased their suspicion of their distinguished visitor.

The interview with the Russian dictator was easily arranged. It is protocol for the Ambassador always to accompany visiting Americans on such occasions and to be present at the interviews. Willkie expressly requested that he be permitted to go alone. When he entered the audience room, however, he found that Stalin was not alone but had with him his Minister of Foreign Affairs, Vyacheslav Molotov. Naturally this was a disappointment to Willkie, as he had expected a man-to-man talk in the most confidential manner with the Russian dictator. Willkie had further opportunity, however, to converse with Stalin at the state dinner accorded him in the Kremlin. As guest of honor at the five-hour banquet, he sat next the Russian dictator. Many toasts were drunk. But one was of special interest. Stalin arose and announced that he wished to propose a toast. He stated that the Americans had consigned to the Soviet Government some 150 airplanes. These planes had not yet arrived. They had been detained by Britain. "Therefore," he said, "I propose a toast to those thieves who stole them from us!"

The British Ambassador, Sir Archibald Clark Kerr (Lord Inverchapel), rose somewhat stiffly and attempted to save the situation by resort to humor. Willkie himself relieved the tension by standing up and declaring that everyone must remember that the British had been sorely pressed and had carried the brunt of the defense of the West. When he sat down, Stalin leaned over and said, through an interpreter, "Mr. Willkie, I like you. I think you are the kind of fellow who would steal airplanes yourself!"

The sequel to the airplane story took place after Willkie had returned to America. He then learned that these planes were diverted from the consignment to Russia to be used a few weeks later in the invasion of North Africa (November 8, 1942). If Stalin had known of their destination he would have felt less grieved, or if he had trusted the Allies who shared with him so generously their short supplies, he would have accepted this diversion with better grace.

Izvestia, the official newspaper of the USSR, published a press interview with Willkie in which he said that the most effective method of winning the war would be for the United States and Great Britain to open the second front. This statement had not been cleared through the Embassy and was considered a dangerous remark. Indeed, the American officials were indignant over such irresponsible comments, which could only make the Russians more critical and more demanding of action in the West, whereas the plans for the invasion of the continent were going forward as fast as possible.

Stalin had turned on his charm for Willkie, as he always did with visitors. Emissaries could be easily flattered by his kind attention and invariably they would return to their homeland to report to the people what a wonderful man the dictator of Russia was and how easy he was to get along with. Such visits always resulted in excellent propaganda for Stalin, which annoyed the diplomats who had the irksome, day-by-day problems to handle. To visitors Stalin appeared, as one embassy official expressed it, more like a sweet old man who should be doing his knitting than as a man of steel. His simple, affable appearance easily beguiled visitors to the Kremlin unless they looked closely at his eyes, which were coldly sharp and piercing. While he cleverly mesmerized many callers, no distinguished personality ever took him in. His policy was based on hard reality.

All the top-ranking officials of the USSR lost confidence in Willkie. While they might enjoy a newspaperman slapping the British for "imperialism," they were surprised that an American representing the President should openly criticize a friendly power. Also they recognized the American Embassy as the official agency of the United States Government, even though they felt unfriendly to it. Nor could the Russians understand an emissary who ignored his own Embassy, and snubbed his Ambassador.

According to official reports from Kuibyshev, Willkie was a child in the hands of Stalin, Molotov and Vishinsky. He never got close to conditions in Soviet Russia and saw only what he was intended to see. In *One World,* he proudly declared that the Soviet Government gave him every opportunity to examine in his own way, war plants, collective farms, schools, libraries, and even the fighting front. Although Willkie actually believed he was under no surveillance, diplomatic reports deny that he had any freedom of movement. For example, there was no inspection tour of the real front. Willkie had been taken to Rzhev, several miles back of the firing line but close enough so that he could hear the cannons.

Willkie took great delight in talking to Russians engaged in a variety of occupations. He made many expeditions around Moscow asking people, through an interpreter, how they liked their work and how they liked communism. In such manner he questioned even the heads of factories. This would be tantamount to asking Charles Wilson how he liked his work and how he liked being an American. In one group that Willkie talked to in his round of visits was a girl who spoke English. She had visited America on Soviet business. Willkie asked her why she was a Communist. As she was a bureaucrat her reply was characteristic. She said that the Communist Government had given her a chance to develop, to become educated, and to travel. Her people had been illiterate peasants, and very poor. Only through the Soviet regime could she have so improved her condition. She avowed her complete freedom saying, "I can do anything I want to do. I can even sleep with you, if I want to!"

To Willkie, it appeared that the Communists had created an effective society which possessed "survival value." The power of this nation, he held, made it necessary for the United States to find a way to work with it when peace at last should come. The future, he said, belonged to America and the Soviet Union. But he advised the President to be tough with Russia. "Stalin is a tough man; he came up the hard way and there is only one language he understands," said Willkie. "Send to Russia as ambassador a strong, two-fisted man who can stand up and talk to Stalin."

Returning to Kuibyshev from Moscow, Willkie prepared to take off for China. He asked one of the members of the embassy staff if he were acquainted with the Ambassador in China. "Yes," said the official, "he is a good friend of mine." "Well," said Willkie, "I want you to cable him not to interfere with me in any way. I want a free hand to do what I want to do." Replied the diplomat coldly, "I am sorry, but I do not know him that well!"

No American official in the war capital of Russia was sorry when on September 28, the giant *Gulliver* took off for its goal four thousand miles away. One official described Willkie as a bully who had been rude to every person in the Embassy. And yet, it was generally agreed that he had received good publicity in the Soviet press, which in turn had produced a favorable and friendly attitude on the part of the Russian people. Some even admitted that there was an advantage in time of war of showing foreign peoples that the opposition party was also behind the policy of the Washington Administration. The effectiveness of Willkie's visit in Russia was entirely with the Russian people. The Soviet diplomats were courteous but unimpressed. It was the populace that was interested in this American citizen who visited their country to talk to them and to try to understand them. He wanted nothing but good will and they responded in kind. Again his work as a publicist was superb.

The flight to China followed the Ili River along the old silk trade route from Tashkent in Central Asia. Nowhere Willkie went did the public response prove so great or the leaders of the Government show more gratitude for his coming than in China. He was the only American visitor of distinction to have come to China in many years. After him soon came Patrick Hurley, Henry A. Wallace, and Donald Nelson. But, coming at a time when the Chinese people were spiritually exhausted after their stubborn resistance to the Japanese invasion for over ten years and their belief that the United States did not fully understand their plight, the visit of Wendell Willkie was most timely. His personality had a stimulating effect in spite of the fact that American prestige had suffered greatly. Ever since the invasion of Manchuria in 1931 China had struggled against Japanese aggression, always hoping that sooner or later the United States and Great Britain would join her. She had waited patiently for that great day. Then came Pearl Harbor and the Japanese declaration of war on the United States. America at last was China's ally. Help could not now be far away. But in rapid succession came the shocking defeats in Malaya, Java, and the Philippines. The military prestige of the white men was questioned. Discouragement again settled over the people of China. The visit of Willkie, therefore, brought to this distracted land a hope and a promise of better times to come.

Willkie landed at Lanchow on the Yellow River in the Kansu Province far up in the northwestern part of the country. He was met by an attaché of the American Embassy and Dr. Hollington K. Tong, Vice-Minister of Information of the Chinese Government. So eager was the Chinese Government that all should go well that the Kuomintang arranged a demonstration for him. Across the main street were banners reading, "The Pacific Is More Important Than the Atlantic" and "Defeat Japan First." This not-too-subtle propaganda was spoken of in the Chinese press as the spontaneous work of the people.

For two weeks before his arrival there had been a clean-up campaign to make the town look its best. For the demonstration, uniformed groups including the Boy Scouts and the Girl Scouts paraded before the distinguished visitor. The morning of the celebration, the people were rounded up from the hovels and the back streets into a parade line. Some of them were so ignorant they could not understand what it was all about. Those in the front rows were given paper American flags to wave as the great man rode past. They waited dumbly in the street for hours and patiently wondered what it meant. The Chinese newspapers were ordered to write editorials on the event. Beneath all the show and fanfare was a degree of pathos. The struggling Government was attempting to emulate a western welcome and western propaganda.

From Lanchow, Willkie stopped at Chengtu, capital of Szechwan Province and the cultural center of Free China, on his way to the war capital of Chungking. Chengtu had become the refugee center of the private colleges in China. Nine universities were here trying to use the facilities of the two local universities in a round-the-clock series of shifts. The Chinese professors and students were attempting to grapple with the real problems of their society.

On the morning of October first, Willkie spoke to a mass meeting of the faculty, students, and townspeople on the campus of the West China Union University. The speech was translated by Dr. Y. P. Mei, acting president of Yenching University. The event had been widely heralded and people came from afar, trudging over the rough, hilly countryside, and through the open fields. Over ten thousand people, including four thousand students, stood on the sloping campus. They presented a magnificent and colorful scene, the hope of the New China.

Willkie spoke to this great audience as he would have talked to college students in Indiana. He did not realize that in China the place of highest respect and honor is that of the scholar. In China, public men do not wisecrack about the learned professions. In ignorance of all this, Willkie expansively said: "I have had many experiences in my life, but this is the first time I have had a college president to translate for me. I rather enjoy this experience because since I left college twenty-six years ago I have wanted to make one of those fellows work for me. As a matter of fact, my six years in the university were not devoted so much to acquisition of facts, but rather to the outwitting of the faculty and the increasing of their discomfiture. I can't tell you how much I am enjoying the passing of this on to you through a college president as my Charlie McCarthy!" Although the people were a little bewildered by such remarks, they were thrilled and encouraged by his very presence. The coming of this great American gave them a spiritual link with the magic country across the sea.

Willkie was still taking advice from Joseph Barnes. Hence the irksome incidents which had happened from Cairo to Moscow were repeated in Chungking. The Ambassador, Clarence Gauss, a career diplomat of long service, offered the hospitality of his house. It is customary for a visitor of distinction to spend the first night in his own Embassy. Mr. Gauss had very limited quarters with only one bedroom. But he had moved out of this space to accommodate his honored guest. However, Willkie refused to cross the river to stay at the Embassy, which was considered a high discourtesy. The Chinese Foreign Office, observing protocol, had arranged his schedule in consultation with the American Embassy. Taking matters into his own hands, Willkie proceeded at once to the charming bungalow provided him by the Chinese Government. Flowers had been placed in all the rooms, and the house was well supplied with American cigarettes and old wine. His bed was made up with sheets of the soft white silk from the famous looms at Szechwan.

To the curious Chinese newsmen who questioned him about his statement in Russia on the second front, he said: "I always have a bad habit of saying what I think." This led the *Army and Navy Journal,* of Washington, D. C., to say in its issue of October 3, "It is fortunate for the war effort of the United Nations that Willkie has ceased to be the 'personal representative' of the President, and in Chungking will be merely a 'visitor'; else he might be demanding with some semblance of authority that a Second Front be established immediately in proximity to Japan as he desires to be done in Europe within fighting distance of Germany." The sharpness of the quip was not diminished by the error as to Willkie's official status which remained the same throughout the trip.

The Ambassador took Willkie to call on the aged President of China, Lin Sen, and on the Generalissimo and Madame Chiang Kai-shek. Willkie was obviously irked by this courtesy, although it had been requested by the Chinese Foreign Office. This was protocol, and without it Willkie would have had no formal standing. As they sat in the outer office waiting to see President Lin Sen, Willkie asked rather pointedly how long Gauss had been in the Far East. A career diplomat, he replied patiently that he had been in various sectors of the East about thirty years. Willkie said, "I suppose you speak Chinese?" "No," replied the diplomat, "I guess I was one who could never master it."

When Willkie returned to the United States he made wide criticism of the Ambassador, especially upon the point of his not speaking the language of the Government to which he was accredited. A short time later he went to a dinner party and fate seated him across the table from a friend of Gauss who twitted him. Said the friend: "What do you think officially of Ambassador Grew?" "A fine man, a fine man," promptly replied Willkie, unthinkingly. "Does he speak Japanese?" the friend shot back. Willkie reddened as he saw the point.

The Embassy had cause to be embarrassed on several occasions during the following five days of the visit. President Lin Sen gave a state dinner for Willkie, who accordingly sat next to the distinguished host. The Americans present were pained to see their countryman lift the glass of wine to his lips before a toast could be proposed to him and with no sign of courtesy to the President. This was not an auspicious beginning, but matters grew worse during the evening. The President had once studied in the United States and he spoke very correct English, but in a slow, halting and high-pitched voice. He attempted to explain certain things to Willkie in English. But Willkie showed his indifference by turning his attention elsewhere.

In like manner, he ignored the Minister of Economics, Dr. Wong Wen-hoa. Willkie had expressed a desire to visit a cotton mill, a paper mill, and the chemical works. Accordingly, this tour had been arranged by the Embassy through the Chinese Foreign Office and it did not provide for any correspondents. The brilliant Dr. Wong, who spoke English well, himself offered to conduct this little expedition. Unimpressed by this gallant courtesy, Willkie himself called together a dozen or so journalists to accompany him and instructed them to keep close by so as to take copious notes of all that he said and did. As they began their itinerary, therefore, the newsmen closed in around Willkie and the Minister of Economics trailed along at the end of the procession with an attaché of the American Embassy. At all points Willkie was too busy with his reporters to ask any questions of Dr. Wong or to receive any information from that learned gentleman.

The meeting with the Generalissimo and Madame Chiang Kai-shek, however, went off with grace and charm. Willkie was captivated by the beauty and delightful personality of Madame Chiang. After the Ambassador made the presentation there were numerous private meetings at which neither the Ambassador nor any other representative of the American Embassy was present. This was contrary to protocol, and caused chagrin at the Embassy.

Dr. T. V. Soong (brother of Madame Chiang), Minister of Foreign Affairs, who was then in Washington, had asked the Chinese Government to make every effort to see that the Willkie visit was a success. He stated that Willkie might be the next President of the United States or, failing that, most likely would be seated at the Peace Conference where issues vital to China would be discussed. Added to this ardent desire to make a friend of one who might become a powerful influence for China was the natural desire of the Chinese to find a direct channel to the White House. The Generalissimo did not like to clear through the American Embassy. At the same time, the President was prone to encourage direct communications, much to the annoyance of the State Department and the embassies.

Upon the second meeting with the Generalissimo and his wife, Willkie proposed that Madame Chiang should return with him to the United States. The Generalissimo sat smiling as Willkie pressed his invitation. The great lady of China seemed fascinated by the idea. Finally she asked if by such a visit she would be likely to secure the planes, tanks, and money so sorely needed by China. With enthusiasm Willkie promised that her visit would get all the planes and machines China desired. It would also do more than anything else, he emphasized, to promote good Chinese-American relations. She would be an ambassador of good will, and the best one that China could possibly send. In a quiet moment aside, she told Willkie that if he would speak to her sister Madame Kung (wife of the Finance Minister), and persuade her to urge the matter upon the Generalissimo, he would consent. It seemed that the Generalissimo was in awe of his sister-in-law and had great respect for her views. Accordingly, Madame Kung was won over, and through her Chiang himself. The trip was arranged, although it was decided she should go to America at a later date and not return with Willkie in his bomber. An invitation from President Roosevelt was dispatched immediately.

Madame Chiang's visit to the United States took place several months later. Her address before Congress was the most brilliant event of the session. Not, however, because of the erudition of her words, but because of her sheer beauty, her great charm and personality, and the simplicity of her plea for aid to China. Afterwards in the cloakroom Congressmen discussed not the logic of her arguments for greater aid to her stricken country, but asked, "Did she use make-up, was her beauty natural?" After captivating Congressmen she spoke in a number of the larger cities to audiences of five and ten thousand people. The press praised her beauty and her wisdom. Indeed she captivated the heart of America, as Willkie had predicted.

In his many speeches in China, Willkie emphasized several themes. The most important was that after the war a new world must be created. All nations, he said, must be free to seek their own aspirations. The imperialistic spheres of influence which had held back China's progress for a century must be abolished, along with the mandate system of the League of Nations. In their place must stand a totally free China entering on a new era in which the traditional poverty of China's masses would be ended.

Another theme he stressed was that the time had come for an all-out offensive. There must be more American arms for China and Russia with immediate "ironclad guarantees against any western imperialism in Asia." More planes, especially, must be sent to China. All the United Nations should help in this broad effort for a world-wide offensive.

And finally he explained to his audience that 22,000,000 people voted for him. He wanted to report to these people the effort that was being made by the peoples of other lands to win victory. By telling his fellow Americans about them and their war work he expected to bring about a better understanding between the two nations.

However, much that Willkie said was garbled in the Chinese

press because of faulty translation. Willkie had placed himself in the hands of Mr. Hollington Tong ("Holly"), who did the translating. The American Embassy was annoyed, but helpless. Thus when Willkie spoke of Woodrow Wilson's dream of a new world, Tong translated it by using a term with the connotation of "illusion." Several times Willkie talked about the Chinese people, meaning the common man, who must have better opportunities in the post-war world. This was translated as the Chinese nation, or China.

His radio speech to the Chinese people just before leaving the war capital presented the plan of action which offered hope not only for winning the war but for a bright new future. He proposed that the United States should keep as large an air force in China as possible. The United States and Britain should at once undertake the recapture of Burma. The United States should send bombing planes against Japanese cities. The United States should consider the Chinese front and the European front as of equal importance. And the United States and China should co-operate to the fullest in winning not only a military victory but even more important in rebuilding a new and better world order in which every people regardless of color, race, or religion should enjoy equal freedom to develop its national life. "So goodbye and good luck. I hope that the next time I meet you again you will all be citizens of a free world," he concluded.

The American Embassy at Chungking was as disturbed by his recommendations for China as had been the Embassy at Kuibyshev by his demand for a second front. On the other hand, Willkie considered the protocol of the service as so much red tape. This, of course, resulted in endless confusion and embarrassment. While his mission was that of a publicist and it was imperative that he get his story into print, it was thought he might have used greater tact and been more observant of international good manners. His relations with the newspapermen were at times rather crass. Shortly after his arrival in Chungking Willkie was at a reception where he was the guest of honor, when the newsmen arrived. At once he left his Chinese hosts for about fifteen minutes while he held a press interview. High Chinese officials accepted the rudeness in Oriental good humor.

Clearly Willkie knew what he wanted to do in China and it was not orthodox. Nevertheless he achieved his objective to make friends of the Chinese people. Willkie enjoyed his expeditions alone among the people and the constant mingling with the crowds along the narrow, ancient streets. He brought them hope and cheer. The people of China were war weary, and worn and despondent. But the fire and confidence of this great American gave courage to valiant millions. He was able to dramatize America to them with all its mystery of untold wealth and priceless supply of planes and weapons of war. Indeed, he promoted generous good will—he put water in that "raisevarr" of good will he so often talked about.

The Generalissimo and his staff felt that the reception of Willkie had gone off well, and that they had made a friend of the "next President" of the United States. From the American viewpoint, probably no more fitting gesture could have concluded the Willkie friendship tour than the announcement by the United States Government on October tenth, just after Willkie had left Chungking, that it was prepared in concert with the British Government to relinquish immediately its century-old extraterritorial rights in China.

On the way to Chungking Willkie had anticipated with eagerness an opportunity to talk with Brigadier General Claire Lee Chennault, the gallant commander of the American Volunteer Group which had recently been inducted into the United States Air Force under the designation of the China Air Task Force. He had long watched the daring exploits of the American volunteer airmen who had protected the Chinese Republic in the darkest days of the Japanese invasion. The "Flying Tigers" had actually held back Japanese air and ground forces from overrunning all of South China.

Willkie was therefore disappointed to find that no arrangements had been made for him to meet Chennault in Chungking. When he realized that General Stilwell, the commanding general of the American Army Forces in China, showed little interest in his request, Willkie began to suspect that the American military officers preferred not to have the meeting take place. On the eve of his departure he insisted upon visiting with the commanding officer of the recent Flying Tigers and was not surprised that Stilwell himself then proposed to accompany him to the CATF headquarters at Peishiyi.

Arriving at Peishiyi, Willkie demanded a private talk with Chennault. Thus, Stilwell was compelled to wait impatiently in the outer office while Chennault and Willkie conversed for two hours. To his amazement, Willkie learned that the spectacular raids against the Japanese air and ground forces were being made with only five bombers and that all of China was being defended with only forty-eight fighter-planes. He had assumed that the Flying Tigers possessed an adequate air force.

"Have you made any recommendations for expansion," asked Willkie.

Chennault replied that he had proposed an American Air Force of 105 fighter-planes, 30 medium bombers and 12 heavy bombers, with replacements of thirty per cent in fighter-planes and twenty per cent in bombers.

"What will you accomplish with these reinforcements?" asked Willkie.

Chennault replied that this air force could not only hold back the Japanese armies in South China but also attack Japanese shipping off the coast. Since the "life-line" between industrial Japan and its overseas conquests in Siam, Cochin-China, Malaya, Java, Burma, and the Philippines lay along the South China coast, the proposal of Chennault offered great strategic possibilities. Willkie readily perceived that this plan would greatly cripple the Japanese war effort and assist General MacArthur.

"Has this plan been laid before the President?" queried Willkie.

Chennault explained he had followed the necessary chain of command. He had formally presented his plan to General Stilwell, his superior officer, but he doubted whether it had been forwarded to General George C. Marshall, Chief of Staff, in Washington. Even if the plan had been sent to the Chief of Staff, Chennault was skeptical of Marshall's approval of it. At a later date, Willkie was to learn that Stilwell had pigeonholed the Chennault plan. Only as a means of wiping out the sting of his Burma defeat did "Vinegar Joe" see any merit in attacking Japanese shipping off the coast of South China.

"Would you present this plan to the President, in case he ordered you to report it?" asked Willkie.

"Certainly," replied Chennault. "The President is Commander-in-Chief of the Army and Navy."

"Then, would you report to the President, in case a representative of the President ordered you to report?" Willkie promptly asked.

Upon Chennault's eager assent, Willkie said:

"I am a representative of the President and I order you to prepare such a report immediately. I myself will carry it to the President."

Chennault was delighted. With his aide, Colonel Merian C. Cooper, he spent several days and nights in hasty preparation of the report to the President. It was dispatched to Willkie by air courier and reached him at Chengtu just before he took off for Siberia and Alaska. After his arrival in Washington, Willkie presented the report to the President, who seemed equally astonished at the lack of support given to General Chennault. The President sent the report to the Secretary of War with a suggestion for a prompt decision.

Although American war effort was feverishly concentrated on Operation Torch (the invasion of North Africa), it was apparent that the fulfillment of promises to the Generalissimo could no longer be postponed. In March, 1943, the Fourteenth Air Force was activated in China; Chennault was made a Major General; and a bomber group of four-engine Liberators (B-24's) arrived at Kunming. The Hump tonnage soon rose to nearly thirteen thousand tons per month. With these reinforcements, Chennault performed miracles in the air. He paralyzed Japanese air power in South China, and struck at the Japanese sea route to Burma, sinking well over two million tons of merchant shipping and forty-four naval vessels. This aid to General Chennault was the concrete accomplishment of Willkie's stay in China. By it he earned the everlasting gratitude of all those in official circles who understood the situation.

Willkie had departed from Chungking on the ninth of October. He first flew to Sian in Shensi Province to visit the fighting front, which was not far distant from this base-city, before quitting Chinese territory. At the conclusion of the visit to Sian, the

Willkie party returned to Chengtu, from which point the *Gulliver* took off to circle northward to Fairbanks, Alaska, then southward to the States. The ATC transport reached Minneapolis on the thirteenth of October. At Minneapolis, Willkie received a message that threw him into a towering rage. Even in China, newspapermen had conveyed to him rumors that the President was highly displeased with his words and actions throughout the tour. The message that he received in Minneapolis confirmed in his mind the criticism he had heard was emanating from the White House during his sojourn abroad. The President had determined that Willkie, as a presidential representative, should make no speeches in the United States until he had reported to the White House and obtained a release on his remarks. Accordingly, Stephen Early, the President's secretary, begged Sam Pryor to undertake the difficult mission of getting Willkie to Washington before he made a public address. By concentrated effort, Pryor reached Willkie only a few minutes after he landed in Minneapolis and informed him of the President's message.

To Willkie, the President's command must have appeared to be nothing less than an attempt to censor him and to intervene between himself and that part of the American public that was willing to listen to him. Nevertheless, he refrained from any public statement and flew directly to Washington to see President Roosevelt. When he was ushered into the President's study, he at once launched into such a tirade as was never heard in that room before. Willkie began by saying, "I know that you are the President and that you can throw me out, but until you do I am going to say a few things to you and you are going to listen." He then proceeded to upbraid the President for criticizing him while he was overseas. The President evidently listened; at least Willkie was not thrown out.

On the twenty-sixth of October, Willkie made his famous report to the people from New York City over the combined networks of Columbia Broadcasting System, the National Broadcasting Company, the Mutual Broadcasting System, and the Blue Network. He told the people where he had been and something of what he had seen. Then he made his criticisms and recommendations on foreign policy. First, he pointed to the "tragically small amount of vital war materials" sent to the other nations. Second, he charged this Government with sending inferior representatives to nations "proud and sensitive," which could only promote unfriendliness. In one instance, he said, a minister did not speak the language of the country to which he was accredited. Again, Russia was hurt, he declared. At no time had a person of Cabinet rank been appointed to a special commission sent to the Soviet Union. This had irritated the Moscovites. And in the Arab-speaking countries of the Near East, no minister had been sent of the rank of ambassador. These people resented their second-class rating. Lastly, he pleaded for a second front to relieve the pressure upon "our superb fighting allies."

More constructive was his thesis upon the peace which was to come. "We must fight our way through not alone to the destruction of our enemies but to a new world idea. We must win the peace." But to achieve this peace it must be planned for, beginning now, on a global basis. The world must be free, and America must take an active, constructive part in bringing it about. Global thinking, he emphasized, was now essential if America was to win the peace. Imperialism must be ended forever. To the people of the Far East, he declared, freedom meant abolition of the colonial system. And they were looking to the United States for leadership.

Willkie dramatized the working relationship of the peoples of the world. "Global unity," he called it. This was an old dream which had stirred him ever since he returned from France in 1919. He had then believed in the League of Nations. Now he believed that world peace could only be achieved by all the peoples, the free peoples of the world, working together.

Although Willkie had absented himself from the country during the height of the 1942 campaign, and had refused to engage in any partisan politics after his return, political commentators were generally agreed that he had made the best speech of the campaign. He had greatly strengthened the internationalist group within the party, and he dispelled the feeling of many people that he was lacking experience and knowledge of international affairs.

Not content with his radio report to the nation, Willkie produced a more enduring report for all to read who might desire.

He wrote an account called *One World*. The small book was published in March, 1943. It was expected that perhaps one hundred and fifty thousand copies might be sold. Eventually two million copies rolled off the presses. Willkie told a simple story of the peoples he had visited. The human qualities of faith, hope, devotion, and labor were the same in all countries. Peoples were actuated by the same motives and responded in like manner the world over. They all wanted freedom. They all wanted peace. This was the hope and the foundation of "One World."

The vivid story gripped the imagination of the people. It crystallized the sentiment for world co-operation and international organization. The very title, *One World,* made people think in terms of global unity. The term sank into the public consciousness and was used and re-used by speakers from coast to coast. The old isolationist view which had become weakened during the war period now crumbled and disintegrated under his compelling enthusiasm. It paved the way for American acceptance of the idea of a new international government under the Charter of the United Nations. It was the most important book to come out of the war period.

Willkie as publicist again touched the lofty heights of enlightened leadership. Others did the planning for the United Nations and blueprinted its organization, but Willkie publicized the idea of "One World." None of the international spokesmen, not even Roosevelt himself, so warmly appealed to the hearts and the imagination of Americans in the cause of global unity and global responsibility. Moreover, the book was widely read in other lands and contributed to the "reservoir of friendship." In all history there have been few books that have created so much general good feeling among the peoples of the earth. It was a triumph that time cannot dull. Willkie made the man on the street as well as the man of public affairs conscious of ONE WORLD.

CHAPTER XVI

A Personality of Contrasts

WILLKIE WAS a man of many moods and swiftly changing facets. He was a man of imagination and temperament, a man of contradictions and contrasts. He was many things to many people. This made him a complicated individual to understand. In fact, he was a stranger to everyone who knew him. Like all undisciplined philosophers, he was guilty of defects in logic. Nonetheless, no one of his countrymen had made a more cogent defense of free enterprise and individualism. Among his literary friends he was more amenable to social change than he was when talking to bankers from Wall Street. Few of his associates had acquaintances with more people in New York City than Willkie, yet he was accounted one of the loneliest persons in the great metropolis. His glowing personality easily attracted numerous friends, yet his ever-thoughtless discourtesies alienated them one by one.

Before a group of a dozen to several hundred persons he was a scintillating speaker, but before an audience of ten thousand he was a disappointment. He possessed an irresistible will to win, yet inevitably he would do the little things to defeat himself. A lawyer trained in logic, a brilliant debater, he was also highly emotional and his violent temper frequently involved him in saying the wrong things. The top executive of a billion-dollar corporation, supposedly a person of caution, he made many decisions hastily, even impetuously, and for this reason was frequently labeled a poor administrator. He loved to argue over ideas but was impatiently contemptuous of those who thought more slowly than did he. He was a great showman, a front man, a magnificent purveyor of ideas, but too temperamental and individualistic to be either a good politician or a good diplomat, yet withal a man of fine courage.

One of Willkie's greatest assets was his talent for making friends. He was informal and casual. At the end of the workday he frequently called unexpectedly upon some friend for a cocktail before going home to dinner. One of his favorite late-afternoon haunts was the home of Helen Rogers Reid, of the *New York Herald Tribune*. Although her husband was the nominal head of the famous newspaper, it was generally recognized that the personality of this great newspaper came from his brilliant wife. At the Reid home, Willkie first met many of his dearest friends.

Willike found stimulation and excitement in a wide variety of people. He so thoroughly enjoyed the encounter of fresh ideas that he would argue about them until early morning. For this reason he had a wide diversity of friends who were like so many antennae extending into the world of literature, journalism, finance and politics. Willkie's friends among the intellectuals were not limited to the masculine sex. Career women, typical of New York's commercial and artistic life, intrigued him. Despite the unhappy home of his youth and the lack of sympathy between him and his mother, he always maintained an admiration for the successful professional woman. When he was in Turkey, on his round-the-world flight, he met in Ankara a woman distinguished in law who was at the time arguing a case before the Turkish Supreme Court. He recounted the story in *One World* and said: "And this was in Turkey. I could not help thinking of my boyhood days when, only forty years ago, my mother's active practice of the law and interest in public affairs were considered unusual—almost peculiar—in central Indiana."

One of the outstanding intellectuals in New York of the last several decades was Irita Van Doren, the divorced wife of Carl

Van Doren. She was literary editor of the *Herald Tribune,* a woman of dynamic energy, and a critic of unusual discernment. Willkie was fascinated by her whimsical logic and catholic interests. Essays that she thought he ought to read were put aside for him. Books in the field of politics and economics were brought to his attention. It was she who encouraged him in politics, and it was she who became the sounding board for many of his ideas. Through her he also met the literary group that gave him unusual mental stimulation. A close bond of friendship and mutual interests bound them together for the last eight years of his life.

The charm and personal attractiveness of Willkie were recorded by Raoul de Roussy de Sales in *The Making of Yesterday,* his vivid account of this distracting era. He told of the first time he had had a close-up of Willkie, at a dinner party at Hamilton Armstrong's in May, 1941. "It was a great surprise. I understand a little better his charm for women: a lock of his hair carelessly falls over his forehead, the eyes which can take on an expression of reverie, the very masculine looks, the good health and a certain warmth of the generous good fellow—all this can be pleasing."

Willkie's personal attraction reached even the man in the street. After the presidential campaign of 1940, which introduced him to millions of voters, demonstrations occurred whenever he appeared in public. Upon his return to New York from his trip to England in early 1941, a crowd of several hundred was at the airport to meet him, although his plane arrived at eight o'clock on Sunday morning. When he returned from his world flight in 1942, he went to Rushville to join his wife. Together they came back to New York by train. En route, they took luncheon in the public dining car. As they left the car everyone rose as one person and remained standing until they had departed. It was a simple tribute of deep respect.

Before he became a candidate for the presidency, the Willkies frequently attended the theater. After the presidential campaign of 1940, the family resumed the practice. Philip often accompanied his father and mother. At the theater, as soon as the family of three found their seats, it was not unusual for a dozen admirers to press around Willkie, requesting his autograph on the theater programs. During the intermission, when father and son went to the foyer for a breath of air, they would soon be surrounded by a crowd of enthusiastic supporters. After the show, not infrequently a police guard was required to conduct the Willkie family through the crowd to a taxicab. In the same theater, at the same time, Governor Thomas E. Dewey came and went almost unnoticed.

Not only the man on the street, but also the most powerful industrialists and financiers, who heard him speak at the Bond Club or the Economic Club, would be captivated by his words. His personality, his appearance, as well as his argumentation, gripped his hearers. Willkie was a big-framed and husky man. His hulking figure had a certain heaviness about it. There was noticeable an innate clumsiness in his movements. He almost lurched or lumbered about the room. This might be accounted for by his size and also perhaps by the fact that as a young man he had never learned to dance. His mannerisms, however, were wholly captivating. The forelock of hair falling over his forehead gave him an earnest, informal appearance; the shining deep blue eyes frequently lighting up in a gay twinkle lent a softness and humor to his speech; and in a public speech the giant-spread arms always gave a dramatic evangelistic sort of entreaty to his words. Physically, Willkie was a commanding figure; he radiated power and magnetism. He could arouse great admiration in any gathering and his remarkable personality always dominated the room. A distinguished economist, C. Reinold Noyes, in describing a wedding which Willkie and his wife attended, remarked that more eyes were fastened on Willkie than on the bride, who was a well-known beauty.

Yet with all his natural gifts of personality and mind, Willkie lost friends almost as rapidly as he made them. Without realizing his discourtesy, he would wound and offend. Although he was extremely sensitive himself, he had a sort of blind spot about the feelings of others. No one was ever close enough to him to censure him and at the same time retain his friendship. He once even warned his staff at the office of the Commonwealth and Southern Corporation that he did not want them to criticize his actions or his statements. When Harold Talbott attempted to point out some of the more flagrant mistakes in the campaign, Willkie savagely replied, "You cannot talk to me like that!" Probably the most sympathetic of all his friends, except Russell Davenport, to whom Willkie could do no wrong, was Sinclair Weeks. He came nearest of all to speaking frankly to him. On several occasions Weeks said, "You can dish it out, but you cannot take it!" Willkie was incredulous and repudiated the charge. He never realized that he was what the musical world calls a prima donna.

Lack of small courtesies frequently chilled his friendships. He often came to Washington, even after the 1940 campaign. But never on these trips did he telephone Charles Halleck or invite him to luncheon, and only rarely did he get in touch with Joe Martin. Nor could he understand why he should extend these courtesies to political associates.

Another habit by which he forfeited the regard and even affection of his associates was his own lack of confidence in them. Too easily he discredited their sincerity and too frequently charged a "double cross." He was often moody, and at these times was oppressed by imaginary grievances. Always deeply concerned with his own problems, he scarcely ever stopped to remember that his friends also had troubles. The loyal support of his colleagues he accepted with rarely any show of appreciation, taking for granted their ever-ready cooperation.

Another curious contradiction was his simplicity and his arrogance. He liked to talk with people: humble and distinguished, young and old, they always held interest for him. Even as a young man he had enjoyed meeting people. He had a real affection for humanity. It was easy for almost anyone to call at his office and see him. Even the manner of his transportation was unassuming. No shining limousine conveyed him around New York. Each morning, from his apartment on upper Fifth Avenue, he took a subway train to reach the financial section in the old historic river area around Trinity Church. Occasionally, if the morning were bright, he would take the more leisurely way of driving down Fifth Avenue by taxicab. It was a matter of press comment, when he went to Brooklyn for his pre-convention campaign speech in June, 1940, that he traveled by subway. Crowded into these trains, hanging on to a strap, brushing shoulders with ordinary people, hearing their conversation he felt in contact with all America.

On the other hand, Willkie had a strange belief in his destiny. This faith in his star gave him on occasions something of the feeling of an exalted being. Rules were made for the rank and file to follow, but big people must establish their own way of accomplishment. Thus he frequently maintained a cavalier contempt for precedents and routine procedure. When the experts attempted to advise him regarding certain matters, he became irked. He intended to chart a new course in politics and in diplomacy. This gave rise to comments that he was stubborn, even "bull-headed." Some ascribed this trait to his German ancestry, some to his faulty early training, and others to his ego.

This loftiness of view, this feeling of superior wisdom, however, was not peculiar to Willkie. It is a common trait among men who achieve high distinction. It was reported that Alf Landon, whom the politicians considered a nice, simple little fellow from the plains of Kansas, became filled with self-importance five minutes after his nomination for the presidency in 1936. Even F.D.R., according to Raymond Moley, with all his attributes of greatness, gradually assumed an air of infallibility that at times was unbearable. Although Willkie never possessed the ridiculous self-righteousness of several contemporaries, he did profess oracular judgment. With this lofty sentiment went the corollary that those about him should act as aides assigned to do little personal errands for him. In the Wisconsin primary campaign, for example, Willkie was entertained at dinner by the Governor. As he was hurriedly leaving his hotel to go to the Executive Mansion, he remembered that flowers should be sent to Mrs. Goodland, the Governor's wife. Pressing a bill into the hand of a distinguished citizen, he directed him to "send roses."

The contrast to this superior and all-wise attitude was his remarkable will to win. Ernest Weir once said that in all his life he never saw anyone so keen on winning. Some friends traced this determination to the days of his childhood. His mother kept parroting to her children that they must always succeed, for the greatest of all crimes was failure! This teaching was in his blood. It gave him a drive and a perseverance that reached almost the level of superhuman effort. Raoul de Roussy de Sales also recognized this trait: "Generally speaking, he seems to believe that a cause which he himself supports must finally triumph because he has faith in it as simple people have faith."

This exceptional stress upon success carried with it the subconscious fear of failure. It produced a quirk in his emotional make-up akin to defeatism. This inner uncertainty was also noticed by his friends. As Frank Altschul watched Willkie, he surmised that there was an element of defeat in every success that he scored. Constantly Willkie did the odd things which would hurt himself. Some people attributed his throat trouble to this subconscious fear of failure. He never started on a political speaking tour but his throat began to hurt him and his voice to grow strained and raucous. Throat specialists insisted there was nothing wrong, nevertheless the discomfort persisted. It is true that he never learned how to use his voice in speaking to large crowds, and it is also true that he punished his voice by speaking frequently from the back end of the train or from an automobile. Yet other politicians go through the same grind without similar ill effect. Furthermore, he could have had the 1944 presidential nomination, but he lost it through sheer folly.

Yet few men who have reached the top have been so modest of their success as was Willkie. He was fond of saying that success was largely a matter of good luck. All anyone could do, he said, was to be good in his job, so good as to attract attention. Whether one could achieve the pinnacle of success would depend "on the breaks one got." He might well have added that native wit and a strong, rugged physique were also helpful.

Willkie was erratic, highly emotional, with many idiosyncrasies. He never owned an automobile because he said that he liked to talk so much that he could not drive with safety. But even more strange was his habit of never carrying a watch. He always maintained that he really did not need a timepiece. Clocks were all over town, in almost every store window and on numerous street corners. In almost any way he looked, wherever he was, he could ascertain the time. One of his colleagues from Commonwealth and Southern told an anecdote which describes a meeting with Willkie about six o'clock one evening in front of the Grand Central Station in New York on the 42nd Street side. After the perfunctory words of greeting, Willkie began to peer to the right and the left. Asked what he was looking for, Willkie replied that he was trying to see what time it was inasmuch as his porter had not yet come with his bags and he was taking a six o'clock train. With considerable amusement, the colleague looked at his own watch and remarked it was then three minutes after the hour and that the porter was probably on the train waiting for him. Thereupon Willkie went loping off through the long passenger tunnel in the hope of catching a train that had already left the station.

A curious characteristic of Willkie was his forgetfulness in small, simple matters. He could meet the same person half a dozen times and never remember either the name or the face. He was always happy to meet new acquaintances, but he forgot them as soon as he passed on. Equally careless was he of hats, coats and even his briefcase with important papers, which were continually left in trains or taxicabs and later retrieved by his capable secretary. Forgetfulness often caused the deepest embarrassment. One evening he had the duty of introducing an old friend and distinguished Senator to a vast audience in New York City, and forgot the name of the speaker. The occasion was a great East-West rally under the auspices of Pearl Buck at the Waldorf-Astoria Hotel. It was the same night that Chiang Kai-shek met with Gandhi in India early in the Second World War. The Senator was Elbert D. Thomas (Utah). They had been friends since the time when both of them had worked for the nomination of Newton D. Baker. Both had been influenced by the same brand of internationalism. Both worshiped at the shrine of Thomas Jefferson. Yet Willkie's introduction of his old friend might better have been performed by the bright boy of the eighth grade in almost any public school in the United States.

"Ladies and Gentlemen, we now have the honor—the pleasure —of listening to the United States Senate—the United States Senator from Oklahoma—the Honorable Elmer Thomas."

A recording was made of these speeches and sent around the world. Those in far-off places who heard a transcript of the broadcast were unaware of the fact that under the name of

Elmer Thomas of Oklahoma they were listening to the voice of Elbert D. Thomas of Utah.

On the other hand, his colleagues admired the power of concentration with which Willkie attacked problems. He would become so immersed in thought as he paced up and down his office that the entrance of his secretary or aide went unnoticed. On such occasions they had literally to shake him out of his trance in order to secure his attention. Frequently, Willkie would send for documents to be brought in from the files but, by the time they arrived, he was again so deep in thought as to be wholly unaware of their arrival or the person who brought them.

Even in his reading, Willkie was a personality of contrasts. The student of his life would expect to find his reading to be largely in the field of economics, since he was the leader of the crusade for free enterprise. On the contrary, his reading was mostly history. Perhaps the one year that he taught history in the high school at Coffeyville, Kansas, confirmed his prejudice for this discipline. At all events his deep interest in history never wavered. The history of the Civil War period and of the Old South fascinated him. He also read extensively in English history of the seventeenth and eighteenth centuries. Internationalist that he was from the end of the First World War to the day of his death, he devoured books on the League of Nations and American foreign policy. Contemporary books on economics, political theory, government and constitutional law were conspicuously absent from his book shelves. He once made a flattering reference in a public address to *Capitalism, the Creator* (1940) by Carl Snyder, a distinguished statistician and a member of the Federal Reserve Board of New York. Snyder had sent a copy of his book to Willkie. A powerful argument for free enterprise, the treatise was considered the best defense of capitalism ever offered by an American scholar. Willkie gave the book only a hurried and superficial glance, although his complimentary reference to it considerably boosted its sales.

Willkie advised his son, Philip, to take his graduate work at Harvard University in history rather than economics. The young man was deeply interested in economics and had intended to pursue graduate studies in this field. "I have had enough of economists in Washington," Willkie said with a laugh. "I don't want to live with one at home."

His preference for history over economics gave another clue to his political philosophy. He believed the American people had the imagination and the stamina to reach unlimited goals of production with an ever-higher increase in living standards. The twentieth century had only touched the fringe of what might be. The frontier of the future, he so often said, would be in scientific development which would make a more glorious America than any progress of the past. He had an abiding faith in America. Because of this great faith the whole New Deal fabrication to him was a philosophy of defeatism born of fear. The bright promise of a free enterprise system he thought was beyond the scope of anything the New Deal could offer.

Although, in the years of the social revolution, he was the sharpest critic and the most articulate opponent of the Roosevelt Government when the war clouds spread over Europe he was the first to call for national unity and to remind the people that Franklin Roosevelt was the President of the United States and "our Commander-in-Chief." It took no less courage for him to shift from being the most vigorous adversary of the White House to the spokesman for unity and loyalty than it had in 1936 when businessmen were so stunned by the strategy of the New Dealers that few dared oppose even the most ridiculous features of the Roosevelt program. Certainly, the President would have faced a most difficult task in those dark days of 1940 and 1941 if it had not been for the honesty and patriotism of Wendell Willkie calling for all-out support of all Administration war measures.

Willkie early discovered that his public life circumscribed his private affairs. By January, 1940, he determined to leave Commonwealth and Southern Corporation, and became committed to a partnership in the distinguished law firm of Miller, Owen, Otis and Bailey. He had an understanding with them that he would not sever his connections with C&S until after the Philadelphia Convention. If he won the nomination he would devote himself to the campaign. Otherwise, he would immediately become active in the firm. As he did secure the nomination his active partnership with Miller, Owen, Otis and Bailey was postponed for a little over a year.

After his defeat for the presidency in 1940, Willkie received some two hundred offers of executive posts. One such offer was from his old friend, Juan Trippe, president of Pan American Airways. Trippe asked Willkie to join his company as a vice-president. But Willkie replied: "No, it would never do. It couldn't possibly work out. You are a one-man organization. You run the company. I am a one-man organization, too!" This incident recalls a story friends told of his boyhood, when he was a pupil in grammar school. The teacher asked each boy in the class to tell what he desired when he grew to manhood. Some did not know, some wanted money, some wanted happiness, but Willkie wanted "power"! As a star he could perform brilliantly, but he never learned team-play or group strategy. Many of his mistakes in politics could be attributed to this characteristic.

In many ways, Willkie had done exceedingly well with Commonwealth and Southern Corporation. For the consumer he had decreased residential rates from five cents to three cents per kilowatt hour and increased service to farms and private homes from 600,000,000 kilowatt hours a year to 1,200,000,000. Sale of appliances jumped from five million dollars in 1933 to nearly nineteen million in 1937. When he became president of C&S, the utility industry was caught in the backlog of the depression. While other companies were laying off men, Willkie engaged five hundred salesmen to increase the demand for electric power. To stimulate further the household use of power, he introduced the "objective rate," or the system whereby a consumer using more than a certain amount of electricity per month would receive a reduced rate. By these devices, he placed the utility business upon a merchandising basis.

Despite his success as president of C&S, Willkie had become restless. The man who had fought the New Deal to a standstill in the Tennessee Valley and who had won for his company a settlement of nearly $30,000,000 additional to the price originally offered—and that from an angry and reluctant Government—had lost interest in the routine management of the great

corporation. Just running a billion-dollar corporation after all
the years of excitement in the congressional hearings and in
presidential politics now seemed insipid. He yearned for the
drama and excitement of the courtroom. Moreover, Willkie was
not primarily an executive. He was a public relations expert.
His great talent was to dramatize a situation, and to develop
ideas.

It cannot be said that the directors of C&S were loath to see
Willkie go. They had been yanked through seven years of
turmoil and emotionalism. Sober and prosaic businessmen, they
were eager to see C&S at last disappear from the headlines of
the newspapers. They wanted to return to normalcy. Even the
greatest admirer of Willkie in C&S would agree that as an
executive, Justin Whiting was a more able officer.

In April, 1941, Willkie concluded his public affairs and was
ready actively to join the legal firm of Miller, Owen, Otis and
Bailey. Harold J. Gallagher had been instrumental in the first
place in bringing Willkie into the firm. As Jeffersonian Democrats, both Gallagher and Willkie had worked together in the
1936 campaign for Landon. He had also been one of the amateurs who boomed Willkie's candidacy in 1940, and later was
manager of his speaking tour. Willkie replaced Nathan L.
Miller, who had been a great trial lawyer and a former governor
of New York and now was retiring from active practice. Willkie,
therefore, was to carry on the tradition of Miller as a trial
lawyer.

Hardly had Willkie opened his desk in the new law firm
reorganized as Willkie, Owen, Otis, Farr and Gallagher than
he was retained for a sensational case. The isolationists had
attacked the motion picture industry as showing pictures favorable to aid to Britain. Finally, in the desperate attempt to reverse public opinion, Senators Wheeler, Gerald P. Nye and
Bennett Champ Clark secured an investigation of the industry
by a subcommittee of the Committee on Interstate Commerce
in the Senate. Willkie was retained to represent the producers
at a reported fee of $100,000.

The proceedings were extremely bitter. Willkie was more
than a match for the isolationists in the Senate, and successfully

defended his client. When the subcommittee denied Willkie the right to cross-examine the witnesses who attacked the industry, Willkie declared that Chairman Nye sought to "divide the American people into discordant racial and religious groups in order to disunite them over United States foreign policy." The country agreed with this assertion. Willkie's plea to Senators to view the accused pictures before condemning the motives of the producers found approval in every state of the Union. Most Americans had already seen these films and heartily approved. The hearing quickly developed into a personal attack on Willkie. Within a few days, amidst the jeers of the internationalists, the investigation completely collapsed. Wheeler, Nye and Clark had lost more than they had gained by this clumsy maneuver. When a few months later came the sneak attack by the Japanese Navy on Pearl Harbor, it seemed incredible to many that with America fighting for her life against the Axis the motion picture industry should have required defense only a few months previously from the extraordinary charge that it was engaged in propaganda against the totalitarian forces of the Axis Powers.

So well did he represent the industry that a short time later he was elected chairman of the board of Twentieth Century-Fox, while his firm was retained as special counsel. The retainer fee was estimated at $200,000 a year. As chairman, however, Willkie was not to perform any executive duties or be actively connected with the operation of the company. The lucrative assignment inspired Senator Rush D. Holt, of West Virginia, to quip that "the barefoot boy of Wall Street had become the glamour boy of Hollywood."

It was his connection with Twentieth Century-Fox that led Willkie to urge the filming of the life story of Woodrow Wilson. He felt that the picture would be a great influence in developing public opinion for a United Nations organization. The picture, which was released during the closing period of the war, pivoted around the war years of the great President who more than any other statesman was responsible for the creation of the League of Nations. Undoubtedly one of the greatest historical pictures ever produced, it renewed the faith of millions of voters in an international organization for promoting international good will. Willkie's one venture in this great medium was a smash hit.

The sensation of the motion picture hearings had hardly ceased when Willkie took part in another equally famous case. He had returned from his world flight only a few weeks earlier when his help was solicited to represent an alleged Communist, William Schneiderman by name, in his appeal before the Supreme Court. Two lower federal courts in California had rendered a decision revoking Schneiderman's citizenship. The appeal was to be heard by the high court in January, 1943. The announcement that Willkie was willing to defend this man was front-page news. While many persons at the time questioned the wisdom of such a defense, this was the period when Willkie thought he understood the Soviet Union. Still fresh in his mind was his friendly meeting with Stalin. Also it should be remembered that Willkie always had a softness towards distressed persons.

William Schneiderman had been brought to the United States at the age of three. In 1922, at the age of sixteen, he became a charter member of the Young Workers (Communist League) in Los Angeles and remained a member until 1930. In the meantime, he had become a member of a group later designated as the Communist Party of the United States. A member in good standing, he attended the Sixth World Congress of the Communist International, held in Moscow in the early fall of 1928. Upon his return to the United States he became the secretary of the Communist Party for the district of California, Arizona and Nevada.

On the eighteenth of January, 1927, he filed a petition for American naturalization which was awarded to him some six months later by the United States District Court for the Southern District of California. According to the Naturalization Act passed by Congress in 1906, an applicant must behave during the five years preceding his petition for citizenship as a man attached to the principles of the Constitution. Had Schneiderman fulfilled this condition?

In 1939, an officer of the Immigration and Naturalization Service of the Department of Labor, as a result of a routine check of the records, discovered the irregularity of Schneiderman's naturalization. He initiated proceedings for the revocation of Schneiderman's citizenship by filing an affidavit contending that Schneiderman's naturalization had been "fraudulently and illegally procured." According to law, the department had the duty of asking the courts to set aside and cancel certificates of citizenship on the ground of fraud or illegal procurement. The government case rested on the fact that at the time of naturalization and five years previously Schneiderman was a member of the Communist Party of the United States which was opposed to the principles of the Constitution and which advocated the overthrow of the Government by force and violence.

According to some authorities, Schneiderman's defense was naive. Although Schneiderman readily admitted that he had continuously subscribed to the philosophy and principles of Marxian socialism as manifested in the writings of Marx and Lenin, he denied that either he or his party advocated the overthrow of the Government of the United States by force or violence. He even considered membership in the Communist Party as wholly compatible with the obligations of American citizenship. He stated that he believed in the retention of personal property for personal use, but had always advocated social ownership of the means of production and exchange, with compensation to the owners. In explanation of his use of the term, "dictatorship of the proletariat," he said he meant that the majority of the people should really direct their own destinies and use the instruments of the state for these truly democratic ends. All of this, of course, was far short of the principles of Marx and Lenin whom Schneiderman professed to follow.

In his defense before the Supreme Court in 1943, Willkie declared that this case was a vital one that might possibly affect every naturalized citizen. Although the petitioner admitted that he was a member of the Communist Party, Willkie stated that the individual liberty of an American citizen, and not the Communist Party, was on trial. He even went so far as to say that the real question was whether free institutions in this country were to be preserved by totalitarian methods or whether freedom of thought would remain as the basic foundation of the American way of life. He argued that until Congress definitely declared the Communist Party to be a cause for denial of citizenship, no court should rule in other than a favorable manner upon a case involving such a fundamental right.

Justice Frank Murphy read the majority decision, concurred in by Justices William O. Douglas, Wiley Rutledge, Hugo L. Black and Stanley F. Reed. Strange to record, Justice Murphy held that the "aim of the Communist Party in the United States in 1927, when Schneiderman was naturalized, was for a peaceful change of government at some indefinite time, rather than by sudden force or violence." Accordingly, the citizenship of Schneiderman was not revoked. The decision was a legal victory for Willkie.

Although Willkie found a majority of the Supreme Court on his side of the case, a calm scrutiny of the controversy, from the vantage point of history, leaves the student amazed at the strained reasoning of both Willkie and the majority of the Court.

Chief Justice Stone read the dissenting opinion, concurred in by Justices Owen J. Roberts and Felix Frankfurter. The Chief Justice tore the argument of Justice Murphy into ribbons. The question, he held, was much more simple than it had been made to appear. It was whether the petitioner in securing his citizenship by naturalization had fulfilled a condition which Congress had imposed on every applicant. The issue was not concerned with freedom of thought or speech or even the present imminent danger to the United States. The issue was simply: Had the plain intent of Congress in the Naturalization Act been met by the petitioner for citizenship?

The Chief Justice pointed to the evidence that the petitioner had attended the meeting of the Third International in 1928, and that he had been active in the Communist Party of the United States. There was abundant documentary evidence, he said, supporting the findings of the two lower courts that the Communist Party diligently circulated printed matter which advocated the overthrow of the American Government by force and violence, and that the petitioner had aided in the circulation and advocacy of such ideas.

Although the Alien Registration Act of 1940 made it a penal

offense against the United States to advocate knowingly the overthrow of the Government, or to help organize any group or society advocating violence, the Communist Party as such was not named. The Supreme Court in its decision of the Schneiderman case failed to declare whether or not the Communist Party was committed to the overthrow of the Government by force and violence. It dodged the logical issue of the case.

Writers and teachers promptly pointed to the text of the resolutions passed by the Communist International in 1928 in which Schneiderman took part. It said that the Communist Party was the vanguard of the working classes based upon the revolutionary theory of Marxism. "The Party personifies the unity of proletarian principles and proletarian revolutionary action. It is a revolutionary organization, bound by iron discipline and strict revolutionary rules of centralism."

The program of the Communist International (1928) then explained how the Communist Party would fulfill its historic mission of achieving the dictatorship of the proletariat. Communists must infiltrate in labor unions, co-operatives and cultural societies. After this had been accomplished and when the revolutionary tide was rising, when the ruling classes were disorganized, when the masses were in a state of revolutionary ferment, then the Party of the Proletariat must lead the direct attack upon the bourgeois state. It was further stated that the Executive Committee of the Communist International (E.C.C.I.) makes the decisions which are then obligatory for all sections (national Communist parties) of the International and must be promptly carried out. Thus it was impossible for Schneiderman to have sworn in good faith his adherence to the American Constitution when he was also bound to carry out the decisions of the high command of the Communist International.

As for Willkie, he had just returned from his world flight, and was full of brotherly love for all enemies of Hitler. He saw no contradiction between his position as the defender of free enterprise and his position as defender of a man who sought to destroy the American system by methods as ruthless as those of the Nazi dictator.

Within the year after his return from the Soviet Union, Willkie had reason to doubt the friendliness of the Communist dictator. He wrote a friendly article concerning Russia, published in the *New York Times* magazine section of January 2, 1944, entitled "Don't Stir Distrust of Russia." It was a warning to his Republican colleagues against adopting a policy of suspicion towards the USSR. He asked for simple American common sense and patience towards the Soviet Union. "We must recognize her for what she is: a mighty nation undertaking huge tasks and responsibilities in the modern world—the world in which we also live." On the other hand, he said, there was real concern by the people of this country over the intentions of the USSR towards the political integrity of the small states around her borders, such as Finland, Poland, the Baltic states and the Balkans. Herein was the most delicate problem facing the United States and the proposed United Nations. He ended: "There is only one way by which we can hope to gain acceptance of our ideas in Russian foreign policy, and that is to regard Russia as an equal with whom we desire to work and live. Our attitude towards her must be demonstrably the attitude of common sense and not of prejudice or passion."

To this moderate and optimistic essay, the Kremlin launched a crude and vehement rebuke. Under the title of "Willkie Is Muddying the Waters," *Pravda* published an article by a political columnist, David Zaslavsky. He charged that Willkie's concern over the border states showed hostility to the Soviet Union. In curt language he said that the question of the Baltic republics was an internal affair of the USSR, which would shape its foreign policy without advice from the American. He called Willkie an "obedient trumpet" reproducing the suspicious cries of those reactionaries who were afraid of a victorious forward movement of the Red Army and the Allied armies. He labeled the Willkie article "an assemblage of words in which there is a rotten smell of familiar anti-Soviet slanders designed to cause mistrust towards the Soviet Union." The article, of course, like all material published in *Pravda,* the official organ of the Communist Party in Russia, had the support of the dictator, Stalin.

The vicious reply to the Willkie article came at a particularly unfortunate time inasmuch as Willkie had told Republican Congressmen only a few weeks before how well he understood the Russian situation and that he above all other Americans knew how to handle Stalin. The *New York Times* commented editorially that the fact *Pravda* had suddenly chosen to berate Willkie for expressing opinions consistent with his own past views offered an inauspicious introduction to the rapidly approaching problem of a political settlement in eastern Europe. "The question from which none of us can escape is whether that settlement will be made by Russia unilaterally, on a basis of force, or within the framework of the United Nations." Edgar Ansel Mowrer, a famous syndicated news-writer, warned that the *Pravda* piece exposed the breakdown of Anglo-American diplomacy. In *Newsweek*, Ernest K. Lindley stated that by any test the attack by *Pravda* was a blunder, and all the more so in case Stalin had been sincere in the commitments made to the Allies at the conferences of Moscow and Teheran.

Thus, the friendship between Willkie and Stalin snapped. Willkie refused to comment publicly on the sudden turn of events. But privately he began to wonder whether there had ever been any friendship between himself and Stalin. Were the conversations and toasts in the Kremlin between himself and the dictator just words—deceitful words? He soon came to the conclusion that Stalin's promises were as worthless as those of Hitler or of any other totalitarian dictator. Even more than this, Willkie belatedly began to realize that the gulf between free America and the bureaucratic dictatorship of Soviet Russia was so great as to constitute a grave danger to the unity of One World. Meanwhile, the President had continued faith in the Russian dictator. A faith that led to Yalta thirteen months later.

The suspicions of the perfidy of Stalin came as a great shock to Willkie. His concept of One World rested on the belief that Soviet Russia was as eager for world co-operation as were the United States and Great Britain. Willkie was not so blind to reality as to assume that doctrines which are contradicted by facts should be assiduously maintained. One World was indeed, in Willkie's mind, a prerequisite for world peace. Its advent might not be as imminent as expected, but Willkie never lost his faith in its eventuality.

The Russian phase of Willkie's career was as replete with contradictions as any other episode in his public life. Willkie had many sides. The man of ideas and imagination is often one of contrasts and contradictions. The true greatness of Willkie lay in the brilliance of his ideas and his unique talent for publicizing these ideas, as well as his courage in standing alone to defend them. Yet the contrasts and contradictions of his personality annoyed his friends and plagued his enemies.

CHAPTER XVII

The Wisconsin Primary

ON A JUNE afternoon in 1942 several devoted friends arrived at the Fifth Avenue apartment of Wendell Willkie to keep an appointment. Conspicuous in the group were Frank Altschul and Alan Valentine. Still loyal to the defender of free enterprise, they believed that he should remain the standard-bearer of the Republican Party and be the presidential candidate in the election of 1944. The defeat of 1940 had alienated many party members, and embittered others. The faithful few who still rallied around the rejected candidate were not unaware of the obstacles in the way of his second nomination. Altschul and his friends were realists. To them it was axiomatic that Willkie must re-establish himself in political circles before the country would accept his candidacy in the presidential election of 1944. Only by election to public office could he erase the memory of the failure of 1940.

Hence these friends now gathered in his apartment to urge upon Willkie the need to enter the gubernatorial race in New York. It was a race that he could easily win. The governor's chair in New York would then be the springboard for the 1944 campaign. Not only would such a victory reinstate him politically, but it would give him most of the votes in the New York delegation at the 1944 Nominating Convention.

Ruefully the little delegation waited a long hour despite the hint from Edith Willkie that she was not expecting her husband to come home early. They were going out to dinner, she said, and Wendell would rush home only in time to dress before leaving for their engagement. Chagrined and disheartened, the group of friends finally took their departure. Willkie had not come nor did he later make the apology demanded by the occasion. On the following morning each friend received a telephone call from Willkie's secretary explaining there must have been some confusion as to the time. The secretary, however, suggested no future appointment.

Chilled by the indifference of the great man, the loyal little group abandoned their plans to promote his political fortunes. His imagination had failed to encompass the strategy offered by the governorship of New York. Two Roosevelts and a Cleveland had successfully used this office as the stepping-stone to the presidency, and Thomas Dewey clearly recognized its advantage.

Despite Willkie's lack of interest in the gubernatorial nomination, rumors persisted that he would accept the nomination. Efforts continued in his behalf by well-meaning friends and acquaintances. Among the most notable of these Willkie boom-movements was the one started by Stanley M. Rinehart, the publisher. All these efforts were finally halted in July when Willkie publicly announced that he would not be a candidate for the governorship. Political forecasters agreed that he could have been elected. His popularity was attested by the Gallup poll of June twentieth which gave Willkie fifty-four per cent of popular approval as compared to forty-eight per cent for Dewey. Some newspapers, in fact, were so persistent that they proposed Willkie should be run as a nonpartisan candidate. This Willkie himself repudiated at once by stressing the need for opposition parties.

Willkie's withdrawal from the field left the state contest to Dewey. Although experienced politicians recognized that this placed Dewey in a superior position of strategy for the presidential nomination, Willkie believed that he had neatly shelved Dewey for the next four years. Ever since Willkie had entered politics, he had his eyes so focused on the White House that he steadfastly refused to consider any lesser post. Meanwhile, as the New York gubernatorial campaign got under way, Willkie was making preparation for his famous world flight.

In the early spring of 1943, John D. M. Hamilton wrote to Sinclair Weeks in reply to questions he had raised on the 1944 presidential nomination. Hamilton stated that he would support Willkie again as he believed the standard-bearer had mended his ways since the impetuous days of 1940. Furthermore, Hamilton stated that he had been impressed with the recent writings of the former candidate. It was thus clear that the great strategist of the Republican Party was ready to forgive and forget the past mistakes of the audacious Willkie.

Meanwhile Willkie had finally realized that it took an experienced politician to win national elections. Belatedly, he recognized that Hamilton was the greatest national chairman of the Republican Party since the days of Mark Hanna. Ironically, Willkie now asked Hamilton to be his campaign manager. Hamilton was seriously considering this proposal when Willkie committed a series of blunders which for all time alienated him.

In August, Willkie visited his farms in Rushville. While in Indiana, he delivered a speech in Indianapolis casting slurs upon the National Republican Committee. Attacking colleagues of his own party had been the cause of much dissension in 1940. Hamilton was troubled when he heard of this new outburst. He was further annoyed when he learned that Willkie had been inviting groups of Republican leaders to come to Rushville for conferences. These exclusive meetings of selected members of the party aroused old suspicions and jealousies. Hence Hamilton reluctantly concluded that Willkie was the same unruly man he had known in the campaign of 1940, and would prove again his inadequacy as a presidential candidate. But Hamilton refrained from any statement of criticism.

Nevertheless, the position of the party on foreign and domestic issues moved definitely in line with Willkie's own views. Some political forecasters even predicted there would now be greater harmony within the party and a more ready acceptance of Willkie's leadership. Harrison E. Spangler, the new chairman of the party, called a meeting of the Republican Post-War Advisory Council to convene at Mackinac Island early in September.

The Advisory Council organized by Deneen Watson, of Chicago, at the beginning of summer, to formulate a party program on foreign and domestic issues in the post-war period, was a magnificent effort to support Willkie and to liberalize the Republican Party. The Mackinac meeting proved to be far more spectacular than anyone had thought possible. It elicited favorable editorial comments throughout the country. In attendance were forty-three party leaders, including Senators Arthur H. Vandenberg, Robert A. Taft, Warren R. Austin, Representatives Joseph W. Martin, Everett M. Dirksen, and Charles Halleck, and eighteen of the twenty-four Republican governors. Conspicuously not invited were Wendell Willkie, Herbert Hoover and Alf Landon.

The exclusion of Willkie from the Mackinac Conference was deliberate. His outspoken advocacy of international co-operation had made him the most provocative influence in the party since the time of Theodore Roosevelt. Had he led the party away from its old position of isolation? If so, then there was need for a more positive expression of the new policy of the Grand Old Party than the resolution accepted by the Republican National Committee in the preceding year. Another vigorous contest over this policy was expected. Thus, the party leaders reckoned that the exclusion of both Willkie and Hoover would promote harmony within the party.

The exclusion of Willkie gave Tom Dewey an opportunity long desired. Although he had done precious little to turn public opinion to internationalism, he was fully prepared to take any advantage of Willkie's great achievement in this field. It had been expected that the Willkie forces would do battle for foreign co-operation. But no one expected the conservative Governor of New York suddenly to take the lead in the issue. It was therefore a matter of some surprise that at the outset of the conference Governor Dewey declared himself for internationalism. His position was at once contested by Senator Taft, who stood by his previous views against any British-American military alliance.

A remarkable feature of the Mackinac Conference was the fact that the governors seized the initiative at the very start and maintained it througout the two-day session. The governors, now led by Dewey, supported the Willkie program and won the victory for world co-operation. The resulting declaration stated: The United States must aid in restoring order and decent living in a distressed world; and America must do its share in a program for permanent peace among nations. In addition the declaration dealt with domestic problems pertaining to employment, liberty, and a return to free enterprise. It was indeed a Willkie platform. By this declaration, the Republican Party committed itself to collective security through a world organization.

Deneen Watson was jubilant. In praise of the Mackinac declaration he said: "We highly commend the members of the Republican Post-War Advisory Council for the statement of foreign policy. It is a splendid step forward." Willkie was also highly pleased, and a few days later in a speech at Los Angeles, he proudly declared that the Republican Party was "drifting rapidly to the viewpoint I have long been advocating." *Time* called the Mackinac declaration the greatest tactical advance politically made by the Republican Party in years. Clearly, the party had now forsaken its position of isolation. It was now twice committed to the new program of its standard-bearer, first in the resolution of the National Republican Committee passed unanimously in April, 1942, and second in this declaration.

Up to this point the political situation looked especially favorable for Willkie. A large and important segment of the party had finally approved his policies. It was a victory for his courageous leadership, and he could justly rejoice in this remarkable success.

Willkie had long delayed formal announcement of his plans for the campaign of 1944. A few weeks after the Mackinac declaration, he presented his candidacy in a strange and dramatic fashion. The entire issue of *Look* was devoted to his pictures and campaign statements, which announced that he would be a candidate if the party committed itself to liberal objectives. These objectives included protection for minorities, efficient management in the federal Government, maintenance of the free enterprise system, social insurance, all-out effort to win the war, and international co-operation in the post-war world. The statement interested the press mainly for its restatement of his thesis on private enterprise. He asked for "a rebirth of enterprise." It must be a genuine not a fake enterprise. America must have competition, invention, expansion, lower rates for the consumer, and lower prices of manufactured goods, he declared. Only thus could the American people create more opportunities, raise the standard of living, and most important of all, maintain *real* jobs for all workers.

Although this was not a formal declaration that he would run, there was no longer any doubt as to his intentions. As the *New York Times* said, "he is in the field with everything but a formal announcement." The unregenerated conservatives were visibly unhappy. But Willkie was oblivious of their dissent. He expected to find compensating support in public opinion.

In late September, he went to the West Coast, partly on a business trip as chairman of the Twentieth Century-Fox Film Corporation and partly to go over the script of his movie, *One World,* which his company was going to produce. But mostly the western journey was a political scouting trip. The excursion was replete with political blunders. If he had seemed unwise in his party conclaves earlier at Rushville and too outspoken against party chiefs, it was only a prelude to what was to follow. In Los Angeles, Willkie boldly declared to newsmen that he would receive on the first ballot in the Republican Convention 400 votes out of the total of 1,058. This meant that Willkie expected to enter the convention of 1944 lacking only 129 votes of the nomination. But he went even further. He actually listed the expected votes of the various state delegations in the convention. Across the country, in Philadelphia, John Hamilton read with astonishment these rash statements in the press.

Already irritated over the Indianapolis speech and the little cliques summoned to Rushville, Hamilton concluded that the Los Angeles declaration was sheer dishonesty. No state could have committed delegates so far in advance of the convention. To Hamilton, Willkie now took the guise of an impostor within the party, one wholly without understanding of party rules, principles and fair play.

Hamilton decided upon action. He promptly arranged for a tour across the country to consult with local politicians. Without fanfare or publicity he left for the Middle West in the latter part

of October. To each local group he asked the same question:
Had they pledged their delegation to Willkie? Upon the invari-
able denial, he produced a copy of the newspaper with the
Willkie release which claimed specified delegates. Indignation
flared. So quietly did Hamilton go about his work that it was
not until he reached Oregon that the press learned of his mission.

The secret of Hamilton's tour was finally divulged through
a young Republican who, although pledged to secrecy, disclosed the story to a *New York Times* correspondent. The newspaperman hastened to telephone his scoop to his editor in New
York. The account appeared in the issue of November fifth, and
reported that Hamilton was touring the country to build a slate
of favorite sons to block the nominating of Willkie. Like all
public men confronted with an unauthorized story, Hamilton
promptly denied it.

Henry Luce, long a staunch supporter of Willkie, hastened
to make use of the information and exploited the story in the
issues of *Life* and *Time* for November fifteenth. He stigmatized
Hamilton as the field manager of the "stop-Willkie-forces," and
the "ambassador of Joseph N. Pew and Edgar M. Queeny."
The Republicans in the hinterland loved Hamilton and believed in his sincerity and honesty. In fact, few who have known
him ever doubted his loyalty or integrity. On the other hand,
many party leaders had been alienated by the coolness of the
candidate himself. Thus, Hamilton in his tour of seventeen
states discovered there was a widespread indifference to Willkie
which only needed to be crystallized.

Following the exposure by Henry Luce of the political motive
of his trip, Hamilton gave a prepared statement to the press in
Los Angeles concerning the Willkie claim as to the number of
his pledged delegates. According to the statement, anyone who
read the polls must know that no man up to this time had captured the public imagination to the extent of one third of the
vote. In view of this situation it might not be out of place to
note that the public agreed with Mr. Willkie's often repeated
phrase of the past campaign: "There is no one indispensable
man."

The skillful attacks upon Hamilton, however, led him to consider that his campaign was finished. He had carefully kept his

cross-country jaunt out of the press until it had broken in the *New York Times*. To his amazement, the response to the unexpected publicity was a deluge of letters and telegrams. Only then did he fully realize that the local politicians had turned against Willkie and that he had merely voiced the seething undercurrent of dissatisfaction. The fight between the organization men and Willkie was now out in the open. The breach was irreparable.

On his return to the East, Willkie stopped at St. Louis to make a futile address which was supposed to be the opening of his campaign. The National Committeeman of Missouri was Edgar Queeny, wealthy industrialist. Although he had been an enthusiastic supporter of Willkie in 1940 and had raised $96,000 for the campaign, he now was bitterly alienated. He had prepared a questionnaire of nine points to force a public declaration by the candidate. One of Queeny's questions was so put as to force Willkie to dissociate himself from various liberal fellow directors of Freedom House in New York. (Freedom House had been organized in October, 1941, to fight against Fascist tendencies at home, and to promote "international economic and political co-operation to assure peace.") Willkie refused to answer any of the questions, and wrote Queeny in defense of his position: "I do not happen to know all the multitude of opinions on a variety of subjects of the various directors of Freedom House whose opinions you cite as determinative of mine." If such a policy of condemnation by "frail association" were pursued, he continued, a case could be made to link him with the philosophy of Norman Thomas. Both were directors of Town Hall. The defection of Queeny and other Republicans in Missouri had been the determining factor in bringing Willkie to St. Louis. He wanted, if possible, to heal the breach, or at least to soften the opposition. Failing in this there was the third alternative of winning public opinion through an evening address so that the party leaders would feel compelled to go along with him regardless of their own inclination.

The *New York Times* reported the Missouri situation as follows: "The very men who, according to local observers, tried to put Mr. Willkie 'on the spot' a month ago with a series of questions, and thus provoke his visit to St. Louis, were today edging into the limelight for tomorrow night's meeting. Furthermore, they were arranging for various side meetings tonight and tomorrow at which Mr. Willkie would meet other leaders and workers in the party."

One such meeting was a luncheon. Recognizing the coolness between Willkie and Queeny, the reception committee did not invite Queeny to the Willkie luncheon. Nevertheless, the Committeeman demanded an invitation, which was accorded; indeed, he was made master of ceremonies.

When Willkie was told of the arrangement he was displeased, but reluctantly agreed to carry through with the plans. As the cameras clicked he shook hands with Queeny and tried to be his charming self. But the possibility of good feeling was quickly dissipated when Queeny began his introductory remarks, which concerned the mistakes of the distinguished guest of honor. Willkie became visibly more and more angry. Finally he was presented.

All feeling of good will and friendship had vanished. Angrily and bluntly he exclaimed: "I don't know whether you're going to support me or not, and I don't give a damn. You're a bunch of political liabilities anyway." The newspapers carried the punch line without telling the story behind it. Opposition of Republican politicians was hardening across the nation. Yet Willkie seemed hardly aware of the danger and significance of what was happening.

In the evening Willkie spoke to an audience of 3,500 in the St. Louis municipal auditorium. To those who expected this speech to be a keynote for his campaign, it was a disappointment. Queeny listened to the speech by radio at his home. To reporters he commented that Willkie would eventually get around to telling his countrymen what he really thought. This was a reference to the unanswered nine-point questionnaire. Yet the applause for the speech had been ample and Willkie could take some encouragement with him from the people of St. Louis.

The national capital was the next stop. Here Willkie addressed the freshman Republicans known as the 78 Club. Although it was an off-the-record speech, it made several Republicans so angry that they talked. *Time* commented that Willkie had demonstrated how NOT to win friends. Within the first few min-

utes of his speech he lost the sympathy even of his most ardent
adherents. He was belligerent. He was arrogant. "Whether you
like it or not," he said, "I am going to be nominated!" If the
leaders of the party should turn against him, he announced, he
would go over their heads directly to the people to win his
nomination.

There were those who said that in coming to this meeting,
Willkie had walked into a lions' den. Certainly, he augmented
the unpleasantness of the situation by charging some of them
with a plot to ask him unpleasant questions. Naming Queeny as
the instigator, he challenged them to "go ahead and ask me those
questions." He looked straight at Louis E. Miller, Missouri
Congressman, and paused. Miller, red-faced and embarrassed,
jumped up and denied that he had been coached to ask anything.
Then the speaker turned to Wat Arnold, also from Missouri,
and said, "How about you, Mr. Arnold!" The uncomfortable
Arnold admitted he had a prepared question to present. "Yes,"
retorted Willkie, "and I can name some others. One of those
questions," he said with asperity, "is: Will I support whoever
is nominated by the party if I do not win myself?" Glancing
around the room dramatically, he replied to his own question:
"My answer is of course not. I will not support anyone who in
my opinion is not the right man to lead the Republican Party.
I would not support Colonel McCormick of the *Chicago
Tribune* or Representative Hamilton Fish."

This procedure created a tense unhappy feeling. The Congressmen resented his arrogance. They deplored his overconfi-
dence. But they resented most another part of his talk, expressing ill-considered remarks about Russia and Stalin. No realist
could deny, he said, that the Russian system had been effective.
Therefore, he charged that the 1944 platform must be clear on
American co-operation with Russia. Only in this way could the
peace of the world be saved. Russia had been antagonized by
the promise of a second front which had not yet been fulfilled.
This blundering was due, he said, to the incompetence of Roosevelt and Churchill. He boasted he understood Stalin and would
know better than Roosevelt how to deal with him. Both of them
had come up the hard way, he said, and understood the tough-

ness of the other. Each had buffeted his way to success. Each admired the strength and mettle of the other.

Although a few of the audience remained to have the speaker autograph his book, *One World,* most of those present left hastily. A columnist reported that there had been cocky candidates and supremely self-confident aspirants for the White House. But the cockiest, the most supremely self-assured that Washington had ever observed "through the eye of living man, was our recent visitor, Wendell Willkie." Instead of winning the warm support of party men in Congress he made more enemies and strengthened the gathering opposition to him.

From Washington, Willkie turned west again for three days of speech-making in Wisconsin, and conferences with politicians. Wisconsin presented a confused and treacherous arena. Although the state had gone Democratic in 1940, there were 679,206 votes for Willkie. A liberal tradition on domestic issues had been built up in Wisconsin, which Willkie hoped to attract. In 1910 Robert M. LaFollette led the insurgent movement composed of farmers, trade unionists, Socialists, American Federation of Labor and liberal weeklies. He drafted a declaration of principles for a Progressive Republican League by which he hoped to liberalize the GOP. There was even some talk that LaFollette might lead the ticket of Progressives. But this group of recalcitrants was promptly captured by the more colorful Theodore Roosevelt. On the other hand, LaFollette was an isolationist and opposed military preparation of the United States in the short weeks which preceded the outbreak of hostilities. He organized an effective filibuster of eleven Senators in February, 1917, to oppose the President's request for the speedy enactment of a bill to arm merchant ships for self-protection against the German submarine menace.

Philip and Robert, Jr., sons of this robust champion of reform, followed the isolationist trend of their father. On the eve of the Second World War, Philip was an active leader of the America First organization. Furthermore, the large German population of the state was opposed to a policy of internationalism. Although most of the German-Americans were anti-Hitler, many of them loyally opposed a war against their beloved fatherland.

Then to be considered was the *Chicago Tribune*. Wisconsin was generally accounted to be *"Tribune* territory." This paper was the leader of the isolationist sentiment in the Middle West. All these factors made Wisconsin a somewhat unattractive testing-ground, and provoked wide warnings and forebodings among the political strategists.

Willkie was strongly supported by John E. Dickinson of West Bend, and Milton R. Polland of Milwaukee. Influential liberals of the party, they offered strong support for Willkie's candidacy. Dickinson was one of the most powerful men in Wisconsin politics. He was chairman of his own Washington County party organization and chairman of the all-county-chairmen in the state, and vice-chairman of the Voluntary Committee. In Wisconsin, the Voluntary Committee was more important than the state Central Committee. (Thomas E. Coleman was chairman of the Voluntary Committee as well as chairman of the state Central Committee.)

Polland had never run for office and engaged in politics for the first time in 1940. He was credited with the success of the unusual campaign of Carl Zeidler for mayor of Milwaukee over the incumbent of twenty-five years, Daniel Webster Hoan. Zeidler named Polland to his place at the Republican National Convention at Philadelphia. There Polland met Willkie and ever afterwards was his enthusiastic supporter.

Curiously, these two men differed upon the advisability of Willkie's entering the Wisconsin primary. Dickinson urged this move and he had even gone East to see Willkie in the spring of 1943. On the other hand Polland was fearful of the isolationists and the Germans in the state. He advised against it. Nevertheless, he worked with earnest loyalty once Willkie had committed himself to the venture.

On his tour of the politicians, Hamilton had visited Thomas Coleman at Madison, Wisconsin. Now on the eleventh of November came Willkie to make friends and give impetus to the group promoting his candidacy. This was his only effort to win support in Wisconsin before he made his campaign in March for the primary election, although Dickinson had urged Willkie to return in February for further speeches and political consultations.

Willkie went first to the State Capitol. Dickinson, using all his influence to arrange a meeting with the aged Governor, had succeeded in securing a dinner invitation at the Executive Mansion. The only other guests were Mr. and Mrs. Coleman. After dinner, Governor and Mrs. Goodland invited some twenty-five friends in to meet Willkie and listen to his informal discussion of politics. Willkie was always superb on such occasions, and this one proved no exception. He made a most favorable impression on everyone. They liked his personality and his skill in defending his faith. But it did not mean endorsement either from the Governor or from Mr. Coleman. The Governor had already committed himself to Harold Stassen and even invited him to file in the spring primaries. But the Governor stated publicly that he had been most favorably impressed with Wendell Willkie and would make him his second choice.

From Madison, Willkie went to West Bend in appreciation of the loyal work of John Dickinson. He spoke at McLane High School the evening of November twelfth, which was the occasion for a political rally of the surrounding countryside. In this brief visit, also, he took time to receive a labor delegation. Representatives of the labor unions, AFL and CIO, wished to show friendship and courtesy to this visitor to West Bend. Arrangements were made for a short interview. They came with warm eagerness to meet a man whom they believed in and admired. Rather abruptly, Willkie declared, "Of course, you know my views. I am for labor." They smiled affably and nodded their heads.

"Ah yes, we have read your speeches on labor," they commented.

"Well, I must make it plain," continued Willkie. "If I am elected labor will have a hell of a lot of house-cleaning to do." The smile quickly faded from their faces. They rose stiffly and took somber leave. Without rhyme or reason, he had again offended. They had asked no commitments, no pledges. It was just a good-will visit. With that queer quirk for defeat which always seemed to bob up at inopportune moments, he had unwittingly alienated them.

On the drive to West Bend from Madison he had asked his companions what was the racial background of the people of this community. He was told they were German Catholics. In addressing these people, therefore, he played upon their common German ancestry. Their forebears and his had come to America for freedom. But there was this difference, he said, he was trying to lift high that torch of liberty which had brought his grandparents to this land. But they were doing nothing about it. They were willing to sit back and watch the destruction of all these precious rights by the Nazi madman of Europe. Their love of the fatherland had outweighed their love of the land of the free! "I believe in fighting to preserve the liberty my ancestors came here to enjoy," he shouted at them. It was a speech that naturally alienated Americans of German ancestry, whether isolationist or not.

That night Willkie was the guest of Dickinson's business associate, Robert Rolfs. The following morning Dickinson joined his two friends for breakfast and later drove Willkie to Milwaukee. During the breakfast talk Willkie eagerly sought discussion on his political "prospects" in the state. Point-blank, Willkie asked if Coleman wasn't on his side. He said he had been very much impressed with the state chairman and pleased with his marked cordiality at the Governor's dinner. For a moment there was flat silence. Then Rolfs bluntly told him the truth! No, Coleman would not support him. Willkie, hurt and taken back, asked if Coleman had recently talked with Hamilton. Upon learning that he had, Willkie gave his interpretation of the Hamilton opposition. The stiffening opposition of the party all along the line was beginning to hurt deeply. Nevertheless, this did not deter him for a moment from the continuation of his campaign. He was very sure of his ability to carry the campaign directly to the people and thus force the political leaders to accept him.

On the evening of the thirteenth Willkie addressed a selected dinner group at the Wisconsin Club in Milwaukee. There were about one hundred and twenty-five guests. His speech was little short of a tirade. He told them that the old days of businessmen being indifferent to the public interest were gone. No enlightened businessman today believes in the nineteenth century adage of the "public be damned." Industrialists must now recognize that they are no longer the owners of wealth, they are merely the custodians of wealth.

The audience was chilled. Sensing this, Willkie lashed out at them. "Some of you are blind, you don't even see what I am driving at. I never read any New Deal textbooks to get my views. I learned them the hard way of business experience. I was president of Commonwealth and Southern where I had to meet the problem of the public interest and adjust to it." At the conclusion of his remarks scarcely ten of those present went to the speakers' table to congratulate him.

Willkie returned to New York. His two months' tour was ended. He had seen numerous party leaders, made many speeches, and conferred with a number of special groups. On the whole he seemed encouraged with his political survey. He thought the rank and file of the people had given evidence of their support. But he had lost the party organization. Clearly, the professionals wanted no part of him. Of the 206 Republicans in the House of Representatives only six were for Willkie as revealed in a poll taken on November 5. Eighty-nine were for Dewey, thirty for MacArthur and even Bricker, Taft and Saltonstall received more votes than did Willkie.

On the seventeenth of November Willkie participated in another of the *New York Herald Tribune* forums. This time he shared the platform with Henry Wallace. Curiously, it was the first time these two men had met. For Wallace it was the only time he ever listened to a Willkie speech. He and the President had boasted that they did not consider it necessary to listen to any of the speeches of their opponent. Confident of success in 1940, they never took the Willkie contest seriously. The size of his vote, therefore, must have been a shock to both of them. The picture of the two men on this occasion showed the mild contempt they had for one another. Willkie annoyed the photographer because he refused to look at his companion.

Meanwhile, another source of opposition developed. It was a sensational book published by C. Nelson Sparks, of Akron, entitled *One Man, Wendell Willkie*. The *Boston Herald* (December 19, 1943) stated that Sparks was only a dummy, as the real writer of the malicious book was Gerald Novius, secretary to Senator Gerald P. Nye. The *Herald* stated the book was "based on brazen lies." It was smear politics at its worst, but it provided the opportunity for Senator Langer, North Dakota

Republican, to introduce a resolution early in December asking for an investigation of "any irregularities" in the 1940 Republican Convention. Sparks had charged in his book that Willkie's nomination was financed and engineered by international banking interests. Describing the charges as ridiculous, Willkie promptly informed his attackers he would be delighted to appear before the investigating committee at their convenience for cross-examination. Better judgment prevailed on the part of the other Senators and the proposed investigation was dropped. The incident is of little value except to show with what bitterness and to what length his enemies attacked him.

Despite the lack of any enthusiastic support by party leaders, Willkie appeared blithely confident of his mesmeric powers. In a discussion with Raymond Moley he boasted of his popularity with the people, which would assure his nomination. Moley was skeptical. Willkie argued his point: "All I have to do to attract a crowd is to stop for a moment in front of any cigar store. I am immediately surrounded." To which the witty Moley replied, "So is a four-fingered man. But you get the nomination by delegates' votes, not curiosity-seekers. And where are you going to get those delegates?" As Moley hastened to point out, there were only fourteen states which held presidential primaries, and these were mostly in unfriendly territory or were dominated by favorite sons.

The little group of friends who urged Willkie to try again for the nomination were Sinclair Weeks, John W. Hanes, who had led the Democrats-for-Willkie in 1940, and Ralph Cake, of Oregon. Cake was a banker from Portland who had recently become prominent in the Willkie fold. He was one of the men Willkie had invited to his "front-porch" conference at Rushville the preceding August. For the most part, the men who had been prominent in the 1940 campaign now opposed him. This created considerable anxiety as to financing the campaign, since the newcomers to his standard lacked both the experience and financial standing of his earlier supporters.

The question of securing delegates to the convention was almost as pressing as that of securing funds for the campaign. Hanes sought commitments from his friends in North Carolina. Delegates to the National Convention in this state were chosen by state party convention. The situation looked promising until Willkie bravely reasserted his stand on Negro equality. That ended any chance of Willkie delegates from North Carolina.

One of the fundamental rules of politics which Hamilton had tried to impress upon him was that appeal to group interests must be clear and sharp. If a candidate declares himself for Negro equality, then he must be prepared to sacrifice his campaign in the South: if he is going to give concrete support to Jewish rights then he must expect a loss of those groups who bitterly assail such minorities. A candidate, of course, need not declare himself on every minority question. But as soon as he makes a bold declaration for one minority group he is bound to lose another such group. By making such sharp cleavages in his appeal, however, a candidate may make some decided gains.

Willkie never was quite able to comprehend the technique of this procedure. His equality speeches elicited an endorsement from Edgar G. Brown, national director of the Negro Council. Brown cited Willkie as having successfully interceded with the motion picture industry to portray the Negro's contribution to the war effort. Notwithstanding such brave support of the Negroes, Willkie made a tour of the South in late November. He told press men that he came a lot closer to representing the views of these Southern Democrats than the present Administration did!

If he had been logical, Willkie would have denounced certain states below the Mason-Dixon Line for their antiquated laws on labor, education and racial discrimination. Then he would have rallied all anti-Southern sentiment. But too frequently he tried to be all things to all men. He talked of the rights of the workers but expected big business to give him unqualified support, he attacked anti-semitism but believed that American First groups should rally to his standard. He maligned his party leaders but was bewildered by their formidable opposition to him. As a Republican he lashed the New Deal for its mistakes and follies yet expected Democrats to vote for him.

Willkie further irritated many of his own party by his speech at the New York Times Hall on February 2, 1944, when he advocated a much larger tax bill than that recommended by the Administration. Congress had rejected the Roosevelt tax program of $10,600,000,000 as unrealistic. Thereupon Willkie proposed a tax levy of nearly double this sum. The *New York Times* commended his stand: "This is a decidedly unorthodox position . . . in an election year. But Mr. Willkie's candor does him credit, and the broad grounds on which he proposes war taxes so heavy that they would actually lower materially the American standard of living are unassailable." Willkie's argument was that heavy taxation in wartime was the best possible insurance against post-war inflation. Furthermore, it would mean that industry could start off after the war with a minimum handicap of a war-inherited debt. His high-tax proposal was another effort to save the American system of free enterprise by paying currently so far as possible the war debt rather than putting a mortgage on enterprise for future generations. "An economic bloodstream composed largely of debt will eventually starve all the cells in the body," he declared. He wanted to encourage the flow of venture capital into new business. He wanted proper rewards for individual enterprise. In place of a government-directed economy dominated by officeholders he preferred a "system operated by free men on their own initiative. A system that will unleash the energies of our citizens, that will give them a chance to get ahead, that will allow the establishment of new industries, that will raise the living standards of the people." Although economically sound, it lacked voting appeal.

As the Willkie advisers surveyed the dismal prospects of convention votes, they decided he should test his strength in New Hampshire, Wisconsin, Nebraska, and Oregon. Three of these primaries came early in March and April, and only Oregon as late as May. This group of states also was selected because it provided a degree of sampling of sectional public opinion.

The New Hampshire primary came the middle of March. The vote was split with six delegates for Willkie, two for Dewey and three uncommitted. This was a small triumph, but it was encouraging. The real test was to be Wisconsin, the heart of isolationism.

Such political experts as Sam Pryor, John Hamilton and Frank Altschul advised Willkie not to risk his prestige in Wisconsin. They considered it political suicide. Even Sinclair Weeks, who had faithfully backed the venture, feared that the

Chicago Tribune would make the odds too great. But Ralph
Cake and John Hanes emphasized that there was little choice as
to states and that the need of committed delegates was pressing.
All agreed that California would have made a better testing-
ground, for here Willkie was very popular. But the opposition of
Governor Warren made this impracticable. Certainly Wisconsin
offered him the challenge of a dramatic victory. If he could win
there, the Middle West would be his. Moreover, Hanes had
assured Willkie that Dewey would not enter the Wisconsin
primary and in fact would not be a contender at all for the 1944
presidential candidacy. So Willkie returned to Wisconsin on
March 18 to begin his thirteen days' campaign. The die was cast.

Now begins another chapter amazing for its confusion, in-
trigue, inefficiency and stupid blundering. Under the best conditions, Willkie had little chance to win in such a state, but the
kind of campaign that was waged made certain total defeat.
Ralph Cake was campaign manager. Although a member of the
National Committee, his bailiwick was Oregon, so that he knew
little either of Wisconsin politics or of big-time strategy.

Cake made several hurried trips to Wisconsin, but on each
occasion he aroused more antagonism than he developed co-
operation. Such clever men as Dickinson and Polland were
ruthlessly shunted aside. Moreover, the campaign was handled
largely from New York. There the decisions were made. Lemuel
Jones, Willkie's publicity secretary, was the liaison man between
the local headquarters and the New York office. Thus the local
men who knew the peculiar situation existing in Wisconsin concerning the Germans and isolationism were denied a voice in the
direction of affairs. No local organization was developed. The
New York headquarters did not consider it necessary. Hence
there was no effort to ring doorbells and talk directly to the
voters. In New York it was decided to build the campaign entirely around Willkie as a personality, in the belief that his
personal appearance would be sufficient to swing the vote. The
Willkie glamour and the Willkie oratory on political issues were
the pattern determined upon. Thus the traditional system of a
political organization developing campaign techniques was rejected.

Now a good organization "runs interference," as it were, for the candidate. It arranges for newsreel pictures of the candidate to be shown in the community where he is speaking, for the proper placing of billboards, the distribution of handbills, press releases, the printing and distribution of speeches, and a string of second speakers recruited among prominent local citizens. None of these things was attempted. No arrangement had even been made with any of the movie houses to show the Willkie newsreel pictures. Polland finally took it upon himself to get the theaters under management of Twentieth Century-Fox to show the films. But he had to appeal to the New York office over the head of the Wisconsin manager of the movie company to secure approval. This despite the fact that Willkie was chairman of the board.

The New York headquarters made no effort to counter the strategy of the Stassen and Dewey forces. Literature vital to the campaign, written by experienced men in the field, was garbled and slashed by the "experts" in New York. Every man in New York who saw it changed the text to conform with his pet ideas. Each was anxious to protect his special kind of philosophy. If a radio speech were to be written by one man another would refuse to o.k. it because he had not written it. The one big question at headquarters seemed to be who could get the credit for what. Thus everyone opposed everybody else. The result was utter confusion. Polland characterized the ineptitude of the organization as a case of definite self-interest on the part of a lot of prima donnas.

While the New York office made all decisions concerning the campaign, the local men were called upon to finance it. About $17,000 was spent, and all of it raised in Wisconsin except about $1,800 which came from the New York headquarters. When the campaign was over, unpaid bills amounted to $7,500 which Willkie and Polland personally split. Yet Polland had been denied any part in the making of important decisions and had to remain silent while the New York "experts" made blunder after blunder. On the other hand, the closing days of the campaign saw a lot of money used by the Dewey adherents. Recklessly they spent money for billboards, signs and publicity of all kinds.

The confusion of the staff and its distance from the field resulted in Willkie's carrying the campaign alone. As he went relentlessly from town to town, he became increasingly aware of the singleness of his fight and realized that his organization had failed to give him supporting assistance. Bravely he talked to the people of Wisconsin about aid to Russia, conscription, Lend-Lease, and other equally unpopular and dangerous issues. Said Polland: "Willkie was there all alone, his giant figure looming at meeting after meeting, throwing out his challenge to the future, speaking truths too advanced for the countryside, truths that later came to be adopted by the Republicans as self-evident." Willkie made twenty-five speeches in thirteen days. Under the strain and disappointment, his throat again gave him trouble, and he sought relief from a specialist.

One of his greatest mistakes in the Wisconsin campaign was his sole emphasis upon principles and issues. He had affronted the organization men, the precinct captains, and the ward committeemen. They supported Dewey. There was nothing in his campaign to attract those men back to his banner. The appeal to the voters was directed in channels to which they were either indifferent or vehemently opposed. Robert McCormick, owner of the *Chicago Tribune,* had read him out of the Republican Party on several occasions and again during the Wisconsin campaign. The *Tribune* is popular in Wisconsin. Willkie returned the honor in his Green Bay speech, and read McCormick out of the party.

The speech at Ripon was built up as one of the important speeches because it was to commemorate the founding of the Republican Party there in 1854. But it was a gloomy disappointment. Willkie was tired and his throat was painful. Although some insisted that the script was good, the speech as delivered was one of his poorest. Even his closest friends would not tell him how badly the speech was received. Added to his own fatigue and the confusion within his own ranks there was, as one observer summarized it, the ten thousand pinpricks of the war.

The regular Republican organization not only gave no support to Willkie but it attempted to defeat him by presenting phantom candidates in opposition. Harold Stassen was now a lieutenant commander stationed on a battleship in the Pacific, but his name was presented in the primary. General Douglas MacArthur was in Australia commanding the armed forces to stem the Japanese advance, yet his name was also presented to the voters. So was that of Governor Dewey, who did not even make a speech in the state, and constantly contended that he was not a candidate. As absentee candidates they were absolved from making any commitments on the stirring issues. Thus none of them was exposed to the devastating rigors of public opinion in Wisconsin.

It was, however, the Stassen candidacy which hurt Willkie most deeply. Willkie felt that he had made Stassen politically by choosing him to be his floor manager at the Philadelphia Convention. With equal justification Stassen felt that he had made Willkie by winning the nomination for him at that time. To his friends Willkie referred to a luncheon that he and Stassen had shortly before the Minnesota Governor joined the Navy. Edith and Philip were also present. At this meeting politics was not discussed except that Stassen volunteered the information that he was going into the Navy and that he was instructing his friends to "support you." And he added that he would not be interested in politics until after the war.

This conversation, apparently, never was repeated to Stassen's supporter, Senator Joseph Ball. Perhaps it was only a passing pleasantry which Stassen did not take seriously or feel bound by. In any event, when he left America for service in the Pacific he expected that Willkie would contend for votes in the far West, where he was known to have strong support. Stassen fully expected his friends to enter his name in Wisconsin, where Governor Goodland had shown great friendliness, and also in Nebraska. Here in the Middle States, Stassen had his strongest support. But in Stassen's mind it did not make too much difference because in the convention the votes of one would be thrown to the other depending upon which was the favorite among the delegates.

Willkie did not look at it this way. To him Dewey was the real opponent. By this division of their strength, the New York Governor was being aided. Hence Willkie was bitter in his denunciation of an old friend. To him, Stassen had "double-crossed him." Of course Stassen knew nothing of all this confusion. In afteryears he expressed regret that there had been this misunderstanding and said that it all could have been easily settled if he had been home. But the old friendship of the days of 1940 was broken.

The real break with Stassen had come earlier. When Willkie landed in Minneapolis on the return from his world flight, he met Stassen at the dinner party given by John Cowles. At this small party, Willkie was somewhat expansive in his views and talked a trifle pompously about world affairs. Stassen broke into the conversation to observe that there were other world-minded persons in the Republican Party. Always very sensitive, Willkie was hurt and resentful. A decided chill came into their association as a result. The two men sat in opposite camps at the meeting of the National Republican Committee meeting several weeks later in St. Louis, where they backed different candidates. But the great widening of the breach came when Stassen reviewed *One World* for the *New York Times,* April 11, 1943. Stassen criticized Willkie for overemphasizing the wrongs of the British colonial system and underestimating the evils of communism. Thus by the time the Wisconsin primary campaign rolled around in March of 1944, Stassen and Willkie were leagues apart.

The primary election was held on April 4. Underground politics had been noticeable all during the campaign. It was a clear "stop-Willkie" movement. But it became clearer on election day. Politicians stood at the legal distance from polling places and asked people not to vote for Willkie, regardless of whom else they might vote for. This tactic was considered highly successful, although it was obvious to all that the Willkie organization had bogged down long before. Yet none of his followers was prepared for the utter defeat the candidate suffered. When the votes were counted, Willkie received not one delegate. Of the twenty-four delegates chosen, Dewey won fifteen, plus two uninstructed delegates who were accredited to him. Stassen won four and MacArthur three.

Willkie had concluded his barnstorming tour in Wisconsin the last of March, and had hastened to Nebraska to electioneer there for that primary held on April eleventh. Thus, he was in Nebraska when the crushing results of the Wisconsin primary were reported to him. To intimates he had declared that if he lost in Wisconsin he would withdraw from the contest. The next night (April 5) he was scheduled to deliver one of his major addresses at Omaha. The speech was a vigorous criticism of American foreign policy, before an audience of four thousand persons in the City Auditorium. At its conclusion the candidate made a dramatic withdrawal from the campaign. He said, "It has been my conviction that no Republican could be nominated for President unless he received at the convention the votes of some of the major midwestern states. For it is in this section of the country that the Republican Party has had its greatest resurgence."

Then he continued, "As I have said many times, this country desperately needs new leadership. . . . I earnestly hope that the Republicans will nominate a candidate and write a platform which really represents the views which I have advocated and which I believe are shared by millions of Americans. I shall continue to work for these principles and policies for which I have fought during the last five years." The following morning newspapers across the country carried the headline news: "Willkie Quits Race!"

The statement was clear and dignified. One could not gather from its lines anything of the surging emotion of the man. Of the four candidates who filed in Wisconsin, he was the only one to campaign and the only one to fail completely. He had spent himself as in no other campaign, so determined was he to make the people understand. No other candidate had the blind confidence that he did in the ability of the people to make a right decision. No other candidate so blithely ignored the rules of politics. He was the white knight leading the people onwards to the high peak of internationalism and good will to all nations. He must not fail. The dreams and hopes of a lifetime were all tied together in the Wisconsin campaign. Not because he wanted power for power's sake, but because he wished to lead the people into the land of promise. Hence lesser political positions held no appeal for him. He could have succeeded to the seat of Kenneth Simpson in the House, he could have been governor of New York, or he could have been senator from New York. But only the presidency could make him leader of the American people.

From first to last he represented himself as heading a crusade. His ideas were bigger than politics, bigger than party and so enveloped the whole nation. That is why he was so sure that the people would support him regardless of party affiliation or political alignment.

The Omaha statement represented more than a defeated candidate. It blighted his hopes for the success of the crusade. Some say that Willkie was really looking to the campaign of 1948, but no man can remain in the public eye that long without a victory. Yet in defeat he found his full stature.

CHAPTER XVIII

The Great Advocate

IMMEDIATELY AFTER his speech in Omaha, withdrawing himself from the presidential campaign, Willkie returned to New York City. Upon his arrival, he was entertained at a dinner given by Malcolm Muir, chairman of the editorial board of *Newsweek*. Raymond Moley was present. Indeed, he had been urged by his host to draw Willkie out regarding the Wisconsin campaign.

Hardly was the dinner served when Moley said: "What happened to you in Wisconsin?"

"The damn county committees were against me," Willkie replied somewhat irritably.

Moley, in one of his flashing witticisms, observed that Willkie was like Enoch Arden. After long years of absence, he had come home to find that his sweetheart had married another man. The years in which Willkie had snubbed the politicians had not been forgotten by the recipients of the slights. Their revenge was swift, and deadly.

"How could you blame them?" asked Moley dryly.

Willkie became angry over this twitting, and plainly showed his bitter disappointment regarding the fiasco of the Wisconsin primary. The ribbing, even by old friends, was like pouring salt into the still-open wound.

The comments that went round the dinner table indicated the general opinion of analysts concerning Willkie's political acumen. By temperament, Willkie was unsuited for party leadership. He offended associates too easily, he talked too often, and he shifted his political advisers too frequently. But most of all he shattered Hamilton's plan for the party organization. Many Republicans, who would have forgotten all else, felt resentment over this.

Yet it was recognized that with all these limitations he rose to a unique position of leadership in the party. No defeated presidential candidate ever exerted such influence either upon his own party or upon national policies as did Wendell Willkie. History will record that he was the most dynamic, resourceful and powerful leader of a defeated party in American politics. He possessed a high sense of responsibility to the voters, which never became dimmed by party expediency, and he led an unwilling party to an understanding and acceptance of this high standard of public conduct. Before the coming of Willkie to party councils, the Republican Party had opposed the Man in the White House for the simple purpose of opposing. Willkie taught his party a technique more serviceable to the American people: oppose when the Administration is wrong but co-operate when it is right.

Charging his party that it must constantly revise its platform to keep up with the changing times, he forced it reluctantly into line with public opinion. Amid the sharp assault of his opponents, he broke the grip of isolationism which had shackled the party. By his spectacular trip around the world in time of war, he dramatized internationalism in a way that had never been done before and which warmly stirred the hearts of his countrymen. His remarkable concept of the loyal opposition and the bipartisan foreign policy was brilliant statesmanship. At a distraught period of national emergency he saved critical war legislation: the Lend-Lease Act, the extension of the Selective Service Act, the occupation of bases in Iceland, the convoy system, and the repeal of the Neutrality Act. He revitalized the thinking of the Republican Party after the discouragement of eight years out of office, and permanently impressed many of his ideas upon party policy. His stamina and faith and even rashness jolted stale party leaders into a fresh appraisal of the American scene. Despite his numerous fumbling mistakes of procedure and the antagonism he created among his colleagues, the real stature of Willkie was that he rose above it all to the sublime heights of unselfish devotion to the American people. In defeat he was greater than most men in victory. In defeat came his glorious opportunity of service to preserve a united nation.

The great contribution to party government made by Willkie was not unnoticed by the news commentators possessed of philosophic outlook. Walter Lippmann, with keen appreciation, wrote: "His part has been to save his country from an irreconcilable partisan division in the face of the most formidable enemies who were ever arrayed against all that America is and means. Historians will say . . . that second only to the Battle of Britain, the sudden rise and nomination of Willkie was the decisive event, perhaps providential, which made it possible to rally the free world when it was almost conquered. Under any other leadership but his the Republican Party would in 1940 have turned its back upon Great Britain, causing all who still resisted Hitler to feel that they were abandoned.

"His rivals for the nomination at Philadelphia . . . [had] made the Republican the isolationist party, [which] would have made it almost impossible thereafter to reinforce our Allies by Lend-Lease and to gain the time we had to have to prepare for war."

It was Lippmann who coined the happy phrase that Willkie was the "conscience of his party." Willkie had been able to hold in check the tendency of the party to drift into "Know-nothingism" and reactionary obstruction. Because of him, said this commentator, the Republican Party survived during those historic years of 1940-1944, and preserved its title and its eligibility to govern the American nation in the world as it now is. Except for Willkie, the nation would have become isolated and divided, and with the victory of Hitler, desperately hard pressed as the last surviving democracy in a conquered world.

The magnitude of his success came from his unusual powers to win public approval of his cause. His strength in rallying his party to responsible politics was based on this unique ability to mobilize public opinion. One of the great advocates of all history, he could dramatize an idea as few publicists have ever been able to do. This gave him power. The glamour which surrounded Willkie as a presidential candidate obscured his more notable contribution as a publicist in the period of 1935 to 1944. On the other hand, the influence of his talent as a great publicist was measurable by the millions of persons attracted to him through the political forum. Among his most famous writings was his article in 1940, "We the People." It created a furore of political thinking and examination. His speech on the "Loyal Opposition," published in the *New York Times* in November, 1940, ranks as the most distinguished speech of creative political thinking ever given by a defeated candidate. With his press release of January 13, 1941, pertaining to Lend-Lease, Willkie rose above partisan strife and attained the full measure of statesmanship. His Lincoln Day address was the turning-point in choking isolationism out of the Republican Party. One of the greatest pamphlets of the modern age was *One World,* which captivated the imagination of men everywhere. And shortly before he died there was published "An American Program." There were many other excellent articles to awaken a national consciousness concerning affairs of state. The list is long, but notable were "With Malice Toward None" in the *Saturday Evening Post* of December 30, 1939, "The Court Is Now His" in the same magazine of March 9, 1940, and "Patriotism or Politics" in the *American Magazine* of November, 1941.

Willkie came to recognize his own ability as a publicist. In the last year of his life he considered the purchase of a newspaper. This would have served as a daily channel for the expression of his views. Like most publishers, he looked upon a newspaper as a reflection of the opinions of its owner.

In an interesting conversation with his old friend Sinclair Weeks, a few weeks before his death, he disclosed his weariness of the practice of law. "I can make money," he said, "but that is not what I want. I want something more than just a law business. Life is bigger than that." Weeks took this poignant confidence with a careless witticism. "You had better make up your mind, you have made a mess of your life so far!" Instantly, he regretted the flippant remark when he saw his companion wince. Willkie abruptly ended the soul-revealing discussion, while the two friends took refuge in a game of gin-rummy.

All his life Willkie had been restless. No success had been satisfying. His law practice at Akron failed to give him the reward he yearned for. He tired of his career as president of Commonwealth and Southern Corporation after the big battle with the Government was ended. His connection with the law firm of Willkie, Owen, Otis, Farr and Gallagher did not yield him the contentment that he had expected. Inwardly, he had been striving for years, and in vain, for an adequate outlet for his ideas and beliefs.

It was at this time that he toyed with the idea of becoming the president of some university. His name was discussed by the board of trustees of Columbia University. But at that time Nicholas Murray Butler was not prepared to retire. That was when his imagination was captivated by the possibility of owning and publishing a newspaper to spread his ideas.

Two definite efforts were made to secure a newspaper. The first decision was to buy the *Indianapolis Star*. In the fall of 1943, the death of John C. Shaffer, of Evanston, Illinois, the owner of the *Star*, caused this newspaper to be put on the market. A Hoosier, who knew Willkie moderately well, conceived the plan of buying the newspaper and offering its management to Willkie, thus affording him an organ of opinion in the Middle West. This admirer was W. S. Woodfill, president of the Grand Hotel on Mackinac Island. Possessing some free time and free capital, he suggested that he would take a part interest in the venture, assuming a silent partnership while Willkie would remain untrammeled as managing editor. So much interested in the proposal was Willkie that he authorized Woodfill to investigate the possibilities, but to keep his name out of the public announcement for the present. Meanwhile, Willkie called upon his old friend and associate of former days, Arthur C. Watt, to pursue an investigation on his own regarding the *Indianapolis Star*. He also asked Watt to prepare for him a statement on the features which make a newspaper "good or bad."

By the time Woodfill had carried out the necessary inquiry

with the necessary caution regarding the *Star*, it had been sold. The purchase was made on April 27, 1944. Strangely enough, on the following day, Frank Knox, the public-minded editor of the *Chicago Daily News*, suddenly died. Woodfill anticipated that this distinguished newspaper would sooner or later be sold. Accordingly, he wrote Willkie of the possibility and received in reply a most enthusiastic expression of interest. Woodfill retained a lawyer to undertake the ensuing negotiations.

The trustees of the Knox Estate were more interested in securing a man with the same staunch views as Colonel Knox than in a few extra dollars per share. When they learned confidentially that Willkie was interested in the paper and that he would move to Chicago and personally take over the management of it, they made a price of $12 per share, which amounted to a total of $1,750,000. Woodfill was to contribute $250,000 of this sum, and Willkie the balance. Further, the trustees agreed not to discuss the sale with anyone else until Willkie had an opportunity of coming to Chicago. A date was arranged for July, which had to be postponed until September.

Immediately after Labor Day in 1944, however, Willkie was taken to a hospital. Accordingly, the negotiations were abruptly broken off. The Knox stock was sold very soon thereafter for $15 a share to John S. Knight, of Akron, Ohio. So ended in futility the dream which would have taken Willkie to the end of destiny. His whole life had been spent striving and searching for the right endeavor. He had once thought it was politics. But actually he was born to be an evangelist carrying on a crusade. That is the very essence of a publicist. A politician must build an organizational structure, founded on compromise and coalitions. The publicist, like Tom Paine or John Milton, spreads ideas. He is more concerned with getting the people to understand and believe in these ideas than he is in being elected to office.

Meanwhile, Willkie had not stood still. Editors of magazines and newspapers were eager to publish articles and statements from his pen. After the Wisconsin primary and his subsequent withdrawal from the campaign of 1944, six Republican newspapers asked him to write a series of seven articles pertaining to the issues due to come before the Platform Committee of the

1944 Republican National Convention. So important were these articles that the *New York Times,* an independent Democratic newspaper, secured a release from the associated Republican newspapers so that it might also publish them. The seven articles, appearing in early June, were later published as a pamphlet called "An American Program."

The articles became the capstone of his success as a publicist. He warned his party that the theory of states' rights was outworn. The United States, he said, cannot be divided into forty-eight separate economic units. We cannot have forty-eight minimum wage laws. The question of states versus the national Government has ceased to be an issue; it is a relic of history. He cautioned the Republicans to refrain from abandoning their traditional platform by an attempt to weaken the federal unit. "The issue today is not that of states' rights versus federal power." The solution lies not in a weakened central government but in the proper and wise use of federal power.

He warned his party not to be blind to minority problems. The Republican Party traditionally was committed to human freedom. Under Republican leadership, the Negro was constitutionally guaranteed the same rights as every other citizen in the United States. "One of these basic rights is the right to vote. Another is the right to live free of the haunting fear and the too-frequent actuality of mob violence," he said. "The Republican Party in its platform and in the declarations of its candidates should commit itself unequivocally and specifically to federal anti-poll tax and anti-lynching statutes." He pointed to the bitter humiliation the Negro people had suffered during the war, when they were excluded from certain branches of the armed forces and relegated to menial jobs in others. To be consistent with the historical platform of the party, the Republicans should assume the responsibility to secure for the Negro the rights to which he is entitled. This, he said, would be a test "of our sincerity and of our moral leadership in the eyes of hundreds of millions all over the world."

He warned his party not to reject social security. All members of society, he said, should be protected against economic disasters sweeping away the bare necessities of life. It is fictitious to think of the alternatives of security or initiative, protection or adventure. We need both. We cannot have the initiative and energy we need for an expanding economy without preserving and increasing the vigor of our human resources. Coverage is still incomplete and eligibility rules are complicated. Social security laws, he said, should include old-age benefits, federal unemployment insurance, a strengthened federal employment agency, disability insurance, maternity benefits, social insurance for the armed forces, agricultural workers and the self-employed, and medical care for all. Need knows no rules of eligibility or coverage. The Republican Party, he declared, should assume the leadership of such an extended program of social security.

He warned his party against economic regression. "We are not going to *return* to anything," he said. The pressure of state-controlled economies in all countries with which the United States must trade would inevitably affect our own society. "Despite the pressure from without and the demands from within, we have an opportunity for a different answer." He proposed that industry, labor and government—local, state, federal—should set up a co-operative mechanism which would act as a clearing house for information and constructive programs. The value of such a procedure would be, he said, that public works could be spread levelly over the years. "But we must be realistic enough to acknowledge that the best efforts of private industry, even supplemented by such intelligent co-operation, will not always be enough. In addition the federal Government must exercise a counter-cyclical influence against depression in order to preserve a reasonably high level of employment." As some of the necessary measures to this end, he listed: direction of the capital market to encourage a flow of new capital when depression threatens and to discourage it in the face of a boom; the undertaking of legitimate government projects at government expense, but by private contract, the moment depression sets in—projects that would improve the health and welfare of the people, create new markets, new purchasing power. He pointed out, however, that if industry was to develop to its fullest possibilities, it must have certain releases and certain safeguards. Capital was necessary—risk capital that would be ready to take a chance on the future. He advocated a drastic revision of the tax laws to encourage risk capital for new investment and new ventures. "The Republican Party cannot meet the need of the post-war period by merely passing resolutions in favor of 'free enterprise.' It must realize the inevitability and the justness of the people's demand for both protection and opportunity, and it must find the answers, answers which exist uniquely within a responsible enterprise system."

He warned his party against a narrow view of labor's problems. He said that there was nothing inherent in the nature of the two parties which justified the roles propagandists had sought to assign them. "Men more zealous than wise are trying to label the Democratic Party the exclusive friend of labor, and the Republican Party its inveterate enemy." Declaring that a 1944 Republican platform should acknowledge the necessary requirements for the protection of labor under conditions existent today—not yesterday—he proposed the continuance and improvement of a federal wage and hour law and federal regulatory machinery for its interpretation and enforcement. He also advocated as fair and necessary an annual wage for workers in plants with periodic shutdowns. But most important, he believed, was that labor be made an essential part of the Government with a real labor representative in the Cabinet. "Like other economic groups it must share in the determination of Government's fiscal, domestic and international policies." On the other hand labor must become responsible and drive from its midst the racketeers, adopt democratic procedures, and account for its funds both to the public and to its own membership. Labor-management co-operation, he felt, had proved fruitful and should be continued. But it was time, he added, for both labor and management to grow up, to recognize each other as essential factors in the same basic enterprise—United States industry—and to settle their affairs among themselves without recourse to Government.

He warned his party against a high tariff policy. In the minds of generations of Americans, he declared, the Republican Party is associated with a high protective tariff, yet at the turn of the century such Republicans as McKinley, Taft and Root were urging modification of the tariff through reciprocal agreements. However, after the last war Republican administrations passed the two highest tariff bills in our history, the Fordney-McCumber and the Hawley-Smoot. Within two years, twenty-five countries had established trade barriers against us. "We are now faced," he said, "with the urgent post-war economic problem of re-establishing a healthy, world-wide trade." Positive steps must be taken "to revive the world economically by opening up international trade." To this end, he said, the Republican Party should propose that through the United Nations Council an attempt should be made to reach general agreement on a clear and uniform code for international economic relations." In addition to ending the many absurdities of the present tariff, he urged the Republican Party to propose steps towards the international stabilization of exchanges.

He warned his party against any return to isolationism. He suggested that the Republican Party demand the immediate creation of a Council of the United Nations as a first step towards the formation of an international organization. The Republican platform should be clear, he emphasized, in its attitude towards sovereignty. "Our sovereignty is not something to be hoarded, but something to be used," he declared. It must be used to create an effective international organization for the good of all peoples everywhere. Three years ago, two years ago, the United States had had the material, the political, the moral leadership of the world. Now we had only the material leadership. We lost political leadership through ineptitude and delay. We lost moral leadership through attempted expediency. "The Republican Party should frame and pursue a foreign policy that will recapture America's lost leadership."

Such was the philosophy Willkie hopefully wrote as a guide in the deliberations of his political colleagues. It was significant that Willkie had shifted his views on social security since the thirties, although he still held strongly to the advantages of the free enterprise system.

On the twenty-sixth of June, 1944, the Republican National Convention met in Chicago. Willkie had urged Cleveland as the convention city because of the isolationist influence of the *Chicago Tribune,* but had been overruled. Even before the convention assembled, Thomas E. Dewey was recognized as the Republican candidate most likely to capture the nomination.

Willkie wanted to discuss with Dewey, before he went to Chicago, certain planks for the Republican platform. Several meetings were arranged for the two Republican leaders by interested friends, but all appointments were broken by the Governor, much to the disappointment of Willkie. The old antagonism flared up on both sides. Dewey had won control of the state organization of the Republican Party and he used his authority to block all efforts to name his rival as a member of the New York delegation. This political slight rankled deeply. The omission was made all the more noticeable by the cold invitation to attend the convention extended to Willkie by Harrison E. Spangler, the National Chairman. The invitation entitled him merely to a seat on the platform of the convention; he could listen to the proceedings but was barred from participation. Willkie had every right to expect an invitation to address the convention. But Dewey and the Old Guard would have none of this. If Willkie came to the convention it would be only in the capacity of a spectator. This was an affront almost without precedent. It was an open and direct denial that he possessed even a small share in the leadership of the Republican Party. On the other hand, Willkie declined to commit himself to any candidate, especially Dewey.

Many of Willkie's friends urged him to attend the convention. Even after it opened, such faithful colleagues as Sam Pryor, Raymond Baldwin and Sinclair Weeks telephoned him to come to Chicago. His presence at the convention, they said, would defeat Dewey, and would insure the nomination of John W. Bricker. But in Willkie's view, the Governor of Ohio was more isolationist even than Dewey. The candidate Willkie favored was Leverett Saltonstall, of Massachusetts, who had no chance of success. So Willkie remained in New York and received frequent reports of the convention proceedings by telephone.

He was so deeply concerned about the platform that he even drafted a model, which he sent to the Resolutions Committee in Chicago. His friends at the convention had little chance, however, to argue in behalf of these proposals before the Resolutions Committee because of the unfriendly feeling towards him. Senator Robert A. Taft held the strategic post of chairman

of the Resolutions Committee, although Senators Vandenberg
and Austin were also members. Senator Baldwin and others of
the Willkie persuasion attempted to form a subcommittee to sit
with the Resolutions Committee. But this proposal Senator Taft
promptly rejected. Nevertheless, the committee hearings were
continued all night long in order that every person who so
desired would have the opportunity to make a statement of his
ideas. No one was excluded.

Willkie's friends at the convention struggled valiantly to
secure for him an advance copy of the platform. But none was
available. All members of the committee were pledged to secrecy
until after the scheduled reading of the platform to the convention on Tuesday afternoon, June twenty-seventh. Senator Taft
and others were determined that Willkie should be prevented
from stampeding the convention into amendments of the platform by any adverse comments which he might issue in New
York. Finally, Willkie turned to a distinguished newspaperman
with a request for a copy of the release issued to the press. Upon
the understanding that he would not use the release until after
the platform had been read to the convention, a copy was given
him on Sunday evening preceding the opening of the convention. Whether Willkie misunderstood the agreement or willfully
broke his promise could only be revealed by the man himself.
In any event, early Monday morning, he held a press conference
in his office at No. 15 Broad Street. He announced keen disappointment in the platform as drafted by the "Taft-dominated
Resolutions Committee." The evening papers carried his bitter
reproaches. The resolutions scuttled his proposals for liberalism
and international co-operation.

The platform, he charged, was similar to the Republican
promises of 1920, which were so broad that Warren Harding
was able to campaign on world co-operation during the presidential campaign and to repudiate the League of Nations after
the election. A Republican President, elected under the proposed platform of 1944, Willkie maintained, could with equal
integrity either lead the United States into a world organization
of states or keep the nation out of such a system. The party
statement said:

We declare our relentless aim to win the war against all our enemies for the attainment of peace and freedom based on justice and security.

We shall seek to achieve such aims through organized international co-operation and not by joining a world state.

Willkie felt that the platform gave only lip-service to internationalism. It contained more than one loophole sufficient to permit an apathetic President to evade the responsibility of leadership in the creation of an international organization capable of suppressing aggression and keeping the peace. Every proposed world organization, he said, could be interpreted as a "world state," and hence condemned by the Republican Party. In concluding his news conference, Willkie assured the reporters that he had no criticism for Warren Austin or Arthur Vandenberg. He only hoped that his objections to the proposed platform would strengthen their position in demanding a forthright commitment on post-war international organization.

The delegates of the Republican Convention were shocked as they read their Tuesday morning newspapers to see the Willkie denunciation of the platform, which had not yet been released. The Old Guard on the Resolutions Committee were infuriated by the discovery that a copy of the platform had fallen into Willkie's hands. Charges and counter-charges of broken faith swept the committee.

At the afternoon session on Tuesday, the draft of the platform, according to plan, was read by Senator Taft. It was immediately adopted without discussion or dissent. Notwithstanding the Willkie opposition, party unity and harmony had been preserved, at least outwardly. With equal precision, the presidential boom of Tom Dewey moved forward. Indeed, on Wednesday, Dewey was nominated on the first ballot. At an early stage of the balloting Pryor had telephoned Willkie in New York to say that Dewey's superb political organization already had captured enough delegates to ensure an early victory. The extraordinary capacity of the New York Governor for strategy had fully demonstrated itself.

As Dewey's advisers hastened to make plans for the coming campaign, their principal worry concerned the reaction of Wendell Willkie to the Dewey nomination. Would the defeated candidate publicly declare his opposition to Dewey and his preference for Roosevelt, and thereby split the Republican Party? Willkie's friends in Chicago telephoned Thomas Lamont urging him to visit Willkie at once and persuade him against any hasty action. Meanwhile, Baldwin, taking a plane back to New York for the graduation of his son from Columbia University, was commissioned by Pryor and Weeks to see Willkie and give him an earnest talk on party loyalty. Faithful to his pledge, immediately upon his arrival in New York, Baldwin hastened to No. 15 Broad Street, and spent two hours alone with Willkie.

He found his old friend and colleague agitated and eager to discuss his lack of confidence in Dewey and his disappointment in the platform. As Willkie paced up and down his office, Baldwin endeavored to appeal to his sense of sportsmanship and party regularity. To desert the GOP, Baldwin argued, would hurt Willkie and his cause as much as the Republican organization. Finally, Willkie stopped his restless pacing and stood squarely before Baldwin. With great emphasis he pounded his clenched fist into the palm of his other hand as he declared: "You can paste this in your hat. I will never support Roosevelt!" With this pledge, torn from Willkie's distressed soul, Baldwin departed.

Willkie sat alone at his desk facing a window overlooking the harbor with its many tugs and shipping cargoes. The office was very quiet. No political associate came to offer comfort. Even the newspapermen had deserted him. He was the forgotten candidate. Slowly he wrote the perfunctory telegram of congratulation to his successful rival, the man he so thoroughly disliked and mistrusted.

It said: "Hearty congratulations on your nomination. You have one of the great opportunities of history." In Republican circles, it was considered a cold passage—he had proffered no help in the ensuing campaign, no pledge of support. Humiliated and hurt, Willkie could not bring himself to offer his support in his usual generous manner. His deep distrust of Dewey never abated.

With Willkie's press release of criticism on the Republican platform, *Collier's* magazine asked him to write two articles analyzing both the Republican and the Democratic platforms. Again his talent as a publicist was superior to his ability as a politician.

He called the action of both parties "cowardice at Chicago." Declaring that Benjamin Disraeli had once defined a practical man as one who practised the errors of his forefathers, Willkie said the definition might be used for those practical politicians who drafted the platforms of the Republican and Democratic parties. Meeting at a moment, he said, the import of which for the country's future was scarcely less than that in which the Government was born or that which saw the great crisis of the Civil War, those men and women chose to borrow from the past neither the bold, imaginative spirit which moved the founding fathers to launch the untried experiment of a republic, nor the kind of courageous meeting of the issues and problems of the day which will make the name of Abraham Lincoln imperishable in history. Instead they borrowed from the past the timidities, the outworn doctrines and mistakes long since rejected by history.

He thought the two platforms paralleled each other in many respects, and revealed the tendency of politcians to conciliate all elements of the population without offending others within or without the party. "This cowardice on the part of both parties occurred at a time when millions of Americans were fighting on a dozen battlefronts and on all the high seas for the preservation of America's principles, principles on which our position expressed through our two great political parties in convention, should have been made so clear that even our enemies could not fail to understand."

Both platforms, he charged, had failed to grapple with the issue of sovereignty. Traditional sovereignty, he held, could not be maintained in an effective international organization. Indeed, there could be no permanent peace without a loss of sovereignty. As a result, all that could be hoped for would be a "consultative pact of peace-loving nations." He declared that an international organization empowered to maintain peace, justice, and security demanded something more. Nevertheless, he considered the Democratic plank on foreign policy better in many ways than the Republican plank. At least it was more forthright on the use of armed force and joint action to preserve the peace.

Willkie scored the Republicans for the secrecy with which they guarded the platform so that even Republican governors who were delegates to the convention could not secure a copy to study before it was read to the convention. Because of the demand for party harmony, he said, it was adopted by a yea-nay vote within twenty seconds after it was read. "The opportunity did not arise, either as a delegate or otherwise, for me to participate in shaping the party's policies in its 1944 convention deliberations," he sadly stated.

Willkie held both platforms were deficient in their statements on foreign policy. Likewise he considered them both as deficient in regard to the Negro citizen, "both of the 1944 political platforms in their pledges to the Negro and their programs for him are tragically inadequate. It must also be said that the Republican platform is distinctly better than the Democratic." Yet he noted that they both evaded clear statements on voting, fair employment practices, and equality in the armed services.

By this sharp analysis of the weakness of both platforms, Willkie hoped to arouse a public opinion that would require the candidates to put aside generalities and evasions. He hoped the candidates would be compelled to deal in concise terms with the great issues before the nation and the world.

The coolness of Willkie towards Dewey soon became a matter of national interest. Roosevelt's aides now attempted to woo him into support of the New Deal Administration. Likewise, the Dewey associates pressed for his committal to the Republican candidate. By withholding support from either candidate, Willkie hoped to force each into a more advanced declaration upon American leadership in promoting a strong international organization. He attempted to play one party against the other, in order to hold both candidates to the pattern of One World. Weary and anxious as to the outcome of foreign policy, Willkie again turned to the task of informing the American people about the issues of the campaign. He was the great advocate pleading his cause.

Willkie's silence regarding the candidates soon proved to be extremely embarrassing. Shrewdly taking advantage of the situation, President Roosevelt summoned Willkie to the White House on the pretext of seeking his advice. But Willkie interpreted these "command visits" as an effort to give the impression to the voters that the President really possessed Willkie's support.

On his side, Dewey tried to entice Willkie out of his Achilles camp. He invited him to come to Albany to discuss foreign policy with his own personal adviser, John Foster Dulles. This would have inevitably ended with the taking of news pictures of Willkie and Dewey in conference, which would have implied a tacit approval of the Republican candidate. To avoid this commitment Willkie suggested that Dulles meet him in New York. Accordingly, the meeting took place on August twenty-first at Dulles' house, on East Ninety-first Street. The two statesmen found that they were in general agreement except on one point. Dulles agreed with Willkie's proposal that the United Nations should have an international police force at its disposal. Both agreed that American participation in the inauguration and use of an international military establishment could properly be effected only through authority conferred upon the President by means of an act of Congress. But here, according to Willkie, congressional control should end. After congressional approval of an international police force was attained, the use of the force must be left to the discretion of the President. Dulles was loath to leave the President free from continuous legislative supervision. Both Willkie and Dulles agreed upon the importance of permitting the participation of all the nations, especially the small nations, in the post-war organization of the United Nations.

As a result of this amicable conference, a joint statement was issued by Willkie and Dulles which was rather colorless but which did present a semblance of party agreement. It read: "We have conferred extensively about various international problems bearing on world organization to assure lasting peace. There was a full exchange of views not animated by partisan consideration or having to do with any candidacy but by the desire of both of us that the United States should play a constructive and responsible part in assuring world order."

The joint statement was one of the last public acts of Wendell Willkie. Late in August he visited the summer home of Sam

Pryor in the forests of Maine. At night, as a group of friends
sat around the campfire under a starlit sky, more than one of
them remarked the strange silence of the distinguished guest.
Unlike his usual self, he seldom spoke. Often his head was
bowed over his folded arms. His massive figure, silhouetted
against the mobile shadows, seemed to embody discouragement,
frustration and utter weariness.

In another week, Willkie had left for Rushville to inspect his
Indiana farms. The weather was hot and humid, but he was
relentless in tramping around his cornfields and meadows. In
the midst of his exertion he suffered a severe heart attack. After
local physicians had eased his pain, he took a train for New
York.

When Mrs. Willkie met him at the Pennsylvania Station, she
was filled with deep apprehension over the weary appearance
of her husband. As he slumped back in the seat of the taxicab,
he murmured, "Billie, I am afraid this is something I can't
lick." After Labor Day, Willkie entered the Lenox Hill Hospital for medical observation. Although still in the prime of
life, being only fifty-two years of age, he was thoroughly exhausted. He had used up his great store of energy in a prodigal
manner. Yet at first the doctors did not view his condition as
serious. They merely advised rest. His condition became worse
several weeks later when a second ailment, a streptococcic throat
infection, developed. Nevertheless the doctor permitted him to
see some visitors and Willkie maneuvered it so that he saw
others. Two days before he died he had a fine visit with his old
friend, Roscoe Drummond, a correspondent of the *Christian
Science Monitor,* although in a surreptitious manner which
indicated that he saw many other people in the same way.

It was Willkie, himself, who telephoned Drummond and
arranged the time of his visit. Willkie explained to his friend
how to slip in the back way and how to reach his room without
being seen. When Drummond arrived at his room by this cir-
cuitous way, Willkie appeared highly pleased with himself for
this successful little deception upon the hospital attendants. The
newspaperman found the patient in excellent spirits with his
usual zest and eager plans for the future. He was not the broken,
discouraged person that some writers later pictured him.

Just before dawn on October 8, Willkie succumbed to an acute cardiac condition brought on by his exhaustion and the toxic effects from the streptococcic infection of his throat.

On the following day, Willkie's body lay in state in the Fifth Avenue Presbyterian Church, while thousands of citizens passed the casket in respect to his memory. Funeral services were held on October tenth. In an eloquent address, the Reverend Dr. John Sutherland Bonnell declared: "Seldom have the American people been so shocked and stunned as when tidings flashed across this nation and around the world that Wendell Willkie had died. Men and women discussed that news in hushed tones and with awed voices. In homes of every class and race and creed, there was something more than a realization of national deprivation. There was a poignant sense of personal bereavement." A crowd of thirty-five thousand men and women, who could not find room in the church, lined the streets and watched in respectful silence.

To many humble folk who had passed by his bier in the church, Willkie was revered as the great defender of the American way of life. To more discerning mourners, Willkie appeared as the eloquent advocate of free enterprise, and the genuine patriot who, at a great crisis in world history, had removed party politics from the conduct of American foreign policy. To American men and women it seemed that as long as there was a Wendell Willkie in the land, no ambitious President could make himself a dictator, or practise executive usurpation, or censor the press, or encroach upon the rights of American citizens. As long as there was a Willkie, a voice would be heard demanding equal opportunity for all citizens, civil liberties for all Negroes and other minority groups, and freedom of speech and conscience for everyone, everywhere. As long as there was a Willkie, the American people would be able to rise above partisan quarrels, to render their judgment upon the great issues of the day by rational processes rather than by blind passion and hatreds, and to maintain a national unity that would be conducive to the public welfare.

While the nation mourned, Secretary of War Henry L. Stimson telegraphed Willkie's widow proposing that the great advocate be buried with the national heroes in Arlington National

Cemetery. Edith was not unmoved by the proposal, but she knew that Willkie belonged to the Middle West, the heart of America. Shortly after the eloquent words of Dr. Bonnell had been uttered, the coffin of Wendell Willkie was placed on board a train for transportation to Rushville, Indiana. Twenty-five years earlier, a young soldier, mustered out of the Army at the end of the First World War, had journeyed to Indiana to re-enter civilian life and to carve out his career as a lawyer. Now, after a short but distinguished service to the nation, this American hero returned to his native prairie forever.

BIBLIOGRAPHY OF PUBLISHED SOURCES

CONGRESSIONAL HEARINGS AND GOVERNMENT REPORTS

Confirmation of Atomic Energy Commission and General Manager: Hearings Before the Senate Section of the Joint Committee on Atomic Energy, Eightieth Congress, First Session, on Confirmation of the Atomic Energy Commission and the General Manager. Washington, D. C. 1947.

Government Competition with Private Enterprise: Report of the Special Committee Appointed to Investigate Government Competition with Private Enterprise, House of Representatives, Pursuant to H. Res. 235 (1933). Washington, D. C. 1935.

Investigation of Lobbying Activities: Hearings Before a Special Committee Investigating Lobbying Activities, United States Senate, Seventy-fourth Congress, First Session, Pursuant to S. Res. 165 and S. Res. 184: Resolutions Providing for an Investigation of Lobbying Activities in Connection with the So-Called Holding Company Bill (S. 2796). Washington, D. C. 1935-1938.

Investigation of Lobbying Activities: Hearings Before a Select Committee to Investigate Lobbying Activities, United States Senate, Seventy-fourth Congress, First Session, Pursuant to S. Res. 165: A Resolution Providing for an Investigation of Lobbying in Connection with the So-Called "Holding Company Bill" (S. 2796). Washington, D. C. 1935.

Investigation of Lobbying Activities: House of Representatives Report No. 2081, Seventy-fourth Congress, Second Session. Washington, D. C. 1936.

Investigation of Lobbying on Utility Holding Company Bills: Hearings Before the Committee on Rules, House of Representatives, Seventy-fourth Congress, First Session, on H. Res. 288: A Resolution Authorizing and Directing the Committee on Rules to Investigate Lobbying Activities with Respect to Utility Holding Companies. Washington, D. C. 1935.

Investigation of the Tennessee Valley Authority: Hearings Before the Joint Committee on the Investigation of the Tennessee Valley Authority, Congress of the United States, Seventy-fifth Congress, Third Session, Pursuant to Public Resolution No. 83 (May-December, 1938). Washington, D. C. 1939.

Investigation of the Tennessee Valley Authority: Report of the Joint Committee on the Investigation of the Tennessee Valley Authority, Congress of the United States, Pursuant to Public Resolution No. 83, Seventy-fifth Congress (April 3, 1939). Senate Document No. 56 (3 parts). Washington, D. C. 1939.

Lend-Lease Bill: Hearings Before the Committee on Foreign Affairs, House of Representatives, Seventy-seventh Congress, First Session, on H. R. 1776. Washington, D. C. 1941.

Muscle Shoals: Hearings Before the Committee on Military Affairs, House of Representatives, Seventy-third Congress, First Session, on H. R. 4859 (April, 1933). Washington, D. C. 1933.

Public Utility Holding Companies: Hearings Before the Committee on Interstate and Foreign Commerce, House of Representatives, Seventy-fourth Congress, First Session, on H. R. 5423 (April, 1935). Washington, D. C. 1935.

Public Utility Holding Company Act: Hearings Before the Committee on Interstate Commerce, United States Senate, Seventy-fourth Congress, First Session, on S. 1725 (April, 1935). Washington, D. C. 1935.

Removal of a Member of the Tennessee Valley Authority: Message from the President of the United States. Senate Document No. 155, Seventy-fifth Congress, Third Session. Washington, D. C. 1938.

Study of Operations Pursuant to the Public Utility Holding Company Act of 1935: Hearings Before the Securities Subcommittee of the Committee on Interstate and Foreign Commerce, House of Representatives, Seventy-ninth Congress, First Session (November 5-15, 1945). Washington, D. C. 1946.

To Amend the TVA: Hearings Before a Subcommittee of the Committee on Military Affairs, Seventy-sixth Congress, First Session, on S. 1796 (May-June, 1939). Washington, D. C. 1939.

To Enlarge Powers of Tennessee Valley Authority: Hearings Before the Committee on Military Affairs, House of Representatives, Seventy-fourth Congress, First Session, on H. R. 6793 (March-April, 1935). Washington, D. C. 1935.

To Establish a Missouri Valley Authority: Hearings Before a Subcommittee of the Committee on Commerce, United States Senate, Seventy-ninth Congress, First Session, on S. 555 (April, 1945). Washington, D. C. 1945.

To Promote the Defense of the United States: Hearings Before the Committee on Foreign Relations of the United States Senate, Seventy-seventh Congress, First Session, on S. 275 (January-February, 1941). Washington, D. C. 1941.

Utility Corporations: Letter from the Chairman of the Federal Trade Commission in Response to Senate Resolution No. 83, Seventieth Congress (1934). Washington, D. C. 1934.

Court Cases

Alabama Power Company v. Ickes (1937). 91 Federal Reporter, 2nd Series, 303.

Alabama Power Company v. Ickes (1938). 302 U. S., 464.

Alabama Power Company v. Tennessee Valley Authority (1937). 92 Federal Reporter, 2nd Series, 413.

Ashwander v. Tennessee Valley Authority (1936). 297 U. S., 288.

Electric Bond and Share Company *v.* Securities and Exchange Commission (1938). 303 U. S., 419.

Railroad Commission of State of California *v.* Pacific Gas and Electric Company (1938). 302 U. S., 388.

Schneiderman *v.* United States (1943). 320 U. S., 118.

Securities and Exchange Commission *v.* Electric Bond and Share Company (1937). 18 Federal Supplement, 131.

Smyth *v.* Ames (1898). 169 U. S., 466.

Southwestern Bell Telephone Company *v.* Public Service Commission of Missouri (1923). 262 U. S., 276.

Tennessee Electric Power *v.* Tennessee Valley Authority (1938). 21 Federal Supplement, 947.

Tennessee Electric Power Company *v.* Tennessee Valley Authority (1939). 306 U. S., 118.

Tennessee Valley Authority *v.* Ashwander (1935). 78 Federal Reporter, 2nd Series, 578.

United States *v.* Schneiderman (1940). 33 Federal Supplement, 510.

GOVERNMENT DOCUMENTS

Annual Reports of the Tennessee Valley Authority. Washington, D. C. 1934 to date.

Congressional Record: Proceedings and Debates. Government Printing Office. Washington, D. C. 1874 to date.

Department of State Bulletin. (Weekly report) Government Printing Office. Washington, D. C. 1939 to date.

Electoral and Popular Votes for President and Congressional Elections Statistics. Compiled by Carl A. Loeffler, Secretary of the United States Senate. Washington, D. C. 1948.

Engineering Report of the Joint Committee Investigating the Tennessee Valley Authority. Senate Document, No. 56, part 3, Seventy-sixth Congress, First Session. Washington, D. C. 1939.

Federal Reporter: Cases Argued and Determined in the Circuit and District Courts of the United States. West Publishing Company. St. Paul. 1880 to date.

Federal Supplements: Cases Argued and Determined in the District Courts of the United States and the Court of Claims. West Publishing Company. St. Paul. 1933 to date.

National Resources Committee. Progress Report: 1939. Washington, D. C. 1939.

Official Opinions of the Attorneys General of the United States Advising the President and Heads of Departments in Relation to Their Official Duties. Government Printing Office. Washington, D. C. 1789 to date.

Papers Relating to the Foreign Relations of the United States. Government Printing Office. Washington, D. C. 1861 to date.

Postwar Foreign Policy Preparation, 1939-1945. Department of State Publication 3580, General Foreign Policy Series 15. Washington, D. C. 1950.

Reports of the National Power Policy Committee. Government Printing Office. Washington, D. C.

Senate Committee on Foreign Relations. A Decade of American Foreign Policy: Basic Documents: 1941-49. Senate Document No. 123, Eighty-first Congress, First Session. Washington, D. C. 1950.

Statistics of the Presidential and Congressional Election of November 2, 1948. Compiled under the direction of Ralph R. Roberts, Clerk of the House of Representatives. Washington, D. C. 1949.

United States Relations with China, with Special Reference to the Period 1944-1949. Department of State Publication 3573, Far Eastern Series 30. (Commonly called the "White Paper on China.") Washington, D. C. 1949.

United States Reports: Cases Adjudged in the Supreme Court. Government Printing Office. Washington, D. C. 1816 to date.

United States Statutes at Large. Government Printing Office. Washington, D. C. 1873 to date.

Vote Cast in Presidential and Congressional Elections, 1928-1944. Bureau of the Census. Washington, D. C. 1936.

Learned Journals

American Economic Review. American Economic Association. Evanston, Illinois. 1911 to date.

American Historical Review. American Historical Association. Washington, D. C. 1895 to date.

American Political Science Review. American Political Science Association. Washington, D. C. 1906 to date.

Annals of the American Academy of Political and Social Science. Philadelphia. 1890 to date.

California Law Review. Berkeley, California. 1912 to date.

Columbia Law Review. New York. 1901 to date.

Contemporary Review. London. 1866 to date.

Economist, The. London. 1843 to date.

Foreign Affairs. Council on Foreign Relations. New York. 1922 to date.

Fortnightly, The. London. 1865 to date.

Harvard Law Review. Cambridge, Massachusetts. 1887 to date.

Illinois Law Review. Chicago. 1906 to date.

Journal of Economic History. Economic History Association. New York. 1941 to date.

Journal of Political Economy. Chicago. 1892 to date.

Journal of Politics. University of Florida. 1939 to date.

Michigan Law Review. University of Michigan. 1902 to date.

National Municipal Review. National Municipal League. New York. 1912 to date.

Political Quarterly. London. 1930 to date.

Political Science Quarterly. Academy of Political Science. Columbia University. New York. 1896 to date.

Public Administration Review. American Society for Public Administration. Chicago. 1940 to date.

Public Opinion Quarterly. School of Public Affairs. Princeton University. 1937 to date.

Quarterly Journal of Economics. Harvard University. 1886 to date.

Review of Politics. Notre Dame University. 1939 to date.

Revue des Deux Mondes, La. 1829 to date.

Revue Politique et Parlementaire. Paris. 1898 to date.

Social Research. New School for Social Research. New York. 1934 to date.

Southern California Law Review. Los Angeles. 1927 to date.

University of Chicago Law Review. Chicago. 1933 to date.

Yale Law Journal. New Haven, Connecticut. 1891 to date.

REPORTS, ARTICLES AND PROCEEDINGS

Alabama Power Company *v.* Ickes: Standing to Protest Against Federal Expenditures, in the *Harvard Law Review* (March, 1932), Vol. 2, no. 5, pp. 897-906.

Albertsworth, E. F. "Constitutional Issues of the Federal Power Program," in the *Illinois Law Review* (March, 1935), Vol. 29, no. 7, pp. 833-866.

Apportionment, Nomination and Election of Delegates to Political Party Conventions. Legislative Reference Service, Library of Congress. Washington, D. C. 1947.

Bulletin of America's Town Meeting of the Air. New York. January 6, 1938.

Clark, J. M. "Toward a Concept of Workable Competition," in the *American Economic Review* (June, 1940), Vol. XXX, pp. 241-256.

Commonwealth & Southern Corporation: Outline of History and Development. New York. 1935.

Commonwealth and Southern Corporation. Analysis of the Annual Report of the Tennessee Valley Authority released on December 31, 1936. New York. 1937.

Dodd, Walter F. "The United States Supreme Court, 1936-1946," in the *American Political Science Review* (February, 1947), Vol. XLI, no. 1, pp. 1-11.

Electric Bond and Share Company *v.* Security and Exchange Commission, in the *Illinois Law Review* (1938), Vol. 32, pp. 875-879.

"Federal Courts: Right of Preferred Shareholder to Enjoin Contract with Allegedly Unconstitutional TVA," in *Harvard Law Review* (April, 1936), Vol. 49, no. 6, pp. 1004-1006.

Green, C. J. *An Analysis of the Real Cost of TVA Power.* Chamber of Commerce of the United States. Washington, D. C. 1948.

Lilienthal, David E., and Robert M. Marquis. "The Conduct of Business Enterprise by the Federal Government," in *Harvard Law Review* (February, 1941), Vol. 54, no. 4, pp. 545-601.

New York Herald Tribune Eighth Annual Forum, 1938. New York. 1939.

Official Party Records and Proceedings of the Democratic National Convention Held at Chicago, Illinois, 1940. Washington, D. C. 1940.

Official Report of the Proceedings of the National Democratic Convention, Chicago, Illinois, 1944. Washington, D. C. 1944.

Official Report of the Proceedings of the Twenty-second Republican National Convention Held in Philadelphia, Pennsylvania, 1940. Judd and Detweiler. Washington, D. C. 1940.

Official Report of the Proceedings of the Twenty-third Republican National Convention Held in Chicago, Illinois, 1944. Judd and Detweiler. Washington, D. C. 1944.

Pound, Roscoe. "Judge Holmes' Contributions to the Science of Law," in the *Harvard Law Review* (March, 1921), Vol. 34, no. 5, pp. 449-452.

Pound, Roscoe. "Administrative Agencies and the Law," in *American Affairs* Pamphlets (April, 1946). Supplement to Vol. 8.

Program for a Dynamic America: A Statement of Republican Principles: Report of Republican Program Committee Submitted to Republican National Committee, February 16, 1940. Washington, D. C. 1940.

Reece, B. Carroll. "Declaration of Republican Post-War Advisory Council" (meeting at Mackinac Island, September 6 and 7, 1943), in the *Congressional Record*. Proceedings and Debates of the Seventy-eighth Congress, First Session, Vol. 89, part II, pp. A3850-3852.

Rising, E. W. Brief on Tennessee Valley Authority. Washington, D. C. 1945.

Rising, E. W. *Shall the TVA Be Extended to Cover the United States?* Washington, D. C. 1944.

Russell, Dean. *The TVA Idea. The Foundation for Economic Education.* Irvington-on-Hudson, New York. 1949.

Tennessee Electric Power Company *v.* Tennessee Valley Authority, in the *Harvard Law Review* (February, 1939), Vol. 52, no. 4, pp. 686-687.

Tennessee Electric Power Company *v.* Tennessee Valley Authority, in the *Southern California Law Review* (January, 1940), Vol. 13, no. 2, pp. 255-257.

Vennard, Edwin. *Dangers of the TVA Method of River Control.* Chicago, Illinois. 1945.

Wolfsohn, Joel David (Executive Secretary of the National Power Policy Committee). *Power Views of Franklin D. Roosevelt.* House of Representatives Document, No. 137, Seventy-fourth Congress, First Session. 1935.

MEMOIRS. BIOGRAPHIES AND PERSONAL PAPERS

Alsop, Joseph, and Robert Kinter. *Men Around the President.* Doubleday, Doran and Company. New York. 1939.

Brandeis, Louis D. *The Curse of Bigness:* Miscellaneous Papers of Louis D. Brandeis. Edited by Osmond K. Fraenkel. The Viking Press. New York. 1934.

Brandeis, Louis D. *The Social and Economic Views of Mr. Justice Brandeis.* Collected Papers with Introductory Notes by Alfred Lief, with a Foreword by Charles A. Beard. The Vanguard Press. New York. 1930.

Chennault, Claire Lee. *Way of a Fighter:* The Memoirs of Claire Lee Chennault. Edited by Robert Hotz. G. P. Putnam's Sons. New York. 1949.

Chiang Kai-shek. *China's Destiny.* Authorized translation by Wang Chunhui. The Macmillan Company. New York. 1944.

Churchill, Winston S. *The Second World War.* Houghton Mifflin Company. Boston. 1948-1952.

Davies, Joseph E. *Mission to Moscow.* Simon and Schuster. New York. 1941.

Deane, John R. *The Strange Alliance:* The Story of Our Efforts at Wartime Co-operation with Russia. The Viking Press. New York. 1947.

De Roussy de Sales, Raoul Jean Jacques Francis. *The Making of Yesterday:* The Diaries of Raoul de Roussy de Sales. Raynal and Hitchcock. New York. 1947.

Farley, James A. *Behind the Ballots.* Harcourt, Brace and Company. New York. 1938.

Farley, James A. *Jim Farley's Story:* The Roosevelt Years. Whittlesey House. New York. 1948.

Flynn, John Thomas. *Country Squire in the White House.* Doubleday, Doran and Company. New York. 1940.

Flynn, John Thomas. *The Roosevelt Myth.* The Devin-Adair Company. New York. 1948.

Forrestal, James V. *The Forrestal Diaries.* Edited by Walter Millis. The Viking Press. New York. 1951.

Frankfurter, Felix (ed.). *Mr. Justice Brandies.* Yale University Press. New Haven, Connecticut. 1932.

Hatch, Alden. *Young Willkie.* Harcourt, Brace and Company. New York. 1944.

Holmes, Oliver Wendell. *The Mind and Faith of Justice Holmes:* His Speeches, Essays, Letters and Judicial Opinions. Edited by Max Lerner. Little, Brown and Company. Boston. 1943.

Holmes, Oliver Wendell. *The Dissenting Opinions of Mr. Justice Holmes.* Arranged with Introductory Notes by Alfred Lief with a Foreword by Dr. George W. Kirchwey. The Vanguard Press. New York. 1929.

Hull, Cordell. *The Memoirs of Cordell Hull.* The Macmillan Company. New York. 1948.

Ickes, Harold L. *The Autobiography of a Curmudgeon.* Reynal and Hitchcock. New York. 1943.

Jones, Jesse H., and Edward Angly. *Fifty Billion Dollars.* The Macmillan Company. New York. 1951.

Leahy, Fleet Admiral William D. *I Was There.* Whittlesey House. New York. 1950.

Lief, Alfred. *Democracy's Norris:* Biography of a Lonely Crusader. Stackpole Sons. New York. 1939.

Lilienthal, David E. *This I Do Believe.* Harper and Brothers. New York. 1949.

Lilienthal, David E. *TVA:* Democracy on the March. Harper and Brothers. New York. 1944.

McIntire, Vice-Admiral Ross T. *White House Physician.* G. P. Putnam's Sons. New York. 1946.

Mason, Alpheus T. *Brandeis:* A Free Man's Life. The Viking Press. New York. 1946.

Mason, Alpheus T. *The Brandeis Way:* A Case Study in the Workings of Democracy. Princeton University Press. Princeton, New Jersey. 1938.

Michelson, Charles. *The Ghost Talks.* G. P. Putnam's Sons. New York. 1944.

Moley, Raymond. *After Seven Years.* Harper and Brothers. New York. 1939.

Neuberger, Richard L., and Stephen B. Kahn. *Integrity:* The Life of George W. Norris. The Vanguard Press. New York. 1937.

Norris, George W. *Fighting Liberal:* The Autobiography of George W. Norris. The Macmillan Company. New York. 1945.

Perkins, Frances. *The Roosevelt I Knew.* The Viking Press. New York. 1946.

Roosevelt, Eleanor. *This I Remember.* Harper and Brothers. New York. 1949.

Roosevelt, Franklin Delano. *F. D. R.:* His Personal Letters. Foreword by Eleanor Roosevelt. Edited by Elliott Roosevelt. Duell, Sloane and Pearce. New York. 1947-1950.

Roosevelt, Franklin Delano. *The Public Papers and Addresses of Franklin D. Roosevelt.* Random House. New York. 1938-1950.

Sherwood, Robert E. *Roosevelt and Hopkins:* An Intimate History. Harper and Brothers. New York. 1948.

Stimson, Henry Lewis. *On Active Service in Peace and War.* Harper and Brothers. New York. 1948.

Welles, Sumner. *Seven Decisions That Shaped History.* Harper and Brothers. New York. 1951.

Welles, Sumner. *The Time for Decision.* Harper and Brothers. New York. 1944.

Welles, Sumner. *Where Are We Heading?* Harper and Brothers. New York. 1946.

Whitman, Willson. *David Lilienthal:* Public Servant in a Power Age. Henry Holt and Company. New York. 1948.

TREATISES

Abrams, Ernest R. *Power in Transition.* Charles Scribner's Sons. New York. 1940.

Adams, James T. *Big Business in a Democracy.* Charles Scribner's Sons. New York. 1945.

Arnold, Thurman W. *Democracy and Free Enterprise.* University of Oklahoma Press. Norman, Oklahoma. 1942.

Arnold, Thurman W. *The Folklore of Capitalism.* Yale University Press. New Haven, Connecticut. 1937.

Arnold, Thurman W. *The Symbols of Government.* Yale University Press. New Haven, Connecticut. 1935.

Bauer, John, and Nathaniel Gold. *The Electric Power Industry.* Harper and Brothers. New York. 1939.

Beard, Charles A. *President Roosevelt and the Coming of the War, 1941:* A Study in Appearances and Realities. Yale University Press. New Haven, Connecticut. 1948.

Blachly, F. F., and M. E. Oatman. *Federal Regulatory Action and Control.* The Brookings Institution. Washington, D. C. 1940.

Bonbright, James C., and Gardiner C. Means. *The Holding Company.* McGraw-Hill Book Company. New York. 1932.

Bonbright, James C. *Public Utilities and the National Power Policies.* Columbia University Press. New York. 1940.

Cardozo, Benjamin N. *The Growth of the Law.* Yale University Press. New Haven, Connecticut. 1924.

Cardozo, Benjamin N. *The Nature of the Judicial Process.* 8th printing. Yale University Press. New Haven, Connecticut. 1932.

Carlson, John Roy. *Under Cover:* My Four Years in the Nazi Underworld of America. E. P. Dutton and Company. New York. 1943.

Ciliberti, Charles. *Backstairs Mission in Moscow.* Booktab Press. New York. 1946.

Colegrove, Kenneth. *The American Senate and World Peace.* The Vanguard Press. New York. 1944.

Collins, Frederick L. *Uncle Sam's Billion-Dollar Baby:* A Taxpayer Looks at the TVA. G. P. Putnam's Sons. New York. 1945.

Cooley, Thomas M. *A Treatise on the Constitutional Limitations Which Rest Upon the Legislative Power of the States of the American Union.* 8th edition. Little, Brown and Company. Boston. 1927.

Corwin, Edward S. *Constitutional Revolution, Ltd.* Claremont Colleges. Claremont, California. 1941.

Corwin, Edwin S. *Court Over Constitution:* A study of Judicial Review as an Instrument of Popular Government. Princeton University Press. Princeton, New Jersey. 1938.

Corwin, Edward S. *The President:* Office and Powers, 1787-1948. 3rd edition. New York University Press. New York. 1948.

Davis, Forrest, and Ernest K. Lindley. *How War Came:* An American White Paper. Simon and Schuster. New York. 1942.

Duffus, R. I., and Charles Krutch. *The Valley and Its People:* A Portrait of TVA. Alfred A. Knopf. New York. 1944.

Editors of the *Economist. The New Deal:* An Analysis and Appraisal. Alfred A. Knopf. New York. 1937.

Feis, Herbert. *The Road to Pearl Harbor.* Princeton University Press. Princeton, New Jersey. 1950.

Gallup, George H., and Saul F. Rae. *The Pulse of Democracy.* Simon and Schuster. New York. 1940.

Hewart, Gordon. *The New Despotism*. Cosmopolitan Book Corporation. New York. 1929.

Holmes, Oliver Wendell. *The Common Law*. Little, Brown and Company. Boston. 1938.

Hoover, Herbert, and Hugh Gibson. *The Problem of Lasting Peace*. Doubleday, Doran and Company. New York. 1942.

Howard, W. V. *Authority in TVA Land*. Kansas City, Missouri. 1948.

Insull, Samuel. *Public Utilities in Modern Life:* Selected Speeches by Samuel Insull. Edited by William E. Keily. Privately Printed. Chicago. 1924.

Johnson, Walter. *The Battle Against Isolation*. University of Chicago Press. Chicago. 1944.

Kemmerer, Edwin W. *Gold and the Gold Standard:* The Story of Gold Money, Past, Present, and Future. McGraw-Hill Book Company. New York. 1944.

Key, V. O. *Politics, Parties and Pressure Groups*. 2nd edition. Thomas Y. Crowell Company, New York. 1950.

Lindley, Ernest K. *Half Way with Roosevelt*. The Viking Press. New York. 1936.

Lippmann, Walter. *U. S. Foreign Policy:* Shield of the Republic. Little, Brown and Company. Boston. 1943.

Lundberg, Ferdinand. *America's Sixty Families*. Vanguard. New York. 1937.

Lutz, Harley L. *Insecurity of the Security Program*. Princeton University Press. Princeton, New Jersey. 1936.

Meriam, Lewis. *Relief and Social Security*. The Brookings Institution. Washington, D. C. 1946.

Moulton, Harold, and others. *The Regulation of the Security Markets*. The Brookings Institution. Washington, D. C. 1946.

Pound, Roscoe. *An Introduction to the Philosophy of Law*. Yale University Press. New Haven, Connecticut. 1922.

Pritchett, C. Herman. *The Roosevelt Court:* A Study in Judicial Politics and Values, 1937-1947. The Macmillan Company. New York. 1948.

Pritchett, C. Herman. *The Tennessee Valley Authority:* A Study in Public Administration. University of North Carolina Press. Chapel Hill, North Carolina. 1943.

Snyder, Carl. *Capitalism the Creator*. The Macmillan Company. New York. 1940.

Strunk, Mildred, and Hadley Cantril. *Public Opinion, 1935-1946*. Princeton University Press. Princeton, New Jersey. 1951.

The Twentieth Century Fund. *Power Industry and the Public Interest:* A Summary of the Results of a Survey of the Relations Between the Government and the Electric Power Industry. Edited by Edward Eyre Hunt. New York. 1944.

Warren, Charles. *Congress as Santa Claus:* Or National Donations and the General Welfare Clause of the Constitution. Michie Company. Charlottesville, Virginia. 1932.

Waterman, Merwin H. *Economic Implications of Public Utility Holding Company Operations,* with Particular Reference to the Reasonableness of the "Death Sentence" Clause of the Public Utility Holding Company Act. University of Michigan, School of Business Administration, Bureau of Business Research. Ann Arbor, Michigan. 1941.

Whitman, Willson. *David Lilienthal:* Public Servant in a Power Age. Henry Holt and Company. New York. 1948.

Whitton, John B. (ed.). *The Second Chance:* America and the Peace. Princeton University Press. Princeton, New Jersey. 1944.

Willoughby, Westel W. *The Constitutional Law of the United States.* 2nd edition. Baker, Voorhis and Company. New York. 1929.

Wilson, G. Lloyd, and others. *Public Utility Regulation.* McGraw-Hill Book Company. New York. 1938.

WENDELL WILLKIE: ADDRESSES AND WRITINGS

An address, "Government and Private Ownership," at the dinner of the American Statistical Association in New York City. September 26, 1934.

An address, "The Other Side of the TVA Program," at the Rotary Club of Birmingham, Alabama. November 9, 1934.

An address, "Government and the Public Utilities," at the joint meeting of the Economic Club of New York and the Harvard Business School Club. January 21, 1935.

An address before the Bond Club, at Newark, New Jersey. February 28, 1935.

An article, "The Campaign Against the Companies," in *Current History.* May, 1935.

An address, "The New Fear," at the 23rd annual meeting of the United States Chamber of Commerce at Washington, D. C. May 1, 1935.

An address, "The Public Utility Problem: Its Recent History and Possible Solution," at the Bond Club of New York City. December 19, 1935.

A radio address over NBC, "Who Pays the Bills for TVA?" March 5, 1936. (Sometimes listed as "Position of the Utilities in the TVA Situation.")

An article, "Horse Power and Horse Sense," in *Review of Reviews.* August, 1936.

An article, "Political Power," in the *Atlantic Monthly.* August, 1937. (Sometimes listed as "Will the Government Take Over the Utilities?")

An article, "The New Deal Power Plan Challenged," in the *New York Times Magazine.* October 31, 1937.

A radio debate with the Honorable Robert H. Jackson, "How Can Government and Business Work Together," on America's Town Meeting of the Air. January 6, 1938.

An address at the University of Indiana on Foundation Day. Bloomington, Indiana. May 4, 1938.

An address, "The True Liberalism," at the *Herald Tribune* Forum in New York City. October 26, 1938.

An article, "Idle Money, Idle Men," in the *Saturday Evening Post*. June 17, 1939.

An article, "Brace Up, America!" in *Atlantic Monthly*. June, 1939.

An article, "What Helps Business Helps You," in *Nation's Business*. June, 1939.

A book review of *The Young Melbourne*, by David Cecil, in the *New York Herald Tribune Book Review*. August 27, 1939.

An address, "The Great American Tripod: All Three Legs Must Reach the Ground," at the Bankers Club in New York City. November 1, 1939.

An address, "We Have Gone Far Enough Down the Road to Federal Control," at the Holland Society Dinner, New York. November 16, 1939.

An article, "Why I Believe in America," in *North American Review*. December, 1939 and condensed in *Readers' Digest*, December, 1939, as "The Faith That Is America."

An address, "The American College," at Wooster College, Wooster, Ohio. January 29, 1940.

An article, "Set Enterprise Free!" in the *Christian Science Monitor*, magazine section. March 2, 1940.

An address, "Government Becomes a Monopoly," at Toledo, Ohio. March 4, 1940.

An article, "The Court Is Now His," in the *Saturday Evening Post*. March 9, 1940.

An address, "Liberalism," at the Commonwealth Club of San Francisco, California. March 15, 1940.

An article, "Fair Trial," in the *New Republic*. March 18, 1940.

Participant on the radio program "Information, Please." April 9, 1940.

An article, "We the People," in *Fortune*. April, 1940.

The Willkie-Ickes debate at American Society of Newspaper Editors Convention. Washington, D. C. April 19, 1940.

An address, "Some of the Issues of 1940," at the Bureau of Advertising, American Newspaper Publishers Association, in New York. April 25, 1940.

An address to the Republicans, at St. Paul, Minnesota. May 11, 1940.

An address at a Republican Rally, Sommerville, New Jersey. May 20, 1940.

An article, "Roosevelt Should Run," in *Look*. June 4, 1940.

An article, "Five Minutes to Midnight," in the *Saturday Evening Post*. June 22, 1940.

An address of acceptance of the Presidental Nomination by the Republican Party. Elwood, Indiana. August 17, 1940.

An article, "I Challenge Roosevelt on These Issues," in *Look*. September 10, 1940.

An article, "America's First Duty," in the *Reader's Digest*. October, 1940.

Addresses, campaign speeches, September 13 to November 2, 1940.

Occasional Addresses and Articles of Wendell Willkie. Privately printed at the Overbrook Press. Stamford, Connecticut. 1940.

A radio address over NBC and CBS, "The Loyal Opposition." New York.

November 11, 1940. (Sometimes listed as "Co-operation but Loyal Opposition; Discord and Disunity Will Arise if Opposition Is Suppressed.")

An article, "Patriotism or Politics?" in the *American Magazine*. November, 1940.

An address, "America Cannot Remove Itself from the World," at the Women's National Republican Club. New York. January 8, 1941.

An address, "The Challenge of Newer Days: Have You Got It in You?" at the Lincoln Day dinner. New York City, February 12, 1941.

An address to Canadians, "Democracy to Live Must Be Expanding." Ontario. March 24, 1941. (Sometimes listed as "Address to Canadians.")

An address, "The Cause of Human Freedom; We Cannot Appease the Forces of Evil." Madison Square Garden, New York. May 7, 1941.

An article, "Americans, Stop Being Afraid," in *Collier's*. May 10, 1941.

A radio address over NBC, "Our Faith in the Union; Let Us Not Be Divided," at the Chicago Unity Rally. Chicago, Illinois. June 6, 1941.

A radio address over NBC, "The Meaning of American Liberty." New York. July 4, 1941.

An article, "Let's Keep the Ball," in *Reader's Digest*. November, 1941.

An article, "Future of the Republican Party," in the *Nation*. December 1, 1941.

A radio address over CBS, "We Cannot Win with Quick Dramatics or Momentary Heroics." New York. December 20, 1941.

An address, "We Need Tanks, Not Talk," at the Annual Dinner of the United States Conference of Mayors. Washington, D. C. January 13, 1942.

An address, "Bring General MacArthur Home," at the Lincoln Birthday dinner of the Middlesex Club in Boston. February 12, 1942.

An article, "Let's Look Ahead," in the *New York Times Magazine*. February 15, 1942.

An address, "World Outlook Needed for Americans; We Cannot Keep Freedom to Ourselves," at Rochester University. April 23, 1942.

An address, "Choose Leaders with Principles Not Poll Wobblers," at the 147th Commencement of Union College. May 11, 1942.

An article, "Case for the Minorities," in the *Saturday Evening Post*. June 27, 1942.

A radio address over the combined networks of CBS, NBC, the Mutual Broadcasting System and the Blue Network on his trip to Russia and China. "Our Reservoir of World Respect and Hope: Deliver the Materials of War—Define Our Peace Aims." New York. October 26, 1942.

An address, "Accord Needed Now," at the *New York Herald Tribune* Forum. New York. November 17, 1942.

An address at Toronto, Canada, on "Aid to Russia." November 25, 1942.

An article, "Give Your Children a World Outlook," in *Parents' Magazine*. November, 1942.

A pamphlet, *One World*. Simon and Schuster. New York. 1943.

An address, "Freedom and the Liberal Arts," at Duke University. January 14, 1943.

An article, "We Must Work with Russia," in the *New York Times Magazine*. January 17, 1943.

An article, "Life on the Russian Frontier," *Reader's Digest*. March, 1943.

An article, "Airways to Peace," in *Travel*. September, 1943.

An article, "How the Republican Party Can Win in 1944," in *Look*. October 5, 1943.

A radio address, "America's Purposes," from St. Louis over NBC. October 15, 1943. (Sometimes given as "Our Task: Problems Facing the Republican Party.")

An address, "Better Management, Please, Mr. President," in *Reader's Digest*. November, 1943.

A pamphlet, *An American Program*. Simon and Schuster. New York. 1944.

An article, "Don't Stir Distrust of Russia," in the *New York Times Magazine*. January 2, 1944.

An address, "Preserve Self-Government; Fiscal Program for War and Post-war Period." Delivered at the first of a series of three meetings under the general title of "America Plans and Dreams," arranged by the *New York Times*. New York. February 2, 1944.

Addresses, campaign speeches in Wisconsin, March 18-30, 1944.

An address withdrawing from presidential race at Omaha, Nebraska, April 5, 1944.

An article, "Our Sovereignty: Shall We Use It?" in *Foreign Affairs*. April, 1944.

An address before the National Association for the Advancement of Colored People in New York, May 26, 1944.

An article, "Cowardice at Chicago," in *Collier's*. September 16, 1944.

An article, "Citizens of Negro Blood," in *Collier's*. October 7, 1944.

INDEX

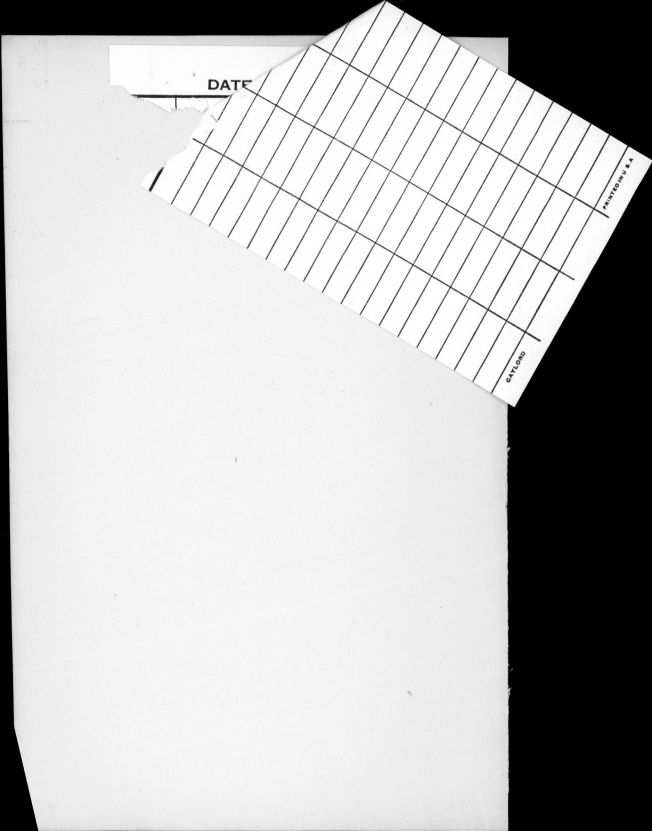

DATE

GAYLORD

PRINTED IN U.S.A